Who Is Rational?

Studies of Individual Differences in Reasoning

Who Is Rational?

Studies of Individual Differences in Reasoning

Keith E. Stanovich
University of Toronto

LAWRENCE ERLBAUM ASSOCIATES, PUBLISHERS
1999   Mahwah, New Jersey   London

Lawrence Erlbaum Associates, Inc., Publishers
10 Industrial Avenue
Mahwah, NJ 07430

Cover design by Kathryn Houghtaling Lacey

Library of Congress Cataloging-in-Publication Data

Stanovich, Keith E., 1950–
Who is rational? : studies of individual differences in reasoning / Keith E. Stanovich

    p. cm.

Includes bibliographical references and indexes.
ISBN 0-8058-2472-3 (hardcover : alk. paper) —
   ISBN 0-8058-2473-1 (pbk. : alk. paper).
1. Reasoning (Psychology) 2. Individual differences. I. Title.
BF442.S73   1998
153.4'3—dc21   98-27738
                                     CIP

Printed in the United States of America
10 9 8 7 6 5 4 3 2 1

For Paula,
who is everything to me

Contents

Preface   xi

CHAPTER 1   *Conceptualizing Rationality: Some Preliminaries*   1

     Descriptive, Normative, and Prescriptive Models   3

     Pretheoretical Positions on Human Rationality   4

     Rationality and Levels of Analysis in Cognitive Science   9

     A Framework for the Intentional Level   12

     Philosophical Problems at the Intentional Level: Is Human Irrationality Possible?   17

     Rationality and Evolution   22

     Rationality and Reflective Equilibrium   24

     Alternative Explanations for the Normative/Descriptive Gap   28

     The Rest of This Book   30

CHAPTER 2   *Performance Errors and Computational Limitations*   32

     (With Richard F. West)

     Individual Differences and Performance Errors   32

     Individual Differences and Computational Limitations   37

     Conclusions Regarding Performance Errors and Computational Limitations   48

CHAPTER 3   *The Inappropriate Norm Argument*   53

     From the Descriptive to the Normative in Reasoning Experiments   56

     Putting Descriptive Facts to Work: The Understanding/Acceptance Principle   61

     Applying the Right Norms: Clues From Individual Differences   63

     Examples of Normative Applications Undermined by the Understanding/Acceptance Principle   68

       Noncausal Base Rates   68

       The False-Consensus Effect   74

Explicating Normative Rules and the Understanding/Acceptance   78
Principle
   The Selection Task: Choosing P(D/~H)   79
   The Selection Task: Choosing the Base Rate   81
   Noncausal Base Rates: The Disease Problem   83
Examination of Other Problems With Controversial Norms   86
   Newcomb's Problem   86
   The Prisoner's Dilemma   88
Summary of Applications of the Understanding/Acceptance Principle   92
The Argument Evaluation Results and Reflective Equilibrium   95
Conclusion   96

CHAPTER 4 *The Problem of Rational Task Construal*   98
The Necessity for Principles of Rational Construal   99
Alternative Construals and Problem Framing   103
Evaluating Principles of Rational Construal: The   105
Understanding/Acceptance Principle Again
The Disease Problem   107
The Laundry Problem   108
Honoring Sunk Costs   109
Summary of Framing and Sunk Cost Results   115
The Overconfidence Effect in Knowledge Calibration   116
The Conjunction Fallacy   121
   The Linda Problem   121
   The Job Problem: An Easier Scenario   124
   The Student Problem: Frequency Estimation   125
Alternative Construals of Conjunction Problems: A Summary   127
Alternative Construals of the Selection Task   128
Models of Selection Task Performance   133
Conclusions   141

CHAPTER 5 *Dual-Process Theories and Evolutionary Adaptation Versus*   142
Normative Rationality
Interactional Intelligence   143
A Generic Dual-Process Framework   144

Alternative Task Construals: Evolutionary Adaptation Versus Normative Rationality   **148**

CHAPTER 6   *Thinking Dispositions and Decontextualized Reasoning*   **153**
(With Richard F. West and Walter C. Sá)

Beyond Computational Limitations: Systematic Associations Among Reasoning Tasks   **154**

Beyond Computational Limitations: Systematic Associations With Thinking Dispositions   **156**

Distinguishing Cognitive Capacities and Thinking Dispositions   **156**

Levels of Analysis and Thinking Dispositions   **158**

Thinking Dispositions: An Empirical Study   **159**

Reasoning Independently of Prior Belief: Thinking Dispositions as Predictors of Argument Evaluation Ability   **162**

A New Analytic Strategy for Assessing Argument Evaluation Ability   **163**

Cognitive Decontextualization   **170**

A Direct Test of the Domain Generality of a Cognitive Decontextualization Skill   **174**

Summary   **189**

CHAPTER 7   *The Fundamental Computational Bias*   **190**

The Pervasiveness of the Fundamental Computational Bias   **193**

The Fundamental Computational Bias and Evolutionary Adaptation   **202**

The Real-World Importance of Cognitive Decontextualization   **203**

CHAPTER 8   *Has Human Irrationality Been Empirically Demonstrated?*   **208**

Performance Errors   **209**

Computational Limitations   **209**

Thinking Dispositions and Rational Thought   **211**

Reversing the Figure and Ground of Competence and Performance   **212**

Alternative Task Construals: A Pyrrhic Victory for the Panglossians   **216**

Alternative Task Construals: A Pyrrhic Victory for the Apologists   **223**

Questionable Task Interpretations   **228**

Why Normative Rationality Will Not Disappear   **231**

The Cultural Transmission of Norms and the Malleability of Computational Limitations   **234**

Education and Normative Rationality   236

Caveats and Clarifications   238

  Assumptions Regarding Evolutionary Rationality and System 1   238
  Processes

  Alternative Interpretations of Relationships With Cognitive Ability   239

  The Plausibility of Computational Limitations in Different Types   241
  of Tasks

  Alternative Construal as a Computational Escape Hatch   241

  Not All System 1 Overrides Are Efficacious   243

  Normative and Evolutionary Rationality and the Rationality₁   243
  and Rationality₂ of Evans and Over (1996)

  Normative Rationality in the Belief Bias Situation: The Knowledge   244
  Projection Argument

Rationality and Pretheoretical Biases   249

References   253

Author Index   283

Subject Index   293

Preface

In this book, I attempt to integrate a decade-long program of empirical research with current cognitive theory. My general goal is to demonstrate, using selected empirical examples, that patterns of individual differences across cognitive tasks can have important implications for current debates about what it means to be rational. Early work in the heuristics and biases tradition of Kahneman and Tversky seemed to indicate that it was quite easy to demonstrate human irrationality experimentally. However, critiques of this work by philosophers and other psychologists during the last two decades have called into question virtually all purported demonstrations of human irrationality—so much so that it has become common for psychologists and philosophers alike to defend models of near-perfect human rationality.

In this volume, I bring new evidence to bear on these issues by demonstrating that patterns of individual differences—largely ignored in disputes about human rationality—have strong implications for explanations for the gap between normative and descriptive models of human behavior. Such normative/descriptive gaps are an empirical reality. What is at issue—and what is extremely contentious—is the theoretical interpretation of such gaps. The tendency in the early heuristics and biases literature was to interpret these discrepancies as indicating systematic human irrationality. However, critics soon argued that the entire heuristics and biases literature was characterized by a proclivity to too quickly attribute irrationality to people, and that there were numerous alternative explanations for discrepancies between descriptive accounts of behavior and normative models.

Across several chapters in the volume, all of the major critiques of purported demonstrations of human irrationality in the heuristics and biases literature are discussed. In these critiques, it has been posited that experimenters have observed performance errors rather than systematically irrational responses, that the tasks have required computational operations that exceed human cognitive capacity, that experimenters have applied the wrong normative model to the task, and that participants have misinterpreted the tasks. The studies presented in this volume demonstrate that gaps between normative and descriptive models of performance on some tasks can be accounted for by positing these alternative explanations but that not all discrepancies from normative models can be so explained. It does seem that some human response tendencies are systematically irrational. The empirical research presented also demonstrates that individual differences in rational thought can in part be predicted by psychological dispositions that are interpreted as characteristic biases in people's intentional-level psychologies.

As a framework for the results, I utilize the two-process theories of S. A. Sloman (1996) and of Evans and Over (1996) that distinguish automatic, heuristic processing operations from controlled, analytic processes. The latter operate to serve the goals of instrumental rationality: maximizing the goal satisfaction of the individual. The former are more directly tied to the evolutionary outcome of reproductive success. Instances of irrationality arise in situations where the instrumental goals of the controlled system conflict with the evolutionary goals of the heuristic system. Irrationality is demonstrated in such situations when the heuristic processes are not overridden by controlled processing.

The pervasive influence of heuristic processing is termed here the *fundamental computational bias* of human cognition and is discussed in chapter 7. The practical importance of understanding conflicts between the fundamental computational bias and the goals of instrumental rationality is stressed because it is argued that modern technological societies vastly increase the probability of such conflicts. Instances of human irrationality will increase as societal complexity increases and the consequences of this irrational cognition will be propagated throughout society as a whole. Thus, it is argued here that the outcome of the so-called "rationality debate" within cognitive science might have profound societal implications.

Discussions of human rationality are contentious because of the normative basis of judgments of rationality. These evaluative connotations have direct implications for how we go about ameliorative efforts and how we view the fundamental nature of human beings. The issues are important because one of the most profound ways that psychology changes society is by changing the way people talk about human behavior. Simply put, folk psychology has social effects by the very way in which it frames human problems. And our folk language of the mental evolves in response to the diffusion of scientific knowledge. "Introversion," "short-term memory," "Freudian slip," "inferiority complex," and "repression" have been woven into the current folk theory of the mental as have notions of information processing from computer science and cognitive psychology.

Bruner (1990) reminded researchers that the ways that they discuss human behavior will eventually affect the social world because the intuitive psychologies of the layperson provide the motivation for social policies. Rationality assumptions of various types form an important part of folk concepts of the nature of human cognition and, as Bruner noted, "it is through folk psychology that people anticipate and judge one another, draw conclusions about the worthwhileness of their lives, and so on. Its power over human mental functioning and human life is that it provides the very means by which culture shapes human beings to its requirements" (p. 15). That this cultural/scientific debate has been contentious should not be surprising as what in essence is being discussed are fundamental conceptions of human nature. Psychology's unique contribution is to condition such cultural debates by empirical evidence about actual human cognition. The unique contribution of this volume is to assure that all possible aspects of the empirical database are used to triangulate these difficult issues that lie on the borderline of philosophy and empirical science.

Structure of the Book

This volume is in part structured around alternative explanations of the gap between descriptive models of human behavior and normative models of the relevant task situation. In the heuristics and biases literature, this gap is taken as indicative of human irrationality. Alternatively, it might be argued that performance discrepancies from normative models might simply represent performance errors (by analogy to linguistics; see Stein, 1996)—minor cognitive slips due to inattention, memory lapses, or other temporary and basically unimportant psychological malfunctions. Another possibility is that it may be that the computational requirements of the problem exceed the capacity of the human brain. Additionally, it can be argued that the experimenter is applying the wrong normative model to the problem. Finally, critics often argue that the subject has a different construal of the task than the experimenter intended and is responding normatively to a different problem. Subsequent chapters discuss how each of these alternative explanations for the normative/descriptive gap—performance errors, computational limitations, incorrect norm application, and alternative task construal—has particular implications for what patterns of individual differences should be observed across different reasoning tasks. Thus, an examination of individual differences promises to give us principled constraints on explanations of the normative/descriptive gap observed in particular task situations.

For those wishing a road map with which to scan ahead, chapters 2, 3, 4, and 6 deal primarily with the empirical research program. Chapters 5, 7, and 8 set the results within the context of current cognitive theory and discuss the implications of the research for the rationality debate. In chapter 1, some basic terminology is introduced that sets the stage for the subsequent discussion. The philosophical context of the debates about human rationality is also introduced. Finally, three pretheoretical positions on human rationality are described—that of the Panglossian, the Apologist, and the Meliorist. These three positions represent preexisting biases on the nature of human rationality that strongly color the experiments that investigators design and their interpretation of the results of those experiments.

Chapter 2 is devoted to demonstrations of the implications of patterns of covariance for explanations for the normative/descriptive gap in terms of performance errors and computational limitations. Chapter 3 is concerned with incorrect norm application and chapter 4 with alternative problem construal. In chapter 5, in order to provide a framework for integrating the patterns of individual differences demonstrated in the series of empirical studies, I outline a framework that links two-process theories of reasoning with the distinction between evolutionary adaptation and normative rationality. Chapter 6 deals with dispositional psychological constructs that predict rational responses and that can be conceptualized at the intentional level. By examining whether such constructs can explain variance in human performance independent of cognitive capacity, it is possible to test the proposition that there is systematic irrationality in the intentional-level descriptions of at least some individuals. This chapter also contains a discussion of the general notion of decontextualizing thought.

In chapter 7, I introduce the notion of the fundamental computational bias—an overarching style that conjoins a number of processing biases that are the reason that evolutionary and normative rationality sometimes dissociate. In chapter 8, I take a step back and attempt to evaluate the practical and theoretical gains to be had from assessing variation in rational thought. It is argued that debates about rational thought might benefit from a reversal of figure and ground. Traditionally these debates have foregrounded issues of competence and backgrounded issues of performance. The results discussed in this volume suggest an inversion of these priorities—an inversion that has some unexpected consequences for the debate among the Panglossians, Apologists, and Meliorists. The chapter concludes with some caveats/qualifications and with some speculations about the pretheoretical views that determine study design and data interpretation in these debates.

ACKNOWLEDGMENTS

My attraction to the field of psychology—and to the research projects I have undertaken—has always been driven by certain Meliorist tendencies. This has been true of my work on literacy and reading disability. It was certainly true of the introductory critical-thinking text I wrote in 1983 (Stanovich, 1998), and it remains true of this more scholarly and abstract product. Despite the seeming practical irrelevance of many theoretical disputes in this research area, the philosophical debates do serve as a context for cognitive remediation efforts. Pondering Stich's (1990) discussion of this context in his (then) just published *The Fragmentation of Reason* during my 1991 sabbatical in Cambridge (thanks are due to Usha Goswami and the Department of Experimental Psychology there) set me ruminating further about both the difficulty and the importance of evaluating human rationality.

Commenting on his own project, Stich (1990) noted that:

> A second concern, one that became increasingly important as work on this volume proceeded, was that if the thesis [that it is impossible to demonstrate human irrationality] were true, then much of the urgency would be drained from the project of assessing strategies of reasoning and inquiry. The interest and vitality of this branch of epistemological research can be traced, in significant measure, to the practical worries it addresses: People out there are reasoning badly, and this bad reasoning is giving rise to bad theories, many of which have nasty consequences for people's lives. But if Davidson and Dennett are right, then these concerns [about irrationality] are overblown. Cognition *can't* be all that bad. Perhaps the reasoning of the man and woman in the street (or the jury box, or the legislature) is not quite normatively impeccable, but we need not worry about them departing in major ways from the normative ideal. This Panglossian doctrine reduces the normative evaluation of inquiry to a rather bloodless, scholastic preoccupation. We can still, if we wish, try to say what it is that makes good reasoning good. But the project can hardly be infused with the reformer's zeal, since we know in advance that there is nothing much to reform. (pp. 15–16)

For the Meliorist with an excess of zeal, this is a disheartening prospect. I thus set about figuring out ways in which the hypothesis of near-perfect human rationality might be tested using an individual differences approach (a fairly neglected approach in this literature). The results of this investigation are summarized in this volume.

This book has had a long gestation period. Although empirical work on the project proceeded throughout the late 1980s and early to mid-1990s, a heavy commitment to research programs on the cognitive consequences of literacy and the cognitive psychology of reading prevented me from bringing the work to fruition in manuscript form. The logjam was finally broken by two things: a research leave granted by the Ontario Institute for Studies in Education of the University of Toronto in 1996 and a Connaught Research Fellowship in the Social Sciences, awarded by the University of Toronto for winter of 1998. The administration of both the Institute and the University are thanked for this support. The empirical research described here was made possible by continuous support received from the Social Sciences and Humanities Research Council of Canada.

My long-time colleague, Richard West, has been central to the empirical parts of this research program. What could one say about a 25-year friendship and collaboration that would speak more eloquently than the longevity of the relationship itself? We hatched many of these experiments together in circumstances that ranged from the sublime to the ridiculous—from the tranquil footpath to Grantchester during my sabbatical in Cambridge to a nasty stretch of highway on the way to Dulles Airport. As always in science, more important than the results obtained was the quest itself—in this case the most joyful of quests with a beloved friend and dedicated scientist. Many thanks are due to Judy West for tolerating my frequent and usually terse requests for her husband to come to the phone. Less directly involved in this book but critical to my intellectual development were former colleagues Anne Cunningham, Larry Lilliston, and Dean Purcell—and Anne Jordan and Linda Siegel, who brought me to Toronto.

Many of our students participated in these projects by collecting and recording data and making our lives easier in various ways. I wish to thank especially Penny Chiappe, Alexandra Gottardo, Jason Riis, Robin Sidhu, Walter Sá, Ron Stringer, and Maggie Toplak.

Intellectual debts to many scholars are evident in the text, and the reference list chronicles this debt. Nevertheless, particular inspiration has been drawn from the work of Daniel Kahneman, Amos Tversky, Jonathan Baron, and Jonathan Evans. Thanks are due to several scholars who critiqued the manuscript, including those who commented on journal versions of the empirical studies that are discussed in this volume. Particularly helpful and generous comments were received from Jonathan Baron, Carole Beal, Peter Dixon, Mike Doherty, Jonathan Evans, Richard Griggs, Phillip Johnson-Laird, Daniel Kahneman, Richard Klaczynski, Nora Newcombe, Mike Oaksford, Keith Oatley, David Over, and Richard Platt.

I have an excellent support staff here at the University of Toronto, but I must single out Mary Macri who is essential to the smooth running of my research projects. She makes the whole operation run, and her efforts are much appreciated. Dan Keating provides a well-run department in which extended projects like this one can flourish.

My editor at Lawrence Erlbaum Associates, Judi Amsel, was enthusiastic about the project from the very beginning but also patient when my deadlines stretched.

And finally, Paula—who has been everything in my life, and means everything to me. There is nothing more commemorative of what we have shared and accomplished together than this book—a symbol of a life shared and of my love.

—*Keith Stanovich*

Conceptualizing Rationality:
Some Preliminaries

The issue of human rationality has provoked contradictory responses within the field of psychology. Some investigators eschew the term rationality and the attendant philosophical debates about normative criteria for thinking and advocate a purely descriptive role for psychology. In contrast, other investigators embrace the philosophical disputes about the normative criteria for evaluating human thought and view empirical findings as a vital context for these debates. In this volume, I throw in my lot with the second group of investigators. I demonstrate that certain previously underutilized aspects of descriptive models of behavior have implications for the evaluation of the appropriateness of normative models of rational thought. Yet assessing the degree to which humans can be said to be responding rationally remains one of the most difficult tasks facing cognitive science. Traditionally, philosophers have been more comfortable analyzing the concept of rationality than have psychologists. Indeed, psychological work that purports to have implications for the evaluation of human rationality has been the subject of especially intense criticism (e.g., Cohen, 1981, 1986; Gigerenzer, 1991b, 1996a; Hilton, 1995; Kahneman, 1981; Kahneman & Tversky, 1983, 1996; Macdonald, 1986; Wetherick, 1995). It is no wonder that many psychologists give the concept a wide berth.

The most intense controversies about human rationality arise when psychologists find that modal human performance deviates from the performance deemed normative according to various models of decision making and coherent judgment (e.g., expected utility theory, the probability calculus). Psychologists have identified many such gaps between descriptive models of human behavior and normative models. For example, people assess probabilities incorrectly, they display confirmation bias, they test hypotheses inefficiently, they violate the axioms of utility theory, they do not properly calibrate degrees of belief, they overproject their own opinions onto others, they allow prior knowledge to become implicated in deductive reasoning, they systematically underweight information about nonoccurrence when evaluating covariation, and they display numerous other information-processing biases (for summaries of the large literature, see Baron, 1994b; Dawes, 1988; Evans, 1989; Evans & Over, 1996; Osherson, 1995; Piattelli-Palmarini, 1994; Plous, 1993; Shafir & Tversky, 1995). Indeed, demonstrating that descriptive accounts of human behavior diverged from normative models was a main theme of the so-called heuristics and biases literature of the 1970s and early 1980s (see Arkes & Hammond, 1986; Kahneman, Slovic, & Tversky, 1982).

Although the empirical demonstration of the discrepancies is not in doubt, the theoretical interpretation of these normative/descriptive gaps is highly contentious (e.g., Baron, 1994a; Cohen, 1981, 1983; Evans & Over, 1996; Gigerenzer, 1996a; Kahneman & Tversky, 1983, 1996; Stein, 1996). Some psychologists have provoked the criticism that they were too quick to interpret the gap as an indication of systematic irrationality in human reasoning competence. It has been argued that the entire heuristics and biases literature is characterized by a proclivity to too quickly attribute irrationality to subjects' performance (Berkeley & Humphreys, 1982; Christensen-Szalanski & Beach, 1984; Cohen, 1982; Einhorn & Hogarth, 1981; Hastie & Rasinski, 1988; Kruglanski & Ajzen, 1983; Lopes, 1991; Lopes & Oden, 1991). Critics argued that there were numerous alternative explanations for discrepancies between descriptive accounts of behavior and normative models.

In subsequent chapters, all of these alternative explanations are examined closely—but with a special focus. In this volume, I attempt to foreground a type of empirical data that has been underutilized by both sides in the debate about human rationality—individual differences. What has largely been ignored is that—although the average person in these experiments might well display an overconfidence effect, underutilize base rates, choose P and Q in the selection task, commit the conjunction fallacy, and so forth—on each of these tasks, *some people give the standard normative response*. It is argued that attention has been focused too narrowly on the modal response and that patterns of individual differences contain potentially relevant information that has largely been ignored.[1] In a series of experiments in which many of the classic tasks in the heuristics and biases literature are examined, it is demonstrated that individual differences and their patterns of covariance have implications for explanations of why human behavior often departs from normative models.

In order to contextualize these demonstrations, however, I must make a number of conceptual distinctions. In the remainder of this chapter, a

---

[1]For exceptions to the general neglect of individual differences in the literature, see Jepson et al. (1983), Rips and Conrad (1983), Slugoski, Shields, and Dawson (1993), and Yates, Lee, and Shinotsuka (1996).

variety of useful distinctions and taxonomies are presented. I begin by adding the notion of a prescriptive model to the well-known distinction between descriptive and normative models.

DESCRIPTIVE, NORMATIVE, AND PRESCRIPTIVE MODELS

Descriptive models—accurate specifications of the response patterns of human beings and theoretical accounts of those observed response patterns in terms of psychological mechanisms—are the goal of most work in empirical psychology. In contrast, normative models embody standards for cognitive activity—standards that, if met, serve to optimize the accuracy of beliefs and the efficacy of actions. For example, in some contexts, subjective expected utility theory serves as a normative model for the choice of actions. Closure over logical implication is sometimes taken as a normative model of belief consistency. Bayesian conditionalization is often used as a normative model of belief updating. Much research accumulated throughout the 1970s and 1980s to indicate that human behavior often deviated from these normative standards (Evans, 1989; Kahneman et al., 1982; Plous, 1993).

As interesting as such divergences between normative and descriptive models are, they cannot automatically be interpreted as instances of human irrationality. This is because judgments about the rationality of actions and beliefs must take into account the resource-limited nature of the human cognitive apparatus (Cherniak, 1986; Gigerenzer & Goldstein, 1996; Goldman, 1978; Oaksford & Chater, 1993, 1995; Osherson, 1995; Simon, 1956, 1957; Stich, 1990). As Harman (1995) explained:

> Reasoning uses resources and there are limits to the available resources. Reasoners have limited attention spans, limited memories, and limited time. Ideal rationality is not always possible for limited beings. Because of our limits, we make use of strategies and heuristics, rules of thumb that work or seem to work most of the time but not always. It is rational for us to use such rules, if we have nothing better that will give us reasonable answers in the light of our limited resources. (p. 178)

More colloquially, Stich (1990) noted that "it seems simply perverse to judge that subjects are doing a bad job of reasoning because they are not using a strategy that requires a brain the size of a blimp" (p. 27).

Acknowledging cognitive resource limitations leads to the idea of replacing normative models as the standard to be achieved with prescriptive models (Baron, 1985a; Bell, Raiffa, & Tversky, 1988; Simon, 1956, 1957). Prescriptive models are usually viewed as specifying how processes of belief formation and decision making should be carried out, given the limitations of the human cognitive apparatus and the situational constraints (e.g., time pressure) with which the decision maker must deal. Thus, in cases where the normative model is computable by the human brain, it is also prescriptive. In a case where the normative model is not computable (Oaksford & Chater, 1993, 1995), then the standard for human performance becomes the computable strategy closest to the normative model. Such a prescriptive strategy is the one that maximizes goal satisfaction given the individual's cognitive limitations and environmental context. Thus, Baron (1985a) pointed out that:

> [Although normative models may not provide] a good prescriptive model for ordinary people, it can be seen as a good prescriptive model for some sort of idealized creature who lacks some constraint that people really have, such as limited time. We may thus think of normative models as prescriptive models for idealized creatures ... . A good prescriptive model takes into account the very constraints on time, etc., that a normative model is free to ignore. (pp. 8–11)

Baron also observed that "prescriptive models are, by definition, possible to follow, which is to say that there is in principle some way to educate people to follow them more closely than they do" (p. 10).

The distinction between normative and prescriptive models lies at the heart of debates about human rationality. It is often the case that investigators on different sides of the issue will agree that an accurate description of human performance deviates from the response dictated by a normative model but disagree about whether or not the response is consistent with a prescriptive model for the task in question. Investigators working in the heuristics and biases tradition (e.g., Kahneman et al., 1982; Nisbett & Ross, 1980; Tversky & Kahneman, 1974) have been prone to assume: (a) that the prescriptive model for most tasks was close to the normative model, (b) that the response that deviated from the normative model was thus also deviant from the prescriptive model, and thus, (c) that an attribution of irrationality was justified. Many critics of the heuristics and biases literature have tended to draw precisely the opposite conclusions—inferring instead: (a) that the prescriptive model for most tasks was quite different from the normative model, (b) that the response that deviated from the normative model was thus not deviant from the prescriptive model, and (c) that an attribution of irrationality was therefore unjustified.

PRETHEORETICAL POSITIONS ON HUMAN RATIONALITY

There are three positions on the relationships between normative, prescriptive, and descriptive models that should be distinguished. These positions might be termed pretheoretical stances or preexisting biases because they largely determine how investigators approach the study of human rationality—determining the types of studies that they design and their data-interpretation proclivities. All three are illustrated in Fig. 1.1. Different relationships between normative, prescriptive, and descriptive models are illustrated as differing distances between the three on a continuum running from optimal reasoning to inefficacious reasoning. The position illustrated at the top is termed the Panglossian position, and it is most often represented by philosophers (e.g., Cohen, 1981; Dennett, 1987; Wetherick, 1995) who argue that human irrationality is a conceptual impossibility. For them, a competence model of actual human performance is coextensive with the normative model (and, obviously, the prescriptive as well). The Panglossian sees no gaps at all between the descriptive and normative.

Of course, in specific instances, human behavior does depart from normative responding, but the Panglossian has a variety of stratagems available for explaining away these departures from normative theory. First,

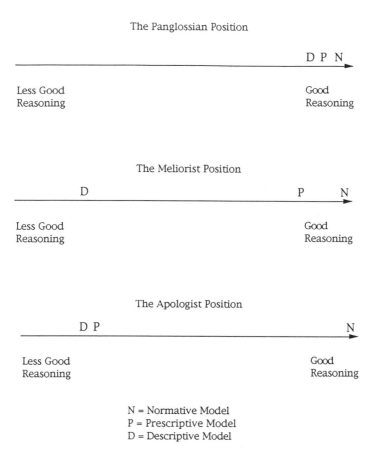

The Panglossian Position

D P N →

Less Good
Reasoning

Good
Reasoning

The Meliorist Position

D

P   N →

Less Good
Reasoning

Good
Reasoning

The Apologist Position

D P

N →

Less Good
Reasoning

Good
Reasoning

N = Normative Model
P = Prescriptive Model
D = Descriptive Model

FIG. 1.1.   Three pretheoretical positions on human rationality.

the departures might simply represent performance errors (by analogy to linguistics, see Cohen, 1981; Stein, 1996)—minor cognitive slips due to inattention, memory lapses, or other temporary and basically unimportant psychological malfunctions. Second, it can be argued that the experimenter is applying the wrong normative model to the problem. Third, the Panglossian can argue that the subject has a different construal of the task than the experimenter intended and is responding normatively to a *different* problem. Each of these three alternative explanations for the normative/descriptive gap—performance errors, incorrect norm application, and alternative task construal—is the subject of extensive discussion in a subsequent chapter.

In addition to the philosophers who argue the conceptual impossibility of human irrationality, another very influential group in the Panglossian camp is represented by the mainstream of the discipline of economics, which is notable for conflating the normative with the descriptive:

> The entire framework of economics—of whatever paradigm or in whatever application—rests on a fundamental premise, namely, that people behave rationally. By "rationally" I mean simply that before selecting a course of action individuals will consider the expected benefits and costs of each alternative and they will then select that course of action which generates the highest expected net benefit. (Whynes, 1983, p. 198)

Such strong rationality assumptions are fundamental tools used by economists—and they are often pressed quite far: "Economic agents, either firms, households, or individuals, are presumed to behave in a rational, self-interested manner ... a manner that is consistent with solutions of rather complicated calculations under conditions of even imperfect information" (Davis & Holt, 1993, p. 435).

These assumptions of extremely tight normative/descriptive connections are essential to much work in modern economics, and they account for some of the hostility that economists often display toward psychological findings that suggest nontrivial normative/descriptive gaps. Yet there are dissenters from the Panglossian view even within economics itself. Thaler (1992) amusingly observed that:

> An economist who spends a year finding a new solution to a nagging problem, such as the optimal way to search for a job when unemployed, is content to assume that the unemployed have already solved this problem and search accordingly. The assumption that everyone else can intuitively solve problems that an economist has to struggle to solve analytically reflects admirable modesty, but it does seem a bit puzzling. Surely another possibility is that people simply get it wrong. (p. 2)

That people "simply get it wrong" was the tacit assumption in much of the early work in the heuristics and biases tradition (e.g., Nisbett & Ross, 1980; Tversky & Kahneman, 1974)—and such an assumption defines the second position illustrated in Fig. 1.1, the Meliorist position. The Meliorist begins with the assumption that the prescriptive, if not identical to the normative, is at least quite close. However, the descriptive model of human behavior, in the Meliorist view, can sometimes be quite far from the normative. Because the prescriptive is close to the normative in this view, actual behavior can be quite far from the most optimal computable response (the prescriptive). Thus, the Meliorist view leaves substantial room for the improvement of human reasoning in some situations by reducing the gap between the descriptive and prescriptive. However, because this view posits that there can be large deviations between human performance and the prescriptive model, the Meliorist is much more likely to impute irrationality. The difference between the Panglossian and the Meliorist on this issue was captured colloquially in a recent article in *The Economist* ("The Money in the Message," 1998) where a subheading asks "Economists Make Sense of the World by Assuming That People Know What They Want. Advertisers Assume That They Do Not. Who Is Right?"

A third position, pictured at the bottom of Fig. 1.1, is that of the Apologist. This position is like the Meliorist view in that it posits that there may be a large gap between the normative and descriptive. However, unlike the Meliorist, the Apologist sees the prescriptive model as closer to the descriptive than to the normative. According to the Apologist, people are quite close to their prescriptive limits. Individuals should not be deemed irrational because of the large deviation of their responses from the normative—although that deviation does mean that from certain omniscient, global perspectives (see Foley, 1991) they may not be reasoning all that well. The Apologist takes seriously the caveat about computational limitations discussed previously and thus this view emphasizes that when human performance deviates from a normative model, irrationality cannot necessarily be imputed.

In short, the Meliorist thinks that sometimes people are not reasoning very well and that they could do much better. The Apologist thinks that sometimes people are not reasoning properly, but that they are doing about as well as they could possibly do. And, finally, the Panglossian feels that people are reasoning very well—indeed, as well as anyone could possibly reason in this best of all possible worlds.

It is clear that from the standpoint of motivating cognitive remediation efforts, these positions have markedly different implications. The Panglossian position provides little motivation for remediation efforts because the Panglossian thinks that reasoning is as good as it could *conceivably* be. The Meliorist position, on the other hand, leaves a wide gap for the motivation of remediation efforts. Actual behavior is sometimes markedly below what is cognitively possible on this view, and the payoff for remediation efforts would appear to be high. The Apologist is like the Panglossian in seeing little that can done given existing cognitive constraints (i.e., the existing computational constraints of our brains and the current way that environmental stimuli are structured). However, the Apologist position does emphasize the possibility of enhancing performance in another way—by presenting information in a way that is better suited to what our cognitive machinery is designed to do (Brase, Cosmides, & Tooby, 1998; Cosmides & Tooby, 1996; Gigerenzer & Hoffrage, 1995). Thus, whereas the Meliorist emphasizes the possibility of getting our cognitive machinery to operate differently, the Apologist emphasizes adapting the world to our cognitive machinery in order to enhance performance.

It is likely that a preexisting bias related to cognitive remediation has partially motivated the positions of the Meliorist reformers in the heuristics and biases literature as well as their critics in the Panglossian and Apologist camps (see Cohen, 1981; Dawes, 1983, 1988; Gigerenzer, 1996a; Jepson, Krantz, & Nisbett, 1983; Kahneman, 1981; Kahneman & Tversky, 1983, 1996; Krantz, 1981). Pretheoretical biases also arise because of different weightings of the relative costs and benefits of different assumptions about the nature of human rationality. For example, if Panglossians happen to be wrong in their assumptions, then we might miss opportunities to remediate reasoning. Thagard and Nisbett (1983) pointed out that a strong Panglossian assumption "preempts the possibilities of criticism and improvement. If we cannot assume actions and judgments to be irrational, then we cannot hope to educate and improve choice strategies and inferential procedures" (p. 263). They worried that such a strong assumption ignores the cultural evolution of reasoning norms and thus may "freeze human behavior in an unprogressive amalgam of late twentieth century procedures" (p. 263).

Conversely, unjustified Meliorism has its associated costs as well. Effort might well be wasted at cognitive remediation efforts. We might fail to appreciate and celebrate the astonishing efficiency of unaided human cognition (Gigerenzer & Goldstein, 1996). Excessive Meliorism might lead to a tendency to ignore the possibility that the environmental change advocated by the Apologists might be an easier route to performance enhancement than cognitive change. Also, exaggerated Meliorism might narrow the nature of our inquiries by prematurely suggesting closure on normative issues that are still in dispute (Gigerenzer, 1991b, 1993; Gigerenzer & Murray, 1987). Additionally, ascriptions of irrationality have moral connotations (Gauthier, 1986; Schmidtz, 1995; Siegel, 1988) and some find distasteful the Meliorist's hastiness toward a judgment of irrationality (Lopes, 1991, e.g., worried about the "social and political implications," p. 65).

Viewpoints in this domain are Necker cubelike. In a chapter titled "The Two Camps on Rationality" (the two camps being the Meliorists and Panglossian/Apologists), Jungermann (1986) referred to the two groups as pessimists and optimists, respectively—Meliorists being pessimists about the possibility of human rationality and Panglossian/Apologists being optimists about the current state of human rationality. I use the term *current state* advisedly because the terms of course reverse if used to refer to the possibility of cognitive betterment—here, it is the Meliorists who are optimists and the Panglossians who are pessimists. In that domain, Jungermann's optimists might well be termed fatalists. Although Lopes (1991) was perhaps right to worry about "social and political implications" (p. 65) of hasty judgments of irrationality, others might find it disturbing that none of our wars, economic busts, technological accidents, pyramid sales schemes, telemarketing fraud, religious fanaticism, psychic scams, environmental degradation, broken marriages, and savings and loan scandals are due to remediable irrational thought. Instead, much more intractable social dilemmas (Hardin, 1968; Komorita & Parks, 1994) and truly evil human desires (see Kekes, 1990; Nathanson, 1994) must be at fault—and this hardly seems "optimistic."

In any case, with this background, Fig. 1.1 serves to situate the alternative explanations for the gap between the normative and the descriptive. From the Meliorist perspective, because there is no computational limitation that separates the prescriptive from the normative, the normative/descriptive gap is attributed to irrationality. From the Apologist perspective, the descriptive model is quite close to the prescriptive model—the normative/descriptive gap is attributed to a computational limitation. The Panglossian perspective denies the possibility of normative/descriptive gaps. Therefore, any observed discrepancies must only be apparent—the result of transitory performance errors, the wrong norm being applied by the experimenter, or an alternative construal of the task on the part of the subject (warranting some other normative model that is then followed perfectly). In the sections of this chapter that follow, I try to further contextualize these alternative explanations in order to set the stage for the subsequent chapters, which contain demonstrations of how individual differences have implications for these various explanations of the normative/descriptive gap.

RATIONALITY AND LEVELS OF ANALYSIS IN COGNITIVE SCIENCE

The resource-limited nature of human information processing—and the notion of a normative/prescriptive gap based on such computational limitations—can be further contextualized by introducing terminology referring to different levels of analysis in a cognitive system. Levels of analysis in cognitive theory have been discussed by numerous investigators (Anderson, 1990, 1991; Dennett, 1978, 1987; Horgan & Tienson, 1993; Levelt, 1995; Marr, 1982; Newell, 1982, 1990; Oaksford & Chater, 1995; Pylyshyn, 1984; Sterelny, 1990). For example, Anderson (1990) defined four levels of theorizing in cognitive science: a biological level that is inaccessible to cognitive theorizing, an implementation level that is basically a comprehensible shorthand approximation to the biological, an algorithmic level concerned with the computational processes necessary to carry out a task, and the rational level. The latter level provides a specification of the goals of the system's computations (what the system is attempting to compute and why) and can be used to suggest constraints on the operation of the algorithmic level. The rational level of analysis is concerned with the goals of the system, beliefs relevant to those goals, and the choice of action that is rational given the system's goals and beliefs (Bratman, Israel, & Pollack, 1991; Dennett, 1987; Newell, 1982, 1990; Pollock, 1995).

Many similar taxonomies exist in the literature (Sterelny, 1990, p. 46, warned of the "bewildering variety of terms" used to describe these levels of analysis). Indeed, Anderson (1990) draws heavily on the work of Marr (1982) and Newell (1982). Table 1.1 presents the alternative, but similar, schemes of Anderson (1990), Marr (1982), Newell (1982), and Dennett (1987). On the far right of the table is the terminology that has been adopted in the present volume, which represents an amalgamation and adaptation of the terminology in the other schemes. The first level of analysis is termed the *biological* level in my taxonomy because I am largely concerned with human information processing rather than computational devices in general. My scheme follows Marr (1982) and Dennett (1987) in collapsing Anderson's algorithmic and implementation levels into one because, for the purposes of the present discussion, the distinction between these two levels is not important. This second level is termed *algorithmic*—a term that is relatively uncontroversial.

In contrast, the proper term for the third level—the main focus of this volume—is variable and controversial. Borrowing from Dennett (1987), I have termed this level of analysis the *intentional* level for the following reasons. First, Anderson (1990) argued that Marr's (1982) terminology is confusing and inapt because "his level of computational theory is not really about computation but rather about the goals of the computation. His basic point is that one should state these goals and understand their implications before one worries about their computation, which is really the concern of the lower levels of his theory" (p. 6). Dennett (1987) reiterated this critique of Marr's terminology by noting that "the highest level, which he misleadingly calls computational, is in fact not at all concerned with computational processes but strictly (and more abstractly) with the question of what function the system in question is serving" (pp. 74–75). The term chosen by Newell (1982)—the knowledge level—is equally inapt in not signaling that this level is concerned with action selection based on expected goal attainment in light of current beliefs.

Anderson's (1990) alternative term—rational level—indicates correctly the conceptual focus of this level of analysis. However, in light of the empirical project outlined in this volume, it has unfortunate question-begging connotations. The term is appropriate for Anderson's pro-

TABLE 1.1
Different Levels of Cognitive Theory as Characterized by Several Investigators and in This Volume

Anderson	Marr	Newell	Dennett	This Volume
Rational Level	Computational Level	Knowledge Level	Intentional Stance	Intentional Level
Algorithmic Level		Program Symbol Level		
	Representation and Algorithm		Design Stance	Algorithmic Level
Implementa- tion Level		Register Transfer Level		
Biological Level	Hardware Implementation	Device	Physical Stance	Biological Level

ject—which is to construct adaptationist models based on an assumption of rationality at this level of analysis. But it is inappropriate here where it is just this assumption that is at issue. In contrast, although Dennett's (1987) assumption that the descriptive models of what he called the intentional level are well matched to normative models is, like Anderson's assumption of rationality, antithetical to the present empirical project (which proceeds with no a priori assumptions about normative/descriptive matches at the intentional level), his term can be used in a more neutral way—as an indication of a particular conceptual level—and it can be employed without the a priori assumption of near-perfect rationality (i.e., without the assumption of a near-perfect normative/descriptive match). Although Sterelny (1990, p. 45) argued that this level of analysis is not necessarily tied to an intentional psychology, in this volume, like Dennett, I do want to conjoin the two—so in the present case, the term is apt.

I have not followed Dennett's (1987) focus on an intentional *stance* but have instead simply employed the more neutral label intentional *level*.[2] Dennett's emphasis flows from his interest in the properties of various predictive strategies (stances) that one can adopt to forecast the behavior of intelligent entities. At the lowest level is the physical stance where we predict behavior by acquiring knowledge of the entity's physical constitution and using the laws of physics. The design stance ignores the physical constitution of the system and instead inquires as to how the entity was designed to behave and then makes the simple assumption that it will

---

[2]The view taken here is more like that of Newell than that of Dennett. In discussing the differences between their two positions, Newell (1982) noted that Dennett's view "does not, as noted, assign reality to the different system levels, but keeps them in the eye of the beholder" (p. 123). In this volume, as in Newell (1982), the intentional level is viewed as a conceptual reality.

"behave as it is designed to behave under various circumstances" (Dennett, 1987, p. 17). Dennett used the prosaic example of an alarm clock—reminding us that we do not care about whether it is battery driven, spring wound, or solar powered in making our predictions about its behavior. We simply use our knowledge that clock alarms sound when they are set to sound and then we monitor whether the alarm is set and what time is indicated (keeping track of background assumptions such as that the clock is running, etc.) in order to predict its behavior.

The intentional stance implicates a third level of explanation where issues of physical constitution and design are set aside and predictions are made by ascribing beliefs and desires to the system and assuming that the system functions (more or less efficiently) to satisfy desires based on current beliefs. It is this third level that is termed here the intentional level. It is at the intentional level where issues of rationality arise. In contrast, at the algorithmic level the key issue is one of computational efficiency. Finally, at the biological level questions such as whether the physical mechanism has the potential to instantiate certain complex algorithms become prominent (Oaksford & Chater, 1993, 1995). It is of course assumed that the intentional-level descriptions are instantiated at the algorithmic and biological levels (and, as is discussed later, limitations at the algorithmic level have important implications for intentional-level explanation).

A FRAMEWORK FOR THE INTENTIONAL LEVEL

Although some quite complex and technical models of intentional-level analysis of cognition exist, I outline only the minimal model necessary for the introduction of the terminology and conceptual distinctions that are needed in later chapters. For extensive discussions of the complexities of intentional-level models and their relation to rationality, see Bratman (1987), Bratman et al. (1991), Newell (1982, 1990), Pollock (1991, 1995), and Stich (1996).

Figure 1.2 displays a minimal model. This minimal intentional system contains a set of beliefs (the system's knowledge), a set of desires (the system's goals), and a mechanism (labeled *action determination*) that derives actions from a consideration of the system's beliefs and desires.

The arrows labeled A are meant to indicate that one way that beliefs are formed is by taking in information about the external world. Modeling of the external world by beliefs can be more or less good and, in the extreme, it may become so poor that we want to call it irrational. Of course, beliefs can be derived without the aid of external information—for example, they can be derived using inferences from other beliefs or from desires (as in wishful thinking, Babad & Katz, 1991; Harvey, 1992). The double-headed arrows labeled B refer to relations among beliefs and relations among desires. These relations may be more or less coherent. Belief inconsistency detection is thus an important determinant of rationality. For example, detection of belief inconsistency might be a sign that belief formation processes have operated suboptimally. Also, detection of belief inconsistency signals that the beliefs and desires that are used in the processes of action determination might be expected to result in a less than satisfactory outcome. Analyses of self-deception (e.g., Gur & Sackheim, 1979; Mele, 1987) have traditionally posited the presence of two contradictory beliefs in an individual's knowledge base (however, see Mele, 1997).

Many potential complications to this model (see Bratman et al., 1991; Pollock, 1995) are not pictured in Fig. 1.2. However, one is pictured in Fig. 1.3. Here, the single-headed arrows labeled C indicate the possibility of desires modifying processes of belief formation and inconsistency detection (Kunda, 1990; Mele, 1997). However, several other processes—such as the formation of desires and beliefs modifying desires (Elster, 1983: Pollock, 1995) are not represented. Nevertheless, with this minimal model, the major components of rational thought that have been the focus of attention in cognitive science have been represented.

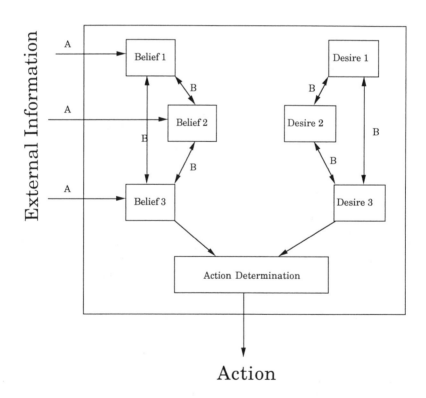

FIG. 1.2.   A minimal model of the intentional level of analysis.

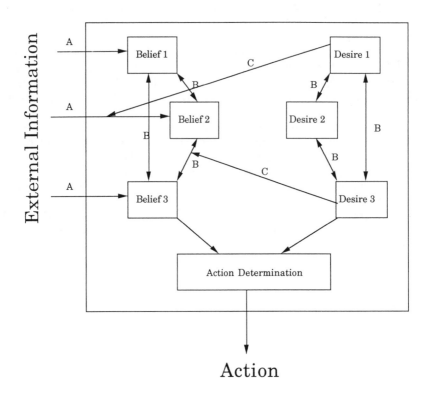

FIG. 1.3. A slightly elaborated minimal model of the intentional level of analysis.

An important distinction that is illustrated in Figs. 1.2 and 1.3 is the distinction between rationality of belief and rationality of action (Audi, 1993a, 1993b; Harman, 1995; Nozick, 1993; Pollock, 1995). The former—how accurately a person's belief network represents the external world—has been variously termed theoretical rationality, evidential rationality, or epistemic rationality (Audi, 1993b; Foley, 1987; Harman, 1995). I follow Foley in terming it *epistemic rationality*. The latter—how well a person maximizes the satisfaction of their desires, given their beliefs—has been variously termed practical, pragmatic, instrumental, or means/ends rationality (Audi, 1993b; Harman, 1995; Nathanson, 1994; Nozick, 1993) and these terms are used interchangeably in this volume.

With this basic model in place, it is possible to sketch some of the difficult problems inherent in attempting to evaluate the rationality of descriptive models of human behavior framed at the intentional level. For example, many debates about rationality focus exclusively on practical rationality. Issues of epistemic rationality are ignored by treating beliefs as fixed and, likewise, the content of desires is often not evaluated. The individual's goals and beliefs are accepted as they are, and debate centers only on whether individuals are optimally satisfying desires given beliefs. Such a view represents what Elster (1983) called a thin theory of rationality because it "leaves unexamined the beliefs and the desires that form the reasons for the action whose rationality we are assessing" (p. 1). Foley (1987, p. 131) termed this thin theory radically subjective because of its total restriction to the preexisting belief network of the actor—independent of the accuracy of the beliefs as representations of the world. The strengths of the thin theory of practical rationality are well known. For example, if the conception of rationality is restricted to a thin theory, many powerful formalisms (such as the axioms of decision theory) are available to serve as normative standards for behavior (Jeffrey, 1983; Pratt, Raiffa, & Schlaifer, 1995; Savage, 1954).

The weaknesses of the thin theory are equally well known (Elster, 1983; Nathanson, 1994; Simon, 1983). In not evaluating desires, a thin theory of rationality would be forced to say that Hitler was a rational person as long as he acted in accordance with the basic axioms of choice as he went about fulfilling his grotesque desires. Likewise, if we submit beliefs to no normative criteria, the psychiatric ward patient who acted consistently on his belief that he was Jesus Christ would be judged a rational person. Although some theorists may feel that these aberrant cases may be worth tolerating in order to gain access to the powerful choice axioms that are available to the thin theorist, others may view with alarm the startlingly broad range of human behavior and cognition that escapes the evaluative net of the thin theory. Elster, for one, argued that "we need a broader theory of rationality that goes beyond the exclusively formal considerations ... and that allows a scrutiny of the substantive nature of the desires and beliefs in action" (p. 15).

Another reason to reject the thin theory is that, as several theorists have argued, in its failure to address epistemic considerations, it ends up by undercutting itself—losing the strong normative criteria it sought to retain by not addressing difficult epistemic issues. This concern about the thin theory is directly related to one of the alternative explanations for the normative/descriptive gap that is discussed in chapter 4—that of alternative task construal. Briefly, to anticipate that chapter, it is being increasingly recognized that if we put no constraints on people's representations of problems—if we simply apply the axioms of rational choice to whatever are their beliefs about the task situation—we will end up with no principles of instrumental rationality at all (Broome, 1990; Schick, 1987, 1997; Sen, 1993; Shweder, 1987; Tversky, 1975). In chapter 4 it is argued that we must accept the challenge of evaluating the rationality of task construals and that psychology can contribute to this complex question.

Moving to a broad theory of rationality—one that encompasses epistemic evaluation as well as a substantive critique of desires—comes with a cost. It means taking on some of the knottiest problems in philosophy (Earman, 1992; Goldman, 1986; Harman, 1995; Millgram, 1997; Nozick, 1993; Richardson, 1997; Schueler, 1995). One problem is that concerns about practical rationality can always seem to trump epistemic rationality in a way that would seem to render a normative evaluation of the latter virtually impossible. For example, Foley (1991) discussed cases where epistemic and practical reasons for belief become separated. That is, generally one's goals will be best served by having a network of beliefs containing many truths and few falsehoods. Truthful beliefs will facilitate the attainment of goals in most cases—but not always. For example, Foley described the case of a person believing that their lover is faithful despite substantial evidence to the contrary. Believing that the lover is faithful satisfies a number of desires (that the relationship continue, that domestic living arrangements not be disrupted), so it is not surprising that were you in such a situation you "may find yourself insisting on higher standards of evidence, and as a result it may take unusually good evidence to convince you of infidelity" (p. 375). Without knowing that there were goals/desires involved, an outside observer might view the criterion for belief as irrationally high. However, a simultaneous consideration of epistemic and practical goals makes the setting of a high epistemic criterion here seem rational. So a simultaneous consideration of practical and epistemic rationality will certainly complicate the application of normative standards (Pollock, 1995).

Likewise, a theory of broad rationality that encompasses the evaluation of the content of desires must address some extremely difficult issues. Nevertheless, various criteria have been proposed for deeming a desire irrational. For example, several theorists (see Nathanson, 1994, for a review) have argued that desires which, upon reflection, we would rather eliminate than fulfill are irrational. Other theorists argue that conflicting desires, or desires based on false beliefs, are irrational. Finally, it could be argued that the persistent tendency to develop goals whose expected utility is different from their experienced utility is a sign of irrationality (Frisch & Jones, 1993; Kahneman & Snell, 1990).

A broad theory of rationality emphasizes the interplay between epistemic and practical concerns (Pollock, 1995). For example, it is relatively uncontroversial that it is rational to have derived goals. One might desire to acquire an education not because one has an intrinsic desire for education but because one desires to be a lawyer and getting an education leads to the fulfillment of that goal. Once derived goals are allowed, the possibility of evaluating goals in terms of their comprehensiveness immediately suggests itself. That is, we might evaluate certain goals positively because attaining them leads to the satisfaction of a wide variety of *other* desires. In contrast, there are some goals whose satisfaction does not lead to the satisfaction of any other desires. At the extreme there may be goals that are in conflict with other goals. Fulfilling such a goal actually impedes the fulfillment of other goals (this is why goal inconsistency is to be avoided).

In the vast majority of mundane cases (nonbizarre, nondegenerate cases), one goal that will serve to fulfill a host of others is the goal of wanting one's beliefs to be true. Generally (i.e., outside of the types of bizarre cases that only a philosopher would imagine), the more that a person's beliefs track the world, the easier it will be for that person to fulfill their goals. Obviously, perfect accuracy is not required and, equally obviously, there is a point of diminishing returns where additional cognitive effort spent in acquiring true beliefs will not have adequate payoff in terms of goal achievement. Nevertheless, other things being equal, the presence of the desire to have true beliefs will have the long-term effect of facilitating the achievement of a host of goals. It is a superordinate goal in a sense and—again, except for certain bizarre cases—should be in the desire network of most individuals. Thus, even if epistemic rationality really is subordinate to practical rationality, the derived goal of maintaining true beliefs will mean that epistemic norms must be adhered to for practical goals to be achieved.

PHILOSOPHICAL PROBLEMS AT THE INTENTIONAL LEVEL: IS HUMAN IRRATIONALITY POSSIBLE?

The model of rationality at the intentional level sketched previously is sufficient to provide a context for a discussion of the reasons for discrepancies between normative and descriptive models. In this and the next two sections, I turn my attention to the arguments that motivate the Panglossian position that there is no normative/descriptive gap—that it is impossible to demonstrate systematic human irrationality. The arguments are largely conceptual, and the theorists who promulgate them believe that the idea of empirically demonstrating systematic deviations from normative responding is misconceived.

There are three popular arguments of this type—the argument from charity, the argument from evolution, and the argument from reflective equilibrium—and these are dealt with in this and the following two sections. The first is most commonly articulated in the writings of philosophers and it derives from what is called the principle of charity (Dennett, 1987; Quine, 1960; Stein, 1996; Stich, 1990). I follow Dennett's version of the charity principle here. Dennett argued that when we approach another intentional system we can accurately predict its behavior only if we make three strong assumptions. First, the intentional stance requires the assumption that "a system's beliefs are those that it *ought to have*, given its perceptual capacities, its epistemic needs, and its biography. Thus, in general, its beliefs are both true and relevant to its life" (p. 49). The second assumption is, analogously, that the system has the desires it ought to have given its biological makeup and its environmental niche. The third assumption is that "a system's behavior will consist of those acts *it would be rational* for the agent with those beliefs and desires to perform" (p. 49).

Note that these three assumptions amount to a claim of near-perfect rationality: Assumption #1 amounts to a statement that the system has nearly perfect epistemic rationality; assumption #2 proposes that the content of the person's desires are rational; and assumption #3 states that the processes of practical rationality are completely optimal. One implication of Dennett's (1987) view that we must ascribe perfect rationality to intentional systems is that empirical evidence from reasoning experiments should never be interpreted as indicating that people are deviating from normative models. All such seeming deviations must only be apparent and should be explained away by positing performance errors or alternative task construals. As Stich (1990) argued, "if Davidson and Dennett are right, then these concerns [about irrationality] are overblown. Cognition *can't* be all that bad" (p. 15). Psychologists could still go about their business of describing human reasoning, but such a project could "hardly be infused with the reformer's zeal, since we know in advance that there is nothing much to reform" (p. 16).

Dennett's (1987) argument for the three strong assumptions of the previous paragraphs is the overall success of the intentional stance in predicting human behavior ("it works with people almost all the time", p. 21). But Dennett went on to argue that this is almost necessarily so because it would not be possible to ascribe beliefs to individuals without these assumptions—persons for whom such an intentional description systematically fails in some sense have no beliefs. The choice, according to Dennett, is to assume perfect rationality or give up on the intentional level and the folk psychological idea of belief (which *is* a real option for some theorists, see Churchland, 1989, 1995; Stich, 1983). He argued that "intentional explanation and prediction cannot be accommodated either to breakdown or to less than optimal design, so there is no coherent intentional description of such an impasse" (Dennett, 1978, p. 20). The idea is that "what makes a mental state count as a belief is the appropriateness of its interactions with other mental states" (Stein, 1996, p. 117). A state that interacted with other beliefs, desires, and processes in no coherent way could not be ascribed as having any content. Hence to have beliefs is to have rationality according to the Dennett view. Because we have beliefs we are rational creatures—and the question of human rationality is not empirically up for grabs in the way that psychologists have tended to think. So goes this philosophical story.

However, many philosophers—in addition to many psychologists —find this story deeply flawed (see Stein, 1996; Stich, 1990; Thagard & Nisbett, 1983). First, the principle of charity applied by Dennett (1987) is extreme and categorical—perfect epistemic rationality, perfect practical rationality, and optimal desire consistency is assumed. But it is not at all clear that the principle has to be applied in such a categorical form. No empirical facts about the predictability of humans as intentional systems dictate such an extreme form of the charity principle. Instead, Thagard and Nisbett suggested that the principle of charity can be conceived as a continuum, and that it is debatable where on the continuum our default assumption should be. Dennett's position defines the extreme point on their continuum (#1):

1. Never interpret people as irrational.
2. Interpret people as irrational only given overwhelming evidence.
3. Do not judge people to be irrational unless you have an empirically justified account of what they are doing when they violate normative standards.
4. Do not give any prior favor to the interpretation that people are irrational.
5. Do not assume a priori that people are irrational.

The other positions on the continuum represent viable alternatives to Dennett's, because it is not at all clear that intentional prediction works as well as Dennett implies. Beyond an (admittedly long) list of mundane examples routinely trotted out by advocates of a strong version of charity (He *believed* the car was coming toward him. He *desired* not to be injured. Therefore, he *decided* to move out of the way), it is not difficult to generate a set of more fine-grained situations—everyday situations in which people have a high stake in their predictions being correct—in which our intentional-level predictions based on an assumption of rationality fail miserably:

- We are surprised by how our colleagues vote on the new curriculum proposal.
- We are shocked when our reliable niece does not pay back our loan to her.
- We shake our heads when the new execrable television series becomes a smash hit.
- We are disappointed when our spouse is unhappy with a Christmas gift that we purchased after much thought.
- We are surprised that our neighbor voted for a flat-tax advocate (particularly given that our neighbor is salaried and has absolutely no capital assets that would go untaxed).
- We are surprised when our numerically sophisticated colleague reveals that he is paying a 16% credit card debt when we are aware that he has sufficient funds in a money-market account to pay it off.

- Juries deadlock because they cannot agree on an intentional-level explanation for a defendant's behavior.

And the list goes on—at least leaving it an open question whether intentional prediction is so good and belief-ascription so assured that they provide a near-tautological argument for perfect human rationality. And, it should be noted, I have charitably not raised the issue of the 3-year-old—or the mother-in-law whose behavior and beliefs are routinely indecipherable (there seem to be no dearth of interactions with our fellow human beings in which "no matter what you do, it's wrong"). Yet (contra Dennett) none of these are cases where we are tempted to say that the actor has no beliefs. To the contrary, we still concoct an intentional-level description of the relevant behavior, but it is a description under the assumption that some component of rational thought has failed—belief formation has gone awry, desires are irrational, action determination is suboptimal, or logical consistency is poor. We make a guess as to which component is faulty and then we ascribe beliefs that cohere with the faulty mechanism to produce the behavior that we initially found unpredictable under the rationality assumption. If we are scientists, we have the possibility of conducting more systematic studies to isolate the irrational component.

Goldman's (1986) view is consistent with that taken in this volume. He claimed that "it is just not clear what it means for a belief system to be logical" (p. 174) and suggested consistency and logical closure as possibilities—but then argued that "deductive closure is especially unattractive. Surely no human being infers all the logical consequences of his beliefs, yet we do not hesitate to ascribe beliefs to people" (p. 174). Goldman admitted that Davidson's (1984) version of charity does not require that beliefs always be consistent—"he only says that propositional attitude attributions commit us to finding a 'large degree' of rationality and consistency in the subjects of our attributions" (p. 175). But precisely in the difference between "large degree" and always is the opening for empirical demonstrations of irrationality: "But then it emerges that there is no a priori determination of the specific logical operations that believers must always, or even regularly, employ. So, as I wish to contend, it presumably rests with empirical science to determine just what these deductive operations are" (p. 175). The situation is even worse in the case of inductive logic:

> Here one hardly knows where to begin. Principles of inductive logic are very controversial, in the first place. Assuming we could settle on some such principles, are they really to be required as conditions for belief ascription? What about principles of probability and statistics? Are creatures who violate such principles necessarily devoid of propositional attitudes? That is extremely dubious. (p. 175)

In summary, it may not be correct that beliefs have no ascribable content in cases where intentional prediction under the rationality assumption fails. As Stich (1985) argued, "there is nothing in the least incoherent or unstable about a description, cast in intentional terms, of a person who has inconsistent beliefs" (p. 122). Similarly, Thagard and Nisbett (1983) argued, "There is no reason, however, why it should not be possible to determine empirically that a system is regularly using some inferential principle or heuristic that departs from standard logical principles, then to use the operation of this heuristic as part of an explanation of the system's behavior" (p. 257).

Thagard and Nisbett's (1983) notion of a continuum of positions on the principle of charity is important because only the most stringent of their ordered set of assumptions renders nonempirical the question of the human irrationality. Every other position short of #1 (see Stein, 1996, pp. 113–136) creates the potential for a gap between the normative and the descriptive and hence the potential for the empirical demonstration of human irrationality. No one knows how much belief ascription under the intentional stance would have to be predictable in order to warrant a default to the strongest charity assumption. Even Dennett (1987, p. 19) admitted that his aforementioned rule #1 (attribute to an intentional system the beliefs it ought to have) might, in normal cases, fail to correctly attribute about 10% of a person's beliefs. As the previous examples indicate, I think it is higher. But even if rationality-based intentional ascription fails 10% of the time, this could have important consequences if the beliefs were important. The 90% accurate belief ascription under assumptions of rationality figure might seem large, but it is "padded" with thousands of mundane, uninteresting inferences. Within the set of the 10% missed by a strong rationality assumption may lie beliefs/desires/actions in domains such as marriage, personal finance, going to war, personal risk, and sexual behavior—precisely where concerns about rational human action are at their greatest.

Even taken at face value, the 90% figure leaves ample room for an empirical psychology of human rationality. As Elster (1983) noted, "once we have established the base line or background of general consistency, one may raise the question of local inconsistency of beliefs" (p. 4). Similarly, Manketelow and Over (1990) emphasized that "a full mental logic might be the only system which would make us completely logical, but some other system might be logical in much of its operation, while still prone at times to bias and error. We can possess this kind of system and still understand what we are saying, even when we fall into error" (p. 151). Such arguments relate to holistic versions of the principle of charity (Stein, 1996) where the intentional system's entire set of beliefs, desires, and actions is posited to achieve a best fit to standards of rationality (see also, Thagard, 1982, 1988, 1992). Such a holistic conception allows for local deviations from rational prescriptions and thus justifies an empirical project for psychology. In summary, the conceptual constraints on how badly people can reason do not seem strong enough to preclude serious irrationality in important domains of human decision making and judgment.

RATIONALITY AND EVOLUTION

The perfect rationality assumption dictated by the strong version of the charity principle in views such as Dennett's (1987) is sometimes intertwined with a second argument in favor of the proposition that human irrationality cannot be experimentally demonstrated: that evolution guarantees human rationality. Dennett's (1987) argument for why the intentional strategy works is typical:

> The first answer to the question of why the intentional strategy works is that evolution has designed human beings to be rational, to believe what they ought to believe and want what they ought to want. The fact that we are products of a long and demanding evolutionary process guarantees that using the intentional strategy on us is a safe bet. (p. 33)

As discussed previously, just how well the intentional strategy works is a debatable question. Putting this objection aside, however, there are other arguments against the argument from evolution. Stich (1990; see also Stein, 1996) demonstrated that it is mistaken to view evolution as necessarily truth preserving. Beliefs need not always track the world with maximum accuracy in order for fitness to increase. Evolution does not guarantee perfect epistemic rationality. Likewise, evolution does not ensure that optimum standards of practical rationality will be attained.

Evolution guarantees that humans are genetic fitness optimizers in their local environments, not that they are truth or utility maximizers as normative theories require. This point has been emphasized by numerous authors (W. S. Cooper, 1989; Skyrms, 1996; Stein, 1996; Stich, 1990). Regarding truth preservation, Stich argued that it is not guaranteed by evolution under either internal or external fitness considerations. Internal fitness concerns the resource demands that a genetic program makes on the organism in order to carry out its function. Stich demonstrated how evolution might fail to select out epistemic mechanisms of high accuracy when they are costly in terms of organismic resources (memory, energy, attention, etc.).

Getting input–output relations mapped in such a way that fitness increases is termed an *external consideration*. Stich (1990) argued that maximum truth preservation might not be selected for here either because:

> A very cautious, risk-aversive inferential strategy—one that leaps to the conclusion that danger is present on very slight evidence—will typically lead to false beliefs more often, and true ones less often, than a less hair-trigger one that waits for more evidence before rendering a judgment. Nonetheless, the unreliable, error-prone, risk-aversive strategy may well be favored by natural selection. For natural selection does not care about

truth; it cares only about reproductive success. And from the point of view of reproductive success, it is often better to be safe (and wrong) than sorry. What we have shown then is that one inferential system may have a higher level of external fitness than another even though the latter, less fit system makes fewer mistakes and gets the right answer more often. (p. 62)

Kitcher (1993; see also Nozick, 1993, pp. 112–114) argued likewise: "The hominid representation can be quite at odds with natural regularities, lumping all kinds of harmless things with potential dangers, provided that false positives are evolutionarily inconsequential and provided that the representation always cues the subject to danger" (p. 300).

The situation is much the same in the domain of practical rationality. Skyrms (1996) devoted an entire book on evolutionary game theory to showing that the idea that "natural selection will weed out irrationality" (p. x) in the instrumental sense is false. He concluded:

If evolutionary game theory is generalized to allow for correlation of encounters between players and like-minded players, then strongly dominated strategies—at variance with both rational decision and game theory—can take over the population.... When I contrast the results of the evolutionary account with those of rational decision theory, I am not criticizing the normative force of the latter. I am just emphasizing the fact that the different questions asked by the two traditions may have different answers. (pp. x–xi)

Skyrms' book articulates the environmental and population parameters under which "rational choice theory completely parts ways with evolutionary theory" (p. 106; see also W. S. Cooper, 1989).

Mechanisms designed for survival in preindustrial times might sometimes even be maladaptive in a technological culture. Our mechanisms for storing and utilizing energy evolved in times when fat preservation was efficacious. These mechanisms no longer serve the goals of people in a technological society where a Burger King is on every corner. The cognitive mechanisms that lead us to stray from normative models that would maximize utility are probably mechanisms that once were fitness enhancing but now serve to thwart our goals (see Baron, 1993a, 1994a, 1998). In short, the evolutionary argument fails at abolishing the normative/descriptive gap. It is possible to grant evolution its role as the creator of potent mental mechanisms (Brase et al., 1998; Cosmides & Tooby, 1994, 1996; Pinker, 1997) and still have room for a research program in psychology that demonstrates human irrationality. The point is that local maximization in the sense of evolutionary fitness is not the same as the maximization of expected utility in the sense of classical decision theory.

Finally, the evolutionary argument seems to ignore the phenomenon of the culturally derived nature of normative standards (Jepson et al., 1983; Krantz, 1981; Thagard & Nisbett, 1983). Normative models for assessing human behavior are social and cultural products that are preserved and stored independently of the genes—they reside in Popper's (1972) "World 3" outside of human bodies. As McCain (1991) pointed out:

> Rationality as a concept is inherently unfinished. The emergence of ratio-
> nality will include (among other phenomena) the emergence of new ratio-
> nales, but also of new methods for validating rationales. Thus (for example)
> we should see the Greek invention of formal logic as an episode in the his-
> toric emergence of rationality. Formal logic is not, after all, a given capacity
> of human beings, any more than felling a tree with a steel axe is: we cannot
> carry out the task until the tool has been invented. And a clear set of rules of
> inference contributes importantly to our capacity to consider the conse-
> quences of our actions—a central aspect of rationality. (pp. 241–242)

The development of probability theory and concepts of empiricism, mathematics, and logic throughout the centuries have provided humans with conceptual tools to aid in the formation and revision of belief and in their reasoning about action. If a college sophomore with introductory statistics under their belt were time transported to the Europe of a couple of centuries ago, they could become rich "beyond the dreams of avarice" by frequenting the gaming tables (or by becoming involved in insurance or lotteries; see Gigerenzer et al., 1989; Hacking, 1975, 1990). The cultural evolution of rational standards is apt to occur markedly faster than human evolution—thus providing ample opportunity for mechanisms of local genetic fitness maximization to dissociate from mechanisms of utility maximization. The implications of this dissociation for studies of human rationality are discussed in chapters 5, 7, and 8.

RATIONALITY AND REFLECTIVE EQUILIBRIUM

The foundation of the final argument for the impossibility of human irrationality derives from an analogy to the competence/performance distinction in linguistics. It is an argument that arises almost exclusively within the philosophical literature (the prototype of this argument is provided by Cohen, 1981; see Stein, 1996, for a detailed discussion and critique). In linguistics, normative principles derive from intuitions about grammaticality. These intuitions about grammaticality are in turn based on our linguistic competence. Thus, in linguistics, normative principles are directly indexed to linguistic competence and the two cannot come apart.

Cohen (1981) imported this argument into the domain of human reasoning by proposing, analogously, that normative principles about what constitutes good reasoning come from our intuitions about what constitutes good reasoning and that our intuitions about what constitutes good reasoning come from our reasoning competence.[3] Thus, as in linguistics,

---

[3]Cohen's (1986) express purpose is to legitimize the practices of analytic philosophers:
  If psychologists were right, what they say would seriously discredit the claims of intuition to provide—other things being equal—dependable foundations for inductive
  reasoning in analytical philosophy. ... If they are right that most people are ...(con't)

normative principles of reasoning are directly indexed to reasoning competence and the two cannot come apart. Normative models of rational thought simply *are* our thought and humans are—by definition—rational. No experimentation is necessary to establish it.

In order to justify the two premises of his argument—that (a) normative principles about what constitutes good reasoning come from our intuitions about what constitutes good reasoning and (b) our intuitions about what constitutes good reasoning come from our reasoning competence—Cohen (1981) made recourse to the concept of reflective equilibrium (Elgin, 1996; Goodman, 1965; Rawls, 1971). Reflective equilibrium is achieved by a process of constraint satisfaction whereby: "Rules and particular inferences alike are justified by being brought into agreement with each other. A rule is amended if it yields an inference we are unwilling to accept; an inference is rejected if it violates a rule we are unwilling to amend. The process of justification is the delicate one of making mutual adjustments between rules and accepted inferences" (Goodman, 1965, p. 64). Reformulated in terms of reflective equilibrium, Cohen's view is that "the normative principles of reasoning come from a process of reflective equilibrium with our intuitions about what constitutes good reasoning as input" (Stein, 1996, p. 142) and that our intuitions about what constitutes good reasoning come from our reasoning competence.

This is the argument that guarantees human rationality according to Cohen (1981), but it has a number of unfortunate implications that have made it singularly unpalatable to psychologists (e.g., Dawes, 1983; Fischhoff, 1981; Jepson et al., 1983; Mynatt, Tweney, & Doherty, 1983). The most important is that it treats as normatively justified a host of principles that we have independent reason to suspect are poor reasoning rules. Stich and Nisbett (1980) discussed how the gambler's fallacy and nonregressive prediction are quite likely to be in reflective equilibrium for most people. Even falling back on the notion of *considered* intuitions (Gauthier, 1986) is unlikely to dislodge the reflective equilibrium involving these two fallacies.

There are several ways to avoid some of these troubling consequences. First, it is possible to fine-tune and enrich the process of justifying normative rules. It is noteworthy that the reflective equilibrium advocated by Cohen (1981) is termed *narrow* reflective equilibrium (see Daniels, 1979, 1996) because only intuitions are brought in to equilibrium with general principles. In contrast, *wide* reflective equilibrium involves a balance between intuitions, normative principles, and other philosophical principles relevant to the intuitions. For example, theoretical arguments about probability theory would be allowed to influence the

---

(cont'd) inherently unfit to practise analytical philosophy in the form in which I have analysed it ... since at many points analytical philosophy has to premiss its accounts of reasoning on the data of human intuitions, its metaphilosophy can hardly afford to ignore this extensive literature. (pp. 149–150)

reflective equilibrium in which the gambler's fallacy seems justified. Such arguments could well disrupt the equilibrium and dislodge the gambler's fallacy as a justified principle.

But what if they failed to dislodge it? This worry has led theorists to further elaborate the process of wide reflective equilibrium by first socializing the process and then by restricting the individuals whose judgment counts in arriving at equilibrium. These changes result in the notion of expert wide reflective equilibrium (Stein, 1996; Stich & Nisbett, 1980)—that "a principle is established as a normative principle of reasoning if it is in reflective equilibrium for those people in a position to assess the relevant considerations" (Stein, 1996, p. 147). The idea derives from Putnam's (1975) concept of a division of linguistic labor whereby most speakers' use of terms piggybacks on the expertise of a smaller group of experts who work on refining the extensional meaning of the term. For example, we all use the term *gold* in ignorance of its chemical composition but with confidence that experts are keeping track of this and that they would tell us if the term's referent changed. In the realm of reasoning, the relevant experts are those who have spent a lifetime studying and thinking about what justifies principles of reasoning. Thus, as a background for their empirical studies, Nisbett and Ross (1980) stipulate that they will "follow conventional practice by using the term 'normative' to describe the use of a rule when there is a consensus among formal scientists that the rule is appropriate for the particular problem" (p. 13).

Combining all of the refinements in the reflective equilibrium concept, we arrive at a notion of normatively justified principles of reasoning as those in wide reflective equilibrium among a group of relevant experts. And something very important has happened in the transition from Cohen's narrow reflective equilibrium to this notion: There is now the possibility of a gap between normatively justified principles and a descriptive account of human behavior. Normative principles are no longer necessarily coextensive with the reasoning competence of untutored individuals. There is now room for experimental demonstrations of human irrationality.

The idea of a strong dissociation between expert wide reflective equilibrium and lay intuitions may nonetheless seem odd if the analogy to language is taken too seriously. But in this case, the latter provides too circumscribed a notion of normative justification. In linguistics there is no court of appeal for the justification of norms outside of linguistic intuitions. But in the domain of reasoning there are mechanisms available outside of intuitions. Practical reasoning norms have consequences if they are followed (see Baron, 1993a, 1994a). Likewise, epistemic reasoning norms, if followed, have consequences for the nature and structure of beliefs and these belief structures can be checked for their congruence with actual information in the world. In short, in the case of reasoning, there is another court of appeal outside of intuitions. That court of appeal is a third-person scientific account of whether a particular set of practical reasoning norms leads to goal satisfaction (Baron, 1993a, 1994a) and whether a particular set of epistemic reasoning norms leads to beliefs that more accurately track the world.

Evidence on the pragmatic effectiveness of various reasoning strategies has had a major role in conditioning the opinion of experts regarding which reasoning principles are normatively justified. In fact, it has probably had more influence than the informed intuitions of the experts themselves—which are often contradicted by the third-person scientific account of the consequences of the reasoning principles. Indeed, in areas of reasoning, the third-person account comes to dominate the primary intuitions of the expert (who has learned to treat such intuitions as highly corrigible). So, for example, in decision science, arguments such as the Dutch Book and the money pump (de Finetti, 1970/1990; Maher, 1993; Osherson, 1995; Resnik, 1987; Skyrms, 1986)—which reveal some of the disastrous consequences of inferior reasoning strategies—have been highly influential and often trump contradictory intuitions among experts.

Thagard (1982) argued that once we have brought in ancillary theories of related domains (e.g., probability theory) and once we have let judgments become influenced by demonstrable pragmatic and epistemic outcomes, then we have moved to a view of normative justification that is similar to that of theory choice in science and that similar criteria (coherence, explanatory power, etc.) apply. Thagard's emphasis on an analogy to theory change in science reminds us that, just as did the evolutionary argument in the previous section, Cohen's view discounts cultural evolution. Norms of reasoning change among the cognitive elite and may well outrun the untutored intuitions of the layperson (Jepson et al., 1983; Krantz, 1981; Thagard & Nisbett, 1983). Primary intuitions are viewed as highly corrigible in Thagard's (1982) account of normative justification and actually, for the expert, may become highly saturated with the third-person account. Some statistics instructors, for example, become unable to empathize with students for whom the basic probability axioms are not transparent. The instructor can no longer remember when these axioms were not primary intuitions.

Like Dennett's (1987) conceptual argument for the charity principle and the evolutionary argument, Cohen's (1981) attack on the possibility of empirical demonstrations of human irrationality fails in the view of most commentators (Kahneman & Tversky, 1983; Stein, 1996; Stich, 1990). However, his arguments have provoked much useful discussion about the justification of normative principles in the study of reasoning and he has provided Panglossians with powerful arguments for dismissing normative/descriptive discrepancies as spurious. Correspondingly, Meliorists have had to think much harder and more carefully about the appropriateness of the normative models that are applied to certain tasks in the heuristics and biases literature (Birnbaum, 1983; Koehler, 1996; Windschitl & Wells, 1997; see chap. 3, this volume).

ALTERNATIVE EXPLANATIONS
FOR THE NORMATIVE/DESCRIPTIVE GAP

Five alternative explanations for the gap between normative and descriptive models have been mentioned throughout this chapter. They are: systematic irrationality in the intentional-level psychology, algorithmic-level limitations, performance errors, incorrect norm application, and alternative problem construal. The Meliorist views the gap as real—the result of human cognition systematically computing a non-normative rule. To the extent that the normative rule is prescriptive, and to the extent that a prescriptive/descriptive gap is by definition what is meant by irrationality, the Meliorist does believe that human irrationality can be experimentally demonstrated. Like the Meliorist, the Apologist accepts the empirical reality and nonspuriousness of normative/descriptive gaps, but the Apologist is much more hesitant to term them instances of irrationality. This is because the Apologist takes very seriously the stricture that to characterize a suboptimal behavior as irrational, it must be the case that the normative model is computable in the cognitive mechanism under study. If there are computational limitations affecting task performance, then the normative model may not be prescriptive, at least for individuals of low algorithmic capacity (an issue that is addressed in detail in the next chapter). From the Apologist's perspective, the descriptive model is quite close to the prescriptive model and the descriptive/normative gap is attributed to a computational limitation. Although the Apologist admits that performance is suboptimal from the standpoint of the normative model, it is not irrational because there is no prescriptive/descriptive gap.

Because the Panglossian does not believe that human irrationality can be experimentally demonstrated, any discrepancies between normative and descriptive models must be illusory or spurious. The Panglossian has three potent strategies for dismissing normative/descriptive gaps. The first is to claim that any discrepancies are mere performance errors—unsystematic responses that result from inattention or memory lapses. The second strategy—to claim incorrect norm application—frequently occurs because psychologists have traditionally appealed to the normative models of other disciplines (probability theory, logic, etc.) in order to interpret the responses on various tasks. A problem arises when there is a lack of consensus on the status of the normative models that are borrowed (Gigerenzer, 1991a, 1991b). Heavy reliance on a normative model that is in dispute often engenders the claim that the gap between the descriptive and normative occurs because the psychologist is applying the wrong normative model to the situation—in short, that the problem is with the experimenter and not the subject.

The third strategy for eliminating normative/descriptive gaps is to argue that although we may be applying the correct normative model to the problem as set, the subject might have construed the problem differently and be providing the normatively appropriate answer to a different problem. Such an argument is not the equivalent of positing that a performance error has been made, because performance errors (attention lapses, temporary memory deactivation, etc.) would not be expected to recur in exactly the same way in a readministration of the same task. Whereas, if the subject has truly misunderstood the task, they would be expected to do so again on an identical readministration of the task. Correspondingly, this criticism is different from the argument that the task exceeds the computational capacity of the subject. The latter explanation puts the onus of the suboptimal performance on the subject. In contrast, the alternative task construal argument places the blame at least somewhat on the shoulders of the experimenter for presenting the task in way that is misleading and that leads the subject away from the desired response—in short, the experimenter has failed to realize that there were task features that might lead subjects to frame the problem in a manner different from that intended. In locating the problem with the experimenter, it is similar to the wrong norm explanation. However, it is different in that in the latter it is assumed that the subject is interpreting the task as the experimenter intended—but the experimenter is not using the right criteria to evaluate performance. In contrast, the alternative task construal argument is that the experimenter may be applying the correct normative model to the problem the experimenter intends the subject to solve, but the subject might have construed the problem in some other way and be providing a normatively appropriate answer to a different problem.

All of the Panglossian alternatives—performance errors, incorrect norm application, and alternative problem construal—render the normative/descriptive discrepancy more apparent than real. All inoculate against the conclusion that an instance of human irrationality has been demonstrated. An interesting aspect of some Panglossian positions is that because the descriptive is simply indexed to the normative, the latter can simply be "read off" from a competence model of the former (Cohen, 1982, termed this the *norm extraction method*). For example, Stein (1996) noted that this seems to follow from the Panglossian view because:

> Whatever human reasoning competence turns out to be, the principles embodied in it are the normative principles of reasoning .... This argument sees the reasoning experiments as revealing human reasoning competence, and, thereby, as also revealing the norms .... The reasoning experiments just give us insight into what our reasoning abilities are; by knowing what these abilities are, we can determine what the normative principles of reasoning are. (pp. 231–232)

Stein (1996) termed this type of Panglossian position the no extrahuman norms view because

> [it] rejects the standard picture of rationality and takes the reasoning experiments as giving insight not just into human reasoning competence but also

into the normative principles of reasoning .... The no extra-human norms argument says that the norms just are what we have in our reasoning competence; if the (actual) norms do not match our preconceived notion of what the norms should be, so much the worse for our reconceived notions (pp. 233–234)

Interestingly, the descriptive component of performance around which Panglossian theorists almost always build their competence models (which index the normative in their view) is the central tendency of the responses (usually the mean or modal performance tendency). But if we are going to "read off" the normative from the descriptive in this way, why is this the only aspect of group performance that is relevant? Do the pattern of responses around the mode tell us anything? What about the rich covariance patterns that would be present in any multivariate experiment? Are these *totally* superfluous—all norm-relevant behavioral information residing in the mode? If we are going to infer something about the normative from the descriptive (and of course not all investigators are agreed that we should—see chap. 3, this volume), it will be demonstrated in subsequent chapters that there is more information available than has traditionally been relied upon.

THE REST OF THIS BOOK

The wide reflective equilibrium of experts regarding principles of instrumental rationality has always been at least partially conditioned by descriptive accounts of actual behavior. In the present volume, I attempt to expand that conditioning beyond the modal response to encompass the rich patterns of variance and covariance that can be captured in a multivariate study. It is demonstrated—using selected examples of empirical results—that these individual differences and their patterns of covariance have implications for explanations of why human behavior often departs from normative models.

Cohen (1982) contrasted what he called the norm extraction method preferred by Panglossians with the (what he viewed as the misconceived) *preconceived norm method* employed by the Meliorists and argued, correctly I believe:

The issue between these two methods is not of the kind that lends itself to being determined by a single crucial experiment since it concerns a whole policy or paradigm of research .... It is essential to consider the issue between the Preconceived Norm Method and Norm Extraction Method in the context of a wide range of different experiments. (p. 252)

Such a survey of performance patterns across a wide range of tasks from the heuristics and biases literature—the literature that has spawned the most vociferous disputes about human rationality—is precisely what is presented in this volume. Cohen was correct that a broad-based approach is necessary, because these are not the type of questions that are likely to be resolved by a single experiment or by a focus on a particular task.

In referring to the four alternative explanations (other than systematic irrationality) for the normative/descriptive gap discussed previously, Rips (1994) warned that "a determined skeptic can usually explain away any instance of what seems at first to be a logical mistake .... To determine whether we are giving people too little credit for correct reasoning, we therefore need to get straight about what would count as a true reasoning error and whether it makes conceptual and empirical sense to postulate such errors" (p. 393). Kahneman (1981) made the same point more humorously in his dig at the Panglossians who seem to have only two categories of errors, "pardonable errors by subjects and unpardonable ones by psychologists" (p. 340). Referring to the four classes of alternative explanation discussed previously—performance errors, computational limitations, alternative problem construal, and incorrect norm application—Kahneman noted that Panglossians have "a handy kit of defenses that may be used if [subjects are] accused of errors: temporary insanity, a difficult childhood, entrapment, or judicial mistakes—one of them will surely work, and will restore the presumption of rationality" (p. 340).

These comments by Rips (1994) and Kahneman (1981) highlight the need for principled constraints on the alternative explanations of normative/descriptive discrepancies. This volume represents an extended study of the possibility of developing such constraints from inferences drawn about patterns of individual differences that are revealed across a wide range of tasks in the heuristics and biases literature. Chapter 2 is devoted to demonstrations of the implications of patterns of covariance for performance errors and algorithmic-level limitations. Chapter 3 is concerned with incorrect norm application and chapter 4 with alternative problem construal. In chapter 5, in order to provide a framework for integrating the patterns of individual differences demonstrated in the series of empirical studies, I outline a framework that links two-process theories of reasoning with the distinction between evolutionary adaptation and normative rationality. Chapter 6 deals with dispositional psychological constructs that predict rational responses and that can be conceptualized at the intentional level. This chapter contains a discussion of the general notion of decontextualizing thought. In chapter 7, I introduce the notion of the *fundamental computational bias*—an overarching style that conjoins a number of processing biases that are the reason that evolutionary and normative rationality sometimes dissociate. In chapter 8, I take a step back and attempt to evaluate the empirical and theoretical gains to be had from assessing variation in rational thought.

Performance Errors
and Computational Limitations

With Richard F. West

In this chapter, two alternative explanations for normative/descriptive gaps are examined. Both center on information-processing problems at the algorithmic level of analysis. Both are used to refute the claim that such gaps represent instances of human irrationality, but they do so in very different ways. One alternative explanation, that of a performance error, is used by Panglossian theorists to essentially deny the existence of a normative/descriptive gap because such errors are transitory. The other alternative explanation, that of a computational limitation, is emphasized by the Apologist camp, which admits the possibility of a normative/descriptive gap. Here, the algorithmic-level processing error is admitted to be nontransitory. However, it is used to deny the existence of a *prescriptive*/descriptive gap and to warn against the premature inference that human irrationality at the intentional level has been demonstrated.

INDIVIDUAL DIFFERENCES AND PERFORMANCE ERRORS

Theorists who argue that discrepancies between actual responses and those dictated by normative models are not indicative of human irrationality (e.g., Cohen, 1981) sometimes attribute the discrepancies to performance errors (see Stein, 1996, pp. 8–9). Borrowing the idea of a competence/performance distinction from linguists, these theorists view performance errors as the failure to apply a rule, strategy, or algorithm that is part of a person's competence because of a momentary and fairly random lapse in ancillary processes necessary to execute the strategy (lack of attention, temporary memory deactivation, distraction, etc.).[1] A descriptive model of human competence that is impeccably rational is maintained under this view—perfect human rationality is preserved, although it is not denied that humans make responses that are suboptimal in particular situations because of transitory algorithmic-level mishaps.

Stein (1996) explained the idea of a performance error by referring to a "mere mistake"—a more colloquial notion that involves:

> A *momentary lapse*, a divergence from some typical behavior. This is in contrast to attributing a divergence from norm to reasoning in accordance with principles that diverge from the normative principles of reasoning. Behavior due to irrationality connotes a *systematic* divergence from the norm. It is this distinction between mere mistakes and systematic violations (between performance errors and competence errors) that is ... implicitly assumed by friends of the rationality thesis when they deny that the reasoning experiments [demonstrate human irrationality]. (p. 8)

Similarly, in the heuristics and biases literature, the term *bias* is reserved for systematic deviations from normative reasoning and does not refer to transitory processing errors ("a bias is a source of error which is systematic rather than random," Evans, 1984, p. 462).

Another way to think of the performance error explanation is to conceive of it within the true score/measurement error framework of classical test theory. Mean or modal performance might be viewed as centered on the normative response—the response all people are trying to approximate. However, scores will vary around this central tendency due to random performance factors (error variance).

The notion of a performance error as a momentary attention, memory, or processing lapse that causes responses to appear non-normative even when competence is fully normative has implications for patterns of individual differences across reasoning tasks. For example, the strongest possible form of this view is that *all* discrepancies from normative responses are due to performance errors. This strong form has the implication that there should be virtually no correlations among performance on disparate reasoning tasks. If each departure from normative responding represents a momentary processing lapse due to distraction, carelessness, or temporary confusion, then there is no reason to expect covariance in performance across various reasoning and decision-making tasks (or covariance among items *within* tasks, for that matter)—error variance should be uncorrelated across tasks. In contrast, positive manifold among disparate rational thinking tasks—and among items within

---

[1]Cohen (1981) and Stein (1996) sometimes encompassed computational limitations within their notion of a performance error. In the present volume, the two are distinguished because their implications for an understanding of the normative/descriptive gap are quite different. Here, performance errors represent algorithmic-level problems that are transitory in nature. Long-term, nontransitory limitations at the algorithmic level that would be expected to recur on a readministration of the task are termed computational limitations.

tasks—would call into question the notion that all variability in respond-ing can be attributable to performance errors. This was essentially Rips and Conrad's (1983) argument when they examined individual differ-ences in deductive reasoning: "Subjects' absolute scores on the proposi-tional tests correlated with their performance on certain other reasoning tests.... If the differences in propositional reasoning were merely due to interference from other performance factors, it would be difficult to ex-plain why they correlate with these tests" (p. 282–283).

It thus is argued that individual differences provide one way of dealing with a recurring problem in theories that emphasize the compe-tence/performance distinction—lack of falsifiability. As Stein (1996) noted, "If every possible divergence from some normative principle of reasoning is unquestionably rejected as a mere performance error, then this is an immunization strategy, an ad hoc procedure that allows an advo-cate of a theory to discount any empirical evidence against her favoured theory" (p. 103). The use of performance errors as an immunization strat-egy in the manner outlined by Stein can thus be precluded by an examina-tion of performance covariance. In fact, a parallel argument has been made in economics where, as in reasoning, models of perfect market ra-tionality are protected from refutation by positing the existence of local market mistakes of a transitory nature (temporary information defi-ciency, insufficient attention due to small stakes, distractions leading to missed arbitrage opportunities, etc.). Thaler (1992) argued, just as out-lined earlier, that variance and covariance patterns can potentially falsify some applications of the performance error argument in the field of eco-nomics:

> A defense in the same spirit as Friedman's is to admit that of course people make mistakes, but the mistakes are not a problem in explaining aggregate behavior as long as they tend to cancel out. Unfortunately, this line of de-fense is also weak because many of the departures from rational choice that have been observed are systematic. (pp. 4–5)

Stanovich and West (1998b) examined whether the strong version of the performance error view can explain any of the discrepancies from normative responding that are observed in the reasoning and deci-sion-making literature. Very little evidence for a strong version of the per-formance error view was found in that study. With virtually all of the tasks from heuristics and biases literature that were examined, there was con-siderable internal consistency. Further, at least for certain classes of task, there are significant cross-task correlations. The direction of these corre-lations was always the same—subjects giving the normative response on one task were usually significantly more likely to give it on another.

A typical set of results is displayed in Table 2.1 (see Stanovich & West, 1998b). The tasks in this study included a syllogistic reasoning task in which the believability of the conclusion contradicted logical validity (Evans, Barston, & Pollard, 1983; Evans, Over, & Manktelow, 1993). The second variable in the table represents a composite of performance on five selection task problems (Wason, 1966). All were without strong thematic content, were difficult to solve, and thus were the type of problem about which there has been considerable debate in the research literature (e.g., Evans & Over, 1996; Newstead & Evans, 1995; Oaksford & Chater, 1996: Sperber, Cara, & Girotto, 1995). Unlike the case of the syllogistic reasoning task, where a substantial number of people give the normative response, the gap between the descriptive and normative for the abstract selection task is unusually large. Fewer than 10% of the subjects give the normative response on the abstract version (Evans, Newstead, & Byrne, 1993). This has led to an unusually vociferous and extended debate in the literature about the reasons for the large normative/descriptive gap (Evans & Over, 1996; Fetzer, 1990; Finocchiaro, 1980; Lowe, 1993; Margolis, 1987; Nickerson, 1996; Oaksford & Chater, 1994, 1996; Wetherick, 1995).

The research literature on deductive reasoning and that on statistical reasoning have developed largely in separation, although some integrative efforts have recently been made (see Evans et al., 1993; Legrenzi, Girotto, & Johnson-Laird, 1993). Because the first two tasks derived from the former, the third task examined by Stanovich and West (1998b) derived from the literature on statistical reasoning and was inspired by the work of Nisbett and Ross (1980) on the tendency for human judgment to be overly influenced by vivid but unrepresentative personal and case evidence and to be underinfluenced by more representative and diagnostic, but pallid, statistical evidence. Studying the variation in this response tendency is important because, as Griffin and Tversky (1992) argued, "the tendency to prefer an individual or 'inside' view rather than a statistical or 'outside' view represents one of the major departures of intuitive judgment from normative theory" (pp. 431–432). The quintessential problem (see Fong, Krantz, & Nisbett, 1986; Jepson et al., 1983) involves choosing between contradictory car purchase recommendations—one from a large-sample survey of car buyers and the other the heartfelt and emotional testimony of a single friend. These problems are presented to par-

TABLE 2.1
Intercorrelations Among Several Reasoning Tasks

Variable	1	2	3
1. Syllogisms			
2. Selection task	.363***		
3. Statistical reasoning	.334***	.258***	
4. Argument evaluation	.340***	.310***	.117

Note. Data from Study 1 of Stanovich and West (1998b).
*** = $p < .001$, all two-tailed. $Ns = 188$ to 195.

ticipants as having no right or wrong answers. As with the selection task, there has been some dispute about the reasons why people's choices sometimes deviate from the choice dictated by the aggregate statistical information that has been considered normative (Gigerenzer, 1991b).

The fourth task was an argument evaluation task (Stanovich & West, 1997) that tapped reasoning skills of the type studied in the informal reasoning literature (Baron, 1995; Klaczynski & Fauth, 1997; Klaczynski, Gordon, & Fauth, 1997; Perkins, Farady, & Bushey, 1991). Important to note, to do well on it, one has to adhere to the Bayesian-like stricture not to implicate prior belief in the evaluation of evidence (i.e., not to implicate prior probabilities in the evaluation of the likelihood ratio). This stricture itself has been the subject of some dispute in the literature (Evans et al., 1993; Koehler, 1993; Kornblith, 1993).

As is apparent in Table 2.1, five of the six correlations between these four tasks were significant at the .001 level. The syllogistic reasoning task displayed significant correlations with each of the other three tasks, as did the selection task. The only correlation that did not attain significance was that between performance on the argument evaluation task and statistical reasoning. Although the highest correlation obtained was that between syllogistic reasoning and selection task performance (.363), correlations almost as strong were obtained between tasks deriving from the deductive reasoning literature (syllogistic reasoning, selection task) and inductive reasoning literature (statistical reasoning).

The significant relationships between most of these reasoning tasks suggests that departures from normative responding on each of them are due to systematic factors and not to nonsystematic performance errors. The positive manifold displayed by the tasks suggests that random performance errors cannot be the sole reason that responses deviate from normative responding because there were systematic response tendencies across very different reasoning tasks. Explaining away these deviations as mere performance errors encounters the same problem that Thaler (1992) pointed out in his arguments against the Panglossians in the domain of economic theory: "This line of defense is weak because many of the departures from rational choice that have been observed are systematic" (p. 5).

In light of the systematic covariance among tasks, it should be emphasized that there is considerable dispute about the appropriate normative model to be applied to several of these tasks (an issue taken up in greater detail in the next two chapters). The selection task is particularly contentious (e.g., Evans & Over, 1996; Nickerson, 1996; Oaksford & Chater, 1994, 1996; Stanovich & West, 1998a). The normative appropriateness of ignoring vivid single-case evidence has also been challenged (Gigerenzer, 1991b; Koehler, 1996). Even the stricture that prior belief should not be implicated in tasks such as syllogistic reasoning and argument evaluation has been questioned (Evans et al., 1993; Koehler, 1993; Kornblith, 1993). It is thus interesting that, despite these disputes, people who gave the standard normative response on one task tended to also give it on another. To state it perhaps more clearly, call the standard normative response the normative$_s$ response. Call the alternative normative response advocated by the critics of the heuristics and biases literature normative$_a$ (alternative normative response). Thus, the outcome of this experiment was that people giving the normative$_s$ response on one task tended to give it on another and the people giving the normative$_a$ response on one tended to give it on another. In short, all of the tasks are either scored in the right direction or in the wrong direction. This is not what one would expect if one or two of the normative$_a$ responses were in fact the correct ones to give. Instead, the results seem to suggest that either all the normative$_s$ responses are correct or all the normative$_a$ responses are. The implications of this covariance for the disputes about the proper interpretation of these tasks is the topic of chapters 3 and 4.

On an individual task basis, however, most of the correlations observed in our studies (see Stanovich & West, 1998b, 1998c) were of a modest magnitude. Nevertheless, it should be emphasized that many of the relationships might be underestimated due to modest reliability. These tasks are not the equivalent of the powerful psychometric instruments that are used in most research on individual differences in cognition and personality (e.g., Ackerman, Kyllonen, & Roberts, in press; Carroll, 1993, 1997). Instead, due to the logistical constraints of a multivariate investigation involving so many different tasks, scores on some of these measures were based on a very few number of trials. The statistical reasoning composite score was based on only seven items, syllogism task performance was based on only eight items, and selection task performance based on just five items. The modest correlations displayed by these tasks must be interpreted with this limitation in mind.

INDIVIDUAL DIFFERENCES AND COMPUTATIONAL LIMITATIONS

As indicated in Footnote 1, the notion of performance error used in this volume does not subsume computational limitations. Instead, performance errors here refer to algorithmic-level problems that are transitory in nature. They might not occur again on a readministration of the same problem. However, long-term, nontransitory limitations at the algorithmic level might also exist and serve to prevent normative models from being computed. Apologists take seriously the caveat that judgments about the rationality of actions and beliefs must take into account the resource-limited nature of the human cognitive apparatus (Baron, 1985a; Cherniak, 1986; Goldman, 1978; Oaksford & Chater, 1993, 1995; Simon, 1956, 1957). Most theorists would agree that to characterize a behavior as irrational via comparison with a normative model, it must be the case that the normative model is computable in the cognitive mechanism under study. To repeat Stich's (1990) memorable phrase, we would not want to attribute irrationality to people if the normative strategy "requires a brain the size of a blimp" (p. 27).

Algorithmic-level limitations are one of the reasons (environmental pressures on performance—e.g., time limits—are another) why the notion of a prescriptive model is needed. Computational limitations might be creating normative/descriptive gaps when in fact there are no prescriptive/descriptive gaps—human cognition may be as close to normative performance as it can be given limitations at the algorithmic level. Sterelny (1990, p. 47) provided an example of a computational limitation in his discussion of color constancy that is preserved in an intentional-level description of the visual system. However, the algorithmic-level mechanisms that preserve color constancy over changes in illumination can fail in unusual conditions such as sodium lighting. The inability to deal with these extreme conditions reflects a computational limitation that will recur in similar conditions. It will not appear and disappear in a random fashion. This computational limitation does not reflect a defect in the intentional-level description of the system but an inability of the relevant algorithms to appropriately process the incoming stimuli under these conditions.

Thus, in contrast to algorithmic-level problems that represent performance errors, computational limitations are not transitory and they should not be conceptualized as representing error variance. Computational limitations represent systematic influences on performance that—unlike performance errors—are not inconsistent with the positive manifold displayed in Table 2.1.

The issue of whether algorithmic-level limitations make prescriptive models for human behavior depart from normative ones is in part an empirical question and it is uniquely illuminated by a study of individual differences. This is because the cognitive capacity of human beings varies—albeit not on such a wide scale as that discussed in the formal literature on computational theory. Nevertheless, there is prima facie evidence that the actual variation in cognitive ability that does exist among human beings might be related to performance on reasoning and decision-making tasks. First, we already know from three decades of work on such tasks that variability in performance does exist. Second, Table 2.1 shows that performance on one task is predictable from that on another. This covariance might well be due to common resource limitations that are affecting performance on all tasks. In a series of studies (Stanovich & West, 1998b, 1998c) our research group has examined the issue of whether there are such limitations at the algorithmic level preventing the computation of the normative response and thus whether—at least for some individuals—the normative response is not prescriptive. Our research program is in the tradition of the project called for by Goldman (1993): "Requirements of rationality, then, should be shaped to fit practical feasibilities, and questions of feasibility are just the sorts of questions which cognitive science often addresses. Thus, cognitive science may be relevant in setting standards for rationality, not just in assessing human prospects for meeting independently given standards" (p. 22).

In a correlational sense—in the aggregate—the tightness of the association between cognitive ability and task performance can be used as a rough indicator of the extent to which computational limitations are implicated in the computation of the normative response. The magnitude of the correlation between performance on a reasoning task and cognitive capacity is viewed as an empirical clue about the importance of algorithmic-level limitations in creating discrepancies between descriptive and normative models. A strong correlation suggests important computational limitations that might make the normative response not prescriptive for those of lower cognitive capacity. In contrast, the absence of a correlation between the normative response and cognitive capacity suggests no computational limitation and thus no reason why the normative response should not be considered prescriptive for every individual.

In our studies, we have operationalized cognitive capacity in terms of well-known cognitive ability and aptitude tasks such as the Scholastic Aptitude Test (SAT), Raven Matrices, and various vocabulary and reading comprehension tests. All are known to load highly on psychometric g (Carpenter, Just, & Shell, 1990; Carroll, 1993, 1997; Lubinski & Humphreys, 1997; Matarazzo, 1972) and such measures have been linked to neurophysiological and information processing indicators of efficient cognitive computation[2] (Caryl, 1994; Deary, 1995; Deary & Stough, 1996; Detterman, 1994; Dougherty & Haith, 1997; Fry & Hale, 1996; Hunt, 1987; Stankov & Dunn, 1993; Vernon, 1991, 1993). Most of the analyses throughout this volume focus on SAT Total scores. The other measures of cognitive ability produced virtually identical results and were largely redundant.

The top half of Table 2.2 indicates the magnitude of the correlation between SAT Total scores and the four reasoning tasks discussed previously. SAT scores were significantly correlated with performance on all four rational thinking tasks. The correlation with syllogistic reasoning was the highest (.470) and the other three correlations were roughly equal in magnitude (.347 to .394). All were statistically significant ($p < .001$).

The remaining correlations in the table are the results from a replication and extension experiment (Study 2 of Stanovich & West, 1998b). Three of the four tasks from the previous experiment were carried over (all but the selection task), and added to this multivariate battery was a covariation detection task modeled on Wasserman, Dorner, and Kao

---

[2]Our focus on a measure with a high g-loading is in part justified by findings indicating that working memory is strongly implicated in tasks with high g-loadings (Bara, Bucciarelli, & Johnson-Laird, 1995; Kyllonen, 1996; Kyllonen & Christal, 1990). In theories of computability, computational power often depends on memory for the results of intermediate computations.

(1990). Three new tasks assessing cognitive biases were also added to this multivariate battery of tests. The first was a hypothesis-testing task modeled on Tschirgi (1980) in which the score on the task was the number of times subjects attempted to test a hypothesis in a manner that did not unconfound variables. Outcome bias was measured using tasks introduced by Baron and Hershey (1988). This bias is demonstrated when subjects rate a decision with a positive outcome as superior to a decision with a negative outcome even when the information available to the decision maker was the same in both cases. Finally, if/only bias refers to the tendency for people to have differential responses to outcomes based on the differences in counterfactual alternative outcomes that might have occurred (Epstein, Lipson, Holstein, & Huh, 1992; Miller, Turnbull, & McFarland, 1990). The bias is demonstrated when subjects rate a decision leading to a negative outcome as worse than a control condition when the former makes it easier to imagine a positive outcome occurring.

The bottom half of Table 2.2 indicates that the correlations involving the syllogistic reasoning task, statistical reasoning task, and argument evaluation task were similar in magnitude to those obtained in the previous experiment. The correlations involving the four new tasks were also all statistically significant. The sign on the hypothesis testing, outcome bias, and if/only thinking tasks was negative because high scores on these tasks reflect susceptibility to non-normative cognitive biases. The correlations on the four new tasks were generally lower (range .172 to .239) than the correlations involving the other tasks (.371 to .410). However, it must again be emphasized that the logistical constraints dictated that the scores on some of the new tasks were based on an extremely small sample of behavior. The outcome bias score was based on only a single comparison and the if/only thinking score was based on only two items.

Schmidt and Hunter (1996) recently cautioned laboratory investigators that "if a subject is observed in an exactly repeated situation, the correlation between replicated responses is rarely any higher than .25. That is, for unrehearsed single responses, it is unwise to assume a test–retest reliability higher than .25" (p. 203). The very modest correlations displayed by a task such as the outcome bias measure must be interpreted with this admonition in mind. Nevertheless, Schmidt and Hunter demonstrated the well-known fact that aggregation can remedy the attenuation caused by the low reliability of single items. Certainly this is true in the present case. The remaining correlations in the table concern composite variables. The first composite involved the three tasks that were carried over from the previous experiment: the syllogistic reasoning, statistical reasoning, and argument evaluation tasks. The scores on each of these three tasks were standardized and summed to yield a composite score. The composite's correlation with SAT scores was .530. A second rational thinking composite was formed by summing the standard scores of the remaining four tasks: covariation judgment, hypothesis testing, outcome bias, and if/only

TABLE 2.2
Correlations Between Performance on the Reasoning Tasks and SAT Total Score

Data from Study 1 of Stanovich and West (1998b)	
Syllogisms	.470*
Selection task	.394*
Statistical reasoning	.347*
Argument evaluation	.358*
Replication and Extension (Study 2 of Stanovich & West, 1998b)	
Syllogisms	.410*
Statistical reasoning	.376*
Argument evaluation task	.371*
Covariation detection	.239*
Hypothesis-testing bias	−.223*
Outcome bias	−.172*
If/only thinking	−.208*
RT1 composite	.530*
RT2 composite	.383*
RT composite, all tasks	.547*

Note. RT1 composite = standard score composite of performance on argument evaluation task, syllogisms, and statistical reasoning; RT2 composite = standard score composite of performance on covariation judgment, hypothesis-testing task, if/only thinking, and outcome bias; RT composite, all tasks = rational thinking composite score of performance on all seven tasks in the replication and extension experiment.

* = $p < .001$, all two-tailed. Ns = 527 to 529 in the replication and extension.

thinking (the latter three scores reflected so that higher scores represent more normatively correct reasoning). SAT Total scores displayed a correlation of .383 with this composite. Finally, both of the rational thinking composites were combined into a composite variable reflecting performance on all seven tasks and this composite displayed a correlation of .547 with SAT scores.

It might be argued that one possible mechanism accounting for the associations displayed in Table 2.2 is differential educational experience. Perhaps, for example, more intelligent individuals have been exposed to superior educational experiences—experiences where they were more likely to be taught the normatively appropriate responses to the tasks. The plausibility of this argument varies greatly across the various tasks that were investigated. The causal aggregate statistical problems are presented to subjects as having no right or wrong answers. These problems did not require any numerical calculation and nothing like them appears in any normal curriculum. Empirically, the correlation between the composite score on the aggregate reasoning problems and formal statistics exposure at the college level was .11 in the replication and extension experiment—a statistically significant relationship because of the large sample size of the study, but one not large enough to sustain a strong explanation in terms of educational experience. Like the statistical reasoning problems, outcome bias and and if/only thinking are unlikely curricular components. In contrast, the selection task and the syllogistic reasoning task would seem to involve reasoning that is more like that taught in formal educational settings. Nevertheless, within the range of variability in the present samples, the effects of educational experience on selection task performance appear to be slight (Cheng & Holyoak, 1985; Griggs & Ransdell, 1986; Jackson & Griggs, 1988; Kern, Mirels, & Hinshaw, 1983).

Stanovich and West (1998b) collected some data relevant to assessing the relationship between educational history and performance in the replication and extension experiment by examining information on the demographics form filled out by the students participating in the study. A 0–4 point scale was constructed that assessed the student's mathematics/statistics course background. Students received 1 point if they had taken a statistics course in college, 1 point if they had taken a statistics course in high school, 1 point if they had taken a mathematics course in college, and 1 point if they had had 4 years of high school mathematics. The mean score on the scale was 2.07 ($SD = .75$).

As Table 2.3 indicates, across the seven tasks in the replication and extension experiment, the mathematics/statistics background composite variable displayed a significant correlation with only one task (argument evaluation). The absolute magnitude of the seven correlations ranged from .045 to .137. Even the composite variable of all seven rational thinking tasks displayed a correlation of only .162 with the mathematics/statistics background variable, considerably lower than that with the SAT Total score (.547). Finally, there was no evidence that more intelligent students were simply more sensitive to demand characteristics that encourage a normative response that happens to be socially desirable. Socially desirable response tendencies were assessed in virtually all of the studies referred to in this volume and a consistent finding was that the students giving the normative response were not more prone to make socially desirable responses. More often, there were slight trends in the opposite direction.

Covariance across tasks from the heuristics and biases literature and the possibility of computational limitations were also examined in the follow-up investigation of Stanovich and West (1998c). Because deviations from Bayesian reasoning have been the focus of much of the research in the heuristics and biases literature, Stanovich and West utilized a task in which two such deviations could be studied simultaneously. The two de-

TABLE 2.3

Correlations Between Performance on the Reasoning Tasks and Mathematics/Statistics Background

Mathematics/Statistics Background	
Argument evaluation task	.137*
Syllogisms	.091
Statistical reasoning	.075
Covariation detection	.088
Hypothesis-testing bias	−.045
Outcome bias	−.071
If/only thinking	−.062
RT1 composite	.145*
RT2 composite	.125*
RT composite, all tasks	.162**

Note. RT1 composite = standard score composite of performance on argument evaluation task, syllogisms, and statistical reasoning; RT2 composite = standard score composite of performance on covariation judgment, hypothesis-testing task, if/only thinking, and outcome bias; RT composite, all tasks = rational thinking composite score of performance on all seven tasks.
* = $p < .01$, ** = $p < .001$, all two-tailed.

viations are most easily characterized if Bayes' rule is expressed in the ratio form where the odds favoring the focal hypothesis (H) are derived by multiplying the likelihood ratio of the observed datum (D) by the prior odds favoring the focal hypothesis:

$$\frac{P(H/D)}{P(\sim H/D)} = \frac{P(D/H)}{P(D/\sim H)} \times \frac{P(H)}{P(\sim H)}$$

From left to right, the three ratio terms represent: the posterior odds favoring the focal hypothesis (H) after receipt of the new data (D), the likelihood ratio composed of the probability of the data given the focal hypothesis divided by the probability of the data given its mutually exclusive complement, and the prior odds favoring the focal hypothesis (see Fischhoff & Beyth-Marom, 1983).

One deviation from Bayesian reasoning that has been the subject of intense investigation is the tendency for individuals to underweight the prior probability, P(H), when it is represented as a statistical base rate—and especially when it has no apparent causal relevance to the focal hypothesis (Bar-Hillel, 1980, 1984, 1990; Fischhoff & Bar-Hillel, 1984; Koehler, 1996; Lyon & Slovic, 1976; Tversky & Kahneman, 1982). This deviation is discussed extensively in chapter 3 because it has been the source of enormous controversy. The deviation that is the focus in this chapter is the tendency to ignore—or at least to pay insufficient attention to—the denominator of the likelihood ratio, $P(D/\sim H)$, the probability of the datum given that the focal hypothesis is false (Beyth-Marom & Fischhoff, 1983; Doherty, Chadwick, Garavan, Barr, & Mynatt, 1996; Doherty, Mynatt, Tweney, & Schiavo, 1979; Einhorn & Hogarth, 1978; Wasserman et al., 1990; Wolfe, 1995).

Although the normative correctness of evaluating $P(D/\sim H)$ is much less controversial than the use of base rates, investigators have questioned the focus on the complement hypothesis that is stressed by the traditional falsificationist research strategy. Klayman and Ha (1987, 1989) illustrated how certain task environments make a hypothesis-testing strategy that concentrates on the focal hypothesis quite efficacious. Similarly, Friedrich (1993) argued that if the human cognitive apparatus is designed to avoid certain types of predictive errors rather than to seek the truth (see Einhorn & Hogarth, 1978; Halberstadt & Kareev, 1995; Stein, 1996; Stich, 1990), then focusing on the focal hypothesis and showing relative inattention to its complement might be a processing pattern that is to be expected (see also McKenzie, 1994).

Stanovich and West (1998c) examined the tendency to process $P(D/\sim H)$ using a selection task in which individuals were not forced to compute a Bayesian posterior, but instead simply had to indicate whether or not they thought $P(D/\sim H)$ was relevant to their decision. The task was taken from the work of Doherty and Mynatt (1990). Subjects were given the following instructions:

Imagine you are a doctor. A patient comes to you with a red rash on his fingers. What information would you want in order to diagnose whether the patient has the disease Digirosa? Below are four pieces of information that may or may not be relevant to the diagnosis. Please indicate *all* of the pieces of information that are necessary to make the diagnosis, but *only* those pieces of information that are necessary to do so.

Subjects then chose from the alternatives listed in the order: percentage of people without Digirosa who have a red rash, percentage of people with Digirosa, percentage of people without Digirosa, and percentage of people with Digirosa who have a red rash. These alternatives represented the choices of $P(D/\sim H)$, $P(H)$, $P(\sim H)$, and $P(D/H)$, respectively.

Of the 596 individuals who completed the task, the normatively correct choice of $P(H)$, $P(D/H)$, and $P(D/\sim H)$ was made by 15.1% of the sample. The most popular choice (43.0% of the sample) was the two components of the likelihood ratio, $P(D/H)$ and $P(D/\sim H)$. The choice of the base rate, $P(H)$, and the numerator of the likelihood ratio, $P(D/H)$—ignoring the denominator of the likelihood ratio—was made by 18.5% of the sample, and 19.1% chose $P(D/H)$ only. These four patterns accounted for over 95% of the choices in our study. Almost all subjects (96.3%) viewed $P(D/H)$ as relevant and very few (2.7%) viewed P(~H) as relevant. Overall, 63.3% of the participants chose P(D/~H) as a necessary component and 35.7% of the sample thought it was necessary to know the base rate, P(H). However, only 18.3% of the sample viewed both the base rate and P(D/~H) as relevant.

The cognitive characteristics of the individuals who chose P(D/~H) as a necessary component are presented in Table 2.4 where the sample is dichotomized based on this choice. Individuals including P(D/~H) in their choices had significantly higher SAT scores than those not choosing P(D/~H), $p < .001$. Similarly, a converging measure of general ability, a vocabulary test, displayed a significant difference ($p < .025$) favoring those who chose P(D/~H). There were also significant differences ($p < .01$) in performance on syllogistic reasoning and statistical reasoning tasks like those described previously. Choosing P(D/~H) was not associated with educational history, as there was no significant difference in mathematics background as assessed by the mathematics background composite variable.

These cognitive ability differences favoring individuals choosing P(D/~H) extended to another paradigm that was examined. This paradigm, the 2 × 2 covariation detection task, requires more active processing of the P(D/~H) information. Additionally, the task was altered to include a belief-bias component (Klaczynski et al., 1997; Levin, Wasserman, & Kao, 1993) in order to increase the complexity of processing as well as the relevance of the task. Participants evaluated 25 contingencies (see Wasserman et al., 1990) that were embedded within the context of 25 different hypothetical relationships. Each of the 25 problems had two parts. In the first part, subjects were asked their opinion on a hypothetical relationship between two variables. They were then asked to evaluate the degree of association between the two variables in the data

TABLE 2.4

Mean Scores of Subjects Including P(D/~H) in Their Choices (n = 377) and Those Not Choosing This Information (n = 219) on the Information Selection Task (Standard Deviations in Parentheses)

Variable	Not Included	Included	t Value
SAT Total	1080 (123)	1120 (127)	3.65**
Vocabulary test	.479 (.169)	.511 (.160)	2.29*
Syllogistic reasoning	16.9 (4.2)	17.9 (4.3)	2.84**
Statistical reasoning	−.389 (2.8)	.275 (2.6)	2.91**
Mathematics background	2.16 (.80)	2.12 (.76)	−0.59

Note. df = 576 for the SAT, 586 for the vocabulary test, 586 for syllogistic reasoning, 593 for statistical reasoning, and 594 for math background.

* = $p < .05$, ** = $p < .01$, all two-tailed.

of a hypothetical research study. For example, in one problem the subjects were asked whether they believed that couples who live together before marriage tend to have successful marriages. They indicated their degree of agreement with this hypothesized relationship on a scale ranging from –10 (strongly disagree) to +10 (strongly disagree) and centered on 0 (neutral). Participants were later told to imagine that a researcher had sampled 250 couples and found that: (a) 50 couples did live together and had successful marriages, (b) 50 couples did live together and were divorced, (c) 50 couples did not live together and had successful marriages, and (d) 100 couples did not live together and were divorced.

These data correspond to four cells of the 2 × 2 contingency table traditionally labeled A, B, C, and D (see Levin et al., 1993). Subsequent to the presentation of the data, the participants were asked to judge the nature and extent of the relationship between living together before marriage and successful marriages in these data on a scale ranging from +10 (positive association) to –10 (negative association) and centered on 0 (no association). The remaining 24 problems dealt with a variety of different hypotheses (e.g., that secondary smoke is associated with lung problems in children, that exercise is associated with a sense of well-being, that eating spicy foods is associated with stomach problems). The cell combinations used in the 25 problems were based on those listed in Table 2 of Wasserman et al. (1990).

Previous experiments have indicated that subjects weight the cell information in the order Cell A > Cell B > Cell C > Cell D—Cell D reliably receiving the least weight and/or attention (see Arkes & Harkness, 1983; Kao & Wasserman, 1993; Schustack & Sternberg, 1981). The tendency to ignore Cell D (and thus to underweight $P(D/\sim H)$—which cannot be calculated without Cell D) is non-normative, as indeed is any tendency to differentially weight the four cells. The normatively appropriate strategy (see Allan, 1980; Kao & Wasserman, 1993; Shanks, 1995) is to use the conditional probability rule—subtracting from the probability of the target hypothesis when the indicator is present the probability of the target hypothesis when the indicator is absent. Numerically, the rule amounts to calculating the Δp statistic: $[A / (A + B)] – [C / (C + D)]$ (see Allan, 1980). For example, the Δp value for the problem presented earlier is +.167, indicating a fairly weak positive association. The Δp values used in the 25 problems ranged from –.600 (strong negative association) to .600 (strong positive association).

Each participant's judgments of the degree of contingency in each of the 25 problems were correlated with the Δp value for each problem, with each of the four cell values, and with their agreement with the hypothesis being tested. The mean individual correlation with Δp was .639 ($SD = .192$) and the median correlation was .676. These average individual subject correlations were somewhat lower than those observed by Wasserman et al. (1990) using the same Δp values (their median correlation was .816)—probably because the Stanovich and West (1998c) problems involved potential belief bias. Indeed, 299 of the 580 participants in the latter investigation displayed significant correlations between their judgments of contingency and their agreement with the hypothesis being tested. The mean correlation was .363.

The mean correlations between contingency judgments and the values of Cells A, B, C, and D were .568, −.523, −.427, and .401, respectively. The signs of these mean correlations are in the appropriate direction of the normative Δp formula: positive for Cells A and D and negative for Cells B and C. However, the normative strategy also dictates equal weighting of the four cells, and the results converged with previous findings indicating that subjects typically weight the cells in the order Cell A > Cell B > Cell C > Cell D (Kao & Wasserman, 1993; Wasserman et al., 1990).

Individual differences in covariation judgment performance were examined by partitioning the sample based on a median split of the weighting of Cell D. As Table 2.5 indicates, participants giving relatively higher weighting to Cell D had significantly higher SAT scores, vocabulary scores, syllogistic reasoning scores, and statistical reasoning scores than did participants giving relatively lower weighting to Cell D. These differences were not due to differences in mathematics background. Thus, the results from the covariation judgment task converged with those from the information selection task in indicating that sensitivity to P(D/~H) was associated with greater facility on other reasoning tasks and with higher cognitive ability scores.

Regarding P(D/~H), performance on the selection task and the covariation detection task was associated. Table 2.6 presents a dichotomization of the sample based on the choice of P(D/~H) in the selection task. Those choosing P(D/~H) displayed significantly higher correlations with the optimal measure of contingency, Δp. They also

TABLE 2.5

Mean Scores of Participants Giving a High Weighting to Cell D in the Covariation Judgment Task ($n = 300$) and Those Giving a Low Weighting ($n = 279$) (Standard Deviations in Parentheses)

Variable	Low	High	t Value
SAT Total	1084 (131)	1133 (117)	4.68**
Vocabulary test	.484 (.170)	.521 (.153)	2.73*
Syllogistic reasoning	16.7 (4.1)	18.4 (4.3)	4.88**
Statistical reasoning	−.359 (2.6)	.340 (2.7)	3.15*
Mathematics background	2.10 (.76)	2.16 (.76)	0.89

Note. $df = 562$ for the SAT, 571 for the vocabulary test and syllogistic reasoning, and 577 for statistical reasoning and math background.

* $= p < .01$, ** $= p < .001$, all two-tailed.

TABLE 2.6

**Mean Scores of Subjects Including P(D/~H) in Their Choices
(n = 377) and Those Not Choosing This Information (n = 219)on the
Information Selection Task on Parameters From the Covariation
Judgment Task (Standard Deviations in Parentheses)**

Variable	Not Included	Included	t Value
Covariation Judgment			
Correlation: Δp	.612 (.208)	.658 (.180)	2.76**
Correlation: Cell A	.554 (.181)	.579 (.159)	1.73
Correlation: Cell B	−.503 (.205)	−.536 (.172)	2.05*
Correlation: Cell C	−.403 (.186)	−.445 (.169)	2.69**
Correlation: Cell D	.382 (.176)	.415 (.175)	2.10*
Correlation: Agreement	.408 (.263)	.342 (.244)	3.03**

Note. $df = 566$; only 568 participants completed both tasks.
* $= p < .05$, ** $= p < .01$, all two-tailed.

displayed higher correlations with the two cells that tend to be underweighted by most subjects in this paradigm—Cells C and D. Consistent with these indications that the P(D/~H) group was more data-driven was the finding that they displayed significantly lower correlations with their agreement with the hypothesis being tested.

CONCLUSIONS REGARDING PERFORMANCE ERRORS AND COMPUTATIONAL LIMITATIONS

As an explanation of the repeated failure of subjects in the heuristics and biases literature to display normatively appropriate behavior, a strong version of the performance error view does not seem tenable. The deviations from normative$_s$ responding have repeatedly been shown to be systematic. Making a normative$_s$ response on one particular task is predictable from performance on unrelated tasks and the direction of the association is always the same. Individuals giving the normative$_s$ response on one task are more likely to give it on another (in the case of the tasks discussed in the present chapter; several exceptions to this trend are discussed in chap. 3). The propensity to give the normative$_s$ response is also modestly predictable from knowledge of the cognitive ability of the subject. None of these systematic covariance patterns would be observed if deviations from normative responding were simply error variance—transitory information-processing fluctuations that unsystematically cause deviations from a competence model centered on the normative response.

It appears that to a moderate extent, systematic discrepancies between actual performance and normative models can be accounted for by variation in capacity limitations at the algorithmic level—at least with respect to these particular tasks. Although performance on many of the reasoning tasks investigated here displayed associations with computational capacity, these should not be viewed as absolute limitations because much variability remained after cognitive ability had been accounted for. The magnitude of many of the correlations leaves much systematic variance unexplained. The substantial unexplained variance leaves considerable room for the possibility that subjects are systematically computing according to non-normative rules (Baron, 1991b; Shafir, 1994) and are not necessarily doing so to circumvent limitations in cognitive capacity (a possibility explored in greater detail in chap. 6).

The loose connections with cognitive capacity can be illustrated by pointing to some specific instances of normative performance. For example, in several of the Stanovich and West (1998b) experiments, many individuals with SAT scores in the 1,000–1,100 range (on the old SAT scale prior to the April, 1995 recentering) gave the aggregate response and ignored the vivid case evidence on at least six out of seven statistical reasoning problems. In Experiment 2 of Stanovich and West, eight individuals with SAT scores less than 900 (substantially below the mean of the sample, 1,108) displayed no outcome bias, as did many students with SAT scores in the 900–1,000 range. In the same experiment, individuals with SAT scores as low as 910 and 960 had near perfectly normative responses on the covariation assessment task (correlations of over .90 with the Δp strategy—see Allan, 1980).

Further examples are provided in the scatterplot illustrated in Fig. 2.1. There, SAT Total scores are plotted against the number (out of eight) of correctly answered syllogistic reasoning problems in which the believability of the conclusion contradicted logical validity (see Experiment 1 of Stanovich & West, 1998b). Although it is true that few individuals with SAT scores below the mean of 1,093 answered all eight items correctly, a substantial number of individuals with SAT scores below the mean answered six or seven items correctly. A stronger relationship—one more suggestive of a computational limitation—is presented in Fig. 2.2. There, SAT Total scores are plotted against the number of selection task problems answered correctly (out of five) in Experiment 1 of Stanovich and West. There, subjects who gave the logically correct P and not-Q response consistently (on three or more problems) were almost uniformly above the mean in cognitive ability. This result is consistent with O'Brien's (1995) argument that for a mental logic without direct access to the truth table for the material conditional, the selection task is, computationally, a very hard problem.

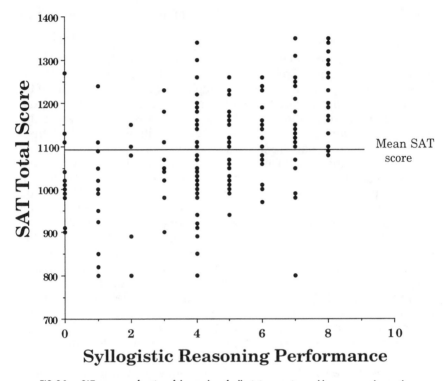

FIG. 2.1.   SAT scores as a function of the number of syllogistic reasoning problems answered correctly.

Collectively, these results indicate that there is some degree of computational limitation on most of the tasks discussed in this chapter, but the
limitation is far from absolute. That is, although computational limitations
appear implicated to some extent in most of the tasks, the normative responses for all of them were computed by some university students who
had modest cognitive abilities (e.g., below the mean in a university sample). Such results help to situate the relationship between prescriptive
and normative models for the tasks in question. For example, even in
cases such as the selection task, where the modal response on the task is
non-normative, individual differences do encompass the normative response. If some humans have sufficient computational power to derive
the normative response, then—whatever might be said about particular
individuals—it is not impossible for humankind in general to compute the
normative model. Additionally, the boundaries of prescriptive recommendations for particular individuals might be explored by examining the
distribution of the cognitive capacities of individuals who gave the normative response on a particular task. This is the role that Stich (1993) saw for
psychology in his pragmatist naturalization of epistemology: "Our norma-

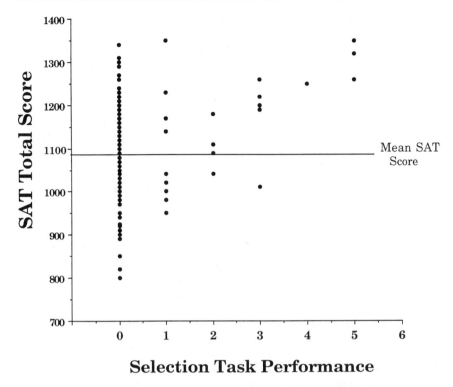

FIG. 2.2.   SAT scores as a function of the number of selection task problems answered correctly.

tive theory will respect the limitations imposed by human psychology and human hardware.... Of course, the more our normative theory ... respects the limits and idiosyncrasies of human cognition, the closer it will resemble the descriptive theory.... But there is no reason to think that the two will collapse" (p. 14).

The "normative theory that respects the limits and idiosyncrasies of human cognition" is of course the prescriptive theory—and with respect to the tasks discussed in this chapter it has indeed not collapsed into the descriptive theory. For most of these tasks, only a small number of the students with the very lowest cognitive ability in this sample would have prescriptive models for any of these tasks that deviated substantially from the normative model for computational reasons (with perhaps the exception of the selection task). Such findings also might be taken to suggest that perhaps other factors might account for variation—a prediction that is confirmed when work on thinking dispositions is examined in chapter 6. Of course, the deviation between the normative and prescriptive model due to computational limitations will certainly be larger in unselected or nonuniversity populations. This point also serves to reinforce the caveat that the correlations observed in Tables 2.1 and 2.2 were undoubtedly attenuated due to restriction of range in the sample.

The finding that the prescriptive model deviates from the normative only for those subjects with the very lowest cognitive ability relates to Stich's (1993) point that:

> [it] may well be the case that there are readily learnable and readily usable strategies of reasoning that would improve on those that were in fact used. … In order to pursue human epistemology in a serious way we will need detailed information about the nature and rigidity of constraints on human cognition. And the only way to get this information is to do the relevant empirical work. This is yet another way in which the sort of naturalized epistemology that I am advocating requires input from empirical science. (p. 14)

For most tasks, it was not difficult to find subjects who gave the normative$_s$ response but who were from the part of the sample with the lowest algorithmic-level capacity. If the normative/prescriptive gap is indeed modest, then there may well be true individual differences at the intentional level—that is, true individual differences in rational thought—and Stich's optimistic conjecture about teachable strategies would indeed be warranted. This will only be known if the normative/prescriptive gap is explored by examining covariation among individual differences on reasoning tasks.

Computational limitations as an explanation of differences between normative and descriptive models are relatively uncontroversial in the literature. Meliorists and Apologists both agree on the importance of assessing such limitations—they differ only in the magnitude of the limitations that they expect empirical studies to reveal. Panglossians will, when it is absolutely necessary, turn themselves into Apologists to rescue subjects from the charge of irrationality. Thus, they too acknowledge the importance of computational limitations in many cases. However, in the next chapter an alternative explanation of the normative/descriptive gap is examined that is much more controversial—the notion that incorrect norms are being used to evaluate human performance.

The Inappropriate Norm Argument

Performance errors and computational limitations as explanations of the normative/descriptive gap both locate the source of the discrepancy in the human cognitive apparatus. The former explanation posits transitory information-processing mishaps; the latter posits permanent algorithmic-level limitations that prevent computation of the normative response. However, a much more contentious alternative explanation is the claim that an inappropriate normative model has been applied to the task. The charge of incorrect norm application locates the problem in the experimenter rather than the subject. It is a potent strategy for the Panglossian theorist to use against the advocate of Meliorism because the latter is quite prone to rely on the heuristics and biases literature (e.g., Baron, 1994b; Dawes, 1988; Gilovich, 1991; Piattelli-Palmarini, 1994; Stanovich, 1998)—precisely the place where the appropriateness of norms has been most at issue.

The possibility of incorrect norm application arises because psychologists have traditionally appealed to the normative models of other disciplines (statistics, logic, etc.) in order to interpret the responses on various tasks. There is a danger in this procedure. The danger arises because there is a less than perfect consensus on the status of the normative models in many of the disciplines from which psychologists borrow. Heavy reliance on a normative model that is in dispute often engenders the claim that the gap between the descriptive and normative occurs because psychologists are applying the wrong normative model to the situation. Such claims have become quite common in critiques of the heuristics and biases literature:

- "Many critics have insisted that in fact it is Kahneman & Tversky, not their subjects, who have failed to grasp the logic of the problem" (Margolis, 1987, p. 158).

- "The standards of rationality themselves are in dispute, so it is unclear, when the intuitions of experimental subjects disagree with the intuitions of the experimenter, whether it is the experimenter or the subject who ought to reform his ideas of rationality" (Kyburg, 1983, pp. 232–233).
- "In the examples of alleged base rate fallacy considered by Kahneman and Tversky, they, and not their experimental subjects, commit the fallacies" (Levi, 1983, p. 502).
- "If a 'fallacy' is involved, it is probably more attributable to the researchers than to the subjects" (Messer & Griggs, 1993, p. 195).
- "The conjunction effect may not be a fallacy after all—that the illusion may be less in the eyes of the subjects than in the eyes of their readers" (Dulany & Hilton, 1991, p. 87).
- "What Wason and his successors judged to be the wrong response is in fact correct" (Wetherick, 1993, p. 107).

Examples of the incorrect norm application argument are provided in the work of Lopes (1982), Birnbaum (1983), and Dawes (1989, 1990). Lopes argued that the literature on the inability of human subjects to generate random sequences (e.g., Wagenaar, 1972) has adopted a narrow concept of randomness that does not acknowledge broad conceptions of randomness that are debated in the philosophical literature. Birnbaum demonstrated that conceptualizing the well-known cab problem (see Bar-Hillel, 1980; Lyon & Slovic, 1976; Tversky & Kahneman, 1982) within a signal-detection framework can lead to different normatively correct conclusions than those assumed by the less flexible Bayesian model that is usually applied. In the cab problem, the subject is told that a cab was involved in a hit-and-run accident at night and that two cab companies, the Green and the Blue, operate in the city in which the accident occurred. The subject is told that: 85% of the cabs in the city are Green and 15% are Blue; that a witness identified the cab as Blue; and that the court tested the reliability of the witness under the same circumstances that existed on the night of the accident and when presented with a sample of cabs (half of which were Blue and half of which were Green) the witness correctly identified each of the two colors 80% of the time. The subject is asked to estimate the probability that the cab involved in the accident was Blue.

The typical Bayesian analysis of the problem assumes that the ratio of the hit rate to the false-alarm rate is independent of signal probability. Birnbaum (1983) pointed out that this might not be true for a human witness who was aware of the base rates, and that it is necessary to generalize the hit/false-alarm ratio from the court's detection experiment (with 50% of each type of cab) to the actual situation. This extrapolation requires the basic formalisms of signal detection theory and, in addition, a theory of judgment that dictates criterion placement in response to changes in signal probability. Depending on which of the latter is adopted, Birnbaum showed how posterior probabilities quite far from the Bayesian solution of .41 might be arrived at and that these alternative probabilities would have some normative justification.

Analogously, Dawes (1989, 1990) argued that social psychologists have too hastily applied an overly simplified normative model in labeling performance in opinion prediction experiments as displaying a so-called false-consensus effect. The false-consensus effect is the tendency for people to project their own opinions when predicting the attitudes, opinions, and behaviors of other people, and it has traditionally been viewed as a non-normative response tendency. It has usually been thought to arise at least in part from egocentric attributional biases (Marks & Miller, 1987; L. Ross, Greene, & House, 1977). Operationally, the false-consensus effect has been defined as occurring when subjects' estimates of the prevalence of their own position exceeds the estimate of its prevalence by subjects holding the opposite position (see Marks & Miller, 1987). However, several authors have argued that the term false consensus when applied to such a situation is somewhat of a misnomer because such a definition of projection says nothing about whether projecting consensus actually decreased predictive accuracy (see J. D. Campbell, 1986; Hoch, 1987).

Hoch (1987) demonstrated that a Brunswikian analysis of the opinion prediction paradigm would render some degree of projection normatively appropriate in a variety of situations. Dawes (1989, 1990) demonstrated that, similarly, a Bayesian analysis renders some degree of projection as normatively appropriate because, for the majority of people, there is actually a positive correlation between own opinion and the consensus opinion. Thus, one's own opinion is, in these social perception paradigms, a diagnostic datum that should condition probability estimates (see also Krueger & Zeiger, 1993, for formal demonstrations that some degree of projection is not necessarily accuracy reducing). Thus, the formal analyses of the social perception experiment by Dawes and Hoch have at least raised doubts about the common interpretation of the consensus effect as a normatively inappropriate egocentric bias (Gilovich, 1991; Greenwald, 1980). Instead, it appears that the consensus effect is not necessarily false—calling it so may be the result of the application of an incorrect normative model.

Perhaps the most consistent advocate of the incorrect norm position is Gigerenzer (1991a, 1991b, 1993, 1996a), who argued that "most so-called errors or cognitive illusions are, contrary to the assertions in the literature, in fact *not* violations of probability theory" (Gigerenzer, 1991b, p. 86). Taking dead aim at the Meliorists in the heuristics and biases camp, Gigerenzer's (1991b) view is that virtually all of the normative/descriptive gaps in that literature are artifacts of the application of the wrong normative model:

Most "errors" in probabilistic reasoning that one wants to explain by heuristics are in fact not errors, as I have argued above. Thus, heuristics are meant to explain what does not exist. Rather than explaining a deviation between human judgment and allegedly "correct" probabilistic reasoning, future research has to get rid of simplistic norms that evaluate human judgment instead of explaining it. (p. 102)

Gigerenzer (1991b, 1993, 1996a; Gigerenzer, Hoffrage, & Kleinbolting, 1991) argued that many tasks involving probabilistic judgment are inappropriately evaluated. For example, he asserted that base-rate neglect (e.g., Bar-Hillel, 1980), the conjunction effect (e.g., Tversky & Kahneman, 1983), and the overconfidence effect in knowledge calibration experiments (e.g., Lichtenstein, Fischhoff, & Phillips, 1982) have all been mistakenly classified as a cognitive biases because of the hasty application of an inappropriate normative model (Gigerenzer, 1991b; Gigerenzer et al., 1991). His argument is that in all of these paradigms, individuals are asked for probabilities of single events and that under some conceptions of probability such single-event subjective judgments are not subject to the rules of a probability calculus. For example, in the knowledge calibration experiment, Gigerenzer (1991b; Gigerenzer et al., 1991) argued that probability theory is not necessarily being violated when the degree of belief in a single event (i.e., that a particular answer is correct) does not equal the relative frequency of correct answers in the long run. He pointed out that many important frequentist theorists (e.g., von Mises, 1957) and subjectivist theorists (e.g., de Finetti, 1989) reject the idea that deviations of subjective probabilities from actual relative frequencies should be considered a reasoning error. For example, he quoted von Mises as stating that a single-event probability "has no meaning at all for us" (p. 11) and concluded that "a discrepancy between confidence in single events and relative frequencies in the long run is not an error or violation of probability from many experts points of view" (Gigerenzer, 1991b, pp. 88–89). Although there are counterarguments to this criticism (Dawid, 1982; Griffin & Tversky, 1992; Howson & Urbach, 1993; Kahneman & Tversky, 1996; Lad, 1984), it is sufficient to establish here that an influential group of theorists have argued that the probability model employed in studies of knowledge calibration, the conjunction effect, and base-rate usage in the traditional heuristics and biases literature has been inappropriate.

FROM THE DESCRIPTIVE TO THE NORMATIVE IN REASONING EXPERIMENTS

The cases just discussed provide examples of how the existence of deviations between normative models and actual human reasoning have been called into question by casting doubt on the normative models used to evaluate performance. Stein (1996) termed an extreme form of this strategy—that of explaining away all normative/descriptive gaps in terms of incorrect norm application—the "reject-the-norm strategy" (p. 239). It is noteworthy that this strategy is used exclusively by the Panglossian camp in the rationality debate, although this connection is not a necessary one.

Specifically, the reject-the-norm strategy is exclusively used to eliminate gaps between descriptive models of performance and normative models. When this type of critique is employed, the normative model that is suggested as a substitute for the normative$_s$ model is one that coincides perfectly with the descriptive model of the subjects' performance—thus preserving a view of human rationality as ideal. It is rarely noted that the strategy could be used in just the opposite way—to *create* gaps between the normative and descriptive. Situations where the modal response coincides with standard normative model could be critiqued, and alternative models could be suggested (normative$_a$ models) that would result in a new normative/descriptive gap. But this is never done. The Panglossian camp, often highly critical of empirical psychologists ("Kahneman and Tversky ... and not their experimental subjects, commit the fallacies"; Levi, 1983, p. 502), is never critical of psychologists who design reasoning tasks in instances where the modal subject gives the response the experimenters deem correct. Ironically, in these cases, according to the Panglossians, the same psychologists seem never to err in their task designs and interpretations.

It is quite clear that Cohen's (1979, 1981, 1986) trenchant criticisms of experimental psychologists would never have been written had human performance coincided with the normative$_s$ models that the psychologists were using. The fact that the use of the reject-the-norm strategy is entirely contingent on the existence or nonexistence of a normative/descriptive gap suggests that the strategy is empirically, not conceptually, triggered (norms are never rejected for purely conceptual reasons when they coincide with the modal human response). What this means is that in an important sense the norms being endorsed by the Panglossian camp are conditioned (if not indexed entirely) by descriptive facts about human behavior. Gigerenzer (1991b) was clear about his adherence to an empirically-driven reject-the-norm strategy:

> Since its origins in the mid-seventeenth century.... When there was a striking discrepancy between the judgment of reasonable men and what probability theory dictated—as with the famous St. Petersburg paradox—then the mathematicians went back to the blackboard and changed the equations (Daston, 1980). Those good old days have gone.... If, in studies on social cognition, researchers find a discrepancy between human judgment and what probability theory seems to dictate, the blame is now put on the human mind, not the statistical model. (p. 109)

One way of framing the current debate between the Panglossians and Meliorists is to observe that the Panglossians wish for a return of the "good old days" where the normative was derived from the intuitions of the untutored layman ("an appeal to people's intuitions is indispensable"; Cohen, 1981, p. 318); whereas the Meliorists (with their greater emphasis on the culturally constructed nature of norms) view the mode of operation during the "good old days" as a contingent fact of history—the product of a period when few aspects of epistemic and pragmatic rationality had been codified and preserved for general diffusion through education.

Thus, the Panglossians who argue for alternative normative models by using the reject-the-norm strategy argue—in parallel with strong charity advocates—that normative models can be literally "read off" from descriptions of human reasoning because the normative is indexed to the descriptive model of reasoning competence—just as it is in linguistics. Their view, in effect, becomes a strong form of the naturalistic fallacy (deriving ought from is). For example, Cohen (1981), like Gigerenzer, felt that the normative is indexed to the descriptive in the sense that a competence model of actual behavior can simply be interpreted as the normative model (see also Overton, 1990). Stein (1996) noted that proponents of this position believe that the normative can simply be "read off" from a model of competence because "whatever human reasoning competence turns out to be, the principles embodied in it are the normative principles of reasoning" (p. 231). The assumption is that when a reasoning experiment reveals a performance divergence from a standard normative model it reveals "only that our reasoning competence diverges from our preconceived ideas of the normative principles of reasoning ... [and that] some of our preconceived ideas about the normative principles of reasoning are mistaken" (p. 231). Such a finding does not establish human irrationality; instead we are to interpret the finding "as giving insight not just into human reasoning competence but also into the normative principles of reasoning" (p. 233) because "whatever human reasoning competence turns out to be, the principles embodied in it are the normative principles of reasoning" (p. 231). According to this view, as an indicator of what the proper normative model is, the descriptive model of competence trumps any consideration of wide reflective equilibrium—scientific theories, empirical evidence on goal satisfaction, Dutch books, and so forth.

Although both endorsed this linking of the normative to the descriptive, Gigerenzer (1991b) and Cohen (1981) did so for somewhat different reasons. For Cohen, it follows from his endorsement of narrow reflective equilibrium as the sine qua non of normative justification. Gigerenzer's endorsement is related to his position in the "cognitive ecologist" camp (to use the term of Piattelli-Palmarini, 1994, p. 183) with its emphasis on the ability of evolutionary mechanisms to achieve an optimal Brunswikian tuning of the organism to the local environment (Anderson, 1990, 1991; Brase et al., 1998; Cosmides & Tooby, 1994, 1996; Oaksford & Chater, 1994; Pinker, 1997).

That Gigerenzer and Cohen concur here—even though they have somewhat different positions on normative justification—simply shows how widespread is the acceptance of the principle that descriptive facts about human behavior condition our notions about the appropriateness of the normative models used to evaluate behavior. In fact, stated in such broad form, this principle is not even restricted to the generic class of Panglossian positions. Even those who adhere to a wide reflective equilibrium of experts as a criterion for normative justification can endorse the principle because the wide expert equilibrium is sometimes conditioned by empirical facts about human behavior. For example, in decision science, there is a long tradition of acknowledging descriptive influences on the normative. Slovic (1995) referred to this "deep interplay between descriptive phenomena and normative principles" (p. 370). Larrick, Nisbett, and Morgan (1993) reminded us that "there is also a tradition of justifying, and amending, normative models in response to empirical considerations" (p. 332). March (1988) referred to this tradition when he discussed how actual human behavior has conditioned models of efficient problem solving in artificial intelligence and in the area of organizational decision making. The assumptions underlying the naturalistic project in epistemology (e.g., Kornblith, 1985, 1993) have the same implication—that findings about how humans form and alter beliefs should have a bearing on normative theories of belief acquisition.

If, as Thagard and Nisbett (1983) argued, "rational inference is inference in accord with the best available rules, and our set of rules is constantly being improved" (p. 260), then it is possible that the "discovery of discrepancies between inferential behavior and normative standards may in some cases signal a need for revision of the normative standards, and the descriptions of behavior may be directly relevant to what revisions are made" (p. 265; see also, Kyburg, 1983, 1991; Shafer, 1988). This position is in fact quite widespread:

- "If people's (or animals') judgments do not match those predicted by a normative model, this may say more about the need for revising the theory to more closely describe subjects' cognitive processes than it says about the adequacy of those processes" (Alloy & Tabachnik, 1984, p. 140).

- "We must look to what people do in order to gather materials for epistemic reconstruction and self-improvement" (Kyburg, 1991, p. 139).

- "When ordinary people reject the answers given by normative theories, they may do so out of ignorance and lack of expertise, or they may be signaling the fact that the normative theory is inadequate" (Lopes, 1981, p. 344).

- "If there is sense in the choice behavior of individuals acting contrary to standard engineering procedures for rationality, then it seems reasonable to suspect that there may be something inadequate about our normative theory of choice" (March, 1988, p. 35).

All of these arguments have something in common—they suggest that we can at least in part derive what people ought to do from a description of their reasoning processes. If the theorists discussed so far are actually committing the naturalistic fallacy, then many of the best minds in cognitive science seem to be doing so. Of course, in this discussion I have conjoined disparate views that are actually arrayed on a continuum. The reject-the-norm advocates represent the extreme form of this view—they simply want to read off the normative from the descriptive: "the argument under consideration here rejects the standard picture of rationality and takes the reasoning experiments as giving insight not just into human reasoning competence but also into the normative principles of reasoning" (Stein, 1996, p. 233). In contrast, other theorists (e.g., March, 1988) simply want to subtly fine-tune and adjust normative models based on descriptive facts about reasoning performance. For example, advocates of wide expert reflective equilibrium as a means of normative justification attempt to bring descriptive facts into equilibrium with a host of other considerations such as money pump and Dutch book arguments (Resnik, 1987) as well as scientific theories.

One thing that all of the various camps in the rationality dispute have in common is that each conditions their beliefs about the appropriate norm based on the central tendency of the responses to a problem. That is, they all seem to view that single aspect of performance as the only descriptive fact that is relevant to conditioning their views about the appropriate normative model to apply. For example, advocates of the reject-the-norm-strategy for dealing with normative/descriptive discrepancies view the mean, or modal, response as a direct pointer to the appropriate normative model.

In this chapter, the scope of descriptive information used to condition our views about appropriate norms is expanded. If we are going to infer something about the normative from the descriptive (and of course not all investigators are agreed that we should—see Baron, 1994a), then the thesis advanced here is that there is more information available than has traditionally been relied on. For example, situations where most people do not give the normative$_s$ response make reject-the-norm advocates question its normative appropriateness. But what would happen if we examined not only how many people responded with the normative$_s$ judgment but also examined the cognitive/personality characteristics of those who did? It is argued here that, before embarking on a wholesale rewriting of normative theory, it may be prudent to consider an aspect of performance that has been greatly underplayed in debates about human rationality: individual differences.

PUTTING DESCRIPTIVE FACTS TO WORK:
THE UNDERSTANDING/ACCEPTANCE PRINCIPLE

How should we interpret situations where the majority of individuals respond in ways that depart from the norm according to the expert reflective equilibrium? Should we search for an alternative, normative$_a$ model as advocates of the reject-the-norm strategy recommend, or should we view the majority who fail to give the normative$_s$ response as displaying systematic irrationality, as the Meliorists tend to conclude? Thagard (1982) called these two different responses the populist strategy and the elitist strategy: "The populist strategy, favored by Cohen (1981), is to emphasize the reflective equilibrium of the average person.... The elitist strategy, favored by Stich and Nisbett (1980), is to emphasize the reflective equilibrium of experts" (p. 39). Thus, Thagard identified the populist strategy with the Panglossian position and the elitist strategy with the Meliorist position.

But there are few controversial tasks in the heuristics and biases literature where *all* untutored laypersons disagree with the experts. There are always some who agree. Thus, the issue is not the untutored average person versus experts (as suggested by Thagard's formulation), but experts plus some laypersons versus other untutored individuals. Might the cognitive characteristics of those departing from expert opinion have implications for how we evaluate the appropriateness of the normative$_s$ response?

Larrick et al. (1993) made just such an argument in their analysis of what justified the cost-benefit reasoning of microeconomics: "Intelligent people would be more likely to use cost-benefit reasoning. Because intelligence is generally regarded as being the set of psychological properties that makes for effectiveness across environments ... intelligent people should be more likely to use the most effective reasoning strategies than should less intelligent people" (p. 333). Larrick et al. were alluding to the fact that we may want to condition our inferences about appropriate norms based not only on what response the majority of people make but also on what response the most cognitively competent subjects make.

Thus, to Thagard and Nisbett's (1983) point that "discovery of discrepancies between inferential behavior and normative standards may in some cases signal a need for revision of the normative standards, and the descriptions of behavior may be directly relevant to what revisions are made" (p. 265) could be added: particularly when the discrepancies are greatest for the subjects who have the greatest measured computational capacity and when there is high covariance across tasks that points in the direction of the normative$_a$ response. Or conversely, we might hesitate to revise our standards if the discrepancies are greatest for the subjects with the lowest measured computational capacity and when the covariance across tasks points in the direction of the normative$_s$ response. Some discrepancies, I argue, are more equal than others. When the most cognitively competent individuals are among the majority who give the normative$_a$ response rather than the normative$_s$ response, this is something that should cause instability in the expert reflective equilibrium. In contrast, if experts and a minority of untutored individuals agree on the normative$_s$ response and among that minority are the most cognitively able individuals, this provides less reason for the expert reflective equilibrium to stray from the normative$_s$ interpretation.

Slovic and Tversky (1974) made essentially this argument years ago, although it was couched in very different terms in their article and thus was hard to discern. Slovic and Tversky argued that descriptive facts about argument endorsement should condition the inductive inferences of experts regarding appropriate normative principles. They conducted a study of subjects' responses to arguments supporting and contradicting the independence axiom of utility theory. They argued that the more that the independence axiom of utility theory was understood, the more it would be accepted ("the deeper the understanding of the axiom, the greater the readiness to accept it," pp. 372–373). Thus, they used the descriptive to justify the normative by finding relevance in patterns of individual differences (associations between axiom acceptance and the depth of understanding).

Slovic and Tversky (1974) felt that finding a congruence between understanding and acceptance would suggest that the gap between the descriptive and normative was due to the failure to fully process and/or understand the task. From their understanding/acceptance principle, it follows that if greater understanding resulted in more acceptance of the axiom, then the initial gap between the normative and descriptive would be attributed to factors that prevented problem understanding (e.g., lack of ability or reflectiveness on the part of the subject). Such a finding would increase confidence in the normative appropriateness of the axioms and/or in their application to a particular problem. In contrast, if better understanding failed to result in greater acceptance of the axiom, then its normative status might be considered to be undermined (or its application to a particular situation brought into question).

Using their understanding/acceptance principle, Slovic and Tversky (1974) found little support for the independence axiom. When presented with arguments to explicate both the Allais (1953) and Savage (1954) positions, subjects found the Allais argument against independence at least as compelling and did not tend to change their task behavior in the normative direction (see MacCrimmon, 1968, and MacCrimmon & Larsson, 1979, for more mixed results on the independence axiom using related paradigms). Although Slovic and Tversky failed to find support for this particular normative axiom, they presented a principle that may be of general usefulness in theoretical debates about why human performance deviates from normative models. The central idea behind Slovic and Tversky's development of the understanding/acceptance principle is that increased understanding should drive performance in the direction of the truly normative principle—so that the direction that performance moves in response to increased understanding provides an empirical clue as to what is the proper normative model to be applied.

One might conceive of two generic strategies for examining the understanding/acceptance principle based on the fact that variation in understanding can be created or it can be studied by examining naturally occurring individual differences. Slovic and Tversky (1974) employed the former strategy by providing subjects with explicated arguments supporting the Allais or Savage normative interpretation (see also Doherty, Schiavo, Tweney, & Mynatt, 1981). Other methods of manipulating understanding have provided consistent evidence in favor of the normative principle of descriptive invariance (see Kahneman & Tversky, 1984). For example, it has been found that being forced to take more time or to provide a rationale for selections increases adherence to descriptive invariance (Larrick, Smith, & Yates, 1992; Miller & Fagley, 1991; Sieck & Yates, 1997; Takemura, 1992, 1993, 1994). Moshman and Geil (1998) found that group discussion facilitated performance on Wason's selection task.

As an alternative to manipulating understanding, the understanding/acceptance principle can be transformed into an individual differences prediction. For example, the principle might be interpreted as indicating that more reflective and engaged reasoners are more likely to respond in accord with normative principles. Thus, it might be expected that those individuals with cognitive/personality characteristics more conducive to deeper understanding would be more accepting of the normative principles of reasoning and decision. This was the emphasis of Larrick et al. (1993) when they argued that more intelligent people should be more likely to use normative cost-benefit principles. Similarly, need for cognition—a dispositional variable reflecting the tendency toward thoughtful analysis and reflective thinking—has been associated with aspects of epistemic and practical rationality (Cacioppo, Petty, Feinstein, & Jarvis, 1996; Kardash & Scholes, 1996; Klaczynski et al., 1997; S. M. Smith & Levin, 1996; Verplanken, 1993).

APPLYING THE RIGHT NORMS:
CLUES FROM INDIVIDUAL DIFFERENCES

It is important to point out that many theorists on all sides of the rationality debate have acknowledged the force of the understanding/acceptance argument (without always labeling the argument as such or citing Slovic & Tversky, 1974). For example, Gigerenzer and Goldstein (1996) lamented the fact that Apologist theorists who emphasize Simon's (1956, 1957, 1983) concept of bounded rationality seemingly accept the classical normative$_s$ models by their tacit assumption that, if computational limitations were removed, individuals' responses would indeed be closer to the behavior those models prescribe.

Lopes and Oden (1991) also wished to deny this tacit assumption in the literature on computational limitations: "discrepancies between data and model are typically attributed to people's limited capacity to process information.... There is, however, no support for the view that people would choose in accord with normative prescriptions if they were provided with increased capacity" (pp. 208–209). Lopes (1992) argued that there is no evidence for the view that "if real subjects were told the optimal response for a task, thus eliminating the need for computations, they would make that response" (p. 234). Lopes—citing the work of Montgomery and Adelbratt (1982) and Slovic and Tversky (1974)—likewise noted that some experiments that have explicated for subjects principles such as expected utility and the independence axiom have not succeeded in driving them toward the normative$_s$ response. In stressing the importance of the lack of evidence for the notion that people would "choose in accord with normative prescriptions if they were provided with increased capacity" (p. 209), Lopes and Oden acknowledged the force of the individual differences version of the understanding/acceptance principle—because examining variation in cognitive ability is just that: looking at what subjects who have "increased capacity" actually do with that increased capacity.

In fact, critics of the heuristics and biases literature have repeatedly drawn on an individual differences version of the understanding/acceptance principle to bolster their critiques. For example, Cohen (1982) critiqued the older "bookbag and poker chip" literature on Bayesian conservatism (Phillips & Edwards, 1966; Slovic, Fischhoff, & Lichtenstein, 1977) by noting that:

> If so-called "conservatism" resulted from some inherent inadequacy in people's information-processing systems one might expect that, when individual differences in information-processing are measured on independently attested scales, some of them would correlate with degrees of "conservatism." In fact, no such correlation was found by Alker and Hermann (1971). And this is just what one would expect if "conservatism" is not a defect, but a rather deeply rooted virtue of the system. (pp. 259–260)

This is precisely how Alker and Hermann (1971) themselves argued in their article:

> Phillips et al. (1966) have proposed that conservatism is the result of intellectual deficiencies. If this is the case, variables such as rationality, verbal intelligence, and integrative complexity should have related to deviation from optimality—more rational, intelligent, and complex individuals should have shown less conservatism. The lack of relationship raises ques-

tions about the type of ideal decision maker the Bayesian model denotes. (p. 40)

Wetherick (1971, 1995) has been a critic of the standard interpretation of the four-card selection task (Wason, 1966) for over 25 years. As a Panglossian theorist, he has been at pains to defend the modal response chosen by roughly 50% of the subjects (the P and Q cards) against the normative$_s$ response given by less than 10% of subjects (the P and not-Q cards). As did Cohen (1982) and Lopes and Oden (1991), Wetherick (1971) pointed to the lack of associations with individual differences to bolster his critique of the standard interpretation of the task:

> In Wason's experimental situation subjects do not choose the not-Q card nor do they stand and give three cheers for the Queen, neither fact is interesting in the absence of a plausible theory predicting that they should. ... If it could be shown that subjects who choose not-Q are more intelligent or obtain better degrees than those who do not this would make the problem worth investigation, but I have seen no evidence that this is the case. (p. 213)

Funder (1987), like Cohen (1982) and Wetherick (1971), used a finding about individual differences to argue that a particular attribution error should not be considered suboptimal or nonnormative. Block and Funder (1986) analyzed the role effect observed by L. Ross, Amabile, and Steinmetz (1977): that people rated questioners more knowledgeable than contestants in a quiz game. Although Ross et al. viewed the role effect as an attributional error—people allegedly failed to consider the individual's role when estimating the knowledge displayed—Block and Funder demonstrated that subjects most susceptible to this attributional "error" were more socially competent, more well adjusted, and more intelligent. Funder used this individual difference finding in just the manner suggested previously—to influence our reflective equilibrium regarding which response should be considered normative in this particular paradigm. He argued that the particular correlates of individual differences in this attribution effect have implications for our intuitions about whether this attributional pattern should be considered a bias or an error. Because more socially competent subjects were more prone to this attributional effect, Funder argued that the view that this attributional pattern is an error is undermined.

Thus, Funder (1987), Lopes and Oden (1991), Wetherick (1971), and Cohen (1982) all made recourse to patterns of individual differences (or the lack of such patterns) to pump our intuitions (see Dennett, 1980) in the direction of undermining the standard normative analysis of the tasks under consideration. These critics of the normative$_s$ interpretations have pointed out that a consideration of patterns of individual differences will sometimes disrupt our reflective equilibrium about what to consider the normative response or the rational construal of the problem (see chap. 4). In other cases, however, such patterns may actually reinforce the expert reflective equilibrium and increase confidence in the normative$_s$ models applied as well as the task construals of the experts who invented the problem.[1]

With these arguments in mind, it is important to note that the correlational tests of the performance error view and of algorithmic-level limitations discussed in chapter 2 were all in fact tests of the individual differences version of the understanding/acceptance principle—and all of these tests came out in the same way. That is, the direction of all of the correlations displayed in Tables 2.1 and 2.2 is consistent with the standard normative models used by psychologists when interpreting tasks in the reasoning and decision-making literature. Individuals giving the normative$_s$ response on one task tended to give it on another—even when the task requirements were quite different. Also, in every single case, cognitive ability was positively associated with giving the normative$_s$ response—individuals of higher intelligence were relatively more likely to give the response considered normative by the designer of the task. Individuals of lower intelligence were relatively more likely to give the normative$_a$ response. This was equally true for tasks where the normative$_s$ response is the subject of great controversy as it was for the relatively uncontroversial tasks such as Tschirgi's (1980) confounded variable hypothesis-testing task and the covariation detection paradigm.

For example, the normative issues surrounding Wason's (1966) selection task have been the subject of intense debate in the last 10 years (e.g., Evans & Over, 1996; Fetzer, 1990; Lowe, 1993; Nickerson, 1996; Oaksford & Chater, 1994, 1996; Wetherick, 1993, 1995) and the modal response on this task is strongly nonnormative (roughly 50% of the subjects respond with P and Q and over 90% choose some combination other than P and not-Q). The normative appropriateness of exclusive reliance on aggregate statistical information in the face of vivid single-case evidence has also been challenged due to concerns about reference class relevance (Gigerenzer, 1991b; Kyburg, 1996; Levi, 1996). The stricture against implicating prior belief in syllogistic reasoning and argument evaluation tasks has also been disputed (Evans et al., 1993; Koehler, 1993; Kornblith, 1993). Yet despite the normative controversies surrounding all of these tasks, each one displayed the same type of association with cognitive ability—more intelligent individuals were more likely to give the response traditionally considered normative. Equally important, all of these tasks displayed intercorrelations among themselves—individuals giving the normative$_s$ response on one were more likely to give it on another.

---

[1]Critics of the normative$_s$ interpretations in the heuristics and biases literature have not indicated how they would modify their positions if the correlations went the other way. For example, Wetherick's (1971) challenge to show that "subjects who choose not-Q are more intelligent" (p. 213) has now been been answered—as shown in Table 2.2 and Fig. 2.2 and in many more extensive analyses reported in chapter 4 (see Tables 4.11 and 4.12).

All of this covariance among tasks and covariance with cognitive ability puts considerable stress on explanations that seek to close the normative/descriptive gap by treating the modal performance as centered on a competence that indexes the truly normative response and all deviations from the central tendency as error variance. To the contrary, all of this covariance suggests that the deviations from the norm are systematic and do not simply represent unpredictable performance errors. Additionally, the directionality of the systematic correlations with intelligence are embarrassing for those reject-the-norm theorists who argue that norms are being incorrectly applied. The correlations are all consistently in the direction predicted by advocates of normative$_s$ models—if we interpret the correlations in terms of the understanding/acceptance principle (a principle endorsed in various forms by a host of Panglossian critics of the heuristics and biases literature: Cohen, 1982; Funder, 1987; Lopes, 1992; Lopes & Oden, 1991; Wetherick, 1971, 1995). Surely we would want to avoid the conclusion that individuals with more computational power are systematically computing the *non*-normative response. Such an outcome would be an absolute first in a psychometric field that is 100 years and thousands of studies old (Brody, 1997; Carroll, 1993, 1997; Lubinski & Humphreys, 1997; Neisser et al., 1996). It would mean that Spearman's (1904) positive manifold for cognitive tasks—virtually unchallenged for 100 years—had finally broken down. Obviously, parsimony dictates that positive manifold remains a fact of life for cognitive tasks and that the response originally thought to be normative, normative$_s$, actually is.[2]

In fact, it is probably helpful to articulate the understanding/acceptance principle somewhat more formally in terms of positive manifold—the fact that different measures of cognitive ability almost always correlate with each other (see Carroll, 1993, 1997). The individual differences version of the understanding/acceptance principle puts positive manifold to use in areas of cognitive psychology where the nature of the normative response is in dispute. The point is that scoring a vocabulary item on a cognitive ability test and scoring a probabilistic reasoning response on a task from the heuristics and biases literature are not the same. The correct response in the former task has a canonical interpretation agreed on by all investigators; whereas the normative appropriateness of responses on tasks from the latter domain has been the subject of extremely contentious dispute (Cohen, 1981, 1982, 1986; Cosmides & Tooby, 1996; Einhorn & Hogarth, 1981; Gigerenzer, 1991a, 1993, 1996a; Kahneman & Tversky, 1996; Koehler, 1996; Stein, 1996). Positive manifold between the two classes of task would be expected only if the normative model being used for directional scoring of the tasks in the latter domain

---

[2]Developmental trends toward the normative$_s$ response (Bara, Bucciarelli, & Johnson-Laird, 1995; Byrnes & Overton, 1986; Jacobs & Potenza, 1991; Klahr, Fay, & Dunbar, 1993; Markovits & Vachon, 1989; Moshman & Franks, 1986; J. Ross & Cousins, 1993; Tschirgi, 1980) would seem to have the same implication.

is correct. Likewise, given that positive manifold is the norm among cognitive tasks, the negative correlation (or, to a lesser extent, the lack of a correlation) between a probabilistic reasoning task and more standard cognitive ability measures might be taken as a signal that the wrong normative model is being applied to the former task or that there are alternative models that are normatively appropriate.[3]

EXAMPLES OF NORMATIVE APPLICATIONS UNDERMINED BY THE UNDERSTANDING/ACCEPTANCE PRINCIPLE

It is not always the case that positive manifold with measures of cognitive ability is obtained when other tasks in the heuristics and biases literature are examined however. I now present some cases of tasks where there has been enormous dispute about the appropriate normative model to be applied and in which an examination of individual differences suggests that the model traditionally applied in the heuristics and biases literature may be questionable. Two of these examples come from the literature on the use of base rates.

Noncausal Base Rates

The statistical reasoning problems utilized in the experiments described thus far (those derived from Fong et al., 1986) have a somewhat less controversial history, because they involved causal aggregate information, analogous to the causal base rates discussed by Ajzen (1977) and Bar-Hillel (1980, 1990)—that is, base rates that had a causal relationship to the criterion behavior. Noncausal base-rate problems—those involving base rates with no obvious causal relationship to the criterion behavior—have had a much more controversial history in the research literature. They have been the subject of over a decade's worth of contentious dispute (Bar-Hillel, 1990; Birnbaum, 1983; Cohen, 1981; Cosmides & Tooby, 1996; Gigerenzer, 1991b, 1993, 1996a; Gigerenzer & Hoffrage, 1995; Kahneman & Tversky, 1996; Koehler, 1996; Kyburg, 1983; Levi, 1983; Macchi, 1995). In several experiments, Stanovich and West (1998b) examined some of the noncausal base-rate problems that are notorious for provoking philosophical dispute. One was the infamous cab problem (see Bar-Hillel, 1980; Lyon & Slovic, 1976; Tversky & Kahneman, 1982) that was mentioned at the beginning of this chapter. It was presented to participants as follows: "A cab was involved in a hit-and-run accident at night. Two cab companies, the Green and the Blue, operate in the city in

---

[3]Interpreted in this manner, our use of a particular cognitive ability indicator (SAT scores) is perhaps less contentious. Regardless of one's attitude toward theories of general intelligence, no one disputes that SAT scores predict performance on a plethora of reasoning tasks—that they are a part of Spearman's positive manifold for mental tasks.

which the accident occurred. You are given the following facts: 85% of the cabs in the city are Green and 15% are Blue. A witness identified the cab as Blue. The court tested the reliability of the witness under the same circumstances that existed on the night of the accident and concluded that the witness correctly identified each of the two colors 80% of the time. What is the probability that the cab involved in the accident was Blue?" Subjects chose from six alternatives (less than 10%, 10%–30%, 30%–50%, 50%–70%, 70%–90%, over 90%).

Responses to the problem were scored in terms of whether subjects relied on the indicant information or displayed some tendency to process the base rate. Bayes rule yields .41 as the posterior probability of the cab being blue. Thus, individuals choosing 70%–90% or over 90% were classified as reliant on indicant information and subjects choosing any of the other categories were classified as Bayesian (see Stanovich & West, 1998b, for a finer-grained classification that does not affect the main conclusions drawn here). Using this classification scheme, 93 subjects were classified as reliant on the indicant and 104 were termed Bayesian (they departed at least somewhat from the indicant probability of 80%).

The top half of Table 3.1 displays the mean scores of these two groups on the other variables examined in the Stanovich and West (1998b) experiment. As indicated in the table, the Bayesian group did not exceed the indicant group on any of the seven other cognitive variables. In fact, there were some mild trends in the opposite direction—for the indicant group to outperform the Bayesian group. The two groups were quite similar in their mean SAT scores, but the indicant group had higher scores on the Raven matrices (a trend that approached significance). The indicant group had a higher mean score on the Nelson–Denny reading comprehension subtest and a syllogistic reasoning task—however only the latter difference attained statistical significance. The indicant group outscored the Bayesian group on a set of selection task problems, causal aggregate statistical reasoning problems identical to those discussed in the previous chapter, and an argument evaluation task also like that previously discussed (Stanovich & West, 1997). Although only the former difference approached significance, it is striking—given that it is traditionally considered the non-normative response—that the direction of six of the differences favored the indicant group. On the seventh variable—SAT test performance—the two groups were identical. Interestingly, this directionality extended to the statistical reasoning problems involving causal aggregate information where the individuals who were most Bayesian on the cab problem were least likely to use causal statistical aggregate information.

The bottom half of Table 3.1 presents the results of a replication experiment from Stanovich and West (1998b). In this replication, the indicant subjects had higher SAT total scores (1,145 vs. 1,114) than the Bayesian subject—a trend that almost attained statistical significance ($p = .0502$).

TABLE 3.1

**Mean Task Performance for the Groups Classified as Indicant
and Bayesian on the Cab Problem**

	Experiment 3A of Stanovich and West (1998b)		
	Indicant (n = 93)	Bayesian (n = 104)	t Value
SAT Total	1094	1093	0.06
Raven	9.95	9.22	1.72*
Nelson–Denny	19.94	19.70	0.59
Syllogisms	4.73	4.07	2.09**
Selection task	1.84	1.14	1.81*
Statistical reasoning	.293	−.262	1.32
AET	.350	.331	0.65

Note. AET = argument evaluation test; df = 2, 181 for SAT, 2, 194 for Raven and Nelson–Denny, 2, 192 for syllogisms, 2, 188 for selection task, 2, 194 for statistical reasoning, 2, 191 for the AET.
* = $p < .10$, ** = $p < .05$, all two-tailed.

	Experiment 3B of Stanovich and West (1998b)		
	Indicant (n = 128)	Bayesian (n = 83)	t Value
SAT Total	1145	1114	1.97*
Raven	9.47	8.83	1.28
Nelson–Denny	20.40	19.89	1.33
Syllogisms	5.23	5.12	0.38
Statistical reasoning	.261	−.402	1.46

Note. df = 2, 198 for SAT, 2, 189 for Raven, 2, 194 for Nelson–Denny, 2, 208 for syllogisms, 2, 208 for statistical reasoning.
* = $p < .10$, ** = $p < .05$, all two-tailed.

Although there were no significant differences on any of the four remaining variables, in each case the difference favored the indicant group. The Bayesian subjects even failed to attain higher statistical reasoning scores on the causal aggregate problems.

In a replication experiment employing 644 subjects, we attempted to clarify a potentially problematic phrase in the cab problem (see Macchi, 1995). The phrase—"the witness correctly identified each of the two colors 80% of the time"—might have encouraged subjects to confuse P(D/H) with P(H/D) and thus seem to be ignoring the base rate (see Braine,

Connell, Freitag, & O'Brien, 1990; Dawes, Mirels, Gold, & Donahue, 1993; Koehler, 1996; Macchi, 1995). Thus, the version used in the replication study clarified the witness identification phrase. The new instructions were as follows: "A cab was involved in a hit-and-run accident at night. Two cab companies, the Green and the Blue, operate in the city in which the accident occurred. You are given the following facts: 85% of the cabs in the city are Green and 15% are Blue. A witness reported that the cab in the accident was Blue. The court tested the reliability of the witness under the same circumstances that existed on the night of the accident and concluded that the witness called about 80% of the Blue cabs blue, but called 20% of the Blue cabs green. The witness also called about 80% of the Green cabs green, but called 20% of the Green cabs blue. What is the probability (expressed as a percentage ranging from 0% to 100%) that the cab involved in the accident was Blue? ___%"

Posterior probabilities greater than or equal to 70% were scored as reliance on the indicant information and probabilities less than 70% were interpreted as indicating some degree of Bayesian amalgamation (finer-grained categorizations do not materially alter the main conclusions). Using this classification scheme, 252 subjects were classified as reliant on the indicant, and 392 subjects were classified as ayesian. The revised instructions did result in more subjects responding in a Bayesian manner (60.9% vs. 45.8%).

Table 3.2 displays the mean scores of these two groups on two cognitive/personality variables included in this study: cognitive ability as measured by the SAT test and need for cognition. The latter variable was mentioned previously and is a dispositional variable reflecting the tendency toward reflective thinking (Cacioppo et al., 1996). The overall SAT scores are higher in this study because scores were derived subsequent to the April 1995 recentering conducted by the Educational Testing Service, which raised the overall mean on the test. As in the second experiment displayed in Table 3.1, the Bayesian group had significantly lower SAT scores. Additionally, they were also significantly lower on the need for cognition variable. Despite the clarification in the problem regarding the witness' identification accuracy (a clarification that did increase the proportion of Bayesian responders), both individual difference variables that were markers for reflective and engaged reasoning (cognitive ability and need for cognition) were higher in the indicant group.

This lack of processing superiority on the part of the Bayesian subjects was replicated in studies of a second noncausal base-rate task—an AIDS-testing problem modeled on Casscells, Schoenberger, and Graboys (1978):

> Imagine that AIDS occurs in 1 in every 1,000 people. Imagine also there is a test to diagnose the disease that always gives a positive result when a person has AIDS. Finally, imagine that the test has a false positive rate of 5%. This means that the test wrongly indicates that AIDS is present in 5% of the

TABLE 3.2

**Mean Scores of Groups Classified as Indicant and Bayesian
on the Cab Problem Replication**

	Indicant (n = 252)	Bayesian (n = 392)	t Value
SAT Total	1,205	1,172	3.90***
Need for Cognition	69.2	67.1	2.12*

* = $p < .05$, ** = $p < .01$, *** = $p < .001$, all two-tailed.

cases where the person does not have AIDS. Imagine that we choose a person randomly, administer the test, and that it yields a positive result (indicates that the person has AIDS). What is the probability that the individual actually has AIDS, assuming that we know nothing else about the individual's personal or medical history?

This version required a singular probability judgment rather than a frequency assessment and thus is the type of problem that is most controversial (Cosmides & Tooby, 1996; Gigerenzer & Hoffrage, 1995). The Bayesian posterior probability for this problem is slightly less than .02. Thus, responses of less than 10% were interpreted as indicating Bayesian amalgamation, response of over 90% were scored as indicating strong reliance on indicant information, and responses between 10% and 90% were scored as intermediate. In Experiment 3A of Stanovich and West (1998b), 107 subjects were classified as strongly reliant on indicant information (responses over 90%), 50 were classified as intermediate (responses between 10% and 90%), and 40 were classified as approximately Bayesian (responses less than 10%). Because over 70% of the responses were either Bayesian or indicant, and because the intermediate group usually scored between these two groups on the cognitive variables, the analyses sketched here focus on the Bayesian and indicant groups (see Stanovich & West, 1998b, for a more detailed partitioning).

As indicated in Table 3.3, the two groups displayed a significant difference in their mean total SAT scores. The mean SAT scores of the subjects strongly reliant on indicant information (1,115) was significantly higher than the mean SAT scores of the Bayesian subjects (1,071). The indicant group also scored significantly higher on the Nelson–Denny reading comprehension subtest. There was a marginally significant difference favoring the indicant group on the causal aggregate statistical reasoning problems. There were no significant differences on the Raven matrices, syllogistic reasoning problems, and selection task problems, but the mean difference favored the indicant group in each case. The two groups performed virtually identically on the argument evaluation measure.

The results displayed at the bottom of Table 3.3 indicate that exactly the same trends were apparent in the replication experiment. The mean SAT scores of the individuals strongly reliant on indicant information (1,153) were significantly higher than the mean score of the Bayesian subjects (1,103). The indicant group also scored significantly higher on the Nelson–Denny reading comprehension measure and statistical reasoning problems. There were no significant differences on the Raven matrices and syllogistic reasoning problems, but the mean difference favored the indicant group in both instances.

These results, taken in conjunction with the milder tendencies in the same direction in the cab problem, indicate that the noncausal base-rate

TABLE 3.3

Mean Task Performance for the Groups Classified as Indicant and Bayesian on the AIDS Problem

Experiment 3A of Stanovich and West (1998b)

	Indicant (n = 107)	Bayesian (n = 40)	t Value
SAT Total	1,115	1,071	1.98**
Raven	10.09	9.40	1.28
Nelson–Denny	20.23	19.05	2.53**
Syllogisms	4.79	4.21	1.45
Selection task	1.61	1.11	1.00
Statistical reasoning	.421	−.537	1.71*
AET	.345	.351	−0.15

Note. AET = argument evaluation test; df = 2, 181 for SAT, 2, 194 for Raven and Nelson-Denny, 2, 192 for syllogisms, 2, 188 for selection task, 2, 194 for statistical reasoning, 2, 191 for the AET.
* = $p < .10$, ** = $p < .05$, *** = $p < .01$, all two-tailed.

Experiment 3B of Stanovich and West (1998b)

	Indicant (n = 118)	Bayesian (n = 36)	t Value
SAT Total	1,153	1,103	2.31**
Raven	9.49	8.64	1.21
Nelson–Denny	20.47	19.47	2.00**
Syllogisms	5.40	4.92	1.25
Statistical reasoning	.726	−1.051	2.93***

Note. df = 2, 198 for SAT, 2, 189 for Raven, 2, 194 for Nelson–Denny, 2, 208 for syllogisms, 2, 208 for statistical reasoning.
* = $p < .10$, ** = $p < .05$, *** = $p < .01$, all two-tailed.

problems display patterns of individual differences quite unlike those shown on the causal aggregate problems of the type examined by Fong et al. (1986). On the latter, subjects giving the statistical response scored consistently higher on measures of cognitive ability and were disproportionately likely to give the normative$_s$ response on other rational thinking tasks (see Tables 2.1, 2.2, and 2.5). This pattern did not hold for the two noncausal base-rate problems. On the cab problem, there was no variable on which the Bayesian group significantly outscored the indicant group. In fact, in each of the 12 comparisons displayed in Table 3.1, the difference was in the opposite direction—the indicant group outscored the Bayesian group. On the AIDS problem, in 11 of 12 cases the indicant group outscored the Bayesian group and in 5 out of 12 of these comparisons the difference was statistically significant. On both of these tasks, subjects strongly reliant on the indicant information scored higher on measures of cognitive ability and were more likely to give the normative$_s$ response on other rational thinking tasks—including base-rate problems of the causal variety (Bar-Hillel, 1980, 1990). These results might suggest that the Bayesian subjects on the AIDS problem might not actually be arriving at their response through anything resembling Bayesian processing (see Cosmides & Tooby, 1996; Gigerenzer & Hoffrage, 1995), because on causal aggregate statistical reasoning problems these subjects were less likely to rely on the aggregate information (see Table 3.3).

Thus, an application of the understanding/acceptance principle serves to undermine confidence in the normative$_s$ interpretation of these two problems. Unlike the case of the tasks examined in chapter 2 where a uniform positive manifold consistently pointed in the direction of the normative$_s$ response, here, positive manifold was either absent altogether or pointing in the direction of the normative$_a$ response.

The False-Consensus Effect

Like the case of noncausal base rates, the social perception experiment—the domain of the so-called false consensus effect (Marks & Miller, 1987; Mullen et al., 1985; L. Ross, Greene et al., 1977)—has also generated contentious dispute regarding normative issues. As mentioned at the beginning of this chapter, the false-consensus effect is the tendency for people to project their own opinions when predicting the attitudes, opinions, and behaviors of other people and it has traditionally been viewed as a non-normative response tendency. The false-consensus effect has usually been thought to arise at least in part from egocentric attributional biases (Marks & Miller, 1987; L. Ross, Greene, et al., 1977). For example, Gilovich (1991) stated that "the false consensus effect is partly a motivational phenomenon that stems from our desire to maintain a positive assessment of our own judgment—a desire that is bolstered by thinking that our beliefs lie in the mainstream" (p. 114).

However, Hoch (1987) demonstrated that a Brunswikian analysis of the opinion prediction paradigm would render some degree of projection normatively appropriate in a variety of situations. Dawes (1989, 1990) demonstrated that, similarly, a Bayesian analysis renders some degree of projection as normatively appropriate, because, for the majority of people, there is actually a positive correlation between own opinion and the consensus opinion. Thus, one's own opinion is, in these social perception paradigms, a diagnostic datum that should condition probability estimates.

The formal analyses of the social perception experiment by Hoch (1987) and Dawes (1989, 1990; Dawes & Mulford, 1996; see also Krueger & Zeiger, 1993) have at least raised doubts about the common interpretation of the consensus effect as a normatively inappropriate egocentric bias. Stanovich and West (1998b, Experiment 4) examined whether high or low projection of consensus is associated with greater predictive accuracy, and explored the cognitive characteristics and other response tendencies of people who differ in their degree of projection.

Subjects were presented with 30 statements used in previous consensus judgment research (e.g., I think I would like the work of a schoolteacher; see Stanovich & West, 1998b). The subject first indicated whether they agreed with the item. Then, for each statement, they answered the question "What percentage of the students participating in this study do you think agree with the statement?" The items elicited a wide range of levels of agreement and perceived consensus. The consensus effect was replicated at the group, or between-subjects level of analysis. On 26 of the 30 items, the percentage estimate of people who endorsed an item was higher than that of nonendorsers, and 24 of these 26 consensus effects were statistically significant. Thus, statistically robust indications of a consensus effect were observed in the data.

However, the between-subjects analysis says nothing about individual differences and is uninformative as to whether or not projecting consensus helps a person more accurately predict the position of others. This was perhaps most clearly demonstrated in Hoch's (1987) Brunswikian analysis of the false consensus effect. Instead of considering performance on individual items aggregated across subjects, Hoch's analysis focuses on the performance of individual subjects aggregated across items. For a particular item, call the actual percentage agreement in the target population the target position (T). Call the subject's own agreement with the item (scored 0/1) own position (O). Call the subject's prediction of the level of agreement in the population the prediction (P). Hoch argued that one index of predictive accuracy is r(T,P): the correlation, across items, between the actual percentage agreement in the target population and the subject's prediction of the level of agreement in the population. The index r(T,P) was calculated for each of the 185 subjects in the Stanovich and West (1998b) study. The mean correlation was .548 (*SD* = .204), indicating a moderate to high predictive accuracy for the sample.

The reason that some degree of projection of one's own opinion may actually be normative is that, by the mathematical definition of majority position, most subjects will have positive correlations between their own opinions (O) and the target position (T)—as long as subjects are members of the target population. This was demonstrated empirically in Hoch's (1987) study and was true in the Stanovich and West (1998b) investigation, where the mean r(T,O) correlation was .532 (*SD* = .170). The degree of perceived consensus is indexed by the correlation r(P,O), which had a mean value of .464 (*SD* = .238) in this sample. A final parameter is calculated in Hoch's analysis: the reliance on other factors in making one's predictions (Z). The "other factors" parameter, Z, is estimated from the residuals when predictions (P) are regressed on own opinions (O). The residuals are thus the variance in predictions not explainable by the subject's own position and presumably are composed of other information on the target opinions that the individual possesses (plus error variance). The mean predictive validity of other factors in our sample—r(T,Z)—was .340 (*SD* = .181).

Because there actually is a correlation between own position and target position for most subjects in this sample [mean r(T,O) = .532], in order to accurately predict the target position, subjects actually did have to perceive consensus and project it. This, plus the fact that the subject's own position is a more valid cue than other factors [mean r(T,O) = .532 > .340 = mean r(T,Z)], suggests that projection might be particularly efficacious in this sample with this particular set of questions. In fact, there was a positive correlation of .689 between the degree of perceived consensus [r(P,O)] and predictive accuracy [r(T,P)]. Also, the degree of perceived consensus [mean r(P,O) = .464] is lower than the degree of actual consensus in the sample [mean r(T,O) = .532], which itself suggests that these subjects may not be overprojecting.

This conclusion is further supported by an analysis of a parameter introduced by Krueger and Zeiger (1993). They suggested that an index of over- (false consensus) or under- (false uniqueness) projection at the individual level that is relative to the actual accuracy achieved can be derived by correlating for each subject, across items, the agreement with the item (0/1) with the difference between the predicted percentage and the target percentage (P minus T). The mean correlation of this index [r(O, P – T)] in the sample was –.093 (*SD* = .255), which was significantly less than zero (*t*(184 = 4.97, *p* < .001). Thus, the sample as a whole displayed a slight false-uniqueness effect—consistent with the finding that degree of perceived consensus was lower than the degree of actual consensus in the sample.

The Krueger and Zeiger (1993) index was used to median split the sample into those subjects displaying relatively strong projection and those displaying relatively weak projection. Table 3.4 displays the comparisons of the 93 subjects (Low-Proj) who were relatively low projecters [mean

TABLE 3.4

**Mean Scores of Subjects High in Projection of Consensus (N = 92)
and Subjects Low in Projection of Consensus (N = 93; Standard
Deviations in Parentheses)**

Variable	Low-Proj	High-Proj	t Value
Consensus Judgment Statistics:			
r(O,P–T)	−.297 (.15)	.113 (.16)	18.40***
O beta (P on T&O)	.082 (.22)	.386 (.17)	10.57***
Perceived consensus, r(P,O)	.338 (.23)	.591 (.17)	8.52***
Actual consensus, r(T,O)	.572 (.14)	.491 (.19)	−3.36***
Other factors, r(T,Z)	.311 (.18)	.369 (.16)	2.24*
Predictive accuracy, r(T,P)	.496 (.23)	.601 (.16)	3.64***
Sum absolute deviations	601 (139)	549 (114)	2.81**
Sum signed deviations	29.7 (190)	−4.5 (156)	−1.34
Other Variables:			
SAT	1,144 (110)	1,128 (117)	−0.93
Raven Matrices	9.1 (3.6)	9.2 (3.5)	0.19
Nelson–Denny comprehension	20.4 (2.4)	20.2 (3.0)	−0.54
Syllogisms	5.42 (2.2)	5.14 (2.0)	−0.89
Statistical reasoning	.382 (3.5)	−.322 (3.2)	−1.44

Note. $df = 183$ for all variables except SAT ($df = 175$), Raven matrices ($df = 165$), and Nelson–Denny ($df = 169$).
$* = p < .05$, $** = p < .01$, $*** = p < .001$, all two-tailed.

r(O, P – T) = −.297] and 92 subjects (High-Proj) who were relatively high projecters [mean r(O, P – T) = .113]. A second measure of projection—the beta weight for own position (O) when P is regressed on T and O—confirmed that the High-Proj group were relatively more prone to projection. The O beta weight—the degree to which overprediction of T is correlated with item agreement—was significantly higher in the High-Proj group ($p < .001$). Consistent with these differences is the fact that the High-Proj group displayed significant higher perceived consensus, r(P,O). This higher perceived consensus was not due to a greater degree of actual consensus, r(T,O), in the High-Proj group. In fact, there was a significant ($p < .001$) difference in the other direction: The actual consensus in the Low-Proj group (.572) was higher than that in the High-Proj group (.491). Nevertheless, the former were less prone to project their higher degree of actual consensus. The next line of the table indicates that there was a slight tendency for other factors to have more predictive validity, r(T,Z), in the High-Proj group.

What were the consequences in terms of accuracy of prediction of the greater degree of projection displayed by the High-Proj group? In fact, the degree of predictive accuracy, as indicated by Hoch's (1987) parameter r(T,P), was significantly higher in the High-Proj group ($p < .001$). Another indicator of predictive accuracy—the sum of the absolute deviations of P from T (see Hoch, 1987)—was significantly lower ($p < .01$) in the High-Proj group (lower summed deviations indicate better predictions). The final measure of predictive accuracy, the sum of the signed deviations was closer to zero for the High-Proj group, but the scores of the Low-Proj group were not significantly different. In summary, there are no indications in the present data that projection is inefficacious for these subjects. Projection of consensus is not "false" in that, if anything, it leads to greater predictive accuracy.

As is indicated in the remainder of Table 3.4, the high- and low-projection groups displayed no significant differences in SAT scores, Raven scores, Nelson–Denny scores, syllogisms, and statistical reasoning. The critics of the interpretation of this task who have argued that zero projection should not be considered the normative response have received some support from these results. More projection is associated with greater accuracy of response and it is not associated with lower cognitive ability or more normative$_a$ responding on other tasks. Performance on the opinion prediction task was thus quite incongruent with its traditional interpretation as an egoistic and maladaptive cognitive bias. Subjects who projected their personal opinions on others were in fact more accurate predictors of the target opinions of others.

EXPLICATING NORMATIVE RULES AND THE UNDERSTANDING/ACCEPTANCE PRINCIPLE

As discussed previously, there are two different ways that the understanding/acceptance principle can be employed: Variation in understanding can be created or it can be studied by examining naturally occurring individual differences. The studies presented so far in this chapter have employed the latter method. The former is now illustrated (in addition to replications of the latter) using the method that Slovic and Tversky (1974) employed—namely, providing subjects with arguments for both the normative$_s$ and the normative$_a$ response to a particular problem. Subsequent to answering the problems for the first time, subjects were presented with arguments explicating normative$_s$ and normative$_a$ principles favoring a given response. At a later point in the experiment, the subject responded again to the same problem. Some of the subjects persevered with their response pattern and some changed their responses subsequent to the arguments. The question addressed was whether there was a greater proportion of subjects moving in the normative$_s$ direction than in the normative$_a$ direction after hearing arguments explicating both normative rules. The method is introduced using the selection paradigm studied by Doherty and Mynatt (1990) and described in chapter 2.

The Selection Task: Choosing P(D/~H)

Recall that in the selection task participants were given the following instructions:

> Imagine you are a doctor. A patient comes to you with a red rash on his fingers. What information would you want in order to estimate the probability that the patient has the disease "Digirosa?" Below are four pieces of information that may or may not be relevant to determining the probability. Please indicate *all* of the pieces of information that are necessary to determine the probability, but *only* those pieces of information that are necessary to do so.

Participants then chose from the alternatives listed in the order: percentage of people without Digirosa who have a red rash, percentage of people with Digirosa, percentage of people without Digirosa, and percentage of people with Digirosa who have a red rash. These alternatives represented the choices of P(D/~H), P(H), P(~H), and P(D/H), respectively.

The results presented in Table 3.5 are from a study of 660 subjects that was a replication of the Stanovich and West (1998c) investigation described in chapter 2. The table illustrates that the finding of the previous experiment (see Table 2.3) was replicated: The mean SAT score of the subjects who chose P(D/~H) was significantly higher than the mean score of those who did not (the overall SAT scores are higher in this study because scores were derived subsequent to the April 1995 recentering of test by the Educational Testing Service). The next row of Table 3.5 indicates, however, that this group was not significantly higher in need for cognition—a dispositional construct encompassing the tendency toward thoughtful analysis, the desire for understanding, and the tendency toward greater information search (Cacioppo et al., 1996).

Subsequent to completing the selection task, 109 of the participants were asked to evaluate the following argument in favor of choosing P(D/~H):

> It is important that we know the percentage of people *without* Digirosa who have a red rash. This is important because if the percentage of people both *with* and *without* Digirosa who have the red rash were the same, then we would know that the presence of the red rash would not help distinguish between those with and without Digirosa.

Subjects rated this argument on a 6-point scale ranging from "extremely weak" to "extremely strong." Subsequent to finishing several other tasks taking about an hour to complete, participants were presented again with the selection task and other tasks (discussed later) that they had completed before. These problems were preceded by the following instructions:

> You have seen some of these problems before, but we would like you to consider them again. Please *disregard* your previous response to it. Examine the problem again with a fresh eye, perhaps considering the arguments that you evaluated. Make what you *currently* think is the best response.

The subjects then completed for the second time an identical version of the Doherty and Mynatt (1990) selection task.

The analyses of responses to the arguments focus on the issue of whether subjects changed their responses from the first administration of the task to the second after seeing a particular argument. On this task, response change could be in one of two directions: making the normative response [choosing P(D/~H)] on the first administration and making the non-normative response [failing to choose P(D/~H)] on the second administration; or making the non-normative choice on the first administration and the normative choice on the second. As the first analysis in Table 3.6 indicates, nearly half (48.9%) of the subjects giving the non-normative response on the first administration chose P(D/~H) when presented again with the task subsequent to evaluating an argument favoring the normative choice. Because only 10.9% of the subjects originally giving the normative response changed in the other direction, there was a significant tendency for responses to change in the normative direction.

The next group of 109 subjects evaluated a single argument *against* choosing P(D/~H) in order to determine whether the movement would be as strong in the non-normative direction if subjects saw a single argument favoring the normative$_a$ response. The argument was the following:

> "The percentage of people *without* Digirosa who have a red rash is irrelevant. The probability to be determined is the probability that the person *has* Digirosa and the key piece of evidence that is needed for that probability is the percentage of people *with* Digirosa who have a red rash. If this percentage is high, then it is necessarily true that it is probable that this person has Digirosa.

In the same sequence as the previous group, this group of subjects evaluated this argument immediately after the first administration of the selection task and then subsequent to completing several further problems were presented again with the selection task preceded by the same instructions reproduced earlier. The second analysis in Table 3.6 indicates that 23.7% of the subjects in this condition moved in the non-normative direction, whereas 22.0% moved in the normative direction—a difference that was not statistically significant.

A third group of 427 subjects was given both arguments to evaluate after the first administration of the selection task (214 receiving the norma-

TABLE 3.5

**Mean SAT and Need for Cognition Scores of Individuals Making
the Normative and Non-Normative Choices on Different Components
of the Selection Task (Number of Subjects in Parentheses)**

Variable	Non-Normative	Normative	t Value
Selection Task, P(D/~H)			
SAT Total	1,173 (296)	1,196 (350)	2.89***
Need for Cognition	67.9 (304)	68.2 (356)	0.34
Selection Task, P(H)			
SAT Total	1,187 (432)	1,183 (214)	−0.39
Need for Cognition	67.2 (444)	69.7 (216)	2.46**

* $= p < .05$, ** $= p < .025$, *** $= p < .01$, all two-tailed.

tive$_s$ argument first and 213 receiving the normative$_s$ argument second). As the third analysis in Table 3.6 indicates, after being presented with both arguments, significantly more subjects moved in the normative direction than in the non-normative direction (34.0% vs. 19.9%). Thus, when presented with arguments explicating reasons for both choices, subjects were more responsive to the argument for the normative$_s$ choice—a result consistent with the greater potency displayed by the normative$_s$ argument when only one argument was presented. This application of the understanding/acceptance principle is consistent with the normative status of choosing P(D/~H)—as is the finding that individuals higher in cognitive ability were more likely to choose P(D/~H).

The Selection Task: Choosing the Base Rate

Table 3.5 displays the results relevant to the choosing of another component in the selection task—the base-rate, P(H). The second set of analyses presented in the table indicate that there was no significant difference in SAT scores between those who chose P(H) and those who did not. However, those choosing the base rate were significantly higher in need for cognition.

Subsequent to completing the selection task, 109 subjects received the following argument in favor of choosing the base rate:

The percentage of people with Digirosa is needed to determine the probability because, if Digirosa is very infrequent in the population and some people *without* Digirosa *also* have red rashes, then the probability of Digirosa might still be low even if the person has a red rash.

TABLE 3.6

**Percentage of Subjects Who Changed Their Responses on the Second
Administration of the Problem After Evaluating the Arguments for
and Against Choosing P(D/~H) in the Selection Task**

Initial Response	*N*	*% Changing Responses*	
One Normative Argument			
Non-normative	45	48.9	$\chi^2(1) = 19.49^{**}$
Normative	64	10.9	
One Non-Normative Argument			
Non-normative	50	22.0	$\chi^2(1) = 0.05$
Normative	59	23.7	
Both Arguments			
Non-normative	206	34.0	$\chi^2(1) = 10.79^{*}$
Normative	221	19.9	

$^* = p < .01, ^{**} = p < .001.$

Participants rated this argument on the same 6-point scale.

The first analysis in Table 3.7 focuses on whether subjects changed their response on the second administration of the task after evaluating a single argument explicating reasons for the choice of P(H). More than 39% changed their responses in the normative$_s$ direction, compared with 15.0% who changed in the other direction, a difference that was statistically significant. The next analysis in Table 3.7 indicates the movement when 109 different subjects were given the following argument for the irrelevance of the base rate:

> The percentage of people with Digirosa is irrelevant because this particular patient has a red rash, and thus the percentage of people who have Digirosa is not needed when trying to determine the probability that someone has Digirosa given that they have a red rash.

A third group of 427 participants was given both arguments to evaluate after the first administration of the selection task (213 receiving the normative$_s$ argument first and 214 receiving the normative$_s$ argument second). As the third analysis in Table 3.7 indicates, after being presented with both arguments, significantly more subjects moved in the normative$_s$ direction than in the normative$_a$ direction (27.2% vs. 11.1%). Thus, when presented with arguments explicating reasons for both choices, subjects were more responsive to the argument for the normative$_s$ choice—a result consistent with the slightly greater potency displayed by the normative$_s$ argument when only one argument was presented. This application of the understanding/acceptance principle is consistent with the normative status of choosing P(H).

Noncausal Base Rates: The Disease Problem

In an extended replication experiment, the effects of argument evaluation on performance on the AIDS problem (now slightly rewritten and termed the disease problem) was examined. Because there are some indications that the term *false positive* can decrease Bayesian responding (Cosmides & Tooby, 1996), the version used in this experiment removed that term. The problem was phrased as follows:

> Imagine that disease X occurs in 1 in every 1,000 people. A test has been developed to detect the disease. Every time the test is given to a person who has the disease, the test comes out positive. But sometimes the test also comes out positive when it is given to a person who is completely healthy. Specifically, 5% of all people who are perfectly healthy test positive for the disease. Imagine that we have given this test to a random sample of Americans. They were selected by a lottery. Those who conducted the lottery had

TABLE 3.7

Percentage of Subjects Who Changed Their Responses on the Second Administration of the Problem After Evaluating the Arguments for and Against Choosing P(H) in the Selection Task

		One Normative Argument	
Initial Response	*N*	*% Changing Responses*	
Non-normative	69	39.1	$\chi^2(1) = 6.99^*$
Normative	40	15.0	
		One Non-Normative Argument	
Initial Response	*N*	*% Changing Responses*	
Non-normative	83	15.7	$\chi^2(1) = 2.91$
Normative	26	30.8	
		Both Arguments	
Initial Response	*N*	*% Changing Responses*	
Non-normative	283	27.2	$\chi^2(1) = 14.52^{**}$
Normative	144	11.1	

$^* = p < .01,$ $^{**} = p < .001.$

no information about the health status of any of these people. What is the chance (expressed as a percentage ranging from 0% to 100%) that a person found to have a positive result actually has the disease?

Recall that the Bayesian posterior probability for this problem is slightly less than .02. Thus, responses of less than or equal to 10% were interpreted as indicating Bayesian amalgamation of the base rate and the likelihood ratio. A small proportion (12.4%) of the responses in this category were less than 1% and thus may have reflected total reliance on the base rate; the results were unchanged when the base-rate responders were removed. Responses greater than or equal to 80% were scored as indicating strong reliance on indicant information, and responses between 10% and 80% were scored as intermediate. As in previous studies similar to this one (e.g., Cosmides & Tooby, 1996), the majority of subjects gave responses that were either Bayesian or that reflected strong reliance on indicant information: 318 were classified as strongly indicant, 242 as Bayesian, and 85 as intermediate. Subsequent analyses focus on the first two groups (these two groups comprise over 85% of the subjects and the two arguments were framed to support these two extreme positions). Table 3.8 presents the mean scores of these groups on the two cognitive/personality variables. The removal of the term *false positive* did increase the proportion of Bayesian responders from 20.3% to 37.5%. However, unlike the results on the false-positive version displayed in Table 3.3, the Bayesian group here had significantly higher SAT scores. However, the two groups did not differ significantly in need for cognition.

Subsequent to completing the disease problem, 90 participants classified as either indicant or Bayesian were asked to evaluate the following argument designed to make subjects pay more attention to the base rate:

The chance that a person with a positive test result has the disease must be low because the test *wrongly* indicates that 5% of the *healthy* people have the disease. Because there are many more healthy people than people with the disease, most of the people with positive test results will *not* have the disease.

TABLE 3.8
Mean Scores of Groups Classified as Indicant and Bayesian on the Disease Problem Replication

	Indicant (n = 318)	Bayesian (n = 242)	t Value
SAT Total	1,182	1,202	−2.35*
Need for Cognition	67.8	68.4	−0.65

* = $p < .05$, two-tailed.

The first analysis in Table 3.9 indicates that after readministration of the task, 43.8% of the indicant group changed their responses in the normative$_s$ direction (were classified as either Bayesian or intermediate), compared with just 16.7% of the Bayesian subjects who shifted in the other direction (were classified as either indicant or intermediate), a difference that was statistically significant. However, the next analysis indicates that the movement was just as strong in the other direction when another group of subjects had to evaluate a single argument emphasizing the indicant:

> The chance that a person with a positive test result has the disease must be very high because, when a person has the disease the test *always* gives a positive result and this guarantees that people with positive results have a high probability of having the disease.

A third group of 365 subjects was given *both* arguments to evaluate after the first administration of the problem (181 receiving the normative argument first and 184 receiving the normative argument second). As the third analysis in Table 3.9 indicates, after being presented with both arguments, significantly more subjects moved in the non-normative (indicant) direction than in the normative (Bayesian) direction (34.9% vs. 18.5%). Thus, when presented with arguments explicating reasons for both choices, subjects were somewhat more responsive to the argument for the normative$_a$ choice.

TABLE 3.9

Percentage of Subjects Who Changed Their Responses on the Second Administration of the Disease Problem

One Normative Argument			
Initial Response	*N*	*% Changing Responses*	
Non-normative	48	43.8	$\chi^2(1) = 7.67^*$
Normative	42	16.7	
One Non-Normative Argument			
Initial Response	*N*	*% Changing Responses*	
Non-normative	50	7.0	$\chi^2(1) = 11.24^{**}$
Normative	44	36.4	
Both Arguments			
Initial Response	*N*	*% Changing Responses*	
Non-normative	216	18.5	$\chi^2(1) = 12.55^{**}$
Normative	149	34.9	

$^* = p < .01,$ $^{**} = p < .001.$

EXAMINATION OF OTHER PROBLEMS WITH CONTROVERSIAL NORMS

In this section, two problems that have been the focus of much contention regarding what should be considered the normative response are examined.

Newcomb's Problem

Newcomb's problem, introduced into the literature by Nozick (1969), has been the subject of intense philosophical dispute (Gibbard & Harper, 1978; Hurley, 1991; Nozick, 1993; see R. Campbell & Sowden, 1985, for a collection of useful readings). The version given to 662 subjects was modeled on Shafir and Tversky (1992) and was as follows:

$20		$250
		or $0

Box A   Box B

Here is a problem that asks you to make use of your imagination. Consider the two boxes above. Imagine Box A contains $20 for sure. Imagine that Box B may contain either $250 or nothing. Pretend your options will be to:

1. Choose both Boxes A and B (and collect the money that is in both boxes).
2. Choose Box B only (and collect only the money that is in Box B).

Imagine now that we have a computer program called the "Predictor" that has analyzed the pattern of the responses you have already made to all of the earlier questions. Based on this analysis, the program has already predicted your preference for this problem and has already loaded the boxes accordingly. If, based on this analysis of your previous preferences, the program has predicted that you will take both boxes, then it has left Box B empty. On the other hand, if it has predicted that you will take only Box B, then it has already put $250 in that box. So far, the program has been very successful: Most of the participants who chose Box B received $250; in contrast, few of those who chose both boxes found $250 in Box B.

Which of the above options would you choose?

a) Choose both Box A and Box B.

b) Choose Box B only.

The choices in Newcomb's problem pit the dictates of evidential decision theory against those of dominance within the framework of causal decision theory (Campbell, 1985; Gibbard & Harper, 1978; Hurley, 1991; Nozick, 1993; Resnik, 1987). The two-box consequentialist choice is clearly viewed as normative by most psychologists who have examined the problem (Shafir, 1994; Shafir & Tversky, 1992), especially in this version, which was specifically designed by Shafir and Tversky to emphasize that the predictor's choice had already been made and to remove some seemingly supernatural elements from the original formulation of the problem (Nozick, 1969). Yet despite these changes in the problem, which make the dominant consequentialist choice quite salient, 65% of Shafir and Tversky's subjects preferred to take only one box—although their sample was somewhat small (only 40 subjects).

Using a much larger sample size (662), Richard West and I replicated their result—62.8% of our sample preferred the one-box option on the first administration of the problem. Table 3.10 indicates that the subjects choosing the two-box alternative had higher SAT scores than those choosing the one-box alternative, but this difference was not significant. However, those choosing two boxes did have significantly higher need for cognition scores.

Subsequent to completing the first administration of the problem, 109 of the participants were asked to evaluate the following consequentialist argument (see Nozick, 1969) in favor of taking both boxes:

> The Predictor has already made the prediction and has already either put the $250 in Box B or has not. If the Predictor has already put the $250 in Box B, and I take both boxes, I get $250 + $20, whereas if I take only Box B, I get only $250. If the Predictor has not put the $250 in Box B, and I take both boxes, I get $20, whereas if I take only Box B I get no money. Therefore, whether the $250 is there or not, I get $20 more by taking both boxes rather than only Box B. So I should take both boxes.

TABLE 3.10

Mean SAT and Need for Cognition Scores of Subjects Making the Normative and Non-Normative Choices on Various Tasks (Number of Subjects in Parentheses)

Variable	Non-Normative	Normative	t Value
Newcomb's Problem			
SAT Total	1,181 (405)	1,192 (242)	1.26
Need for Cognition	67.1 (415)	69.5 (246)	2.40*
Prisoner's Dilemma			
SAT Total	1,176 (264)	1,191 (383)	1.83
Need for Cognition	68.3 (272)	67.8 (389)	−0.59

* $= p < .025$, two-tailed.

The first analysis in Table 3.11 indicates that 35.8% of the sample changed their responses in the normative direction, compared with 7.1% who changed in the other direction, a difference that was statistically significant. However, the next analysis indicates that the movement was almost as strong in the other direction when another group of subjects had to evaluate a single argument in favor of taking only one box. This argument, adapted from Nozick (1969), was the following:

> If I choose both boxes, the Predictor almost certainly would have predicted this and would not have put the $250 in Box B, and so therefore I will get only $20. If I take only Box B, the Predictor almost certainly would have predicted this and will have put the $250 in Box B, and so therefore I will get the $250. Thus, if I take both boxes, I almost certainly will get only $20. But, if I take just Box B, I almost certainly will get $250. Therefore, I should choose just Box B.

A third group of 436 subjects was given both arguments to evaluate after the first administration of the problem (217 receiving the normative$_s$ argument first and 219 receiving the normative$_s$ argument second). As the third analysis in Table 3.11 indicates, after being presented with both arguments, significantly more subjects moved in the normative$_s$ (two-box) direction than in the normative$_a$ (one box) direction (24.3% vs. 7.5%). Thus, when presented with arguments explicating reasons for both choices, subjects were more responsive to the argument for the normative choice.

An analysis of the impact of all three factors relevant to understanding (argument evaluation, cognitive ability, need for cognition) on normative choices revealed the following. Among those 130 subjects in the lower half of the distributions of both cognitive ability and need for cognition, only 41 chose two boxes (31.5%) on the first administration of the task. In contrast, after evaluating both arguments, 53.8% of the 106 subjects in the upper half of the distributions of both cognitive ability and need for cognition chose two boxes. Thus, the combined effects of evaluating arguments both for and against the normative choice, high cognitive ability, and high need for cognition resulted in a 70.8% increase (22.3/31.5) in the proportion of subjects making the normative two-box choice. However, the following (similarly contentious) problem indicates that this outcome does not always obtain.

The Prisoner's Dilemma

The prisoner's dilemma has generated an enormous literature (e.g., Hargreaves Heap & Varoufakis, 1995; Rapoport & Chammah, 1965; Rasmusen, 1989; Skyrms, 1996). The version given to 661 subjects was modeled on Shafir and Tversky (1992) and was as follows:

TABLE 3.11

Percentage of Subjects Who Changed Their Responses on the Second Administration of Newcomb's Problem

	One Normative Argument		
Initial Response	N	*% Changing Responses*	
Non-normative	67	35.8	$\chi^2(1) = 11.39^{**}$
Normative	42	7.1	
	One Non-Normative Argument		
Initial Response	N	*% Changing Responses*	
Non-normative	71	5.6	$\chi^2(1) = 13.24^{**}$
Normative	42	31.0	
	Both Arguments		
Initial Response	N	*% Changing Responses*	
Non-normative	276	24.3	$\chi^2(1) = 19.21^{**}$
Normative	160	7.5	

$^{**} = p < .001.$

Intercollegiate Computer Game

This game was originally designed to be played by pairs of students who were sitting in front of different computers on the same computer system. Since we are not using computers today, *please use your imagination*, and pretend that you are sitting in front of a computer and playing the Intercollegiate Computer Game with another student.

In this game you will be presented with a situation involving you and one other player who is sitting at a computer in another room. You cannot communicate with each other. The situation requires that you make a strategic decision: to cooperate or to compete with the other player. The other player will have to make the same decision.

The situation is represented by a payoff matrix that will determine how much money each of you earns depending on whether you compete or cooperate. The matrix looks like the following:

	Other Cooperates	Other Competes
You Cooperate	You: 20 Other: 20	You: 5 Other: 25
You Compete	You: 25 Other: 5	You: 10 Other: 10

According to this matrix, if you both cooperate you will both earn $20 each. If you cooperate and the other person competes, the other will earn $25 and you will earn only $5. Similarly, if you compete and the other person cooperates, you will earn $25 and the other person will earn only $5. Finally, if you both choose to compete, you will each earn $10. Not knowing what the other person will choose to do, what would you choose?

(a) I would choose to compete

(b) I would choose to cooperate

Competing is the dominant action for each player in this situation because whatever the other player does, each person is better off competing than cooperating. The fact that this individually rational (dominant) action leads to an outcome that is suboptimal for both ($10, when each could have had $20 by cooperating) is what has piqued the interest of social scientists and philosophers in this problem. As Nozick (1993) put it: "The combination of (what appears to be) their individual rationalities leads them to forgo an attainable better situation and thus is Pareto-suboptimal" (p. 50).

However, in the one-shot game (with no communication between players or repeated play) the compete strategy is usually championed as rational—sometimes using parallels between the logic of the prisoner's dilemma and the logic underlying Newcomb's problem. This connection between the two problems has been discussed by several authors (R. Campbell & Sowden, 1985; Hurley, 1991; Lewis, 1979; Nozick, 1993). For example, Shafir and Tversky (1992) pointed out that:

> In both cases, the outcome depends on the choice that you make and on that made by another being—the other player in the Prisoner's Dilemma and the Predictor in Newcomb's problem. In both cases one option (competing or taking both boxes) dominates the other, yet the other option (cooperating or taking just one box) seems preferable if the being—the Predictor or the other player—knows what you will do, or will act like you. (p. 460)

But in neither case can anything you do affect what the Predictor or the other player has already done. Nevertheless, Shafir and Tversky found a cooperation rate of 37% using a one-shot problem similar to that presented previously.

In a much larger sample of 661 participants, we observed a similar cooperation rate of 41.2%. Table 3.10 indicates that the subjects choosing to compete had higher SAT scores than cooperators but this difference did not reach significance. However, the difference in need for cognition was in the other direction—subjects choosing to compete had lower scores—although again the difference was not significant.

Subsequent to completing the first administration of the problem, 109 of the participants were asked to evaluate the following consequentialist argument in favor of competing:

> No matter what the other person does, I am better off competing. If the other person cooperates and I compete, I get $25 rather than $20. If the other person competes and I compete, I get $10 rather than $5. Competing is always the better strategy for me, so it is the better choice.

The first analysis in Table 3.12 indicates that, when the task was re-administered, over half of the cooperators (51.4%) changed their responses compared with only 6.9% of the competers who changed in the other direction, a difference that was statistically significant. However, the next analysis indicates that there was a strong (but not quite as large) change in the other direction when another group of subjects had to evaluate a single argument in favor of cooperating. This argument is adapted from Hurley's (1991) discussion of the notion of collective action as the source of the attractiveness of the cooperative response:

> The rational thing for both of us to do is to both cooperate and get $20 rather than to both compete and get only $10. The other player probably realizes this, too, just like I do. Therefore, I should cooperate so that we both end up with $20, rather than $10.

TABLE 3.12
Percentage of Subjects Who Changed Their Responses on the Second Administration of the Prisoner's Dilemma

One Normative Argument			
Initial Response	N	% *Changing Responses*	
Non-normative	37	51.4	$\chi^2(1) = 28.07^{**}$
Normative	72	6.9	
One Non-Normative Argument			
Initial Response	N	% *Changing Responses*	
Non-normative	43	7.0	$\chi^2(1) = 8.07^{*}$
Normative	68	29.4	
Both Arguments			
Initial Response	N	% *Changing Responses*	
Non-normative	191	23.0	$\chi^2(1) = 2.72$
Normative	245	16.7	

$^{*} = p < .01,\ ^{**} = p < .001.$

A third group of 436 participants was given both arguments to evaluate after the first administration of the problem (218 receiving the normative$_s$ argument first and 218 receiving the normative$_s$ argument second). As the third analysis in Table 3.12 indicates, there was no significant difference in the proportions of subjects who moved in the normative direction compared with those who moved in the non-normative direction. Thus, deeper understanding of the logic of the prisoner's dilemma situation—as evidenced by considering arguments for both responses or by the tendency to engage in reflective thought (need for cognition) or the ability to successfully engage in such thought (cognitive ability)—was not associated with the compete response that is traditionally considered normative in the one-shot problem.

SUMMARY OF APPLICATIONS
OF THE UNDERSTANDING/ACCEPTANCE PRINCIPLE

In this chapter, the focus has been on problems in which the appropriate normative model to be applied has been hotly debated. Slovic and Tversky's (1974) understanding/acceptance principle was applied to these problems. The essence of their principle is that the greater the understanding of a normative rule the greater will be the willingness to accept it. Thus, the direction of the correlation between performance and understanding provides a clue as to the nature of the appropriate norm for the problem. Use of the principle represents a pretheoretical commitment to a type of naturalistic epistemology that is widely endorsed in decision science. The understanding/acceptance principle was operationalized in two different ways. First, individual difference variables related to the tendency to engage in reflective thought (cognitive ability and need for cognition) were examined. Second, the argument evaluation procedure of Slovic and Tversky was employed—subjects were presented arguments both for and against the normative$_s$ principle and the directionality of response change was examined.

Unlike the tasks examined in chapter 2 where positive manifold was consistently observed, the controversial tasks examined in this chapter displayed a variety of different patterns. Results were most consistent with respect to $P(D/\sim H)$ in the selection task. There, subjects choosing that component had significantly higher SAT scores and—as described in chapter 2—they tended to give the normative response on a host of other tasks. After evaluating a single argument for the normative response, subjects moved significantly in that direction, but subsequent to a single non-normative argument there was no significant tendency for responses to move in the non-normative direction. After hearing one normative and one non-normative argument, subjects were significantly more likely to alter their responses in the normative direction.

The results were considerably more mixed in the case of the base-rate component of the selection task, P(H). Differences in cognitive ability between choosers and nonchoosers of this component have not been observed (see Table 3.5 and Stanovich & West, 1998c), however those choosing this component were significantly higher in need for cognition. Also, as indicated in Table 3.7, when presented with one normative and one non-normative argument, subjects were significantly more likely to alter their responses in the normative direction.

The same pattern was apparent on Newcomb's problem. There was not a significant difference between those choosing one box and those choosing two boxes in SAT scores, but there was a significant difference in need for cognition scores favoring those making the consequentialist two-box choice. Likewise, after evaluating arguments for both the one-box and two-box choice, significantly more subjects moved in the direction of the two-box choice that is traditionally considered normative in the psychological literature (Shafir & Tversky, 1992).

However, an application of the understanding/acceptance principle did not serve to justify the competitive response in the prisoner's dilemma problem. This task yielded quite ambiguous results. There were no significant differences between those competing and those cooperating on the SAT test or in need for cognition. The nonsignificant mean differences were in the direction of the compete response on the former and in the direction of the cooperation response on the latter. When presented with one argument for competing and one argument for cooperating, there was no significant difference in the proportion of subjects changing their responses in either direction.

Argument evaluation was not employed as a method in the consensus task, but analyses of individual differences consistently yielded null results—differences in cognition and reasoning were particularly unsuccessful in explaining the gap between the descriptive and the normative on the opinion prediction task. Thus, the discrepancy between descriptive and normative models of behavior in such a situation cannot be attributed to algorithmic-level limitations. If the gap also cannot be attributed to performance errors, then there are two other important possibilities. One is that humans are systematically computing a non-normative rule (Baron, 1991b; Kahneman & Tversky, 1996; Shafir, 1994). The other is that there is something wrong with the assumptions about how subjects should represent the task (see chapter 4) or with the normative models that have been used to evaluate task performance. Other aspects of the data presented in Table 3.4 reinforce the latter critique. For example, when predictive accuracy is analyzed, the data indicated that projecting one's own opinion is actually efficacious. This finding might be viewed as reinforcing the previous critiques of the standard normative analysis of the false-consensus effect (Dawes, 1989, 1990;

Hoch, 1987), which have questioned whether total lack of projection of one's own position is actually normative.

Two of the problems completely failed to show trends in the direction of the normative$_s$ response. Both were noncausal base-rate problems (the cab problem and the AIDS/disease problem). Here the trends were in the direction that would be expected under the assumption that an incorrect norm was being applied. For example, in two out of three comparisons (see Tables 3.1 and 3.2) the SAT scores of the indicant responders on the cab problem were significantly higher than those of the Bayesian responders, and the indicant responders also outscored the Bayesian responders on the need for cognition scale (see Table 3.2). On the AIDS problem with the "false positive" wording (Table 3.3), the SAT scores of the indicant responders were significantly higher than those of the Bayesian responders. On the disease problem with the "false positive" wording removed, this trend reversed (Table 3.8). However, in the test of response to argument evaluation, when presented with one argument for the indicant response and one argument for a Bayesian response, significantly more subjects moved in the indicant direction (see Table 3.9).

Thus, these particular noncausal base-rate problems are truly different in terms of the understanding/acceptance principle. As is clear from Tables 2.1, 2.2, 2.4, and 2.5, causal base-rate problems of the type examined by Fong et al. (1986) display positive manifold with cognitive ability and with other reasoning tasks. As argued previously, because positive manifold for cognitive tasks has been the expected finding at least since Spearman (1904; see Carroll, 1993), one way to reconcile the reversed sign on the associations involving these two noncausal base-rate problems is to call into question the normative model that is being applied to them. The signs all reverse and positive manifold is restored if the interpretation of the indicant and Bayesian response is reversed. The contentious literature spawned by these two tasks appears to have been justified.

With respect to other tasks, however—Newcomb's problem, choosing $P(D/\sim H)$ in the selection task, and the tasks discussed in chapter 2—an application of the understanding/acceptance principle serves to reinforce the normative analysis traditionally applied to the task. The results with respect to these tasks provide a response to the claim of Lopes and Oden (1991) that there is "no support for the view that people would choose in accord with normative prescriptions if they were provided with increased capacity" (p. 209). The results with respect to the tasks listed in Tables 2.2, 2.4, 2.5, and 3.5 indicate that they would. In contrast, their claim appears to be right on the mark with respect to the two noncausal base rate tasks and perhaps with respect to the prisoner's dilemma as well.

THE ARGUMENT EVALUATION RESULTS
AND REFLECTIVE EQUILIBRIUM

One important issue that is raised by the attempt to manipulate understanding by presenting normative and non-normative arguments is the issue of the lability of the responses that are the subject of debate in the heuristics and biases literature. What invariably provokes these critiques—often by philosophers defending the notion of impeccable human rational competence—is the finding that the modal subject departs from the normative$_s$ response. Trying to avoid the conclusion that human cognition is systematically irrational in some domain, critics committed to the principle of virtually ideal rational competence (e.g., Cohen, 1981; Wetherick, 1995) argue either that experimenters are applying the wrong normative model to the task or that, alternatively, they may be applying the correct normative model to the problem as set, but they have presented the problem misleadingly so that the subject adopts a different problem construal and ends up providing a normatively appropriate answer to a different problem (see chapter 4). Cohen and other critics (e.g., Gigerenzer, 1996a; Macdonald, 1986; Wetherick, 1995) were at pains to show that any normative/descriptive gaps can be so explained. But this entire critique is misguided if the finding that spawned it—that typical human performance departs from a specified normative$_s$ model—displays systematic lability.

The focus of these critiques—what they purport to explain—is modal or mean performance that departs from the response deemed normative under the model being applied. But these are normative/descriptive gaps that are uninformed by any analysis of the degree of understanding of the subject—of any analysis based on the understanding/acceptance principle. Specifically, it is assumed that these non-normative responses are in reflective equilibrium. But the results reported here would seem to suggest that in many cases this assumption is unjustified.

Consider how labile were responses on some of these problems. Collapsed across all of the problems in this chapter that were tested with the argument evaluation procedure, when presented with an argument on each side of the question, an average of 22.1% altered their responses on a readministration of the task. When presented with a single normative argument, 42.5% of the non-normative subjects switched to the normative response on a readministration of the task. Note that, in the procedure used, subjects were *not* told that the argument was correct. They were simply told to evaluate the argument, and were free to rate it as very weak if it conflicted with their previous response. Similarly, subjects in the both-arguments condition were perfectly free to rate as weak the argument that conflicted with their response and to view the compatible argument as strong and thus as justification for persisting with their previous response. Nevertheless, fully 25.4% of the non-normative subjects shifted after seeing one conflicting argument along with a compatible one.

Consider further how the modal response on these tasks can change as criteria for reflectiveness and cognitive engagement are imposed. Of the 661 subjects who completed the first administration of the Doherty and Mynatt (1990) selection task, only 217 (32.8%) chose the base rate, P(H). Thus, failure to choose the base rate is the clear modal response on the first administration. If we wished to explain this deviation from Bayesian logic without positing a systematic deviation from rational principles, we might wish to criticize the experimenter's application of the normative model and/or the formulation of the problem. For example, we might be prone to start thinking about whether the experimenter has used an inappropriately broad reference class in defining the base rate (Kyburg, 1996; Levi, 1996) or perhaps whether the subjects' concept of probability is Baconian rather than Pascallian (Cohen, 1983). However, a much simpler assumption is that perhaps many of the subjects had failed to fully think through the implications of the base rate. The latter assumption would seem to have the advantage of parsimony—particularly in light of the following empirical finding: After seeing one normative and one non-normative argument, 52.8% of the subjects in the upper half of the SAT and need for cognition distributions chose the base rate! Subsequent to a very slight intervention, choosing the base rate becomes the modal response; and because choosing it coincides with the normative$_s$ model assumed by the authors of this problem, there is now no need to assume error on their part (as mentioned previously, the critiques of the heuristics and biases literature tend to ignore all situations where the modal response coincides with the normative model being applied—experimenters apparently make no mistakes in these situations).

Newcomb's problem yields the same reversal in the modal response after the three factors associated with greater reflectiveness are applied. Of the 662 subjects who completed the first administration of the problem, only 246 (37.2%) chose two boxes. Again, the nonconsequentialist one-box choice was the modal response. However, after seeing one normative and one non-normative argument, 53.8% of the subjects in the upper half of the SAT and need for cognition distributions chose two boxes. Among this group who were more reflective and who had the advantage of problem explication, the two-box choice was the modal response. In short, a normative/descriptive gap that is disproportionately created by subjects with superficial understanding and/or low task engagement provides no warrant for amending the application of standard normative models.

CONCLUSION

In this chapter, selected experimental examples have been presented to illustrate how variation and instability in responses can be analyzed—in conjunction with tools such as the understanding/acceptance principle—in ways that shed light on debates about the reasons why descriptive and normative models of human reasoning sometimes do not coincide. The expected positive manifold among reasoning tasks provides a tool for conditioning expert reflective equilibrium. Following in the tradition of decision science where notions of normative performance are conditioned by empirical evidence about actual human performance (Larrick et al., 1993; March, 1988; Slovic, 1995), failure to obtain positive manifold can be conceived as the type of descriptive finding that calls into question the normative model being applied. Recall that it was the behavioral (descriptive) discrepancies with normative$_s$ models in the heuristics and biases literature that spawned the last 20 years worth of debate in this field in the first place. There would have been no debate (or at least much less of one) had people behaved in accord with the then-accepted norms. The debate itself is, reflexively, evidence that the descriptive models of actual behavior condition expert notions of the normative. The present volume has as one of its goals adding new descriptive patterns to the debate about reasoning norms.

The Problem of Rational Task Construal

Theorists who resist interpreting the gap between normative and descriptive models as indicating human irrationality have one more strategy available in addition to those previously described. In the context of empirical cognitive psychology, it is a commonplace argument, but it is one that continues to create enormous controversy and to bedevil efforts to compare human performance to normative standards. It is the argument that although the experimenter may well be applying the correct normative model to the problem as set, the subject might be construing the problem differently and be providing the normatively appropriate answer to a different problem—in short, that subjects have a different interpretation of the task (see, e.g., Adler, 1984, 1991; Broome, 1990; Henle, 1962; Hilton, 1995; Levinson, 1995; Margolis, 1987; Schick, 1987, 1997; Schwarz, 1996).

Such an argument is somewhat different from any of the critiques examined thus far. It is not the equivalent of positing that a performance error has been made, because performance errors (attention lapses, etc.) would not be expected to recur in exactly the same way in a readministration of the same task. Whereas, if the subject has truly misunderstood the task, they would be expected to do so again on an identical readministration of the task.

Correspondingly, this criticism is different from the argument that the task exceeds the computational capacity of the subject. The latter explanation puts the onus of the suboptimal performance on the subject. In contrast, the alternative task construal argument places the blame at least somewhat on the shoulders of the experimenter for presenting the task in way that is misleading and that leads the subject away from the desired response (or at least that the experimenter has failed to realize that there were task features that might lead subjects to frame the problem in a manner different from that intended).[1]

As with the incorrect norm explanation, the alternative construal argument locates the problem with the experimenter. However, it is different in that in the wrong norm explanation it is assumed that the subject is interpreting the task as the experimenter intended—but the experimenter is not using the right criteria to evaluate performance. In contrast, the alternative task construal argument allows that the experimenter may be applying the correct normative model to the problem the experimenter intends the subject to solve—but posits that the subject has construed the problem in some other way and is providing a normatively appropriate answer to a different problem.

It seems that in order to comprehensively evaluate the rationality of human cognition, it is necessary to evaluate the appropriateness of various task construals. This is because—contrary to thin theories of means/ends rationality that treat the subject's task construal as fixed (Elster, 1983; Nathanson, 1994)—it is argued in this chapter that if we are going to have any normative standards at all, then we must also have standards for what are appropriate and inappropriate task construals. The chapter begins with a sketch of the arguments of philosophers and decision scientists who have made just this point. Then it is argued that: (a) in order to tackle the difficult problem of evaluating task construals, criteria of wide reflective equilibrium come into play; (b) it is necessary to use all descriptive information about human performance that could potentially affect expert wide reflective equilibrium; (c) included in the relevant descriptive facts are individual differences in task construal and their patterns of covariance. This argument again makes use of the understanding/acceptance principle of Slovic and Tversky (1974) that was employed in chapter 3.

THE NECESSITY FOR PRINCIPLES OF RATIONAL CONSTRUAL

It is now widely recognized that the evaluation of the normative appropriateness of a response to a particular task is always relative to a particular interpretation of the task. For example, Schick (1987) pointed out that "how rationality directs us to choose depends on which understandings are ours ... [and that] the understandings people have bear on the question of what would be rational for them" (pp. 53, 58). Likewise, Tversky (1975) argued that "the question of whether utility theory is compatible with the data or not, therefore, depends critically on the interpretation of the consequences" (p. 171).

---

[1]A further possibility, discussed in chapter 8, is that the subject may use a different task interpretation as an "escape hatch" to avoid the computational burden of the normative$_s$ task construal.

Schick (1987) used the Allais (1953) paradox to illustrate the importance of differences in construing outcomes. Allais proposed the following two choice problems:

Problem 1. Choose between:

A: 1 million dollars for sure

B: .89 probability of 1 million dollars
    .10 probability of 5 million dollars
    .01 probability of nothing

Problem 2. Choose between:

C: .11 probability of 1 million dollars
    .89 probability of nothing

D: .10 probability of 5 million dollars
    .90 probability of nothing

Many people find Option A in Problem 1 and Option D in Problem 2 to be the most attractive, but these choices violate the independence axiom of utility theory. Savage's (1954) explanation is that .89 of the probability is the same in both sets of choices. In both Problem 1 and Problem 2, in purely numerical terms, the subject is essentially faced with a choice between .11 probability of $1,000,000 versus .10 probability of $5,000,000 and .01 probability of nothing. If you chose the first in Problem 1, you should choose the first in Problem 2. That is, Options A and C are numerically identical, as are B and D. The choices of A and D are incoherent.

However, Schick (1987) pointed out that if we allow a construal of the options that incorporates psychological factors such as regret (Bell, 1982; Loomes & Sugden, 1982), then Choices A and D no longer violate the independence axiom. He argued that we might view the zero-money outcome of Option B as something like "getting nothing when you passed up a sure chance of a million dollars!" The equivalent .01 slice of probability in Option D is folded into the .90 and will never be psychologically coded in the same way. Schick's point is that we do not know whether a particular subject coded psychological factors into the zero-money outcome of Option B and that the possibility of this alternative construal prevents us from saying that the choice of A and D represents a violation of the independence axiom. This is why Hilton (1995) advised that theories of judgment must "include a front-end component that determines how the incoming message is interpreted in its context" (p. 249).

However, others have pointed to the danger inherent in too permissively explaining away non-normative responses by positing different construals of the problem. Normative theories will be drained of all of their evaluative force if we adopt an attitude that is too charitable toward alternative construals. Broome (1990) illustrated the problem by discussing the preference reversal phenomenon (Grether & Plott, 1979;

Lichtenstein & Slovic, 1971; Slovic, 1995). In a choice between two gambles, A and B, a person chooses A over B. However, when pricing the gambles, the person puts a higher price on B. This violation of procedural invariance leads to what appears to be intransitivity. Presumably there is an amount of money, M, that would be preferred to A but given a choice of M and B the person would choose B. Thus, we appear to have B > M, M > A, A > B.

Broome (1990) pointed out that when choosing A over B the subject is choosing A and is simultaneously rejecting B. Evaluating A in the M versus A comparison is not the same. Here, when choosing A, the subject is not rejecting B. The A alternative here might be considered to be a different prospect, and if it is so considered there is no intransitivity. Broome argued that whenever the basic axioms such as transitivity, independence, or descriptive or procedural invariance are breached, the same inoculating strategy could be invoked—that of individuating outcomes so finely that the violation disappears. His discussion of individuating outcomes (how we go about classifying outcomes as similar or different) centers around how fine-grained or coarse-grained to make the outcome categories. Broad categories of outcomes would disregard superficial problem differences and (possibly ephemeral, malleable, highly labile) psychological attitudes. Thin categories would result if such factors were coded. Broome's point is that the thinner the categories, the harder it will be to attribute irrationality to a set of preferences if we evaluate rationality only in practical or instrumental terms ("using the finest individuation leads to trouble. It prevents you from ruling any pattern of preferences as irrational," p. 140). Foley (1987, p. 131) concurred by emphasizing the radical subjectivity of pure means/ends rationality. This very subjectivity is what allows the differential construal argument to undercut many of the strictures of a normative theory of practical rationality.

Two intuitions are thus in sharp conflict here. Consider that most people are not complete relativists—they feel that there are at least *some* principles of cognitive evaluation. But another intuition—that all subject interpretations of a problem, even the most bizarre—must be honored and treated equally, is sharply at odds with the notion that there are any rational standards. If we want any standards of rationality at all, we cannot accept every problem interpretation.

Broome (1990) contended that the only way out of this impasse is that in addition to the formal principles of rationality, principles that deal with content must be developed so as to enable us to evaluate the reasonableness of a particular individuation of outcomes. Broome acknowledged that "this procedure puts principles of rationality to work at a very early stage of decision theory. They are needed in fixing the set of alternative prospects that preferences can then be defined upon. The principles in question might be called 'rational principles of indifference'" (p. 140). Broome admitted that "many people think there can be no principles of rationality apart from the formal ones. This goes along with the common view that rationality can only be instrumental ... [however] if you acknowledge only formal principles of rationality, and deny that there are any principles of indifference, you will find yourself without any principles of rationality at all" (pp. 140-141). Broome cited Tversky (1975) as concurring in this view:

> I believe that an adequate analysis of rational choice cannot accept the evaluation of the consequences as given, and examine only the consistency of preferences. There is probably as much irrationality in our feelings, as expressed in the way we evaluate consequences, as there is in our choice of actions. An adequate normative analysis must deal with problems such as the legitimacy of regret in Allais' problem.... I do not see how the normative appeal of the axioms could be discussed without a reference to a specific interpretation. (p. 172)

Others agree with the Broome–Tversky analysis (see Bacharach & Hurley, 1991; Baron, 1993a, 1994a; Frisch, 1994; Sen, 1993). For example, Schick (1997) rejected the relativism of those disputing the possibility of rational principles of task construal: "I reject this libertine view, though I have no good case against it" (p. 143). More positively, Shweder (1987) reiterated that:

> The problem with the idea of abstract or formal axioms is not that the axioms are false but rather the implication that one can focus on them alone (ignoring content and framing) and still comprehend or predict actual functioning. If you can succeed at predicting functioning, it is because you know more than you realized about the content and the proper way to frame things. (pp. 168–169)

Finally, Einhorn and Hogarth (1981) reiterated that "even if one were to accept instrumental rationality as the sole criterion for evaluating decisions, knowledge of how tasks are represented is crucial since people's goals form part of their models of the world. Moreover, their task representation may be of more importance in defining errors than the rules they use within that representation" (p. 60).

Thus, although there is some support for Broome's (1990) generic argument, the dauntingly difficult task he set has barely been broached. The contentious disputes about rational principles of indifference and rational construals of the tasks in the heuristics and biases literature (Adler, 1984, 1991; Berkeley & Humphreys, 1982; Cohen, 1981, 1986; Gigerenzer, 1993, 1996a; Kahneman & Tversky, 1983, 1996; Krantz, 1981; Lopes, 1991; Nisbett, 1981) highlight the difficulties to be faced when attempting to evaluate problem construals.

ALTERNATIVE CONSTRUALS AND PROBLEM FRAMING

Disputes about the proper individuation of outcomes and principles of rational task interpretation have become common in the literature on framing effects. The Disease Problem of Tversky and Kahneman (1981) has been the subject of much contention:

> Problem 1. Imagine that the U.S. is preparing for the outbreak of an unusual disease, which is expected to kill 600 people. Two alternative programs to combat the disease have been proposed. Assume that the exact scientific estimates of the consequences of the programs are as follows: If Program A is adopted, 200 people will be saved. If Program B is adopted, there is a one-third probability that 600 people will be saved and a two-thirds probability that no people will be saved. Which of the two programs would you favor, Program A or Program B?
> Problem 2. Imagine that the U.S. is preparing for the outbreak of an unusual disease, which is expected to kill 600 people. Two alternative programs to combat the disease have been proposed. Assume that the exact scientific estimates of the consequences of the programs are as follows: If Program C is adopted, 400 people will die. If Program D is adopted, there is a one-third probability that nobody will die and a two-thirds probability that 600 people will die. Which of the two programs would you favor, Program C or Program D?

Many subjects select Alternatives A and D in these two problems despite the fact that the two problems are redescriptions of each other and that Program A maps to Program C rather than D. This response pattern violates the assumption of descriptive invariance of utility theory and such a violation severely undermines ascriptions of rationality (Shafer, 1988; Tversky, Sattath, & Slovic, 1988). However, Berkeley and Humphreys (1982) argued that the Programs A and C might not be descriptively invariant in subjects' interpretations. They argued that the wording of the outcome of Program A ("will be saved") combined with the fact that its outcome is seemingly not described in the same exhaustive way as the consequences for Program B suggests the possibility of human agency in the future that might enable the saving of more lives (see also Kuhberger, 1995). The wording of the outcome of Program C ("will die") does not suggest the possibility of future human agency working to save more lives (indeed, the possibility of losing a few more might be inferred by some people). Under such a construal of the problem, it is no longer non-normative to choose Programs A and D. Likewise, Macdonald (1986) argued that, regarding the "200 people will be saved" phrasing, "it is unnatural to predict an exact number of cases" (p. 24) and that "ordinary language reads 'or more' into the interpretation of the statement" (p. 24).

Similarly, Jou, Shanteau, and Harris (1996) argued that the Disease Problem's assumed underlying formula (Total Expected Loss – Number

Saved = Resulting Loss) is without rationale and may be pragmatically odd for various reasons. For example, they asserted that "the deaths could be construed as occurring immediately after the decision to save 200 lives, or at some indefinite time in the future. If the deaths were construed as occurring at some unknown future time, they would not likely be seen as a consequence of saving 200 lives. Hence saving the lives will not be conceived as entailing the death of 400 people" (p. 3).

Another example of a dispute about principles of rational task construal is provided by Over and Manktelow's (1993) suggestion of an alternative construal for another one of Tversky and Kahneman's (1981) problems—that many subjects would travel 20 minutes to another branch of a store to save $5 on a $15 calculator but would not make the same trip to save $5 on a $125 jacket. They suggested that the standard economic analysis of these two situations (that they are the same—both involving a choice between foregoing $5 and expending resources on a trip) fails to include factors such as unfairness and the detection of cheating as aspects in the representation of the outcomes. Over and Manktelow noted that a store that charges $15 for an item that costs $10 elsewhere might be thought to be overcharging and in the long run it might be efficacious to avoid transactions at such an establishment. In contrast, the store charging $125 for a jacket selling for $120 elsewhere would not raise the same suspicions of being cheated and would not necessitate the same cautions. In short, considerations of fairness and possible cheating might well make the two situations seem different.

Finally, Gigerenzer (1996b) discussed an example drawn from Sen (1993) on the internal consistency condition of independence of irrelevant alternatives. The principle can be illustrated by the following humorous imaginary situation. A diner is told by a waiter that the two dishes of the day are steak and pork chops. The diner chooses steak. Five minutes later, the waiter returns and says "Oh, I forgot, we have lamb as well as steak and pork chops." The diner says "Oh, in that case, I'll have the pork chops." The diner has chosen x when presented with x and y, but prefers y when presented with x, y, and z, thus violating the principle of independence of irrelevant alternatives. Yet consider a guest at a party faced with a bowl with one apple in it. The individual leaves the apple—thus choosing nothing (x) over an apple (y). The host puts another apple (z) in the bowl. A moment later, the guest takes the first apple. The diner has just chosen x when presented with x and y, but has chosen y when presented with x, y, and z. Has the independence of irrelevant alternatives been violated? Most would answer no. Choice y in the second situation is not the same as Choice y in the first—so the equivalency required for a violation of the principle seems not to hold. Whereas Choice y in the second situation is simply "taking an apple," Choice y in the first is contextualized and probably construed as "taking the last apple in the bowl when I am in public" with all of its associated negative utility inspired by considerations of politeness.

EVALUATING PRINCIPLES OF RATIONAL CONSTRUAL: THE UNDERSTANDING/ACCEPTANCE PRINCIPLE AGAIN

Discrepancies between the task interpretations that experimenters expect and those that subjects adopt might arise for two basic reasons corresponding roughly to the alternatives "it's the experimenter's fault" and "it's the subject's fault." That is, one possibility is that the experimenter has overlooked an ambiguity in the problem wording and that the subject has come to a reasonable, but different, construal of the problem. If the subject's choices then violate a normative rule based on the experimenter's construal, we would not want to impute irrationality to their choices. Alternatively, the experimenter may not have introduced a great deal of ambiguity into the problem, but nevertheless the subject might have come to a different, relatively unreasonable interpretation.

These two alternatives are really not two separate categories but instead lie on a continuum (Broome, 1990). Certainly some of these alternative construals seem better than others. For example, the argument that a 33% price differential might be grounds for suspicion seems more convincing than the argument that the statement "200 people will be saved" always leads to the inference "and maybe more." Even more strongly, construing the two apple choices as different seems eminently reasonable. But given current arguments that principles of rational construal are necessary for a full normative theory of human rationality (Broome, 1990; Einhorn & Hogarth, 1981; Jungermann, 1986; Schick, 1987, 1997; Shweder, 1987; Tversky, 1975), how are such principles to be derived?

When searching for principles of rational task construal, the same mechanisms of justification used to assess principles of instrumental rationality will be available. Perhaps in some cases—instances where the problem structure maps the world in an unusually close and canonical way—problem construals could be directly evaluated by how well they serve the decision maker in achieving their goals (Baron, 1993a, 1994a). In such cases, it might be possible to prove the superiority or inferiority of certain construals by appeals to Dutch Book or money pump arguments (Osherson, 1995; Resnik, 1987; Skyrms, 1986).

Also available will be the expert wide reflective equilibrium view discussed in chapter 1. There are of course dissenters from this view. For example, Baron (1993a, 1994a) and Thagard (1982) argued that rather than any sort of reflective equilibrium, what is needed here are "arguments that an inferential system is optimal with respect to the criteria discussed" (Thagard, 1982, p. 40). But in the area of task construal, finding optimization of criteria may be unlikely—in the case of evaluating different task construals, there will be few money pumps or Dutch Books to point the way. If in the area of task construal, there will be few money pumps or Dutch Books to prove that a particular task interpretation has disastrous consequences, then the field will be thrust back on the debate that Thagard called the argument between the populists and the elitists: "The populist strategy, favored by Cohen (1981), is to emphasize the reflective equilibrium of the average person.... The elitist strategy, favored by Stich and Nisbett (1980), is to emphasize the reflective equilibrium of experts" (p. 39).

Presumably psychologists will again find the alternative of wide expert reflective equilibrium more attractive than narrow individual equilibrium (see chap. 1). But here again lurks the conundrum that has plagued attempts to evaluate whether people follow the axioms of instrumental rationality (e.g., the independence axiom): How do we interpret situations where the majority of subjects construe tasks in ways that depart from the expert reflective equilibrium? One of the few tools that are available to help adjudicate between alternative task construals is the understanding/acceptance principle of Slovic and Tversky (1974) discussed in chapter 3. That chapter also contained an extensive discussion of how the reflective equilibrium of experts regarding principles of instrumental rationality has always been at least partially conditioned by descriptive accounts of actual behavior. In parallel to the arguments presented there, it might likewise be thought that descriptive facts about human behavior would have implications for evaluating alternative task construals. For example, there are few controversial tasks in the heuristics and biases literature where all untutored laypersons interpret tasks differently from those of the experts who designed them. Some untutored laypersons agree with the experts. Thus, the issue is not the untutored average person versus experts, but experts plus some laypersons versus other untutored individuals. The cognitive characteristics of those departing from the expert construal might—for reasons parallel to those argued in chapter 3—have implications for how we evaluate particular task interpretations. It is argued here that Slovic and Tversky's assumption ("the deeper the understanding of the axiom, the greater the readiness to accept it," pp. 372–373) can again be used as a tool to condition the expert reflective equilibrium regarding principles of rational task construal.

There has been a small amount of experimental work on framing effects that has exploited Slovic and Tversky's (1974) understanding/acceptance principle. Both methods of exploiting the principle—by manipulating understanding and by examining naturally occurring individual differences—have been examined in this research. For example, it has been found that being forced to take more time or to provide a rationale for selections reduces framing effects (Larrick et al., 1992; P. M. Miller & Fagley, 1991; Sieck & Yates, 1997; Takemura, 1992, 1993, 1994). The individual differences prediction derived from the understanding/acceptance principle—that individuals more prone to reflective thought should be more accepting of the task construals endorsed by expert reflective equilibrium—has received a small amount of support. S. M. Smith and Levin (1996) found that two different framing effects (one analogous to the famous Disease Problem of Tversky & Kahneman, 1981) were smaller among individuals higher in need for cognition (a dispositional variable associated with thoughtful analysis, deep reflection, and greater information search; see Cacioppo et al., 1996).

In research conducted with my colleague Richard West, the individual differences prediction was examined with measures of cognitive ability and need for cognition (Stanovich & West, in press). Both measures served as markers for the central assumption of the understanding/acceptance principle—that more reflective and engaged reasoners, and those with greater ability to fully understand the problem, will be more likely to adopt rational task construals. Framing effects are ideal vehicles for examining whether the understanding/acceptance principle can provide evidence relevant to alternative task construals. First, it has already been demonstrated that there are consistent individual differences across a variety of framing problems (Frisch, 1993). Second, framing problems have engendered much dispute about what are appropriate and inappropriate task interpretations.

THE DISEASE PROBLEM

The Disease Problem of Tversky and Kahneman (1981) discussed previously was one of the problems examined by Stanovich and West (in press). Two hundred and ninety-two subjects completed both versions of the problem, with 148 subjects completing the positively framed version first (termed Order 1) and 144 subjects completing the negatively framed version first (termed Order 2). The two versions were separated by several unrelated tasks.

On a between-subjects basis (i.e., considering the first problem received by both groups), an overall framing effect was demonstrated, with 67.6% of the subjects making the risk-averse choice in the positive frame and only 34.7% making the risk-averse choice in the negative frame. On a within-subjects basis, framing effects of roughly equal magnitudes were observed for the subjects in both order conditions. However, an analysis of response patterns among individual subjects also converged with earlier findings (e.g., Frisch, 1993; Schneider, 1992) in indicating that only a minority of subjects demonstrated framing effects. Across both task orders, 202 of the 292 subjects were consistent on both trials (101 were consistently risk averse and 101 were consistently risk seeking). That 69.2% of the subjects responded consistently in a within-subjects administration of this problem is in accord with the 63.6% figure obtained by Frisch. Framing effects in the expected direction (risk-seeking responses in the negative frame and risk-averse responses in the positive frame) were observed in 25.0% of the sample (73 subjects) and 5.8% of the sample (17 subjects) displayed reverse framing effects (risk-averse responses in the negative frame and risk-seeking responses in the positive frame).

Table 4.1 presents the mean SAT scores of the subjects as a function of the pattern of responding on the Disease Problem. As is apparent from Table 4.1, the subjects giving a consistent response on both problems had significantly higher SAT scores (1,115) than those subjects displaying a framing effect (1,075). The small number of subjects displaying a reverse framing effect had mean SAT scores that were intermediate between the other two groups (1,098). Thus, on the Disease Problem, the framing effect is a minority phenomenon (see Frisch, 1993; Schneider, 1992) and it is disproportionately displayed by those lower in cognitive ability. The originators of the Disease Problem (Kahneman & Tversky, 1984; Tversky & Kahneman, 1981) viewed displaying a framing effect on it as a violation of the normative principle of descriptive invariance because they viewed the two versions of the problem as isomorphs. As discussed previously, some investigators have defended interpretations of the two versions that are not isomorphic. However, the results displayed in Table 4.1 indicate that a majority of subjects concur with Tversky and Kahneman that the versions are isomorphic and these subjects were disproportionally of higher cognitive ability. This is not always the outcome, however.

THE LAUNDRY PROBLEM

Frisch (1993) discussed how the framing effect has been used in both the "strict" and the "loose" sense (see also, Sieck & Yates, 1997, for a discussion). In her studies, Frisch classified as loose "pairs of problems that aren't exactly the same, but which are equivalent from the perspective of

TABLE 4.1

Mean SAT Scores as a Function of Pattern of Responding on Various Framing and Sunk Cost Problems (Number of Subjects in Parentheses)

Problem	Framing Effect	Consistent	Reverse Framing	F Ratio
Framing Problems				
Disease Problem	1,075[a] (73)	1,115[b] (202)	1,098 (17)	3.52*
Laundry Problem	1,113[a] (190)	1,078[b] (80)	—— (7)	5.51**
Sunk Cost Problems				
Tennis Problem	1,086 (113)	1,112 (129)	1,121 (45)	2.38
Movie Problem	1,098 (164)	1,112 (127)	—— (2)	1.12

Response Patterns

Note. $df = 2, 289$ for Disease Problem; 1, 268 for the Laundry Problem; 2, 284 for the Tennis Problem; 1, 289 for the Movie Problem.
* $= p < .05$, ** $= p < .025$.
a, b = means with different superscripts are significantly different (Scheffe post hoc).

economic theory" (p. 399). Thus, Stanovich and West (in press) examined a loose framing problem in which rather large framing effects have been found—a situation in which buying and selling prices differ markedly despite the expectation under certain economic frameworks that WTP (willingness to pay) and WTA (willingness to accept) should be quite similar (Kahneman, Knetsch, & Thaler, 1990, 1991; Thaler, 1980). One such problem, the Laundry Problem, was drawn from Frisch:

1. How much would you pay someone to do your laundry for a month? $ ____
2. How much would someone have to pay you to do their laundry for a month? $ ____

Two hundred and seventy-seven subjects completed both versions of this problem, with 143 subjects completing the WTP version first and 134 subjects completing the WTA version first. The problems were separated by several unrelated tasks. On a between-subjects basis (i.e., considering the first problem received by both groups), the overall framing effect was quite large. Subjects were willing to pay someone an average $16.21 to do their laundry but would demand $69.63 to do someone else's laundry, $t(275) = 5.88, p < .001$.

An analysis of response patterns among individual subjects indicated that 190 of the 277 subjects responded with WTA > WTP, 80 subjects responded with WTA = WTP, and only 7 subjects had WTP > WTA. In Table 4.1 it is apparent that the group showing WTA > WTP had significantly higher SAT scores than the group displaying WTA = WTP. Thus, the patterns on the Laundry Problem are opposite of those on the Disease Problem.

HONORING SUNK COSTS

A person is said to be mistakenly honoring sunk costs when they persist in a nonoptimal activity because previous resources have been spent on the activity (for numerous examples, see Arkes, 1996; Arkes & Blumer, 1985; Bornstein & Chapman, 1995; Frisch, 1993; Thaler, 1980). The tendency to honor sunk costs is viewed as irrational economic behavior under traditional analyses, because actions should be determined only by future consequences, not past expenditures (Baron, 1993a, 1994a, 1998).

Frisch (1993) examined sunk cost effects as a class of framing problem because the alternative choices in the two versions of a problem were the same but one version represented an opportunity to honor sunk costs. However, under some classifications this sunk cost manipulation would not be termed a framing effect (D. Kahneman, personal communication, September 2, 1997). Stanovich and West (in press) followed Frisch's terminology in terming this a loose framing effect, but whether or not it is classified as such has no bearing on the issues discussed here. Their version of the tennis problem was adapted from Frisch (1993) and Thaler (1980). The two versions were as follows:

1. Imagine you have paid $300 to join a tennis club for 6 months. During the first week of your membership, you develop tennis elbow. It is extremely painful to play tennis. Your doctor tells you that the pain will continue for about a year. Estimate the number of times you will play tennis in the next 6 months. ____

2. Imagine you enjoy playing tennis. One day, on the court you develop tennis elbow. It is extremely painful to play tennis. Your doctor tells you that the pain will continue for about a year. Estimate the number of times you will play tennis in the next 6 months. ____

Two hundred and eighty-seven subjects completed both versions of this problem. Overall, there was a large framing effect in the direction of honoring sunk costs. When people imagined that they had paid $300 to join a club, they estimated that they would have played 5.9 times in the next six months; whereas under the same conditions, had they not paid to join a club, they estimated that they would have played 4.2 times, $t(286) = 3.64, p < .001$.

An analysis of response patterns among individual participants showed that 113 out of 287 indicated that they would have played more had they paid the $300 fee, 129 indicated that they would have played the same number of times in both circumstances, and 45 subjects displayed a reverse sunk cost effect (they indicated that they would have played fewer times had they paid the fee). Table 4.1 presents the mean SAT scores as a function of the response pattern on the Tennis Problem. There were no significant differences in cognitive ability among the three groups, although the group displaying a sunk cost effect did have the lowest mean.

After responding to the two versions of the Tennis Problem, participants were asked to respond to a comparison question adapted from Frisch (1993):

How do you compare Question 1 above to Question 2 above?

    a. the situations in 1 and 2 are really the same
    b. the situations in 1 and 2 are subjectively different
    c. the situations in 1 and 2 are objectively different

For the analyses involving this question, the group showing a sunk cost and reverse sunk cost effect were combined in order to ensure a larger N in several of the categories and because the patterns for these two groups were very similar. Table 4.2 displays a contingency table that indicates that there was a significant difference in how the two groups responded to this question ($\chi^2(2) = 84.10, p < .001$). Very few people who displayed a framing effect of some type thought that the two versions were really the same. Instead, over 50% thought that they were subjectively different and over 40% thought that they were objectively different. In sharp contrast, almost 50% of the subjects who responded identically to the two versions thought they were the same. Interestingly, however, 35.7% of the subjects who responded identically on the two versions thought that they were subjectively different.

Table 4.2 also presents the SAT scores of the individuals in the six different groups defined by the cross-classification of framing and response to the comparison question. A 2 (framing vs. consistent) × 3 (comparison question: same, subjectively different, objectively different) analysis of variance (ANOVA) conducted on the data indicated that there was a significant effect of framing response ($F(1, 281) = 7.17, p < .01$), a significant effect of comparison question response ($F(2, 281) = 4.72, p < .01$), but no interaction ($F(2, 281) = 2.26, p > .10$). The direction of the effects indicated that the subjects responding consistently tended to have higher SAT scores and the subjects who thought that the versions were subjectively different tended to be higher in cognitive ability. The highest SAT scores were obtained by the 46 people who responded similarly on the two versions but nevertheless thought that they were subjectively different. These individuals apparently thought that the subjective difference did not warrant a different response to the situation and it was these subjects who were the highest in cognitive ability.

Stanovich and West (in press) examined another sunk cost problem taken from Frisch (1993). The the two versions of the Movie Problem were:

1. You are staying in a hotel room on vacation. You paid $6.95 to see a movie on pay TV. After 5 minutes you are bored and the movie seems pretty bad. Would you continue to watch the movie or not?
   a. continue to watch
   b. turn it off

TABLE 4.2

Number of Subjects Displaying a Framing Effect on the Tennis Problem as a Function of Response on the Comparison Question and Mean SAT Scores of the Various Groups

| | Response Pattern | | | | | |
| | Framing Effect | | | Consistent | | |
	SAT	N	%	SAT	N	%
Comparison Question Response:						
Same	980	6	3.8%	1,103	64	49.6%
Subjectively Different	1,109	86	54.4%	1,128	46	35.7%
Objectively Different	1,089	66	41.8%	1,103	19	14.7%

2. You are staying in a hotel room on vacation. You turn on the TV and there is a movie on. After 5 minutes you are bored and the movie seems pretty bad. Would you continue to watch the movie or not?

   a. continue to watch

   b. turn it off

Two hundred and ninety-three subjects completed both versions of this problem. Overall, there was a large framing effect in the direction of honoring sunk costs; 62.5% of the sample thought they would watch the movie if they had paid for it, whereas only 7.2% of the sample thought they would watch the movie if they had not paid for it.

An analysis of response patterns among individual subjects indicated that 164 displayed a framing effect in which sunk costs were honored (they would watch the movie if they had paid for it but not if they had not paid for it), 127 subjects responded consistently (19 watching the movie in both cases and 108 not watching it in both cases), and 2 subjects displayed a reverse framing effect (the latter were eliminated in the analyses that follow). Table 4.1 presents the mean SAT scores of the subjects as a function of their response pattern on the Movie Problem. The difference between the group displaying a sunk cost effect and those responding consistently was not statistically significant, although the group displaying a sunk cost effect did have the lower mean.

As with the Tennis Problem, the subjects were also asked whether the two situations were really the same, subjectively different, or objectively different. Table 4.3 displays a contingency table that indicates that there was a significant difference in how the two groups responded to this question ($\chi^2(2) = 62.05$, $p < .001$). Very few subjects who displayed a framing effect thought that the two versions were really the same. Instead, 50% thought that they were objectively different and almost 50% thought they were subjectively different. In sharp contrast, over 35% of the people who responded identically to the two versions thought that they were the same. Interestingly, however, 33.9% of the subjects who responded identically on the two versions thought that they were subjectively different and 30.7% thought that they were objectively different.

Table 4.3 also presents the SAT scores of the individuals in the six different groups defined by the cross classification of framing and response to the comparison question. An ANOVA run on these SAT scores failed to yield significant effects; however, as in the Tennis Problem, the highest SAT scores were obtained by the 43 participants who responded similarly on the two versions but nevertheless thought that they were subjectively different. These individuals apparently thought that the subjective difference did not warrant a different response to the situation, and it was these subjects who were the highest in cognitive ability.

In another experiment in which over 600 individuals were tested, the Movie Problem was examined using the argument evaluation procedure described in chapter 3. The participants were administered the Movie

TABLE 4.3

Number of Subjects Displaying a Framing Effect on the Movie Problem as a Function of Response on the Comparison Question and Mean SAT Scores of the Various Groups

	Response Pattern					
	Framing Effect			*Consistent*		
	SAT	*N*	*%*	*SAT*	*N*	*%*
Comparison Question Response:						
Same	1,040	2	1.2%	1,109	45	35.4%
Subjectively Different	1,104	80	48.8%	1,134	43	33.9%
Objectively Different	1,094	82	50.0%	1,091	39	30.7%

TABLE 4.4

Mean SAT and Need for Cognition Scores as a Function of Pattern of Responding on the Movie Problem (Number of Subjects in Parentheses)

Variable	*Framing Effect*	*Consistent*	*t Value*
SAT Total	1,173 (262)	1,194 (385)	2.54*
Need for Cognition	66.4 (267)	69.1 (394)	2.80**

* $= p < .05$, ** $= p < .01$, all two-tailed.

Problem twice—with an intervening argument evaluation task. On the first administration of the task, an analysis of response patterns among individual subjects indicated that 268 displayed a framing effect in which sunk costs were honored (they would watch the movie if they had paid for it but not if they had not paid for it), 394 subjects responded consistently (15 watching the movie in both cases and 379 not watching it in both cases), and one subject displayed a reverse framing effect (this subject was eliminated from the analyses that follow). Table 4.4 indicates that the subjects displaying a sunk cost effect had significantly lower SAT scores than those responding consistently (the overall SAT scores are higher in this study because scores were derived subsequent to the April 1995 recentering by the Educational Testing Service, which raised the overall mean on the test). Additionally, individuals displaying a sunk cost effect were significantly lower in need for cognition than those responding normatively.

Subsequent to completing the Movie Problem, 105 of the participants were asked to evaluate the following argument against honoring sunk costs:

> The two situations are very similar. Once I have paid the $6.95, it is water under the bridge. Fifteen minutes after turning on the TV, I am in the same situation in both A and B: I am faced with the choice of whether it is more enjoyable to continue watching the movie or to watch regular TV. I can't get the $6.95 back, so I should forget about the money. If my enjoyment is increased by turning off the movie and watching regular TV, I should turn it off whether or not I paid for the movie. Continuing to watch the movie just because I paid $6.95 is like throwing good time after bad money. The only thing that matters is doing the thing that is most enjoyable *now*, regardless of how I arrived at the present situation.

The first analysis in Table 4.5 focuses on whether subjects changed their response pattern on the second administration of the task after evaluating a single argument explicating reasons for avoiding sunk costs. More than 44% changed their responses in the normative direction, compared with 2.9% who changed in the other direction, a difference that was statistically significant. The next analysis in Table 4.5 indicates that presenting an argument in favor of honoring sunk costs was ineffective in causing changes in the non-normative direction. The argument utilized

TABLE 4.5

Percentage of Subjects Who Changed Their Responses on the Second Administration of the Movie Problem

	One Normative Argument		
Initial Response	*N*	*% Changing Responses*	
Framing Effect	36	44.4	$\chi^2(1) = 28.75^{**}$
Consistent	69	2.9	
	One Non-Normative Argument		
Initial Response	*N*	*% Changing Responses*	
Framing Effect	45	15.6	$\chi^2(1) = 1.54$
Consistent	63	7.9	
	Both Arguments		
Initial Response	*N*	*% Changing Responses*	
Framing Effect	176	27.8	$\chi^2(1) = 46.76^{**}$
Consistent	240	4.2	

$^{**} = p < .001.$

one of the most common rationales for honoring sunk costs—that failing to do so entails waste (see Arkes, 1996)—and was as follows:

> The two situations are very different. If I had paid $6.95 for the movie and then didn't watch it, I would have wasted $6.95. If I did watch the movie, even if I was bored and didn't like it, I would have gotten something for my money so it wouldn't be a total waste. Whereas, if I had paid nothing for the movie and turned it off, nothing would be wasted.

Even after seeing this argument, more subjects moved in the normative direction than the reverse (15.6% vs. 7.9%).

A third group of 416 participants was given both arguments to evaluate after the first administration of the sunk cost task. As the third analysis in Table 4.5 indicates, after being presented with both arguments, significantly more people moved in the normative direction than in the non-normative direction (27.8% vs. 4.2%). Thus, when presented with arguments explicating reasons for both choices, subjects were much more responsive to the argument for the normative choice—avoiding honoring sunk costs. This result is consistent with the greater potency displayed by the normative argument when only one argument was presented and with the fact that the subjects responding normatively were higher in cognitive ability and need for cognition.

SUMMARY OF FRAMING AND SUNK COST RESULTS

For three of the four problems that have been considered, an application of the understanding/acceptance served to reinforce the expert consensus on the proper construal of the problem. In the Stanovich and West (in press) study, there were mild tendencies for the subjects honoring sunk costs to have somewhat lower SAT scores. For both sunk cost problems, the subjects with the highest SAT scores were those subjects who thought that the versions were subjectively different yet nonetheless responded the same to both. These may well be subjects who were conscious of having two systems of thought in conflict—a heuristic system prone to honor sunk costs because of automatically activated schemata and an analytic reasoning system prone to objective comparison and consequentialist decisions (see Evans, 1984, 1989; Evans & Over, 1996; Sloman, 1996). That the latter system ultimately determined the response is consistent with these subjects being high in analytic cognitive resources (see later discussions). In a replication experiment, subjects honoring sunk cost were significantly lower in both cognitive ability and need for cognition (see Table 4.4). Subjects were also much more responsive to an argument against honoring sunk costs than they were to an argument favoring (see Table 4.5).

The majority of subjects agree with the expert consensus that the two versions of the Disease Problem should be treated as descriptively invari-

ant. The minority who assessed the two versions differently were disproportionately of lower cognitive ability. In short, the majority of
respondents, the majority of experts, and the untutored individuals with
the greatest capacity for considered judgment all agree on a principle of
rational task construal that classifies the two versions of this problem as
descriptively invariant. As Slovic and Tversky (1974) argued, this finding
might be seen as reinforcing the expert reflective equilibrium about the
appropriate interpretation of this problem.

In sharp contrast, however, are the results on the Laundry Problem.
Not only do the majority of subjects reject the principle that WTP should
be quite close to WTA for this problem, but it is disproportionately rejected by the more cognitively able individuals. A number of hypotheses
have been put forth to explain discrepancies between WTP and WTA, including the concepts of endowment effects and status quo effects (Davis
& Holt, 1993; Kahneman et al., 1991). Rather than seeing these effects as
mechanisms leading to biased decisions, it might be thought that they are
rational principles of task construal in some situations such as the Laundry Problem. Alternatively, there may be ambiguities in the problem that
make it reasonable to code into problem representations some
nonconsequentialist factors. For example, some individuals might have
viewed one alternative as personal and the other as a transaction with a
commercial laundry. Also, it is unclear whether some subjects viewed the
question in terms of goods that could be traded or as a special one-off situation. Whatever is the case, the pattern of individual differences appears
to support a task construal where the rough equivalence for WTA and
WTP does not hold.

THE OVERCONFIDENCE EFFECT IN KNOWLEDGE CALIBRATION

Another alleged cognitive bias that has been the subject of considerable
controversy is the overconfidence effect in knowledge calibration experiments (Lichtenstein et al., 1982). In this task situation, people answer
multiple-choice or true–false questions and, for each item, provide a
judgment indicating their subjective probability that their answer is correct. It has traditionally been assumed that perfect one-to-one calibration
is the normatively appropriate response—that the set of items assigned a
subjective probability of .70 should be answered correctly 70% of the
time, that the set of items assigned a subjective probability of .80 should
be answered correctly 80% of the time, and so forth. The standard finding
of overconfidence on this task (that subjective probability estimates are
consistently higher than the obtained percentage correct) has been considered normatively inappropriate (Fischhoff, 1988; Lichtenstein et al.,
1982; Lichtenstein & Fischhoff, 1977).

However, Gigerenzer et al. (1991; Gigerenzer & Goldstein, 1996; see
also Juslin, 1994; Juslin, Winman, & Persson, 1994) argued that if the sub-

ject construes the task situation in a certain way, then some degree of overconfidence might well be considered normative. Their critique of the standard task interpretation is conceptualized within their Brunswikian theory of probabilistic mental models (PMM). In the PMM theory, people are posited to base confidence judgments on probabilistic cues that they retrieve from memory that are related to the target judgment. That is, when asked whether Philadelphia or Columbus, Ohio, has more people, an individual might retrieve the cue that Philadelphia has a major league baseball team and Columbus does not. This cue has a certain validity in the natural environment of U.S. cities (in a random selection of pairs of cities in which one has baseball team and another does not, the former has a greater than 50% probability of being the larger).

It is hypothesized that people use such probabilistic cues not only to derive the answer to the question but to determine their level of confidence. The use of cues with high ecological validity in the Brunswikian sense (Leary, 1987; Petrinovich, 1989) will lead to high degrees of confidence. Gigerenzer et al. (1991) assumed that the cue validities stored in memory are well adapted to the actual environment: "cue validities correspond well to ecological validities" (p. 510). However, overconfidence results when people employ cue validities stored in memory that are well adapted to the information in the actual environment to derive degrees of confidence about questions that have been nonrandomly sampled. For example, the baseball team cue, although highly valid for a random selection of U.S. cities, would not be as diagnostic for the types of pairs that are usually employed in knowledge calibration experiments. Such experiments most often select items that would be analogous to the comparison between Columbus and Cincinnati (here, the generally valid baseball team cue leads the assessor astray).

When in the unrepresentative environment of the typical knowledge calibration experiment, reliance on cue validities that are generally well adapted to a representative environment to derive confidence judgments will result in overconfident estimates of knowledge. In short, Gigerenzer et al. (1991) proposed that if subjects construe the task situation as appropriate for the use of their environmentally optimized cues, then overconfidence is normative. Zero overconfidence bias is only the normatively appropriate outcome if the subject construes the situation as unrepresentative and recalibrates cue validities accordingly. The fact that most studies in the literature observe a greater than zero overconfidence bias might simply indicate that most subjects adopt the former task construal (however, see Brenner, Koehler, Liberman, & Tversky, 1996; Griffin & Tversky, 1992).

Stanovich and West (1998b, Experiment 4) examined individual differences in knowledge calibration as well as another cognitive bias: the hindsight bias. The hindsight effect occurs when people overestimate what they would have known without outcome knowledge (Fischhoff, 1975, 1977; Hawkins & Hastie, 1990). It is thought to arise at least in part from egoistic or esteem-preserving motivations (J. D. Campbell & Tesser, 1983; Greenwald, 1980; Haslam & Jayasinghe, 1995; Hawkins & Hastie, 1990), and it has usually been interpreted as a non-normative response tendency: "These experiments show that people rapidly rewrite, or fabricate, memory in situations for which this seems dubiously appropriate" (Greenwald, 1980, p. 607).

The methods and analyses used in the Stanovich and West (1998b) experiment were similar to those employed in the extensive literature on knowledge calibration (Fischhoff, 1982; Ronis & Yates, 1987; Yates et al., 1989). Subjects answered 35 general knowledge questions in multiple-choice format with four alternatives. The items were not sampled randomly but were instead chosen to be relatively difficult. After answering each question, subjects made percentage estimates of their degree of confidence in their answer. The mean bias score—the mean percentage confidence judgment minus the mean percentage correct—in the sample was 7.5% (SD = 11.1), significantly different from zero ($t(200)$ = 9.67, p < .001). The positive sign of the mean score indicates that the sample as a whole displayed overconfidence, the standard finding with items of this type. An overconfidence bias was displayed by 154 (76.6%) of the 201 individuals completing this task.

Several additional measures of calibration accuracy were calculated—all standard in the literature. *Calibration-in-the-small* (termed simply calibration by Lichtenstein & Fischhoff, 1977) refers to the mean squared difference between the probability label of the category and the percentage correct in that category across all the categories (see Yates et al., 1989). It is minimized at a value of zero when a subject gets 25% of the items correct in the category labeled .25 probability, 35% of the items correct in the category labeled .35, and so forth. Two measures of discrimination were calculated for each subject. One, termed *resolution*, is the mean squared difference between the percentage correct in each category and the overall mean correct percentage summed across all the categories (see Lichtenstein & Fischhoff, 1977; Yates et al., 1989). Resolution measures "the ability of the responder to discriminate different degrees of subjective uncertainty by sorting the items into categories whose respective percentages correct are maximally different.... a steep curve shows great resolution. The higher the resolution score, the better" (Lichtenstein & Fischhoff, 1977, p. 162). Finally, a measure related to resolution is the correlation between the correctness of the subject's response (scored 0/1) and the probability judgment.

One consistent finding in the knowledge calibration literature is that the overconfidence effect is larger for more difficult items (Lichtenstein & Fischhoff, 1977, 1980; Lichtenstein et al., 1982). This fact creates problems for individual difference analyses that focus on the overconfidence effect. If a sample is partitioned based on subjects' degree of overconfidence calculated via the traditional bias score, then individuals displaying low overconfidence will inevitably have attained a higher percentage correct on the knowledge measure. Thus, any variable that correlates with knowledge (SAT scores, e.g.) will almost invariably display a negative correlation with the degree of overconfidence. This problem can be addressed by creating groups of subjects who were roughly equal in their performance on the knowledge test but who differed in their degree of overconfidence.

A 2 × 2 classification of the sample was created by a median split on the percentage of items answered correctly (creating high- and low-general-knowledge groups: high-GK and low-GK) and on the degree of overconfidence bias (creating high and low overconfidence groups: high-OC and low-OC). The performance of the high-GK/high-OC subjects was then compared to the high-GK/low-OC subjects and the performance of the low-GK/high-OC subjects was compared to that of the low-GK/low-OC subjects. Table 4.6 presents the comparisons between the performance of the two groups high in general knowledge: high-GK/low-OC and high-GK/high-OC. As is clear from the table, the groups answered roughly equal percentages of the items correct, but the

TABLE 4.6

Mean Scores of Subjects With High (N = 27) and Low (N = 53) Overconfidence Scores Who Were High Scorers on the General Knowledge Test (Standard Deviations in Parentheses)

Variable	Low-OC	High-OC	t Value
Knowledge Calibration Task			
General knowledge, % correct	62.8 (5.1)	61.6 (6.2)	−0.92
Probability estimates	61.5 (7.7)	73.8 (6.3)	7.10***
Over/underconfidence	−1.9 (5.9)	13.1 (5.5)	10.96***
Calibration	.032 (.02)	.039 (.02)	1.73
Resolution	.061 (.03)	.048 (.02)	−1.85
Correct/estimate correlation	.389 (.18)	.349 (.18)	−0.95
Hindsight Task			
Hindsight bias	2.7 (7.3)	12.7 (6.0)	6.12***
Other Variables			
SAT	1,140 (114)	1,196 (109)	2.08*
Raven matrices	10.4 (3.2)	10.5 (3.1)	0.17
Nelson–Denny comprehension	20.7 (2.2)	20.6 (2.2)	0.21
Syllogisms	5.38 (2.4)	5.85 (1.4)	0.95
Statistical reasoning	.374 (3.3)	.768 (3.3)	0.50

Note. df = 78 for all variables except SAT (df = 77), Raven matrices (df = 71), Nelson–Denny (df = 75).
* = p < .05, ** = p < .01, *** = p < .001, all two-tailed.

estimated probabilities of the high-GK/high-OC group were significantly higher, thus resulting in a significant higher overconfidence bias. In fact, the high-GK/low-OC group displayed no overconfidence at all. There was a slight tendency for the low-OC group to be better calibrated and to have better resolution, but these tendencies did not reach significance. The high-OC group did display significantly more hindsight bias ($p < .001$). The high-OC group actually had significantly higher SAT scores, although there were no significant differences obtained on the Raven matrices, Nelson–Denny comprehension, syllogistic reasoning, and statistical reasoning tasks.

Table 4.7 presents the comparisons between the performance of the two groups low in general knowledge: low-GK/high-OC and low-GK/low-OC. The low-OC group was significantly better calibrated, but neither measure of discrimination displayed a significant difference. The high-OC group did display significantly more hindsight bias ($p < .001$), thus replicating the pattern displayed by the high-GK groups. Also similar to the findings with the high-GK groups, the two low-GK groups did

TABLE 4.7

Mean Scores of Subjects With High ($N = 35$)
and Low Overconfidence ($N = 29$) Scores Who Were
Low Scorers on the General Knowledge Test
(Standard Deviations in Parentheses)

Variable	Low-OC	High-OC	t Value
Knowledge Calibration Task			
General knowledge, % correct	49.7 (5.3)	47.8 (3.5)	−1.66
Probability estimates	51.0 (7.1)	64.4 (8.1)	6.97***
Over/underconfidence	1.5 (5.6)	16.7 (7.2)	9.29***
Calibration	.032 (.02)	.064 (.03)	4.87***
Resolution	.062 (.04)	.053 (.03)	−1.02
Correct/estimate correlation	.358 (.21)	.325 (.15)	−0.72
Hindsight Task			
Hindsight bias	13.1 (7.9)	20.6 (7.3)	3.95***
Other Variables			
SAT	1,087 (108)	1,108 (66)	0.90
Raven matrices	8.4 (3.1)	8.8 (3.0)	0.52
Nelson–Denny comprehension	20.5 (2.8)	19.9 (2.8)	−0.76
Syllogisms	5.07 (2.3)	5.00 (1.7)	−0.14
Statistical reasoning	.334 (3.4)	−.659 (3.1)	−1.21

Note. $df = 62$ for all variables except SAT ($df = 59$), Raven matrices ($df = 55$), and Nelson–Denny ($df = 54$).
*** $= p < .001$, all two-tailed.

not display significant differences on the Raven matrices, Nelson–Denny comprehension, syllogisms, and statistical reasoning tasks. However, unlike the case with the high-GK groups, there was no significant difference in SAT scores.

Low overconfidence (the absence of calibration bias) failed to correlate with higher scores on any of the cognitive ability measures. Likewise, lack of bias in calibration judgments was not associated with normative$_s$ responding on other reasoning tasks. The only significant association to be found in any of these comparisons was in the opposite direction: Subjects with a low overconfidence bias who were high in general knowledge had significantly lower SAT scores. Subjects high in overconfidence bias did display greater hindsight bias. Thus, subjects who were overconfident that they *did* answer correctly (in the knowledge calibration part of the experiment) were also more overconfident that they *would have* answered correctly a problem where the correct response was indicated (in the hindsight part of the experiment). Thus, from an individual differences point of view, this task did not converge with other reasoning or cognitive ability measures in either direction. Neither the normative$_s$ response (calibration bias of zero) nor the normative$_a$ response (moderate positive calibration bias) displayed consistent correlations with other general ability or reasoning measures.[2]

THE CONJUNCTION FALLACY

Perhaps no finding in the heuristics and biases literature has been the subject of as much criticism as Tversky and Kahneman's (1983) claim to have demonstrated a conjunction fallacy in probabilistic reasoning. Most of the criticisms have focused on the issue of differential task construal, and several critics have argued that there are alternative construals of the tasks that are, if anything, more rational than that which Tversky and Kahneman regarded as normative (Adler, 1984, 1991; Hilton, 1995; Levinson, 1995; Macdonald & Gilhooly, 1990).

The Linda Problem

An example of the task interpretation criticism is provided by the most famous problem in this literature, the so-called Linda Problem (Tversky & Kahneman, 1983):

> Linda is 31 years old, single, outspoken, and very bright. She majored in philosophy. As a student, she was deeply concerned with issues of discrimination and social justice, and also participated in anti-nuclear demonstra-

---

[2]However, reliable individual differences in overconfidence bias observed across differing calibration tasks (Stankov & Crawford, 1996; West & Stanovich, 1997) may be problematic for the PMM account.

tions. Please rank the following statements by their probability, using 1 for the most probable and 8 for the least probable.

a. Linda is a teacher in an elementary school
b. Linda works in a bookstore and takes Yoga classes
c. Linda is active in the feminist movement
d. Linda is a psychiatric social worker
e. Linda is a member of the League of Women Voters
f. Linda is a bank teller
g. Linda is an insurance salesperson
h. Linda is a bank teller and is active in the feminist movement

Because Alternative h is the conjunction of alternatives c and f, the probability of h cannot be higher than that of either c or f, yet 85% of the subjects in Tversky and Kahneman's (1983) study rated Alternative h as more probable than f, thus displaying the conjunction fallacy.

It has been argued that this response pattern should not be considered a reasoning error because there are subtle linguistic and pragmatic features of the problem that serve to block the use of the conjunction rule from probability theory. Macdonald and Gilhooly (1990) argued that it is possible that:

> [Subjects will] usually assume the questioner is asking the question because there is some reason to suppose that Linda might be a bank teller and the questioner is interested to find out if she is.... If Linda were chosen at random from the electoral register and "bank teller" was chosen at random from some list of occupations, the probability of them corresponding would be very small, certainly less than 1 in 100.... the question itself has suggested to the subjects that Linda could be a feminist bank teller. Subjects are therefore being asked to judge how likely it is that Linda is a feminist bank teller when there is some unknown reason to suppose she is, which reason has prompted the question itself. (p. 59)

Hilton (1995; see Dulany & Hilton, 1991) provided a similar explanation of subjects' behavior on the Linda Problem. Under the assumption that the detailed information given about the target means that the experimenter knows a considerable amount about Linda, then it is reasonable to think that the phrase "Linda is a bank teller" does not contain the phrase "and is not active in the feminist movement" because the experimenter already knows this to be the case. If "Linda is a bank teller" is interpreted in this way, then rating h as more probable than f no longer represents a conjunction fallacy.

Morier and Borgida (1984) pointed out that the presence of the unusual conjunction "Linda is a bank teller and is active in the feminist movement" itself might prompt an interpretation of "Linda is a bank teller" as "Linda is a bank teller and is not active in the feminist movement." To avoid such an interpretation, Morier and Borgida ran a condition in which "Linda is a bank teller and is not active in the feminist movement" was included as an alternative along with "Linda is a bank teller," but this manipulation did little to reduce the conjunction fallacy. Actually, Tversky and Kahneman (1983) themselves had concerns about such an interpretation of the "Linda is a bank teller" alternative and ran a condition in which this alternative was rephrased as "Linda is a bank teller whether or not she is active in the feminist movement." They found that conjunction fallacy was reduced from 85% of their sample to 57% when this alternative was used. Macdonald and Gilhooly (1990) did observe a much larger reduction in the fallacy with the wording "Linda is a bank teller who may or may not be active in the feminist movement" (along with some other problem alterations).

Several other investigators have suggested that pragmatic inferences lead to seeming violations of the logic of probability theory in the Linda Problem (see Adler, 1991; Dulany & Hilton, 1991; Politzer & Noveck, 1991; Slugoski & Wilson, in press). Hilton (1995) summarized the view articulated in these critiques by arguing that "the inductive nature of conversational inference suggests that many of the experimental results that have been attributed to faulty reasoning may be reinterpreted as being due to rational interpretations of experimenter-given information" (p. 264). In short, these critiques imply that displaying the conjunction fallacy is a rational response triggered by the adaptive use of social cues, linguistic cues, and background knowledge (see Hilton, 1995). Because the group displaying the fallacy is in fact the majority in most studies—and because the use of such pragmatic cues and background knowledge is often interpreted as reflecting adaptive information processing (e.g., Hilton, 1995)—it might be expected that these individuals would be the subjects of higher cognitive ability.

Stanovich and West (in press) examined the performance of 150 subjects on the Linda Problem presented earlier. A within-subjects version of

TABLE 4.8
Mean SAT Total Scores of Subjects Who Gave the Correct and Incorrect Responses to the Three Conjunction Problems (Number of Subjects in Parentheses)

	Incorrect	Correct	t Value	Effect Size[a]
Linda Problem	1,080 (121)	1,162 (29)	3.58***	.746
Job Problem	1,072 (57)	1,111 (92)	2.06*	.349
Student Problem	1,075 (35)	1,103 (107)	1.28	.250

Note. $df = 148$ for the Linda Problem, 147 for the Job Problem, and 140 for the Student Problem.
* = $p < .05$, ** = $p < .01$, *** = $p < .001$, all two-tailed.
[a] Cohen's d.

the conjunction-judgment task, it represents what Tversky and Kahneman (1983) called a "direct-subtle" test of susceptibility to the conjunction fallacy—where the conjunction and its constituents are directly compared by the same subjects, but the inclusion relation is not emphasized. Consistent with the results of previous experiments on this problem (Tversky & Kahneman, 1983), 80.7% of the sample (121 participants) displayed the conjunction effect—they rated the feminist bank teller alternative as more probable than the bank teller alternative. Table 4.8 presents the mean SAT Total scores of those subjects who displayed the conjunction fallacy and those who did not. The 29 individuals who did not display the conjunction fallacy had significantly higher SAT scores, and the difference of 82 points was quite sizable. It translates into an effect size of .746, which Rosenthal and Rosnow (1991) classified as "large" (p. 446).

The Job Problem: An Easier Scenario

Reeves and Lockhart (1993) demonstrated that the incidence of the conjunction fallacy can be decreased if extensional reasoning is more strongly cued by using problems that describe the event categories in some finite population. The Job Problem was adapted from their article and used in the Stanovich and West (in press) study:

> John is a student having trouble paying his tuition. To improve his financial situation, John has applied for three different part-time jobs. For the variety-store job, there are five other applicants; for the bookstore job, there are seven other applicants; and for the shoe-sales job, there is only one other applicant. Please rank the following statements by their probability, using 1 for the most probable and 8 for the least probable. When ranking, please use each of the numbers from 1 to 8:
>
>   a. John will be offered the variety-store job
>   b. John will not be offered any job
>   c. John will be offered the shoe-sales job
>   d. John will be offered the variety-store job and the shoe-sales job
>   e. John will be offered the variety-store job or the bookstore job
>   f. John will be offered the bookstore job
>   g. John will be offered more than one job
>   h. John will be offered the bookstore job and the shoe-sales job

In contrast to the Linda Problem, where 80.7% of the sample displayed the conjunction fallacy, only 38.3% (57 subjects) rated d as more probable than a (the least probable of the two conjuncts). Table 4.8 indicates that the 92 individuals who did not display the conjunction fallacy had significantly higher SAT scores, but the difference was not as large as that displayed in the Linda Problem. The effect size of .349 is between "moderate" (.50) and "small" (.20) according to Rosenthal and Rosnow

TABLE 4.9

Mean SAT Total Scores as a Function of Performance on the Two
Additional Conjunction Problems Conditionalized on Performance
on the Linda Problem (Number of Subjects in Parentheses)

	Linda Problem	
	Incorrect	Correct
Job Problem Incorrect	1,071 (52)	——— (5)
Job Problem Correct	1,087 (68)	1,180 (24)
Student Problem Incorrect	1,065 (31)	——— (4)
Student Problem Correct	1,085 (83)	1,167 (24)

(1991, p. 446). Furthermore, as Table 4.9 indicates, the higher SAT scores
of those responding correctly on the Job Problem were almost entirely
due to those who also responded correctly on the Linda Problem. Of the
92 responding correctly on the Job Problem, the 24 who also responded
correctly on the Linda Problem had mean SAT scores of 1,180; whereas
the 68 who responded incorrectly on the Linda Problem had mean SAT
scores that were much lower (1,087) and that were not significantly different from those responding incorrectly on the Job Problem as well (1,071),
$t(118) = .80, p > .10$.

The Student Problem: Frequency Estimation

Tversky and Kahneman (1983) and Fiedler (1988) reduced the incidence
of the conjunction fallacy by having subjects estimate the frequency of the
categories rather than judge probabilities (see Gigerenzer, 1991b, 1993).
We employed the following problem (modeled on Fiedler), which encouraged the subjects to operate in frequentistic mode:

A survey of a random sample of 100 high school seniors in Columbus,
Ohio, was conducted. Please give your best estimate of the following
values:

a. How many of the 100 students were planning on attending a university
   or community college?
b. How many of the 100 students had smoked marijuana and had had in-
   tercourse?
c. How many of the 100 students had experimented with cocaine?
d How many of the 100 students participated on interscholastic sports
   teams?
e. How many of the 100 students had at least a B average and were planning on attending a university or community college?

f. How many of the 100 students had a full-time job lined up after graduation?

g. How many of the 100 students had at least a B average?

In contrast to the Linda Problem, where 80.7% of the sample displayed the conjunction fallacy, only 24.6% (35 of 142 subjects) gave Alternative e a higher frequency estimate than g (the least frequent of the two conjuncts). Table 4.8 indicates that the 107 subjects who did not display the conjunction fallacy had somewhat higher SAT scores than those who did display the fallacy, but the difference was not statistically significant and it was not nearly as large as that displayed in the Linda Problem. Furthermore, as Table 4.9 indicates, of the 107 responding correctly on the Student Problem, the 24 who also responded correctly on the Linda Problem had mean SAT scores that were quite high (1,167); whereas the 83 who responded incorrectly on the Linda Problem had mean SAT scores that were much lower (1,085) and that were not significantly different from those responding incorrectly on the Student Problem as well (1,065), $t(112) = .88, p > .10$.

Table 4.10 displays even more clearly the pattern of cognitive ability differences on the three conjunction problems. The major pattern is easily summarized. It is correct responding on the Linda Problem specifically that is associated with higher cognitive ability. As Table 4.10 indicates, subjects getting either the Job or the Student Problem correct but not the Linda Problem had SAT scores (1,076 and 1,083, respectively) only modestly higher than those subjects displaying the conjunction fallacy on all three problems (1,051). Subjects responding correctly to both the Job and Student Problems but who did not respond correctly on the Linda Problem had SAT scores (1,086) barely higher than those getting only one of the former problems correct; but subjects responding correctly on those two and the Linda Problem had substantially higher scores (1,182).

TABLE 4.10

Mean SAT Total Scores as a Function of Performance on the Three Conjunction Problems (Number of Subjects in Parentheses)

	Mean SAT Total Score
All Three Problems Incorrect	1,051 (13)
Job Problem Only Correct	1,076 (18)
Student Problem Only Correct	1,083 (35)
Job & Student Problems Correct[a]	1,086 (48)
All Three Problems Correct	1,182 (21)

[a] Linda Problem Incorrect.

ALTERNATIVE CONSTRUALS OF CONJUNCTION PROBLEMS:
A SUMMARY

Large cognitive ability differences were observed on the Linda Problem. Unlike the Disease Problem, where the framing effect was a minority phenomenon, the conjunction fallacy was displayed on this problem by a substantial majority of the subjects (80.7%); however, the minority who avoided the fallacy were considerably higher in cognitive ability. The SAT differences were substantially smaller on two problems (the Job Problem and the Student Problem) that contained features that reduce conjunction effects (event categories from an obviously finite population and frequency estimation, respectively). There has been little controversy over the construals of these two problems, however. In contrast, the proper construal of the Linda Problem has been the subject of continuing dispute. Several critics (e.g., Adler, 1984, 1991; Hilton, 1995; Levinson, 1995; Macdonald & Gilhooly, 1990) have argued that rational conversational implicatures dictate construals different from those championed by Tversky and Kahneman (1983), who themselves discussed the issue of conversational implicatures in laboratory experiments (see pp. 132–135 of Kahneman & Tversky, 1982). It has repeatedly been argued that the traditional task interpretations in the heuristics and biases literature should be revised:

- "Many critics have insisted that in fact it is Kahneman & Tversky, not their subjects, who have failed to grasp the logic of the problem" (Margolis, 1987, p. 158).

- "If a 'fallacy' is involved, it is probably more attributable to the researchers than to the subjects" (Messer & Griggs, 1993, p. 195).

Indeed, Macdonald (1986) asked, "Why do Tversky and Kahneman differ from the rest of the world in the answers to their problems?" (p. 15). As the data presented in Table 4.1 indicate, Tversky and Kahneman's interpretation does not differ from "the rest of the world" on the Disease Problem. A within-subjects comparison of choices on both versions of that problem indicates that only a minority of subjects display a framing effect and they are disproportionately of lower cognitive ability—just as the understanding/acceptance principle predicts under the assumption that the original task interpretation is appropriate.

Tversky and Kahneman's interpretation of the Linda Problem does differ from that of the majority of untutored subjects but, interestingly, their interpretation is endorsed by those who were high in analytic cognitive ability. If we accept that such individuals, like those high in need for cognition (see S. M. Smith & Levin, 1996), are more likely to deeply comprehend the problem (an assumption for which there is some evidence; see Ackerman & Heggestad, 1997; Baron, 1985b; Carroll, 1993) then according to Slovic and Tversky's (1974) understanding/acceptance principle, we might infer that this covariance between performance and cognitive ability further validates the standard construal of this problem.

ALTERNATIVE CONSTRUALS OF THE SELECTION TASK

Another problem that has spawned many arguments about alternative construals is Wason's (1966) selection task. The subject is shown four cards lying on a table showing two letters and two numbers (A, D, 3, 7). They are told that each card has a number on one side and a letter on the other and that the experimenter has the following rule (of the if P, then Q type) in mind with respect to the four cards: "If there is an A on one side of the card, then there is a 3 on the other side." The subject is then told that he or she must turn over whichever cards are necessary to determine whether the experimenter's rule is true or false. Performance on such abstract versions of the selection task is extremely low (Evans, Newstead, & Byrne, 1993; Newstead & Evans, 1995). Typically, less than 10% of subjects make the correct selections of the A card (P) and 7 card (not-Q). The most common incorrect choices made by subjects are the A card and the 3 card (P and Q) or the selection of the A card only (P).

Early on in the investigation of the selection task it was thought that the use of a real-life, but arbitrary rule such as the so-called Destination Problem ("Every time I go to Manchester I travel by train") would facilitate performance, but subsequent research has demonstrated that this is not the case (Dominowski, 1995; Evans, 1989, 1995; Griggs & Cox, 1982; Manktelow & Evans, 1979). However, one particular rule introduced by Griggs and Cox (1982) has consistently produced substantially improved performance. When testing the rule "if a person is drinking beer, then the person must be over 19 years of age" (hereafter termed the Drinking-Age Problem) and when given the four cards beer, Coke, 22, and 16 to represent P, not P, Q, and not Q, respectively, performance is markedly superior to that on the abstract selection task (Dominowski, 1995; Griggs & Cox, 1982, 1983; Pollard & Evans, 1987).

A vigorous debate has ensued over which theory can explain the robust content effects observed with rules of the type exemplified in the Drinking-Age Problem. Cosmides (1989; see also Gigerenzer & Hug, 1992) argued that such rules activate a Darwinian algorithm concerned with social exchange. In contrast, Cheng and Holyoak (1985; Cheng, Holyoak, Nisbett, & Oliver, 1986) argue that the Drinking-Age Problem triggers a pragmatic reasoning schema—a content-bound set of production rules that have been abstracted from experience with similar situations. Performance on the Drinking-Age Problem is facilitated because it fits a preexisting set of production rules for permission schemata (Holyoak & Cheng, 1995a, 1995b); whereas rules with familiar but arbitrary content ("Every time I go to Manchester I travel by train") would not trigger the same set of preexisting production rules and hence would not lead to facilitation (for extensive discussions of the ongoing controversy concerning these interpretations, see Chater & Oaksford, 1996; Cummins, 1996; Holyoak & Cheng, 1995a, 1995b; Liberman & Klar, 1996; Over & Manktelow, 1995).

Although quite different in their specifics, many of these theories seem to have the implication that the type of reasoning (or task interpretation) involved when deontic rules (reasoning about rules used to guide human behavior—about what "ought to" or "must" be done; see Manktelow & Over, 1991) are used in selection tasks is different from the type of reasoning (or task interpretation) involved when abstract rules are employed (see Griggs & Cox, 1993; Manktelow & Over, 1990). Manketelow, Sutherland, and Over (1995) argued that "deontic reasoning can be contrasted with indicative reasoning roughly along the lines of the philosophical distinction between theoretical and practical reasoning: theoretical reasoning aims to infer what is, was, or will be the case; practical reasoning, or deontic reasoning in the present context, aims to infer what one should, may, or must do" (p. 201).

The preponderance of P and Q responses in nondeontic tasks has most often been attributed to a so-called matching bias that is automatically triggered by surface-level relevance cues (Evans, 1996; Evans & Lynch, 1973), but some investigators have championed an explanation based on an alternative task construal. For example, Oaksford and Chater (1994, 1996; see also Nickerson, 1996) argued that rather than interpreting the task as one of deductive reasoning (as the experimenter intends), many people interpret it as an inductive problem of probabilistic hypothesis testing. They showed that the P and Q response is actually the expected one if an inductive interpretation of the problem is assumed along with optimal data selection (which they modeled with a Bayesian analysis).

Stanovich and West (1998a) examined individual differences in responding on a variety of abstract and deontic selection task problems. The pattern of results on a commonly used nondeontic problem with content, the Destination Problem (e.g., Manktelow & Evans, 1979), is illus-

TABLE 4.11

Mean SAT Total Scores as a Function of Response Given
on a Selection Task Using the Destination Rule
(Number of Subjects in Parentheses)

Correct	1,190	(24)
P	1,150	(38)
All	1,101	(21)
P, Q	1,095	(144)
P, Q, NQ	1,084	(14)
Other	1,070	(53)

trated in Table 4.11, which displays the mean SAT scores of subjects giving a variety of response combinations. Respondents giving the deductively correct P and not-Q response had the highest SAT scores followed by the subjects choosing the P card only. All other responses, including the modal P and Q response, were given by subjects having SAT scores some 100 points lower than those giving the correct response under a deductive construal.

In the study presented in Table 4.11 and in other studies reported in Stanovich and West (1998a) there was a consistent tendency for the incorrect response P to be associated with high SAT scores. This finding might be interpreted as indicating that Margolis (1987) was correct that some individuals develop an open reading of the task (in terms of choosing categories) rather than a closed reading (in terms of choosing cards) and that this is a reasonable construal given that it is one that is attractive to the more cognitive able individuals. Margolis demonstrated the distinction by suggesting a selection task in which subjects are given the rule: "If it says swan on one side of a card, it must say white on the other." Given the four categories of cards—swan, raven, black, white—the subjects are asked which categories they would need to examine exhaustively to test whether there has been a violation of the rule. Many people familiar with selection task do not recognize that this is not a selection task in the traditional sense. The correct answer is not that categories P and not-Q should be picked. In this open scenario, only P or not-Q need be chosen, but not both. Examining all swans will reveal any violations of the rule—as will examining all black things. But examining both provides only a redundant opportunity to see a violation. This open scenario (where one chooses categories) is different from the closed selection task scenario where one must check designated exemplars of the stated rule. If the subject views the task from an open scenario, then P-only is a reasonable choice. It is thus intriguing that the subjects opting for the P choice had, with the exception of the correct responders, the highest SAT scores.

In fact it is ironic that the hapless subject in Wason's (1969) famous "Mensa protocol" may well have had an open interpretation of the task. Perhaps it has been unfair of us to have been deriving amusement from him for over two decades! This subject, a male chemistry major, was probed about his reaction to the rule "every card that has a red triangle on one side has a blue circle on the other side." Like most people, this subject initially failed to see the relevance of the card with red circle on it (the not-Q card). Even when this card was flipped over to reveal a falsifying instance, the subject was extremely reluctant to alter his original choices and in the end announced to the experimenter "I am a member of Mensa. I wasn't going to tell you that until afterwards" (p. 479). But despite our tendency to chuckle at this, there is evidence in the protocol that the subject had an open, Margolis-type interpretation of the task, particularly when he said that "there is only one card which needs to be turned over to

TABLE 4.12

Mean SAT Total Scores of Subjects Who Gave the Correct and
Incorrect Responses to Three Different Selection Task Problems
(Numbers in Parentheses are the Number of Subjects)

	Incorrect	P & Not-Q (Correct)	t Value	Effect Size[a]
Nondeontic Problem:				
Destination Problem	1,187 (197)	1,270 (17)	3.21***	.815
Deontic Problems:				
Drinking-Age Problem	1,170 (72)	1,206 (143)	2.39**	.347
Sears Problem	1,189 (87)	1,198 (127)	0.63	.088
	P & Q	P & Not-Q	t Value	Effect Size[a]
Nondeontic Problem:				
Destination Problem	1,195 (97)	1,270 (17)	3.06***	.812

Note. df = 212 for the Destination and Sears Problems and 213 for the Drinking-Age Problem; df = 112 for the P&Q comparison on the Destination Problem.

* = p < .05, ** = p < .025, *** = p < .01, all two-tailed.
[a] Cohen's d.

prove the statement exactly: the red triangle. Strictly speaking, you don't need the blue circle. You must find every card with a red triangle on it and turn it over, but there is only one" (p. 479). In other words, the subject was arguing that in an open reading only the P category need be picked—which is correct. The fact that he was in Mensa is thus consistent with the pattern in Table 4.11 and other results reported by Stanovich and West (1998a) indicating that individuals choosing P only in the selection task tend to be of high intelligence.

The results from another study in the Stanovich and West (1998a) investigation are presented in Table 4.12 (the overall SAT scores are higher in this study because scores were derived subsequent to the April 1995 recentering of the test by the Educational Testing Service). The table presents the mean SAT scores of subjects responding correctly (as traditionally interpreted—with the responses P and not-Q) on various versions of selection task problems. One was the nondeontic Destination Problem. Those who responded correctly had significantly higher SAT scores than those who responded incorrectly and the difference was quite large in magnitude (effect size of .815).

Also presented in the table are two well-known problems (Dominowski, 1995; Griggs, 1983; Griggs & Cox, 1982, 1983; Newstead & Evans, 1995) with deontic rules—the Drinking-Age Problem mentioned previously (presented without accompanying scenario; see Stanovich &

West, 1998a) and the Sears Problem (Any sale over $30 must be approved by the section manager, Mr. Jones). Both are known to facilitate performance and this effect is clearly replicated in the data presented in Table 4.12. However, it is also clear that the differences in cognitive ability are much less in these two problems. The effect size is reduced from .815 to .347 in the case of the Drinking-Age Problem and it fails to even reach statistical significance in the case of the Sears Problem (effect size of .088). The bottom half of the table indicates that exactly the same pattern was apparent when the P and not-Q responders were compared only with the P and Q responders on the Destination Problem—the latter being the response that is most consistent with an inductive construal of the problem (see Nickerson, 1996; Oaksford & Chater, 1994, 1996).

Table 4.13 presents two contingency tables relating performance on the Destination Problem to performance on each of the two deontic problems. From the first table it is clear that the subjects who answered both the Destination and Drinking-Age Problems correctly had very high SAT scores (1,286). However, if subjects did not answer the Destination Problem correctly, then whether or not they answered the Drinking-Age Prob-

TABLE 4.13

Performance on Two Deontic Problems as a Function of Performance on the Nondeontic Destination Problem

	Drinking-Age Problem Incorrect	Drinking-Age Problem Correct
Destination Problem		
Incorrect	71 (66.3)	126 (130.7)
	[SAT = 1,173]	[SAT = 1,196]
Correct	1 (5.7)	16 (11.3)
	[——]	[SAT = 1,286]

phi coefficient = .173. $\chi^2(1) = 6.38$, $p < .025$

	Sears Problem Incorrect	Sears Problem Correct
Destination Problem		
Incorrect	85 (80.1)	111 (115.9)
	[SAT = 1,187]	[SAT = 1,187]
Correct	2 (6.9)	15 (10.1)
	[——]	[SAT = 1,270]

Note. Numbers in parentheses are the expected frequencies in that cell based on statistical independence, and numbers in brackets are the mean SAT scores.
phi coefficient = .174. $\chi^2(1) = 6.47$, $p < .025$.

lem correctly had only a very weak relationship with SAT scores. Among participants responding incorrectly on the Destination Problem, the mean SAT score of those answering the Drinking-Age Problem correctly was only 23 points higher than those answering the Drinking-Age Problem incorrectly (1,196 vs. 1,173). Similar relationships held for the Destination and Sears Problems as indicated in the second contingency table. Only the subjects answering both problems correctly had high SAT scores. Among participants responding incorrectly on the Destination Problem, the mean SAT score of those answering the Sears Problem correctly was identical to the mean score of those answering the Sears Problem incorrectly. Both tables indicate that participants answering the deontic problem correctly but failing to answer a nondeontic version of the selection task correctly failed to display significantly higher SAT scores.

Interestingly, just as in the case of the conjunction fallacy, on the selection task cognitive ability differences are strong in cases where there is a dispute about the proper construal of the task (in nondeontic tasks); but, in cases where there is little controversy about alternative construals—the deontic rules of the Drinking-Age and Sears problems—cognitive ability differences are markedly attenuated (compare Tables 4.8 and 4.12). In the next section, it is argued that an examination of individual differences among participants who complete both types of selection task might enable an elaboration of two major models of selection task performance. In chapter 5, a theoretical interpretation that spans both tasks is explored.

MODELS OF SELECTION TASK PERFORMANCE

As has been known for decades, people answering nondeontic problems correctly are few in number. The results presented in Tables 4.11 and 4.12 (and in Fig. 2.2) counter a long-standing assumption in the selection task literature that whether an individual answered correctly or not could not be predicted (see also Dominowski & Ansburg, 1996, and other studies in Stanovich & West, 1998a). For example, over 25 years ago, Wason and Johnson-Laird (1972) declared that, regarding performance on the selection task, "only the rare individual takes us by surprise and gets it right. It is impossible to predict who he will be" (p. 173). Although agreeing with Wason and Johnson-Laird on just about nothing else, Wetherick (1971) agreed with them on the unpredictability of correct responding: "in Wason's experimental situation subjects do not choose the not-Q card nor do they stand and give three cheers for the Queen, neither fact is interesting in the absence of a plausible theory predicting that they should" (p. 213). Interestingly, Wetherick used the lack of data regarding individual differences on the task to skewer Wason's assumptions about what represents correct responding: "If it could be shown that subjects who choose not-Q are more intelligent or obtain better degrees than those who do not this would make the problem worth investigation, but I have seen no evidence that this is the case" (p. 213). The studies reported in this chapter (and in chap. 2, see Fig. 2.2) in fact provide such evidence. The effect sizes of solving versus not solving a nondeontic task on SAT performance were in fact reasonably large, ranging from .502 to .859 across all of the Stanovich and West (1998a) studies and averaging .673—which is larger than moderate in most classifications of effect sizes (Rosenthal & Rosnow, 1991).

In contrast, the pattern of associations with cognitive ability on the Drinking-Age and Sears Problems is entirely different from that on nondeontic problems. These problems displayed much smaller effects of cognitive ability. Additionally, when only those participants answering nondeontic problems incorrectly were considered, there was little difference in SAT scores between solvers and nonsolvers of the Drinking-Age and Sears Problems. This finding is consistent with the conjecture that there might be a small number of individuals who respond nonheuristically to the nondeontic problems and it might be assumed that these individuals might also respond analytically on the Drinking-Age Problem. But when these people are eliminated, it cannot be assumed that the remaining solvers of the Drinking-Age Problem are responding analytically at all.

In a discussion of performance on deontic selection tasks, Manktelow et al. (1995) noted that a consideration of the pragmatic reasoning theories and social exchange theories leads inevitably to the question of "whether subjects do much indicative or theoretical reasoning as such in selection tasks" (p. 204). This quote from Manktelow et al. is simply the latest example of a long line of conjectures that the reasoning styles and/or task interpretations triggered by deontic versions of the selection task are fundamentally different from those implicated in abstract versions. Griggs (1983) argued explicitly against the view that content facilitated logical reasoning and pointed to the lack of transfer effects from thematic forms to abstract forms as one basis for his argument (see Klaczynski & Laipple, 1993). Similarly, Tweney and Yachanin (1985) argued that subjects fail "to utilize the rules of conditional logic correctly except when instructions and content change the task to one not requiring such logic" (p. 162).

However, other investigators see a certain type of continuity in the processing involved in deontic and nondeontic tasks. As discussed previously, Oaksford and Chater (1994) argued that under an inductive construal, a Bayesian model of optimal data selection fits individual choices quite well—including the modal choice of P and Q on the nondeontic task. For the deontic selection task, Oaksford and Chater developed the Bayesian model in terms of the utilities of the cards rather than their information value. They demonstrated that under certain assumptions, their model could predict the predominant choice of P and Q in the nondeontic task and P and not-Q in the deontic versions of the task. Their view is that in both tasks people are essentially optimal information processors as they perform a task that they construe as inductive and probabilistic rather than deductive. Patterns of performance in both abstract and deontic versions are optimal on a rational analysis that emphasizes optimization to the environment rather than conformity to a normative model (Anderson, 1990, 1991; Oaksford & Chater, 1994). Thus, at the broad level of optimality there is a commonality between both versions of the task in their view.

In his heuristic-analytic framework, Evans (1984, 1989, 1995, 1996) posited that people use the same generic mechanism to solve both tasks. He proposed a two-stage process of heuristic, followed by analytic, processing (the implications of the discussion that follows also hold for the more parallel conception of Evans & Over, 1996). In the first stage, basic stimulus relevance is determined by preconscious heuristic processes. A conscious analytic process then operates to justify focusing on the cards that have been given attention due to the heuristic relevance judgment ("analytic reasoning, while present, does not alter the choices made and serves only to rationalise or confirm them," Evans, 1995, p. 169). Evans (1995) hypothesized that heuristics deriving from linguistic function cue responses in the abstract selection task and that in deontic tasks "card choices are still determined by relevance, but relevance is now cued pragmatically and not linguistically" (p. 169). Thus, although the triggering cues differ, choices in both types of task are determined by heuristic processing.

The patterns of response among individuals who complete both types of selection task have implications for the dual-process framework of Evans (1984, 1995, 1996; Evans & Over, 1996) and the optimal data selection model of Oaksford and Chater (1994). Both models predict that the modal response pattern of individuals completing both tasks should be P and not-Q on deontic tasks and P and Q on nondeontic tasks (or, collectively, the set of responses traditionally considered "incorrect" on this task, [P]; [P,Q, not-Q]; etc.). Beyond this group of modal individuals, there may be processing implications depending on the distribution of participants in the remaining cells (individuals getting both items correct; those getting the deontic problem incorrect and the nondeontic problem correct; etc.). For example, the individuals in the remaining cells may simply represent error variance around the modal response—that is, probabilistic straying from optimal data selection as conceived in the model of Oaksford and Chater. If this is the case, the bivariate distribution of responses should be characterized by statistical independence. Alternatively, some individuals straying from the modal bivariate response might represent a subgroup of individuals who are systematically deviant from the response predicted by the rational model of Oaksford and Chater (and the two-process view of Evans) because they *are* viewing the nondeontic task as a problem of deductive logic and are reasoning analytically to their choices (rather than just rationalizing the heuristically determined responses, as in the two-process view). If such a subgroup exists, then we might expect the cell representing correct responding on both deontic and nondeontic tasks to be overrepresented. Thus, unlike the view that individuals deviating from the modal response are error variance, the subgroup hypothesis predicts a dependence in responding across the two tasks. The magnitude of the dependence in responding could be viewed as an index of the size of the subgroup of analytic responders.

The first contingency table displayed in Table 4.13 indicates that performance on the Destination and Drinking-Age Problems was significantly associated ($\chi^2(1) = 6.38, p < .025$). Although 94.1% of the participants getting the Destination Problem correct also got the Drinking-Age Problem correct, only 64.0% getting the Destination Problem incorrect got the Drinking-Age Problem correct. Another theoretically important way of viewing the association is to note that individuals making the modal selection on the Drinking-Age Problem (P and not-Q) were more likely to make a particular *non*modal selection on the nondeontic problem (again, P and not-Q). As the discrepancies between the observed and expected cell frequencies indicate, there was an excess of individuals in the incorrect/incorrect and correct/correct cells.

The next contingency table indicates that there was a similar dependence between performance on the Destination Problem and Sears Problem that attained statistical significance. The significant association was again in the direction where the incorrect/incorrect and correct/correct cells were over-represented. Thus, in the case of each of these comparisons, individuals responding with the P and not-Q choice on one problem were disproportionately likely to respond by choosing that pair on the other. The significant deviation from statistical independence that consistently tends in this direction is probably due to the existence of a subset of individuals who are viewing the nondeontic task as a problem of deductive logic and are reasoning analytically to their choices.

A slight modification of the dual-process view (Evans, 1996; Evans & Over, 1996) might also explain the tendency for the correct/correct cell to be overpopulated in Table 4.13. Part of the title of a recent article (Evans, 1996)—"deciding before you think"—sums up the two-process framework. Evans argued that abstract or other nondeontic versions of the selection task "may not be a reasoning task at all, in the sense that it may fail to elicit any cognitive process of the type we would wish to describe as reasoning" (p. 224). If we view the responses of the vast majority of incorrect responders in nondeontic versions as dominated by a preconscious relevance judgment (see Evans and Over, 1996, for the most recent discussion of the dual-process view), we are still left with the small proportion of correct responders. Are these individuals random variation (as the earlier quotes from Wetherick and Wason & Johnson-Laird seem to assume), or might these be individuals who are approaching the task in a more analytic manner? Perhaps instead of an analytic stage dominated by attempts to justify the early heuristic attentional responses, some individuals use the analytic processing stage to critically examine the implications of turning all of the cards—not just the ones brought to attention through a preconscious relevance judgment. That is, some individuals might actually think before they decide. And if we view intelligence as encompassing important self-regulatory and metacognitive components (Byrnes, 1995; Sternberg, 1985), then we might well expect the individuals who think before they decide to be individuals of higher cognitive ability.

In short, what the results like those presented in Table 4.12 may be indicating is that in the abstract task, and in various versions of nondeontic problems with thematic content, a considerable amount of thinking is required before deciding—because the early heuristic relevance judgments must be overcome. However, in the Drinking-Age Problem, it is possible to be correct by deciding without thinking because the early pragmatic relevance judgments cue the correct response. With this rule, it is fine to think only after you decide because preconscious heuristics lead to the correct response.

The heuristic-analytic framework fits particularly well with the Stanovich and West (1998a) results because Evans and Over (1996) linked their notion of preconscious, heuristic processing with work in the implicit learning tradition (Reber, 1993). Specifically, they endorsed Reber's view of such preconscious, tacit processes as evolutionarily more ancient, more robust in the face of insult, less variable, and less related to intelligence than conscious processes. The latter assumption, for which there is some empirical evidence (McGeorge, Crawford, & Kelly, 1997; Reber, Walkenfeld, & Hernstadt, 1991), is the crucial one for the purposes of explaining the cognitive ability differences apparent in Tables 4.11 and 4.12. In nondeontic selection tasks, the preconscious relevance heuristic cues a response (P and Q) that is different from the one that will be deemed correct under a deductive construal. The latter construal will result only if conscious, analytic processing overcomes the heuristic cuing. Because the conscious mechanism is related to intelligence, individuals adopting this construal will tend to be of higher cognitive ability.

In contrast, in deontic problems, both deontic and rule-based logics are cuing construals of the problem that dictate the same response (P and not-Q). Whatever is one's theory of responding in deontic tasks—preconscious relevance judgments, pragmatic schemas, Darwinian algorithms, or evolutionarily maximized expected utility (for extensive discussions of the ongoing controversies, see Chater & Oaksford, 1996; Cheng & Holyoak, 1989; Cosmides, 1989; Cummins, 1996; Gigerenzer, 1995; Gigerenzer & Hug, 1992; Holyoak & Cheng, 1995a, 1995b; Kirby, 1994; Liberman & Klar, 1996; Over & Manktelow, 1995)—the mechanisms are likely tacit in the sense of Evans and Over (1996) and Reber (1993) and thus are unlikely to be strongly associated with analytic intelligence.

Hence, such processes will draw subjects of both high and low analytic intelligence to the same response dictated by the rule-based system and thus will serve to dilute cognitive ability differences between correct and incorrect responders.

An informal simulation of how individual differences in cognitive ability are manifested and attenuated in selection tasks is presented in Table 4.14. Following Evans (1995), we propose that the matching response (P and Q) is triggered by a preconscious linguistic heuristic. The top of Table 4.14 indicates that, on an abstract problem from Study 2 of Stanovich and West (1998a), the 140 individuals who gave this response had mean SAT scores of 1,091. The 34 individuals choosing P and not-Q had a mean SAT score of 1,159. These are assumed to be individuals who reasoned analytically to the correct solution. As a simplifying assumption, the individuals in the remaining response categories (P; All; P,Q,not-Q; Other) are assumed to be individuals for whom analytic processing also overrode heuristic processing but who did not analytically reason to the correct solution. These individuals had mean SAT scores higher than the heuristic responders (1,107 vs. 1,091), but lower than the correct responders. The sizable number of analytic processors who did not solve the problem is consistent with O'Brien's (1995) argument that for a mental logic without direct access to the truth table for the material conditional, the selection task is a very hard problem. This subgroup, when combined with the heuristic responders, yields an overall SAT mean for the incorrect responders of 1,098—61 points below the mean of the correct responders.

The next analysis in Table 4.14 simulates how the difference between correct and incorrect responders would change upon presentation of a deontic problem such as the Drinking-Age Problem. Two strong assumptions are made, but moderate relaxation of either assumption leaves the essential lesson to be drawn from the simulation unchanged. The first assumption is that the heuristic processors remain heuristic processors, but the relevance cue is now pragmatic rather than linguistic (see Evans, 1995) and in the context of the Drinking-Age Problem cues the correct response (P & not-Q). The second assumption is that the analytic processors remain analytic processors. The simulated means indicate that the shift in heuristics has totally eliminated the difference in mean SAT scores between the groups of correct and incorrect responders. It is also easy to see that a relaxation of the second assumption (that the analytic processors remain analytic processors) would have virtually no effect on this pattern.

In short, it is posited that correct responders on nondeontic tasks are largely analytic processors; whereas, the group of correct responders on deontic tasks such as the Drinking-Age and Sears Problems is comprised of a small number of analytic processors and a much larger group of heuristic processors. Once the former are removed from the group of correct responders, the latter are no more likely to be of high cognitive ability than

TABLE 4.14

Simulation of Differences in Mean SAT Scores
Assuming the Heuristic-Analytic Account of Individual Differences
(Number of Participants in Parentheses)

Actual Data From Abstract Task of Study 2 in Stanovich and West (1998a)

	Incorrect	Correct
Heuristic 1 (Linguistic Relevance; see Evans, 1995) Response = P&Q	1,091 (140)	
Analytic Failure (P; All; P,Q,not-Q; Other)	1,107 (120)	
Analytic Success P and not-Q		1,159 (34)
Actual Mean	1,098	1,159

Simulated Drinking-Age Problem Results Based on a Total Heuristic Change

	Incorrect	Correct
Heuristic 1 (Linguistic Relevance; see Evans, 1995) Response = P&Q	——	
Heuristic 2 (Pragmatic Relevance; see Evans, 1995) Response = P & not-Q		1,091 (140)
Analytic Failure (P; All; P,Q,not-Q; Other)	1,107 (120)	
Analytic Success P and not-Q		1,159 (34)
Simulated Mean	1,107	1,104
Actual Mean	1,110	1,104

are those who gave an incorrect response (see Table 4.13). Consistent with Evans and Over's (1996) and Reber's (1993) speculations about individual differences, it is responses determined by analytic processing that create differences in cognitive ability. In contrast, correct responses determined by heuristic processes serve to dilute such differences.

The results of our studies thus suggest a refinement in the theories of optimal data selection that assume that people view the task as an inductive problem of probabilistic hypothesis testing (e.g., Evans & Over, 1996; Nickerson, 1996; Oaksford & Chater, 1994). Such theories may well account for the performance of the majority of individuals. However, the results reported by Stanovich and West (1998a) suggest that perhaps 10% of the participants—disproportionately those of higher cognitive ability—do view the task as a deductive problem, do reason analytically, and thus will display performance patterns that will not be well fit by these theories. Who these individuals are can be predicted by their performance on other nondeontic problems and by their general cognitive ability. For example, in one of Stanovich and West's (1998a) studies, participants who were above the median in cognitive ability and who answered two other nondeontic problems correctly had an over 85% chance of answering a further nondeontic problem correctly. Models of optimal data selection should fit selection task results better if these individuals are eliminated from the analysis, because individuals of higher cognitive ability may be more likely to override evolutionarily optimized computations in order to pursue a normative solution.

Finally, these results have implications for the arguments of the champions of human rationality who have been at pains to defend the modal response of P and Q on abstract tasks and P and not-Q on deontic tasks as arising from the same basic and rational thought processes (Wetherick, 1995). The pragmatic reasoning theories and social exchange theories appear problematic for this view. As Dominowski and Ansburg (1996) argued:

> Although the formally-correct cards are selected, there might be no reasoning taking place—i.e., the person might simply have learned what to do in the situation presented. At best, success might reflect narrow reasoning processes strictly tied to a particular kind of content. No content-free reasoning processes are assumed to play a role. In short, these accounts characterize successful performance on thematic problems as rather isolated behavior. (p. 5)

This was precisely Wetherick's concern. He rejected the "theoretical superstructures that have been erected to explain apparently 'correct' performance on these aberrant versions of the four-card task [because the pragmatic and social exchange theories are] irrelevant. Ordinary logic is sufficient to show that, in every case, intelligent subjects do what intelligent subjects would be rationally expected to do" (p. 439).

As discussed in chapter 3, Wetherick (1995) is a Panglossian theorist who seeks support in findings about individual differences when attempting to defend the idea of perfect human reasoning competence. In this case, he sought support in some unpublished findings reported by Dominowski and Dallob (1991; see also Dominowski & Ansburg, 1996). They reported that performance on abstract and thematic tasks was correlated and was also related to scores on several general reasoning tests. Wetherick argued that these results contradict the view that different mental mechanisms are involved in the abstract and deontic versions of the task. Instead, Wetherick viewed the results as supporting the notion that both types of task "call on the same mental processes. I would argue that the preceding argument of this section suggests strongly that these processes are the processes of ordinary logic" (p. 440).

But Wetherick's (1995) citing of Dominowski and Dallob's study in this context is puzzling because that study (as did all of the selection task studies discussed in this chapter) revealed correlations with what is *typically* considered to be the normative response on the abstract task (P and not-Q)—not with the response Wetherick considered to be normative and rational (P and Q; in fact, he argued that people who fail to give the P and not-Q response "are to be congratulated," Wetherick, 1970, p. 214). Similarly, in Dominowski's work—as in ours—it was the P and not-Q responders who displayed higher cognitive ability, not the P and Q responders.

CONCLUSIONS

The sampling of results just presented has produced a varied pattern of outcomes resulting from the application of the understanding/acceptance principle. Application of the principle to the knowledge calibration experiment failed to adjudicate between the traditional interpretation of overconfidence as a cognitive bias and overconfidence as the expected finding when using environmentally optimized cues in an unrepresentative knowledge calibration environment. The magnitude of the overconfidence effect was unrelated to cognitive ability and to normative$_s$ responding on other tasks. In contrast, the results indicated that the normative$_s$ response on a well-known framing problem (the Disease Problem), on the Linda Problem (a conjunction problem), and on the nondeontic selection task was consistently associated with higher cognitive ability. How might we interpret this consistent pattern displayed on three tasks from the heuristics and biases literature where alternative task construals have been championed? In the next chapter, a unifying framework for conceptualizing the results from these three tasks is introduced.

Dual-Process Theories
and Evolutionary Adaptation
Versus Normative Rationality

In chapter 4, three tasks from the heuristics and biases literature displayed large individual differences in cognitive ability between those who solved the problem and those who did not. One possible interpretation of the consistent pattern across these three problems is in terms of two-process theories of reasoning (Epstein, 1994; Evans, 1984, 1996; Evans & Over, 1996; S. A. Sloman, 1996). For example, Sloman distinguished an associative processing system with computational mechanisms that reflect similarity and temporal contiguity from a rule-based system that operates on symbolic structures having logical content. The key feature that signals the operation of both systems in a reasoning situation is that of simultaneous contradictory belief—"a feeling or conviction that a response is appropriate even if it is not strong enough to be acted on" (Sloman, 1996, p. 11). Certainly such a conflict can be said to be present for the 50.4% of the subjects who responded identically to both versions of the Tennis Problem despite viewing them as subjectively or objectively different (and the 64.6% who did so in the Movie Problem).

S. A. Sloman (1996) viewed the Linda Problem as the quintessence of this type of situation. He quoted Stephen Gould's (1991) introspection that "I know the [conjunction] is least probable, yet a little homunculus in my head continues to jump up and down, shouting at me—'but she can't be a bank teller; read the description'" (p. 469). According to Sloman, the associative system responds to the similarity (representativeness in the terminology of Tversky & Kahneman, 1983) in the conjunction; whereas the rule-based system engages probabilistic concepts that dictate that bank teller is more probable. A parallel analysis could be made using the dual-process theory of Evans (1996; Evans & Over, 1996) "in which tacit and parallel processes of thought combine with explicit and sequential processes in determining our actions" (Evans & Over, 1996, p. 143).

INTERACTIONAL INTELLIGENCE

It is conjectured here that large differences in cognitive ability will be found only on problems that strongly engage both reasoning systems and in which the reasoning systems cue opposite responses. This is because individual differences in the two systems are identified with different types of intelligence. Clearly, the rule-based system embodies analytic intelligence of the type measured on SAT tests and identified with psychometric g (Brody, 1997; Carroll, 1993, 1997; Lubinski & Humphreys, 1997). The associative system, in contrast, might be better identified with what Levinson (1995) termed interactional intelligence. He speculated that evolutionary pressures were focused more on negotiating cooperative mutual intersubjectivity than on understanding the natural world (see also Cummins, 1996; Gigerenzer, 1996b). Because he viewed the primary evolutionary pressures as intraspecific, he posited that there is "a systematic bias in human thinking in other domains which might be attributed to the centrality of interactional intelligence in our intellectual makeup" (p. 223). Having as its goals the ability to model other minds in order to read intention and to make rapid interactional moves based on those modeled intentions, interactional intelligence is composed of the mechanisms that support a Gricean theory of communication that relies on intention-attribution. These pragmatic heuristics have, according to Levinson, the property of speed and also of nonmonotonicity. They are subjectively determinate rather than probabilistic.

The interactional intelligence behind conversational understanding operates with an important default—that the conversational puzzles it is trying to solve were "*designed* to be solved and the clues have been designed to be sufficient to yield a determinate solution" (p. 238). Levinson (1995) proposed that this assumption poses "spill-over" problems when interactional intelligence—rather than analytic intelligence—is used to decode nondeterminate and nondesigned problems such as theories about nature and the human body. As a result:

> We see design in randomness, think we can detect signals from outer space in stellar X-rays, suspect some doodles on archaeological artifacts to constitute an undiscovered code, detect hidden structures in Amazonian myths. If we are attuned to think that way, then that is perhaps further evidence for the biases of interactional intelligence: in the interactional arena, we must take all behaviour to be specifically designed to reveal its intentional source. (p. 245)

Levinson (1995) pointed out the formal similarity of the properties of interactional intelligence to some of the properties of Tversky and

Kahneman's (1974, 1981, 1983) heuristics (salience, prototypicality, representativeness). However, Levinson, like Hilton (1995), viewed the pragmatic heuristics not as "logically suboptimal rules of thumb" (Hilton, 1995, p. 265) to be used when time or energy limitations do not permit the optimal response to be computed with more accurate mechanisms. Instead, the pragmatic heuristics are rational solutions to problems in another domain. The former view predicts, for example, that increasing incentives should result in the abandonment of rule-of-thumb heuristics for more accurate mechanisms. In contrast, Hilton argued that "it is not clear why increasing the financial stakes in an experiment should cause respondents to abandon an interpretation that is pragmatically correct and rational.... Incentives are not going to make respondents drop a conversationally rational interpretation in favor of a less plausible one in the context" (pp. 265–266). It is interesting that although Hilton thought financial incentives will not have such an effect, more cognitive resources (Stanovich & West, 1998a, in press), more engagement with the problem (S. M. Smith & Levin, 1996), and more time (Takemura, 1992) do seem to move subjects away from the "conversationally rational interpretation" of several of the problems discussed in this book. More so than financial incentives, cognitive ability, engagement, and time all result in a higher ratio of the analytic to interactional resources that are committed to the problem.

A GENERIC DUAL-PROCESS FRAMEWORK

A summary of the two-process view that provides the framework for the remainder of this volume is presented in Table 5.1. The dual-process terms of several major theorists are presented in the table. Although the details and technical properties of these dual-process theories do not always match exactly, nevertheless there are clear family resemblances (for discussions, see Evans & Over, 1996; Gigerenzer & Regier, 1996; Sloman, 1996). In order to emphasize the prototypical view that is adopted here, the two systems have simply been generically labeled System 1 and System 2. The key differences in the properties of the two systems are listed next. System 1 is viewed as encompassing primarily the processes of interactional intelligence. It is automatic, largely unconscious, and relatively undemanding of computational capacity. Thus, it conjoins properties of automaticity and heuristic processing as these constructs have been variously discussed in the literature. System 2 conjoins the various characteristics that have been viewed as typifying controlled processing. System 2 encompasses the processes of analytic intelligence that have traditionally been studied in psychometric work and that have been examined by information-processing theorists trying to uncover the computational components underlying psychometric intelligence.

The work of Pollock (1991) is included in the table in order to indicate that aspects of the two-process conception are shared by some investiga-

TABLE 5.1

The Terms for the Two Systems Used by a Variety of Theorists and the Properties of Dual-Process Theories of Reasoning

	System 1	System 2
Dual-Process Theories:		
Sloman (1996)	associative system	rule-based system
Evans (1984, 1989)	heuristic processing	analytic processing
Evans & Over (1996)	tacit thought processes	explicit thought processes
Reber (1993)	implicit cognition	explicit learning
Levinson (1995)	interactional intelligence	analytic intelligence
Epstein (1994)	experiential system	rational system
Pollock (1991)	quick & inflexible modules	intellection
Hammond (1996)	intuitive cognition	analytical cognition
Klein (1998)	recognition-primed decisions	rational choice strategy
Properties:	associative	rule-based
	holistic	analytic
	automatic	controlled
	relatively undemanding of cognitive capacity	demanding of cognitive capacity
	relatively fast	relatively slow
	acquisition by biology, exposure, and personal experience	acquisition by cultural and formal tuition
Task Construal:	highly contextualized	decontextualized
	personalized	depersonalized
	conversational and socialized	asocial
Type of Intelligence Indexed:	interactional (conversational implicature)	analytic (psychometric IQ)

tors attempting to implement intelligence and rationality in computer models—and also because he theorized explicitly about the override function of System 2. In his view, System 1 is composed of Q&I (quick & inflexible) modules that perform specific computations. System 2 processes are grouped under the term intellection in his model and refer to all explicit reasoning in the service of theoretical or practical rationality: "The advantage of Q&I modules is speed. The advantage of intellection, on the other hand, is extreme flexibility. It seems that it can in principle deal with any kind of situation, but it is slow" (p. 192).

As an example, Pollock (1991) mentioned the Q&I trajectory module that predicts the movement path of objects in motion. The Q&I module for this computation is quite accurate, but it relies on certain assumptions about the structure of the world. When these assumptions are violated, then the module must be overridden by System 2 processing. So when a baseball approaches a telephone pole, "we had best wait until it ricochets before predicting its trajectory. Our built-in trajectory module cannot handle this situation accurately, so we use intellection to temporarily override it until the situation becomes one that can be handled accurately by the trajectory module" (p. 191). Pollock stressed, however, that Q&I modules do not just operate in the domains of movement and perception but instead that "everyday inductive and probabilistic inference is carried out by Q&I modules" (p. 191).

For the purposes of the present discussion, the most important difference between the two systems is that they tend to lead to different types of task construals. Construals triggered by System 1 are highly contextualized, personalized, and socialized. They are driven by considerations of relevance and are aimed at inferring intentionality by the use of conversational implicature even in situations that are devoid of conversational features (see Margolis, 1987). In chapter 7 these properties of contextualization and personalized construal are discussed further and are labeled the *fundamental computational bias*. In contrast, System 2's more controlled processes serve to decontextualize and depersonalize problems—this system is more adept at representing in terms of rules and underlying principles. System 2 can accept the asocial nature of certain problems and is not dominated by the goal of attributing intentionality or by the search for conversational relevance.

Using the distinction between System 1 and System 2 processing, it is conjectured here that in order to observe large cognitive ability differences in a problem situation, two conditions are necessary. First, the task must engage both the associative and the rule-based system. This will happen quite often because, as Evans and Over (1996) noted, "almost all reasoning tasks show evidence of a logical and non-logical component of performance" (p. 144). Second, these two systems must strongly cue different responses.[1] It is not enough simply that both systems are engaged. If both cue the same response (as in deontic selection task problems), and if most people's responses are more strongly determined by the associative system, then this could have the effect of severely diluting any differences in cognitive ability (see the demonstration illustrated in Table 4.14).

One reason that this outcome is predicted is that it is assumed that individual differences in interactional intelligence bear little relation to individual differences in analytic intelligence. This is a conjecture for which there is a modest amount of evidence. Reber (1993) showed precon-

---

[1]Of course, another way that cognitive ability differences might be observed is if the task engages only the rule-based system. For the present discussion, this is an uninteresting case.

scious processes to have low variability and to show little relation to analytic intelligence. For example, individual differences in implicit associative induction have displayed much smaller correlations with analytic intelligence than have individual differences in rule-based reasoning (McGeorge et al., 1997; Reber et al., 1991). Furthermore, direct indicators of interactional intelligence have displayed very low correlations with measures of analytic intelligence (Jones & Day, 1997; Matthews & Keating, 1995).

If these conjectures are correct, then the associative system will equally cue subjects of high and low analytic intelligence. Thus, if the associative system is the dominant cue to a response that is also signaled by the rule-based system, it will tend to dilute any cognitive ability differences by drawing equally to the response individuals high and low in analytic intelligence. In contrast, if the two systems cue opposite responses, the rule-based system will tend to differentially cue those of high analytic intelligence and this tendency will not be diluted by the associative system nondifferentially drawing subjects to the same response (again, refer to Table 4.14). For example, the Linda Problem maximizes the tendency for the associative and rule-based systems to prime different responses and this problem produced a large difference in cognitive ability. As Kahneman and Tversky (1996) noted, "the within-subjects design addresses the question of how the conflict between the heuristic and the rule is resolved" (p. 587). The other two conjunction problems removed some of the conflicts between the two systems (primarily the tendency for the associative system to cue a nonextensional response) and the cognitive ability difference decreased on these two problems.

Similarly, in nondeontic selection tasks there is ample opportunity for the two systems to cue different responses. A deductive interpretation conjoined with an exhaustive search for falsifying instances yields the response P and not-Q. This interpretation and processing style is likely associated with S. A. Sloman's (1996) rule-based system (System 2)—individual differences in which underlie the psychometric concept of analytic intelligence. In contrast, within the heuristic-analytic framework of Evans (1984, 1989, 1996), the matching response of P and Q reflects the heuristic processing of System 1 (in Evans' theory, a linguistically cued relevance response).

In contrast, in deontic problems, both deontic and rule-based logics are cuing construals of the problem that dictate the same response (P and not-Q). Whatever is one's theory of responding in deontic tasks—preconscious relevance judgments, pragmatic schemas, or Darwinian algorithms—the mechanisms triggering the correct response resemble heuristic or modular structures that fall within the domain of System 1. These structures are unlikely to be strongly associated with analytic intelligence (Cummins, 1996; Levinson, 1995; McGeorge et al., 1997; Reber, 1993; Reber et al., 1991), and hence they operate to draw subjects of both high and low analytic intelligence to the same response dictated by the rule-based system—thus serving to dilute cognitive ability differences between correct and incorrect responders (see Table 4.14).

ALTERNATIVE TASK CONSTRUALS: EVOLUTIONARY ADAPTATION VERSUS NORMATIVE RATIONALITY

The experimental results reviewed in chapter 4 have demonstrated that the construal favored by the inventors of the Linda Problem (Tversky & Kahneman, 1983), Disease Problem (Tversky & Kahneman, 1981), and selection task (Wason, 1966) is the construal favored by people of high analytic intelligence. The alternative construals favored by the critics of the heuristics and biases literature were the choices of the individuals of lower analytic intelligence.[2] In the remainder of this chapter, we explore the possibility that these alternative construals may be triggered by heuristics that make evolutionary sense, but that subjects higher in a more flexible type of analytic intelligence are more prone to follow normative rules that maximize personal utility. In a restricted sense, such a pattern might be said to have relevance for the concept of rational task construal.

When interpreting these outcomes, it helps to distinguish between evolutionary adaptation and instrumental rationality (utility maximization given goals and beliefs). The key point is that for the latter (variously termed practical, pragmatic, or means/ends rationality), maximization is at the level of the individual person. Adaptive optimization in the former case is at the level of the genes (Dawkins, 1976, 1982). For example, Anderson (1990, 1991) emphasized this distinction in his treatment of adaptionist models in psychology. In his advocacy of such models, Anderson eschewed Dennett's (1987) assumption of perfect rationality in the instrumental sense (hereafter termed *normative rationality*) for the somewhat different assumption of evolutionary optimization (i.e., evolution as a local fitness maximizer). Anderson (1990) accepted Stich's (1990; see also W. S. Cooper, 1989; Skyrms, 1996) argument that evolutionary adaptation (hereafter termed *evolutionary rationality*) does not guarantee perfect human rationality in the normative sense:

> Rationality in the adaptive sense, which is used here, is not rationality in the normative sense that is used in studies of decision making and social judgment.... It is possible that humans are rational in the adaptive sense in the domains of cognition studied here but not in decision making and social judgment. (p. 31)

---

[2]Again, the reader is reminded that the results do not always go in this direction (see chap. 3 and the results on the overconfidence effect and Laundry Problem reported in chap. 4).

Thus, Anderson (1991) acknowledged that there may be arguments for "optimizing money, the happiness of oneself and others, or any other goal. It is just that these goals do not produce optimization of the species" (pp. 510–511). As a result, a descriptive model of processing that is adaptively optimal could well deviate substantially from a normative model. This is because Anderson's (1990, 1991; see also Oaksford & Chater, 1994) adaptation assumption is that cognition is optimally adapted in an evolutionary sense—and this is not the same as positing that human cognitive activity will result in normatively appropriate responses.

Similarly, Gigerenzer (1996b; see also W. S. Cooper, 1989) pointed out that neither rats nor humans maximize utility in probabilistic contingency experiments. Instead of responding by choosing the most probable alternative on every trial, subjects alternate in a manner that matches the probabilities of the stimulus alternatives. This behavior violates normative strictures on utility maximization, but Gigerenzer demonstrated how probability matching could actually be an evolutionarily stable strategy (see Skyrms, 1996, for many such examples). Again, in this example, evolutionary rationality has dissociated from normative rationality—where the latter is viewed as utility maximization for the individual organism (instrumental rationality) and the former is defined as survival probability at the level of the gene (Dawkins, 1976, 1982).

Such a view can encompass both the impressive record of descriptive accuracy enjoyed by a variety of adaptionist models (Anderson, 1990, 1991; Oaksford & Chater, 1994, 1996) as well as the fact that cognitive ability sometimes dissociates from the response deemed optimal on an adaptionist analysis (Stanovich & West, 1998a). As discussed earlier, Oaksford and Chater (1994) have had considerable success in modeling the nondeontic selection task as an inductive problem in which optimal data selection is assumed (see also, Oaksford, Chater, Grainger, & Larkin, 1997). Their model predicts the modal response of P and Q and the corresponding dearth of P and not-Q choosers. Similarly, Anderson (1990) modeled the 2 × 2 contingency assessment experiment (see chap. 2; Stanovich & West, 1998c; Wasserman et al., 1990) using a model of optimally adapted information processing. He demonstrated that an adaptive model can predict the much-replicated finding that the D cell (cause absent and effect absent) is vastly underweighted and concluded that "this result makes the point that there need be no discrepancy between a rational analysis and differential weighting of the cells in a 2 × 2 contingency table" (p. 160). Anderson's (1990) adaptionist model predicts the modal departure from the normative$_s$ analysis of the task—the Δp statistic of conditional probability, which dictates that the cells be equally weighted (see Allan, 1980; Kao & Wasserman, 1993; Shanks, 1995). Finally, a host of investigators (Adler, 1984, 1991; Dulany & Hilton, 1991; Hilton, 1995; Levinson, 1995) have stressed how a model of rational conversational implicatures predicts that violating the conjunction rule in the Linda Problem reflects the adaptive properties of interactional intelligence.

Yet in all three of these cases—despite the fact that the adaptionist models predict the modal response quite well—individual differences analyses demonstrate associations that also must be accounted for. Correct responders on the nondeontic selection task (P and not-Q choosers—not those choosing P and Q) are higher in cognitive ability. In the 2 × 2 covariation detection experiment, it is those subjects weighting cell D more equally (not those underweighting the cell in the way that the adaptionist model dictates) who are higher in cognitive ability and who tend to respond normatively on other tasks (see Tables 2.5 and 2.6). Finally, despite conversational implicatures indicating the opposite, individuals of higher cognitive ability disproportionately tend to adhere to the conjunction rule. These patterns make sense if it is assumed that the two systems of processing are optimized for different situations and different goals and that these data patterns reflect the greater probability that the analytic intelligence of System 2 will override the interactional intelligence of System 1 in individuals of higher cognitive ability.

It is hypothesized that the features of System 1 are designed to very closely track increases in the reproduction probability of genes. System 2, though also clearly an evolutionary product, is primarily a control system focused on the interests of the whole person. Although its overall function was no doubt fitness enhancing, it is the primary maximizer of an individual's *personal* utility.[3] Maximizing the latter will occasionally result in sacrificing genetic fitness (Barkow, 1989; W. S. Cooper, 1989; Skyrms, 1996).

Thus, the hypothesis is that System 1 is more specifically attuned than is System 2 to evolutionary rationality. System 1 processes represent the collection of the processes that are goal maximizing for the genes—the reproductive goals of fecundity, longevity, and replication accuracy (Dawkins, 1976, 1982). System 2, in contrast, maximizes goal satisfaction for *people*—the survival machines for the genes (to use Dawkins' 1976 memorable phrase). Because System 2 is more attuned to normative rationality, it is System 2 that will seek to fulfill the individual's goals in the minority of cases where those goals conflict with the responses triggered by System 1.

Of course, in most (but not all) cases, fulfilling the organism's goals will also be fitness enhancing. Likewise—and equally obviously—in the vast majority of mundane situations, the evolutionary rationality embodied in System 1 processes will also serve the goals of normative rationality. Accurately navigating around objects in the natural world fostered evolutionary adaptation, and it likewise serves our personal goals as we carry out our lives in the modern world (i.e., navigational abilities serve normative rationality as well). Nevertheless, the assumption that we are adapted

---

[3]Evidence for this assumption comes from voluminous data indicating that analytic intelligence is related to the very type of outcomes that normative rationality would be expected to maximize. For example, the System 2 processes that collectively comprise the construct of cognitive ability are moderately and reliably correlated with job success and with the avoidance of harmful behaviors (Brody, 1997; Gottfredson, 1997; Lubinski & Humphreys, 1997).

in the evolutionary sense—the assumption made in so many of the adaptionist models (Anderson, 1990; Oaksford & Chater, 1994)—does not entail normative rationality (as argued in chap. 1). Thus, situations where evolutionary and normative rationality dissociate might well put the two processing systems in conflict with each other.

It is proposed that just such conflicts are occurring in the three tasks discussed in the previous chapter (the Disease Problem, the Linda Problem, and the selection task). This conjecture is supported by the fact that evolutionary rationality has been conjoined with Gricean principles of conversational implicature by several theorists (Gigerenzer, 1996b; Hilton, 1995, Levinson, 1995) who emphasize the principle of "conversationally rational interpretation" (Hilton, 1995, p. 265). According to this view, the pragmatic heuristics are not simply inferior substitutes for computationally costly logical mechanisms that would work better. Instead, the heuristics are optimally designed to solve a particular evolutionary problem—attributing intentions to conspecifics and coordinating mutual intersubjectivity so as to optimally negotiate cooperative behavior (Cummins, 1996; Levinson, 1995; Skyrms, 1996).

Thus, the heuristics triggering alternative task construals in various heuristics and biases paradigms may well be adaptive evolutionary products as Levinson (1995) and others argued. However, as Stich (1990) pointed out, this does not guarantee normative rationality (see also Shafir, 1993; Skyrms, 1996; Stein, 1996). The latter is defined as the maximization of the organism's current goal achievement (Baron, 1985a; Larrick et al., 1993; Sternberg & Detterman, 1986)—and some of these goals might well have become detached from their evolutionary context (see Barkow, 1989). Our analytic intelligence registers the fact that, in our current environment, maximizing fat intake does not satisfy our life goals for health and longevity even though biological drives—that make perfect evolutionary sense—trigger positive affective responses to fatty foods. As Morton (1997) aptly put it: "We can and do find ways to benefit from the pleasures that our genes have arranged for us without doing anything to help the genes themselves. Contraception is probably the most obvious example, but there are many others. Our genes want us to be able to reason, but they have no interest in our enjoying chess" (p. 106).

Thus, we seek "not evolution's end of reproductive success but evolution's means, love-making. The point of this example is that some human psychological traits may, at least in our current environment, be fitness-reducing" (see Barkow, 1989, p. 296). And if the latter are pleasurable, analytic intelligence achieves normative rationality by pursuing them—not the adaptive goals of our genes. This is what Larrick et al. (1993) argued when they spoke of analytic intelligence as "the set of psychological properties that enables a person to achieve his or her goals effectively. On this view, intelligent people will be more likely to use rules of choice that are effective in reaching their goals than will less intelligent people" (p. 345).

In his inimitable style, Dawkins (1976) made the same point in *The Selfish Gene*: "We are built as gene machines and cultured as meme machines, but we have the power to turn against our creators. We, alone on earth, can rebel against the tyranny of the selfish replicators" (p. 201). That rebellion might consistent of our gene-built brain trying to maximize its own utility function rather than the reproduction probability of its creators in situations where the two are in conflict. Thus, high analytic intelligence may lead to task construals that track normative rationality; whereas the alternative construals of subjects low in analytic intelligence (and hence more dominated by System 1 processing) might be more likely to track evolutionary rationality in situations that put the two types of rationality in conflict—as is conjectured to be the case with the problems discussed previously. If construals consistent with normative rationality are more likely to satisfy our current individual goals (Baron, 1993a, 1994a) than are construals determined by evolutionary rationality (which are construals determined by our genes' metaphorical goal—reproductive success), then it is in this restricted sense that individual difference relationships such as those discussed in chapter 4 tell us which construals are "best."

Thinking Dispositions and Decontextualized Reasoning

With Richard F. West and Walter C. Sá

As demonstrated in chapter 2, any correlation between cognitive ability and performance on a reasoning or decision-making task can be interpreted as indicating some degree of algorithmic-level limitation—at least for some individuals. In theory, correlations close to unity represent the idealized version of the Apologist's position—every individual performing at the limits of their computational capacity. The descriptive model would exactly equal the prescriptive model of performance in such a case, and there would be no reason to impute irrationality to any subject. However, the actual results fell considerably short of this extreme. Even when corrected for attenuation due to the modest reliabilities of many of the reasoning tasks (Schmidt & Hunter, 1996), the associations observed in several of the studies were considerably less than perfect. Thus, the computational limitations that have been implicated in performance on some of the tasks do not represent absolute limitations. The moderate correlation between cognitive ability and performance on these tasks thus leaves considerable residual variance. Given that computational limitations can explain only a portion of the normative/descriptive gap, this chapter examines whether there are clues in the residual variance that might help to explain why a normative/descriptive gap remains.

In order to simplify the discussion, in this chapter we set aside those cases where an inappropriate normative model may have been applied (e.g., false-consensus effect) and those cases where there is an alternative task construal that appears equally rational (e.g., overconfidence effect) and focus only on cases where the direction of the computational limitation pointed in the direction of the normative$_s$ model and the original task construal. The question addressed is whether the residual variance (after computational limitations are accounted for) is systematic or whether instead it appears to be error variance. If the latter, then the appropriate model for the normative/descriptive gap would seem to be one that posited some degree of computational limitation plus random performance errors. Such a model—as discussed in chapter 1—could preserve the assumption of perfect human rationality. Differences in the prescriptive and normative models would explain part of normative/descriptive gap and any remaining deviations from the prescriptive could be attributed to performance errors. There would be no need to posit a systematic deviation from rationality at the intentional level of analysis. In contrast, evidence that the residual variance (after partialing cognitive ability) was systematic would mean that not all of the normative/descriptive gap could be attributed to computational limitations and performance errors, and it would support the idea that the intentional-level model of behavior is characterized by systematic irrationality.

There are two different ways in which the nature of the residual processing variance can be examined. One is to determine the covariance among reasoning tasks after cognitive ability has been partialed out. The second is to examine whether there are cognitive/personality variables that can explain the normative/descriptive discrepancies that remain after computational limitations have been accounted for. These two methods of examining residual the variance are discussed in the following sections.

BEYOND COMPUTATIONAL LIMITATIONS: SYSTEMATIC ASSOCIATIONS AMONG REASONING TASKS

In chapter 2, associations among the reasoning tasks in Study 1 of Stanovich and West (1998b) were examined. These correlations are repeated below the diagonal in Table 6.1. The reasoning tasks were a syllogistic reasoning task in which the believability of the conclusion contradicted logical validity, five nondeontic selection task problems, statistical reasoning problems tapping the tendency to prefer aggregate information over vivid but unrepresentative case evidence, and an argument evaluation task (discussed in more detail later in this chapter).

Recall that five of the six correlations among the tasks (see bottom half of Table 6.1) were significant at the .001 level and that all four tasks displayed significant correlations with SAT Total scores (see Table 2.2). Thus, it is possible that the significant associations among these reasoning tasks occur because they all share common computational limitations. The uniformly moderate correlations with cognitive ability raise the possibility that no covariance will be shared among the tasks once computational capacity is controlled (thus supporting a view of the normative/descriptive gap as solely the product of algorithmic-level limitations and performance errors). The partial correlations in the top half of Table 6.1 address this question directly. These represent the correlations among the tasks

TABLE 6.1

Intercorrelations Among Several Reasoning Tasks

Variable	1.	2.	3.	4.
1. Syllogisms		.237**	.222**	.213**
2. Selection task	.363***		.150	.215**
3. Statistical reasoning	.334***	.258***		−.014
4. Argument evaluation	.340***	.310***	.117	

Note. These data are from Study 1 of Stanovich and West (1998b). Zero-order correlations are below the diagonal and correlations with SAT Total score partialed out are presented above the diagonal.

$* = p < .05, ** = p < .01, *** = p < .001$, all two-tailed.

$Ns = 188$ to 195.

after differences in cognitive ability have been statistically removed. The results indicate that four of the six associations were still significant even after variance in SAT scores had been partialed out.

A similar analysis was carried out on the composite variables (see Table 2.2) formed from performance on several of the tasks examined in Study 2 of Stanovich and West (1998b). The first composite score (RT1, see Table 2.2) was a standard-score composite of performance on the syllogistic reasoning, statistical reasoning, and argument evaluation tasks. A second rational thinking composite (RT2, see Table 2.2) was formed by summing the standard scores of the remaining four tasks: covariation judgment, hypothesis testing, if/only thinking, outcome bias. The two composite scores—despite being composed of vastly different reasoning tasks—displayed a significant correlation of .395 ($p < .001$, $n = 546$). However, both RT1 and RT2 displayed significant correlations with SAT scores (.530 and .383, respectively, both $p < .001$). Thus again the possibility remains that the association between the two rational thinking indices derives from their common association with cognitive ability. However, the correlation between RT1 and RT2 when the variance due to SAT scores was partialed out remained significant (partial $r = .242$, $F(1, 526) = 32.82$, $p < .001$).

In summary, the two studies discussed here both produced evidence indicating that there is systematic variance in various rational thinking tasks that is not explained by variation in cognitive ability. Of course, the caveat discussed in chapter 2 must be repeated here: Most of the correlations observed in these studies were of a modest magnitude. But the caveat must also be contextualized in the same manner as in chapter 2—that the correlations may be underestimated due to modest reliability. Because they were embedded in a multivariate investigation, most of the tasks represent a very thin slice of behavior (e.g., selection task performance was based on just five items, the outcome bias score was based on only a single comparison). The modest correlations displayed by these tasks must be interpreted with these limitations in mind (see Schmidt & Hunter, 1996). Nevertheless, the overall conclusion from these analyses is that there are reliable individual differences in the normative/descriptive gap even after computational limitations and performance errors are accounted for.

BEYOND COMPUTATIONAL LIMITATIONS: SYSTEMATIC ASSOCIATIONS WITH THINKING DISPOSITIONS

The results presented in the previous section indicated that the residual variance in rational thinking tasks that remains after variance in computational limitations is accounted for is systematic. Another way of examining whether this residual variance is systematic—by examining whether it is consistently associated with cognitive/personality variables at the intentional level of analysis—is explored in this chapter. If the residual variance is unsystematic (the result of performance errors), then it should not reliably associate with other cognitive/personality variables. In contrast, if the residual variance does reflect systematic deviations from normative responding, then reliable associations with other cognitive variables might be expected. It is argued here that the latter expectation might be particularly true for intentional-level cognitive dispositions having epistemic significance. In this (and the following) section, the potency of thinking dispositions as predictors of rational thought is explored.

Distinguishing Cognitive Capacities and Thinking Dispositions

In many areas of psychology, there is increasing attention being paid to behavioral/cognitive concepts that reside at the borderline of cognitive psychology and personality (Ackerman & Heggestad, 1997; Goff & Ackerman, 1992; Keating, 1990; Nickerson, 1988; Perkins, 1995; Perkins, Jay, & Tishman, 1993; Siegel, 1993; Stanovich & West, 1997; Sternberg, 1997; Sternberg & Ruzgis, 1994; Swartz & Perkins, 1989). Moshman (1994), for instance, reminded us of the importance of "considerations of will and disposition [because they] lie at the interface of cognition with affect, motivation, social relations, and cultural context" (p. 143), and Sternberg (1988) likewise noted that "intellectual styles represent an important link between intelligence and personality, because they probably represent, in part, a way in which personality is manifested in intelligent thought and action" (p. 218). Terminology surrounding such notions is remarkably varied. The term *thinking dispositions* is used in this chapter (see Baron, 1988; Ennis, 1987; Perkins, 1995), although other theorists—in dealing with similar concepts—prefer terms such as *intellectual style* (Sternberg, 1988, 1989), *cognitive emotions* (Scheffler, 1991), *habits of mind* (Keating,

1990), *inferential propensities* (Kitcher, 1993), *epistemic motivations* (Kruglanski, 1990), *constructive metareasoning* (Moshman, 1994), and *cognitive styles* (Messick, 1984, 1994). Despite this diversity of terminology, most authors use such terms similarly—to refer to relatively stable psychological mechanisms and strategies that tend to generate characteristic behavioral tendencies and tactics (see Buss, 1991). In the present chapter, it is proposed that cognitive capacities and thinking dispositions are constructs at different levels of analysis in cognitive theory. As such, their joint relationship to performance on various reasoning and decision-making tasks provides clues to the interpretation of discrepancies between descriptive and normative models of thinking and reasoning.

The distinction between cognitive capacities and thinking dispositions has been drawn by many theorists (e.g., Baron, 1985a, 1988, 1993b; Ennis, 1987; Moshman, 1994; Norris, 1992; Perkins et al., 1993; Schrag, 1988). For example, in Baron's (1985a, 1988) conceptualization, capacities refer to the types of cognitive processes studied by information-processing researchers seeking the underlying cognitive basis of performance on IQ tests. Perceptual speed, discrimination accuracy, working memory capacity, and the efficiency of the retrieval of information stored in long-term memory are examples of cognitive capacities that underlie traditional psychometric intelligence and that have been extensively investigated (Carpenter et al., 1990; L. A. Cooper & Regan, 1982; Deary & Stough, 1996; Estes, 1982; Fry & Hale, 1996; Hunt, 1978, 1987; Lohman, 1989; Vernon, 1991, 1993). These cognitive capacities are what Baltes (1987) termed the "mechanics of intelligence." Psychometric g provides an overall index of the cognitive efficiency of a wide variety of such mechanisms in a given individual (Carroll, 1993, 1997). According to Baron's (1985a) conception, cognitive capacities cannot be improved in the short term by admonition or instruction. They are, nevertheless, affected by long-term practice.

Thinking dispositions, in contrast, are better viewed as cognitive styles that are more malleable: "Although you cannot improve working memory by instruction, you can tell someone to spend more time on problems before she gives up, and if she is so inclined, she can do what you say" (Baron, 1985a, p. 15). Rational thinking dispositions are those that relate to the adequacy of belief formation and decision making, things like "the disposition to weigh new evidence against a favored belief heavily (or lightly), the disposition to spend a great deal of time (or very little) on a problem before giving up, or the disposition to weigh heavily the opinions of others in forming one's own" (Baron, 1985a, p. 15).

By and large, psychometric instruments such as IQ tests have tapped cognitive capacities almost exclusively and have ignored cognitive styles and thinking dispositions (Baron, 1985a, 1988; Stanovich, 1994). Because thinking dispositions and cognitive capacity are thought to differ in their degree of malleability, it is important to determine the relative proportion of variance in reasoning tasks that can be explained by each. To the extent that thinking dispositions explain variance in a rational thinking skill independent of cognitive capacity, theorists such as Baron (1985a, 1988, 1993b) would predict that the skill would be more teachable.

Levels of Analysis and Thinking Dispositions

Baron (1988) has argued that, in ignoring dispositions, the IQ concept "has distorted our understanding of thinking. It has encouraged us to believe that the only general determinants of good thinking are capacities, and this attitude has led to the neglect of general dispositions" (p. 122). Rephrased in terms of the issues that are the focus of this volume, the argument is that an exclusive focus on cognitive capacities limits potential explanations of normative/descriptive gaps to algorithmic limitations only. It is argued here that the study of thinking dispositions balances this tendency by directing attention to the possibility of systematically suboptimal systems at the intentional level of analysis.

The remaining analyses in this chapter are framed by an assumption that is often either ignored or unarticulated in the psychological literature: that cognitive capacities and thinking dispositions are constructs at different levels of analysis in a cognitive theory and that they may do separate explanatory work in a descriptive theory of human reasoning performance. Specifically, each level of analysis in cognitive theory frames a somewhat different issue. At the algorithmic level the key issue is one of computational efficiency, and at the biological level the paramount issue is whether the physical mechanism has the potential to instantiate certain complex algorithms. In contrast, it is at the intentional level that issues of rationality arise. Thus, to fully understand variation in human performance on argument evaluation tasks, for instance, we might need to consider variation at the intentional level as well as at the algorithmic level of cognitive analysis.

Omnibus measures of cognitive capacities such as intelligence tests are thus indexing individual differences in the efficiency of processing at the algorithmic level. In contrast, thinking dispositions as traditionally studied in psychology (e.g., Cacioppo et al., 1996; Kardash & Scholes, 1996; Klaczynski et al., 1997; Kruglanski & Webster, 1996; Schommer, 1990, 1993, 1994; Stanovich & West, 1997) index individual differences at the intentional level of analysis. They are telling us about the individual's goals and epistemic values—and they are indexing broad tendencies of pragmatic and epistemic self-regulation. For example, in his model of mind as a control system, Sloman (1993) viewed desires as control states that can produce behavior either directly or through a complex control hierarchy by changing intermediate desire states. He viewed dispositions (high-level attitudes, ideals, and personality traits) as long-term desire states that "work through a control hierarchy, for instance, by changing other desire-like states rather than triggering behaviour" (p. 85).

Thus, thinking dispositions are reflective of intentional-level psychological structure. They can potentially serve as explanatory mechanisms in accounts of discrepancies between normative and descriptive models of behavior. If thinking dispositions correlate with individual differences in the normative/descriptive gap, then this will be prima facie evidence that the gap is caused by actual differences in intentional psychology. However, any such association might well arise because the variation in thinking dispositions is coextensive with differences in computational capacity. Thus, it will be important to examine whether intentional-level cognitive dispositions can explain unique variance—independent of cognitive capacity. If so, this would represent the strongest evidence of a real intentional-level problem and would be consistent with the notion that human irrationality is empirically demonstrable. In contrast, if computational limitations and performance errors exhaust the explanatory mechanisms that can account for individual differences in the normative/descriptive gap, then there would seem to be no reason not to adopt the Apologist's position that no systematic human irrationality has been demonstrated (because there is no prescriptive/descriptive gap).

THINKING DISPOSITIONS: AN EMPIRICAL STUDY

Study 2 of Stanovich and West (1998b) contained an extensive examination of the associations between cognitive ability, thinking dispositions, and performance on a variety of tasks from the heuristics and biases literature. The left column of figures in Table 6.2 recapitulates the results regarding cognitive ability that were discussed in chapter 2. All of the tasks, including the composite performance indices, are indicated in the table.

The second column of figures includes the correlations with a composite measure of thinking dispositions that was employed in that study. This measure is the additive combination of several questionnaire subscales designed to tap epistemic self-regulation (Goldman, 1986; Harman, 1995; Nozick, 1993; Thagard, 1992). The subscales thus overrepresented dispositions with potential epistemic significance; for example, "the disposition to weigh new evidence against a favored belief heavily (or lightly), the disposition to spend a great deal of time (or very little) on a problem before giving up, or the disposition to weigh heavily the opinions of others in forming one's own" (Baron, 1985a, p. 15). Baron (1985a, 1988, 1993b) called such tendencies dispositions toward activity open-minded thinking. Overall, the subscales in this thinking dispositions measure the following dimensions: epistemological absolutism, willingness to perspective-switch, willingness to decontextualize, and the tendency to consider alternative opinions and evidence. Established subscales were included (e.g., Rokeach, 1960) as well as subscales new to the literature (such as an activity open-minded thinking scale based on Baron's 1985a, 1988, work). Several of the subscales had strong similarities to other related measures in the literature (Cacioppo et al., 1996; Schommer, 1990, 1993, 1994; Schommer & Walker, 1995; Webster & Kruglanski, 1994). Perhaps the strongest similarities were with the two dispositional factors that Schommer (1990, 1993) called "belief in simple knowledge" and "belief in certain knowledge." However, aspects of the need for cognition (Cacioppo et al., 1996) and need for closure (Kruglanski & Webster, 1996) constructs were also represented in the Stanovich and West (1998b) composite scale. Item scores were reflected so that high scores on the total scale indicated greater tendencies toward open-mindedness and cognitive flexibility.

The second column of correlations in Table 6.2 indicates that the thinking dispositions composite score (TDC) displayed significant correlations with each of the tasks in the Stanovich and West (1998b) study. In each case, the direction of the relationship was the same as that observed for cognitive ability—thus reinforcing the issues about the direction of the correlation and the appropriateness of normative models discussed in chapter 3. In most cases, the correlations involving the TDC were lower than those involving the SAT, but in several cases (outcome bias, if/only thinking) the magnitude of the correlations was similar. The correlations between the TDC and the three composite indices of rational thinking were moderate in size (.413, .324, and .442, respectively).

TABLE 6.2
Correlations Between the Reasoning Tasks and SAT Total Score and
Thinking Dispositions Composite Score

	SAT Total	TDC
Argument evaluation task	.371*	.296*
Syllogisms	.410*	.329*
Statistical reasoning	.376*	.263*
Covariation detection	.239*	.176*
Hypothesis testing bias	−.223*	−.167*
Outcome bias	−.172*	−.175*
If/Only thinking	−.208*	−.205*
RT1 Composite	.530*	.413*
RT2 Composite	.383*	.324*
RT Composite, All Tasks	.547*	.442*

Note. The data are from Study 2 of Stanovich and West (1998b). TDC = Thinking dispositions composite score; RT1 Composite = standard score composite of performance on argument evaluation task, syllogisms, and statistical reasoning; RT2 Composite = standard score composite of performance on covariation judgment, hypothesis-testing task, if/only thinking, and outcome bias; RT Composite, All Tasks = rational thinking composite score of performance on all seven tasks.
* = $p < .001$, two-tailed.

There appears to be no question that there are consistent and replicable relationships between intentional-level thinking dispositions and normative$_s$ responding on a variety of tasks from the heuristics and biases literature. To find out whether the thinking dispositions explained unique variance after algorithmic-level limitations were controlled, a series of regression analyses were conducted. The first analysis used the first rational thinking composite variable (RT1)—a standard-score sum of performance on the argument evaluation, statistical reasoning, and syllogistic reasoning tasks. SAT Total scores and the TDC attained a multiple R with this criterion variable of .600 ($F(2, 526) = 148.15, p < .001$). Thus, a substantial amount of variance (36.0%) on these rational thinking tasks was jointly explained by these two predictors. SAT Total was a significant unique predictor (partial correlation = .478, unique variance explained = .190, $p < .001$) as was the TDC (partial correlation = .332, unique variance explained = .079, $p < .001$).

A second rational thinking composite was formed by summing the standard scores of the remaining four tasks: covariation judgment, hypothesis testing, if/only thinking, outcome bias (the latter three scores reflected so that higher scores represent more normatively correct reasoning). SAT Total scores and the TDC attained a multiple R with this rational thinking composite of .447 ($F(2, 526) = 65.53, p < .001$). SAT Total was a significant unique predictor (partial correlation = .325, unique variance explained = .094, $p < .001$) as was the TDC (partial correlation = .249, unique variance explained = .053, $p < .001$).

Finally, both of the rational thinking composites were combined into a composite variable reflecting performance on all seven tasks. SAT Total scores and the TDC attained a multiple R with this criterion variable of .627 ($F(2, 526) = 170.56, p < .001$). SAT Total was a significant unique predictor (partial correlation = .496, unique variance explained = .198, $p < .001$) as was the TDC (partial correlation = .366, unique variance explained = .094, $p < .001$). Thus, there were consistent indications in the data of Stanovich and West (1998b) that thinking dispositions do in fact explain variance on a variety of reasoning and decision-making tasks after the variance in cognitive ability has been accounted for. The residual variance does appear to be systematic and predictable. These results refute the notion that all of the normative/descriptive gap can be accounted for by algorithmic limitations and performance errors. Indicators of intentional-level epistemic attitudes—the thinking dispositions subscales—are consistent unique predictors of normative$_s$ response tendencies.

In another study, we examined a reasoning domain (argument evaluation) in which we thought that epistemically related thinking dispositions would be especially likely to account for unique variance.

REASONING INDEPENDENTLY OF PRIOR BELIEF: THINKING
DISPOSITIONS AS PREDICTORS OF ARGUMENT EVALUATION ABILITY

Discussions of critical thinking consistently point to the importance of decontextualized reasoning styles that foster the tendency to evaluate arguments and evidence in a way that is not contaminated by one's prior beliefs. In the critical-thinking literature, the disposition toward such unbiased reasoning is almost universally viewed as a characteristic of good thinking. For example, Norris and Ennis (1989) argued that one fundamentally important characteristic of critical thinking is the disposition to "reason from starting points with which we disagree without letting the disagreement interfere with reasoning" (p. 12). Zechmeister and Johnson (1992) listed as one characteristic of the critical thinker the ability to "accept statements as true even when they don't agree with one's own position" (p. 6). Similarly, Nickerson (1987) stressed that critical thinking entails the ability to recognize "the fallibility of one's own opinions, the probability of bias in those opinions, and the danger of differentially weighting evidence according to personal preferences" (p. 30). This sentiment is echoed by many critical-thinking theorists (e.g., Baron, 1991a; Brookfield, 1987; Kuhn, 1991, 1996; Lipman, 1991; Perkins, 1995; Perkins et al., 1993). The growing literature on informal or practical reasoning likewise emphasizes the importance of detaching one's own beliefs from the process of argument evaluation (Baron, 1991a, 1995; Klaczynski et al., 1997; Klaczynski & Gordon, 1996; Kuhn, 1991, 1993; Voss, Perkins, & Segal, 1991).

In the assessment of critical thinking, the issue of belief bias has been dealt with in two different ways—neither satisfactory. The first strategy is to adopt a more ability-like definition of critical thinking and to downplay the dispositional aspects of critical thinking (e.g., Norris, 1992) that are most closely related to belief bias. This strategy seeks to avoid content that would strongly engage a prior belief either by choosing neutral content (content without affective valence) or content unfamiliar to all participants (e.g., the Moorburg "overnight parking" letter from the *Ennis–Weir Critical Thinking Essay Test, Ennis & Weir, 1985; Level X of the Cornell Critical Thinking Test*, Ennis & Millman, 1985). The content-neutral strategy tends to define critical thinking as following good standards of deductive and inductive reasoning and as avoiding certain textbook fallacies. Such a strategy eliminates the belief bias issue by removing the sources of the belief bias effect—but at the steep cost of failing to assess what many theorists view as a central component of critical thinking.

The second common strategy is to acknowledge that the issue of belief bias is central to most definitions of critical thinking and thus to actually use material that would be most likely to provoke potential belief biases (Kunda, 1990). The problem is that assessment devices employing this strategy never actually attempt to measure the prior belief, but instead try to distribute arguments of varying quality across issues varying in their controversial nature. From the point of view of assessing individual differences in critical thought, this is problematic. The quality of the argument that participants are supposed to evaluate varies unsystematically with the respondent's prior beliefs about the issue in question—thus making the argument evaluation task unusually difficult for some subjects and unusually easy for others (depending on the chance correlation between the quality of the argument and the participant's prior belief).

As an example of this problem, consider an exercise on the *Watson–Glaser Critical Thinking Appraisal* (Watson & Glaser, 1980), which requires that respondents evaluate three arguments concerning the proposition: Groups in this country who are opposed to some of our government's policies should be permitted unrestricted freedom of press and speech. Two arguments refute the proposition and, of these two, one is weak and the other is strong. A third argument supports the proposition and happens to be a strong argument. Thus, assuming that prior belief does have some effect, by a margin of two to one, individuals in agreement with the proposition will have an easier task when answering these three items. Even worse is the situation with respect to another proposition on the Watson–Glaser test: that pupils should be excused from public schools to receive religious instruction in their own churches during school hours. Two arguments refute the proposition and they are scored as strong and two arguments support the proposition and they are both scored as weak. Thus, these four items on the test will be vastly easier for someone who opposes the proposition at the outset.

The basic problem here is that the respondent's prior attitude is not only uncontrolled (obviously), but that it is in no way taken into account when performance on the task is assessed. No account is taken of how chance correlations between prior opinion and argument quality serve to artificially enhance or inhibit the argument evaluation process. Such tasks do not result in an individualized assessment of the ability to evaluate the quality of an argument independent of personal biases about the proposition at issue (although they may be useful for certain types of group comparisons).

A New Analytic Strategy for Assessing Argument Evaluation Ability

The logic of the task designed by Stanovich and West (1997) was aimed directly at this problem. With this task—the argument evaluation test (AET)—we introduced an analytic technique for deriving an index of a person's reliance on the quality of an argument independent of their own personal beliefs about the issue in question. Our methodology involved assessing, on a separate instrument, the participant's prior beliefs about a series of propositions. On an argument evaluation measure, administered at a later time, the participants evaluated the quality of arguments related to the same propositions. The arguments had an operationally determined objective quality that varied from item to item. Our analytic strategy was to regress each subject's evaluations of the argument simultaneously on the objective measure of argument quality and on the strength of the belief he or she had about the propositions prior to reading the argument. The standardized beta weight for argument quality then becomes an index of that subject's reliance on the quality of the arguments independent of their beliefs on the issues in question. The magnitude of this statistic becomes an index of argument-driven, or data-driven processing (to use Norman's, 1976, term) independent of knowledge-based or opinion-based processing.

The Stanovich and West (1997) methodology is different from the traditional logic used in critical-thinking tests, and it is a more sensitive one for measuring individual differences. Rather than merely trying to balance opinions across items by utilizing a variety of issues and relying on chance to ensure that prior belief and strength of the argument are relatively balanced from respondent to respondent, in the AET the prior opinion is actually measured and taken into account in the analysis (for related techniques, see Klaczynski & Fauth, 1997; Klaczynski & Gordon, 1996; Klaczynski et al., 1997; Kuhn, 1991, 1993; Kuhn, Amsel, & O'Loughlin, 1988; Slusher & Anderson, 1996).

The technique allowed us to examine thought processes in areas of "hot" cognition where biases are most likely to operate (Babad & Katz, 1991; Kunda, 1990; Pyszczynski & Greenberg, 1987). With one exception, the propositions used in the Stanovich and West (1997) experiment all concerned real social and political issues on which people hold varying, and sometimes strong, beliefs (e.g., gun control, taxes, university governance, crime, automobile speed limits). For example, in one item, the target proposition was: The welfare system should be drastically cut back in size. In the first part of the AET—the prior belief section—participants indicated their degree of agreement with a series of 23 target propositions such as this on a 4-point scale: strongly agree (scored as 4), agree (3), disagree (2), strongly disagree (1). The AET prior belief items varied greatly in the degree to which the sample as a whole endorsed them—from a low of 1.79 for the item "It is more dangerous to travel by air than by car" to a high of 3.64 for the item "Seat belts should always be worn when traveling in a car."

After completing several other questionnaires and tasks, the participants completed the second part of the AET. The instructions introduced the subjects to a fictitious individual, Dale, whose arguments they were to evaluate. Each of the 23 items on the second part of the instrument began with Dale stating a belief about an issue. The 23 beliefs were identical to the target propositions that the subjects had rated their degree of agreement with on the prior belief part of the instrument (e.g., "The welfare system should be drastically cut back in size"). Dale then provides a justification for the belief (in this case, e.g., "The welfare system should be drastically reduced in size because welfare recipients take advantage of the system and buy expensive foods with their food stamps"). A critic then presents an argument to counter this justification (e.g., "Ninety-five percent of welfare recipients use their food stamps to obtain the bare essentials for their families"). The subject is told to assume that the facts in the counterargument are correct. Finally, Dale attempts to rebut the counterargument (e.g., "Many people who are on welfare are lazy and don't want to work for a living"). Again assuming that the facts in the rebuttal are correct, the subject is told to evaluate the strength of Dale's rebuttal to the critic's argument. The subject then evaluates the strength of the rebuttal on a 4-point scale: very strong (scored as 4), strong (3), weak (2), very weak (1).

The analysis of performance on the AET required that the subjects' evaluations of argument quality be compared to some objective standard. We employed a summary measure of eight experts' evaluations of these rebuttals as an operationally defined standard of argument quality. Specifically, three full-time faculty members of the Department of Philosophy at the University of Washington, three full-time faculty members of the Department of Philosophy at the University of California, Berkeley, and the two authors of the scale (Stanovich & West, 1997) judged the strength of the rebuttals. The median correlation between the judgments of the eight experts was .74. Although the problems were devised by the two authors, the median correlations between the authors' judgments and those of the external experts were reasonably high (.78 and .73, respectively) and roughly equal to the median correlation among the judgments of the six external experts themselves (.73). Thus, the median of the eight experts' judgments of the rebuttal quality served as the objective index of argument quality for each item.

As an example, on the aforementioned item, the median of the experts' ratings of the rebuttal was 1.5 (between weak and very weak). The mean rating given the item by the subjects was 1.93 (weak) although the participants' mean prior belief score indicated a neutral opinion (2.64).

One indication of the validity of the experts' ratings is that the experts were vastly more consistent among themselves in their evaluation of the items than were the subjects. Because the median correlation among the eight experts' judgments was .74, a parallel analysis of consistency among the subjects was conducted in order to provide a comparison. Forty-three groups of eight subjects were formed and the correlations among the argument evaluations for the eight individuals in each group were calculated. The median correlation for each of the 43 groups was then determined. The highest median across all of the 43 groups was .59. Thus, not one of the 43 groups attained the level of agreement achieved by the eight experts. The mean of the median correlations in the 43 groups was .28, markedly below the degree of consistency in the experts' judgments.

A further validation of the experts' ratings comes from comparing the zero-order correlation of SAT scores and the beta weight for the experts' ratings (.35) with the zero-order correlation of SAT scores and the beta weights based on the mean ratings of argument quality given by the subjects (.23). This difference in dependent correlations was statistically significant ($t(346) = 3.20$, $p < .01$), indicating that subjects of higher cognitive ability were more likely to agree with the experts in their judgments of argument quality than with their fellow subjects of lower cognitive ability. High-ability students and the experts rate the arguments more similarly than do the high-ability students and low-ability students.

Individual regression analyses (one for each subject) were conducted in which the subject's evaluations of argument quality served as the criterion variable. The evaluation scores were regressed simultaneously on both the argument quality scores and the prior belief scores. For each subject, these analyses resulted in two beta weights—one for argument quality and one for prior belief. The former beta weight—an indication of the degree of reliance on argument quality independent of prior belief—is the primary indicator of the ability to evaluate arguments independent of one's beliefs.

The mean multiple correlation across the 349 separate regressions was .451 ($SD = .158$). The mean standardized beta weight for argument quality was .330 ($SD = .222$). These values varied widely—from a low of −.489 to a high of .751. Only 30 of 349 subjects had beta weights less than zero. The correlates of the ability to evaluate arguments independently of prior belief were examined by splitting the sample in half based on the argument quality beta weight. A median split of the sample resulted in a subsample of 174 subjects with mean beta weights for argument quality of .504 (termed HIARG because of their high reliance on argument quality) and 175 low-scoring subjects having mean argument quality beta weights of .156 (termed LOARG because of their low reliance on argument quality). The difference in beta weights was of course statistically significant, $t(347) = 23.56$, $p < .001$.

As indicated in Table 6.3, the mean SAT total scores of the HIARG group were significantly ($p < .001$) higher than those of the LOARG group, indicating that the group more reliant on argument quality for their judgments was higher in cognitive ability. This finding was confirmed by the existence of differences in favor of the HIARG group on a vocabulary test ($p < .001$).

The remainder of Table 6.3 presents comparisons of the two groups on the different scales of a Thinking Dispositions Questionnaire that was partially overlapping in its subscales with the questionnaire used in Stanovich and West (1998b) and discussed previously. The HIARG group scored significantly higher on the flexible-thinking scale designed to tap Baron's (1985a, 1988, 1993b) concept of actively open-minded thinking—a construct encompassing the cultivation of reflectiveness rather than impulsivity, the seeking and processing of information that disconfirms one's belief (as opposed to confirmation bias in evidence seeking), and the willingness to change one's beliefs in the face of contra-

TABLE 6.3

**Mean Scores of Subjects With Highest (n = 174) and Lowest (n = 175)
Argument Quality Scores on the Argument Evaluation Test
(Standard Deviations in Parentheses)**

Variable	LOARG	HIARG	t Value
SAT Total	1,080 (106)	1,133 (103)	4.64***
Vocabulary Checklist	.528 (.160)	.592 (.150)	3.89***
Thinking Dispositions			
Flexible Thinking Scale	44.2 (4.6)	45.5 (4.9)	2.59*
Openness-Ideas	32.5 (6.3)	34.6 (6.4)	3.00**
Openness-Values	34.4 (5.4)	36.8 (5.4)	4.06***
Absolutism Scale	30.1 (5.7)	28.0 (6.1)	−3.25**
Dogmatism Scale	30.5 (5.5)	28.2 (5.7)	−3.84***
Categorical Thinking	8.2 (2.7)	7.0 (2.6)	−4.05***
TDC Composite	42.3 (21.7)	53.6 (22.9)	4.71***
Superstitious Thinking	18.2 (6.0)	16.7 (5.4)	−2.36*
Counterfactual Thinking	8.2 (2.6)	9.0 (2.4)	3.12**
Social Desirability Scale	14.9 (3.6)	15.2 (3.8)	0.84

Note. $df = 347$ for vocabulary checklist, 338 for SAT total, and 346 for the thinking dispositions scales. TDC Composite = (Flexible Thinking Scale + Openness-Ideas + Openness-Values) − (Absolutism Scale + Dogmatism Scale + Categorical Thinking).
* = $p < .05$, ** = $p < .01$, *** = $p < .001$, all two-tailed.

dictory evidence. Some items on this subscale tapped the disposition toward reflectivity ("If I think longer about a problem I will be more likely to solve it," "Difficulties can usually be overcome by thinking about the problem, rather than through waiting for good fortune," "Intuition is the best guide in making decisions,"—the latter reverse scored); others tapped willingness to consider evidence contradictory to beliefs (e.g., "People should always take into consideration evidence that goes against their beliefs"); some tapped willingness to consider alternative opinions and explanations ("A person should always consider new possibilities"); and still others tapped tolerance for ambiguity combined with a willingness to postpone closure ("There is nothing wrong with being undecided about many issues").

The two groups scored differently on two openness subscales of the Revised NEO Personality Inventory (Costa & McCrae, 1992), with the HIARG group displaying significantly higher scores on both. Conversely, the HIARG group scored significantly lower on a measure of absolutism based on the Perry scheme (Erwin, 1981, 1983; Perry, 1970), a measure of dogmatism (Robinson, Shaver, & Wrightsman, 1991; Rokeach, 1960), and a measure of categorical thinking (Epstein & Meier, 1989). A thinking dispositions composite score (TDC), formed by a linear combination of these six scales, displayed a statistically significant ($p < .001$) difference. The HIARG group also displayed significantly lower scores on a superstitious-thinking scale (W. Jones, Russell, & Nickel, 1977; Stanovich, 1989) and significantly higher scores on the two-item counter factual-thinking scale (Stanovich & West, 1997). None of the response patterns were due to a tendency for the HIARG group to give more socially desirable responses, because the groups did not differ on that variable.

As the results displayed in Table 6.3 indicate, a consistent pattern of differences on the thinking dispositions measures was observed. The HIARG group of subjects consistently displayed more openmindedness, cognitive flexibility, and skepticism, and less dogmatism and cognitive rigidity—replicating the pattern displayed in Table 6.2. There appear to be consistent and replicable relationships between intentional-level thinking dispositions and the ability to evaluate arguments in the face of prior belief. However, as Table 6.3 also indicates, the groups differed in cognitive ability (SAT and vocabulary scores).

To find out whether the thinking dispositions explained unique variance after algorithmic-level limitations were controlled, a series of regression analyses were conducted. The analyses displayed in Table 6.4 were structured to examine the question of whether thinking dispositions can predict performance on the AET even after cognitive ability has been partialed out. The criterion variable was the beta weight for argument quality. Entered first into the regression equation was the SAT Total score which, not surprisingly given the results displayed in Table 6.3, accounted for a significant proportion of variance. Listed next are alternative second steps in the hierarchical analysis. As the table indicates, the TDC composite score accounted for significant variance in performance on the AET even after SAT scores were entered into the equation. In fact, regression analyses using each component of the TDC as the second step indicated that five of six of its components considered separately was a significant unique predictor. Although the proportion of variance in some cases was small, it again must be noted that no subscale contained more than 10 items and the categorical-thinking subscale had as few as three. Finally, both the superstitious-thinking and counter-factual-thinking measures were also unique predictors. Thus, the linkage between the thinking dispositions and performance on the AET illustrated in Table 6.3 is not entirely due to covariance with cognitive ability. Various measures of thinking dispositions are predictors independent of SAT scores. Intentional-level thinking dispositions are unique predictors of ability to evaluate arguments in the face of prior belief. Performance on the latter is not simply a function of computational limitations.

TABLE 6.4

Hierarchical Regression Analyses Predicting Beta Weight for Argument Quality on the Argument Evaluation Test

Step	Variable	R	R^2 Change	F Change
1.	SAT Total	.353	.124	47.86***
2.	TDC Composite	.401	.037	14.76***
2.	Flexible-Thinking Scale	.380	.021	8.01**
2.	Openness-Ideas	.363	.007	2.75
2.	Openness-Values	.377	.018	6.96**
2.	Absolutism Scale	.379	.020	7.51**
2.	Dogmatism Scale	.394	.031	12.23***
2.	Categorical Thinking	.401	.037	14.66***
2.	Superstitious Thinking	.368	.012	4.36*
2.	Counterfactual Thinking	.380	.020	7.80**

$* = p < .05, ** = p < .01, *** = p < .001.$

Although the number of relevant studies is still small, there are increasing indications in the literature that intentional-level thinking dispositions can predict the tendency toward decontextualized thought. Schommer (1990) found that a measure of belief in certain knowledge predicted the tendency to draw one-sided conclusions from ambiguous evidence even after verbal ability was controlled. Kardash and Scholes (1996) found that the tendency to properly draw inconclusive inferences from mixed evidence was related to belief in certain knowledge and need for cognition scores. Furthermore, these relationships were not mediated by verbal ability. Likewise, Klaczynski et al. (1997) found that the reasoning biases disrupting the ability to critique experimental studies for flaws were associated with the need for cognition and thinking dispositions drawn from Epstein's (1994; Epstein & Meier, 1989) two-process theory.

Why is performance on many of the tasks examined in the Stanovich and West (1997, 1998b) studies associated? Why do indicators of thinking dispositions in the epistemic domain predict residual performance on the heuristics and biases tasks and argument evaluation tasks examined by Stanovich and West and others (Kardash & Scholes, 1996; Klaczynski et al., 1997; Schommer, 1990)? It is conjectured here that the reason is that many of the tasks share a requirement for cognitive decontextualization that accounts for both of these covariance patterns. In the next section, this conjecture is examined.

COGNITIVE DECONTEXTUALIZATION

Adult interviewer: What is three and one more? How many is three and one more?

RM (aged 4 years, 7 months): Three and what? One what? Letter? I mean, number? [He was referring presumably to magnetic numerals used in an earlier game.]

Adult interviewer: How many is three and one more?

RM: One more what?

Adult interviewer: Just one more, you know.

RM (disgruntled): I don't know. (from Donaldson, 1993, p. 89)

Donaldson (1993) used this example to illustrate the important role of detaching from context in cognitive development. She argued that:

What is involved in the mind's movement from "seven fishes" to "seven" is abstraction indeed, but it is more: it is a dramatic decontextualization. In the contexts of our ordinary life we have to deal with quantities of fishes but we never encounter seven. (p. 90)

She emphasized how, in order to master a variety of abstract rule systems (mathematics, logic, etc.), decontextualization must become a comfortable thinking style for a learner:

If the intellectual powers are to develop, the child must gain a measure of control over his own thinking and he cannot control it while he remains unaware of it. The attaining of this control means prising thought out of its primitive unconscious embeddedness in the immediacies of living in the world and interacting with other human beings. It means learning to move beyond the bounds of human sense. It is on this movement that all the higher intellectual skills depend. (Donaldson, 1978, p. 123)

Many different theorists have emphasized the importance of the processes of decontextualization in the development of higher level thought processes. For example, Piaget's (1972) conceptualization of formal operational thought places mechanisms of decontextualization in positions of paramount importance, because according to his view, "one of the essential characteristics of formal thought appears to us to be the independence of its form from reality content" (p. 10). In her earlier work, Donaldson (1978) used the term *disembedding*, and discussed how individual differences in home backgrounds made some children more accepting of the disembedded style that is demanded of children during formal schooling. The literature of developmental psychology contains many related concepts, such as Sigel's (1993) idea of distancing strategies.

Likewise, many writers in the critical-thinking literature have emphasized modes of decontextualization as the foundational skills of rational thought (see Paul, 1984, 1987; Siegel, 1988). Kelley (1990) argued that "the ability to step back from our train of thought ... is a virtue because it is the only way to check the results of our thinking, the only way to avoid jumping to conclusions, the only way to stay in touch with the facts" (p. 6). Neimark (1987) lumped the concepts of decentering and decontextualizing under the umbrella term *detachment*. One component of detachment she termed *depersonalizing*: being able to adopt perspectives other than one's own. This aspect of detachment is closely analogous to Piaget's (1926) concept of decentration. Neimark's second component of detachment—detaching from context—is more like Donaldson's concept of disembedding in that it involves breaking the bounds of situational constraint and local context. Neimark emphasized how associations built up over time will tend to activate a decision for us automatically and unconsciously if we are not reflective and cannot detach from situational cues.

The danger of response patterns that are determined too strongly by overlearned cues is a repeated theme in the reasoning literature (Arkes, 1991; Baron, 1994a; J. Brown & Langer, 1990; Evans, 1984, 1989; Wason & Evans, 1975; T. D. Wilson & Brekke, 1994). For example, Baron argued that many departures from consequentialism in decision making are due to inappropriate generalizations. For example, the act-omission distinction is hypothesized to arise because harmful acts are usually more intentional than harmful omissions; but this distinction continues to be made even when there is no difference in intention. In short, to act in consequentialist fashion, the features of the actual context (intention, etc.) must be abstracted and compared componentially. Such decontextualizing cognitive habits represent one line of defense against overlearned associations that might trigger non-normative responses.

The development of decontextualizing cognitive styles has also been examined by researchers studying the cultural context of literate thought (see Akinnaso, 1981; Goody, 1977, 1987; Havelock, 1963, 1980; Luria, 1976; Olson, 1977, 1986, 1994; Ong, 1967, 1982). Luria's classic work among illiterate Uzbeks in central Asia provides some prototypical examples of refusal to adopt a decontextualizing processing style to the syllogistic reasoning task. In reviewing this literature, Denny (1991) made a strong claim for cognitive decontextualization, which he defined as "the handling of information in a way that either disconnects other information or backgrounds it" (p. 66). Denny defended the thesis that all of the characteristics that have long been associated with the rise of literacy in the literature of cognitive anthropology—reliance on logic rather than social context, induction from a variety of examples rather than salient anecdotes, empirical observation rather than folk theories, and styles that involve criticizing underlying assumptions—are in fact traceable to the decontextualizing effects of literacy.

Interestingly, Denny (1991) structured his theory of the cultural context of rational thought around the capacity/disposition distinction that was discussed earlier. He argued that "all humans are capable of and do practice both … contextualized and decontextualized thought. However, different cultures make some of these thought patterns fluent and automatic, whereas the opposite patterns remain unusual and cumbersome" (p. 66). Denny viewed the basic psychological processes that support both propositional thinking and mental modeling as something akin to cognitive capacities (in the sense of that discussed previously). For him, decontextualization is a cognitive style that determines how basic cognitive capacities will be deployed.

Most of the tasks examined in the Stanovich and West (1998b) studies might be said to involve some type of decontextualization skill—that is, skills enabling reasoning processes to operate independently of interfering context (world knowledge, prior opinion, vivid examples). These skills are perhaps best termed decontextualizing, or abstracting, or disembedding thinking styles to distinguish them from abstract problem solving itself. They do not refer to the ability to solve problems that have been decontextualized—problems already in abstract form. Instead, they relate to the propensity or disposition of the thinker to decontextualize the problem.

Consider some of the tasks used in the Stanovich and West (1998b) investigation. In their syllogistic reasoning task, people are presented with premises and then asked if the conclusion follows logically from them. To turn the task from a purely reasoning task into one that required decontextualizing thought, Stanovich and West employed conclusions that contradicted world knowledge when the syllogism was valid and that were consistent with world knowledge when the syllogism was invalid. An example of the former is: All animals love water. Cats do not like water. Cats are not animals. The belief bias effect in syllogistic reasoning occurs when people endorse conclusions based on their believability or truth in the world rather than on logical validity and it has been much investigated (Evans et al., 1983; Markovits & Nantel, 1989; Newstead, Pollard, Evans, & Allen, 1992; Oakhill, Johnson-Laird, & Garnham, 1989). The task of reasoning about syllogisms with conflicts between factual content and logical form puts a heavy premium on the ability to decontextualize. In order to concentrate on logical form, the person must decouple (see Navon, 1989a, 1989b) the content of the items from the reasoning process and reason as though the terms of the syllogism were neutral symbols rather than words connected to world knowledge in highly overlearned ways. Such reasoning embodies what later interpreters of Piaget's theories have viewed as a crucial aspect of his notion of formal thought: "the ability to reason with hypothetical propositions irrespective of their empirical status" (Markovits & Vachon, 1989, p. 399; see also Byrnes, 1988).

The argument evaluation task used by Stanovich and West (1998b) was like the syllogistic reasoning task in that it required individuals to reason in the face of potentially interfering contextual information. Whereas in the case of the syllogisms that information was factual knowledge about the world, in the AET it was the nature of the subjects' prior opinions about the focal issue in the argument they were evaluating.

The statistical reasoning problems investigated by Stanovich and West (1998b) were inspired by the work of Nisbett and Ross (1980) on the tendency of human judgment to be overly influenced by vivid but unrepresentative personal and case evidence and to be underinfluenced by more representative and diagnostic, but pallid, statistical evidence. The quintessential problem (see Fong et al., 1986; Jepson et al., 1983) involves choosing between contradictory car purchase recommendations—one from a large-sample survey of car buyers and the other the heartfelt and emotional testimony of a single friend. The choice of the statistical evidence could be viewed as a response reflecting greater decontextualization because recognizing its greater diagnosticity requires the individual to ignore the salience and seeming personal relevance of the case evidence.

Similarly, solution of the nondeontic selection problems employed by Stanovich and West (1998b) might be said to require a type of cognitive decontextualization. Of course, there are many other alternative explanations of performance on this much investigated task. However, regardless of whether one's favored explanation of selection task performance is in terms of confirmation bias (Wason, 1966); in terms of automatic and preconscious relevance judgments (Evans, 1989); in terms of restrictive focussing (Legrenzi et al., 1993); in terms of a heuristic responses to cues that are differentially associated to items mentioned in the rule (Pollard, 1982); or in terms of utility considerations overriding logical considerations (Kirby, 1994)—in each case a certain type of decoupling (see Navon, 1989a, 1989b) is involved when a person chooses the deductively correct P and not-Q combination. Either a tendency for confirmation-driven search must be decoupled before a logical analysis of the problem can take place, or an automatic linguistic association must be resisted, or a preconscious priming from the task instructions must be inhibited, or the choice utilities of the task must be prevented from overwhelming the inferential component. Regardless of which of these theoretical views one adopts, a type of decontextualization is involved. Most of the alternative explanations fall under some rubric of overly focused reasoning (Legrenzi et al., 1993) or concrete thinking, which Shafir (1994) defined as "relying heavily on information that is explicitly available, at the expense of other information which remains implicit" (p. 418).

Thus, a consideration of the four tasks employed in one of the Stanovich and West (1998b) studies shows that all seem to involve a decoupling operation of a slightly different type. In the syllogisms task, the people must decouple their knowledge of the world from the processes they use in evaluating the syllogism. To perform well on the argument evaluation test, the subject must decouple their prior opinion on the issue from the evaluation of the argument. In the statistical reasoning problems, the subject must look beyond the vividness and immediacy of the testimonial evidence in order to realize that the abstract statistical information has greater validity. Finally, in the selection task the context is the linguistic form itself—the subject must resist the salient linguistic cues that seem to compel a test of only those items actually named in the rule.

The performance linkages among these tasks are perhaps due to the underlying decontextualization requirements that the tasks seem to share—and the common reasoning property leading to superior performance might be the operation of some type of decoupling mechanism as discussed by Navon (1989a, 1989b) in his model of attention. He conceived of attentional phenomena as epiphenomenal outcomes of the operation of a decoupling mechanism in an intelligence system composed of semiautonomous modules. In his model, the coupler resolves and assesses the actions and goals and decouples modules low in the current activation/goal hierarchy.

The motivation to sustain decoupling seems at least partially like a disposition and not solely a cognitive capacity (i.e., ability) in Navon's (1989a, 1989b) account. Indeed, in parts of his article he explicitly translated folk terms such as *willpower* into his conceptualization: "Willpower may presumably amount to the skill of exercising selective decoupling to the effect of minimizing the visibility of distracting modules" (Navon, 1989b, p. 217). In Navon's (1989a) account, decoupling becomes at least partly dispositional:

> Because effort is aversive, motivation is needed to override the aversion, so that decoupling can be carried out. Motivation in itself, so it seems, is a continuum of states rather than a scarce commodity. The amount of decoupling actually exerted at any moment probably depends on the balance of motivation to accomplish the goal and the aversion.... The function of attention, according to the present view, is not to manage the supply of scarce resources, but rather to determine an optimal agenda for a multiple-entity community. (pp. 203–204)

A DIRECT TEST OF THE DOMAIN GENERALITY OF A COGNITIVE DECONTEXTUALIZATION SKILL

As mentioned previously, discussions of critical thinking in the educational psychology literature consistently point to the importance of decontextualized reasoning styles that foster the tendency to evaluate arguments and evidence in a way that is not contaminated by one's prior beliefs. This literature has two salient characteristics. First, the ability to evaluate evidence in an unbiased manner is treated as a global trait. Second, unbiased evidence evaluation is assumed to be efficacious. That is, it is assumed that unbiased reasoning styles have some degree of domain generality and that they are normatively appropriate. Despite their popularity, there exist few empirical data that relate to either assumption (domain generality and normative appropriateness), and theoretical critiques have been leveled at each. Before describing one of the few empirical studies of these assumptions, the critiques of each of the traditional assumptions are discussed in order to establish a rationale for opposing empirical predictions.

In the critical-thinking literature, there has been a strong tendency to treat the tendency to decontextualize as a domain-general phenomenon. For example, when Nickerson (1987) warned against "differentially weighting evidence according to personal preferences" (p. 30), the domain of the preferences was not specified. Likewise, when Zechmeister and Johnson (1992) championed the ability to "accept statements as true even when they don't agree with one's own position" (p. 6), they did not specify a statement domain. Throughout the entire critical-thinking literature, domain generality is assumed for the various thinking dispositions that are listed as the key properties of critical thinking (e.g., Ennis, 1987; Lipman, 1991; Wade & Tavris, 1993). Indeed, Baron (1985b) made some degree of domain generality a defining feature of his notion of a thinking style: "Cognitive styles ought to be general. By ought I mean that evidence against the generality of a style is taken to make the style less interesting" (pp. 379–380). This view leads to an obvious individual difference prediction, that "we should expect some correlation across individuals between style in one situation and style in another, regardless of how discrepant the situations are" (Baron, 1985b, p. 380). However, there have been virtually no such multivariate studies reported on the tendency toward decontextualization. Whether the phenomenon has any degree of domain generality or whether it is domain specific (and thus, under Baron's criterion, does not warrant its treatment as a thinking disposition in the critical-thinking literature) is almost completely unknown.

In contrast to the assumption of domain generality in the critical-thinking literature, the contextualist tradition within developmental psychology emphasizes the point that the exercise of cognitive skills is often quite situation specific (Bronfenbrenner & Ceci, 1994; J. S. Brown, Collins, & Duguid, 1989; Ceci, 1993, 1996; Lave & Wenger, 1991; Rogoff & Lave, 1984). Within this framework, it is argued that many so-called basic cognitive processes are so dependent on familiarity with the specific stimulus domain and its context that it seems almost a misnomer to call them "basic" (see Ceci, 1996). Stigler and Baranes (1988) stressed this point in particular:

> What differentiates participants who exhibit expert performance from those who perform at a lower level is not the presence of higher levels of general cognitive abilities, but rather is a greater accumulation of knowledge specific to the domain of expertise…. It is more and more difficult, within modern cognitive theory, to draw a division between basic processes and "mere" content. (p. 257)

Theorists in the contextualist tradition of cognitive developmental psychology thus emphasize the domain specificity of the exercise of a cognitive skill or style. They question the existence of thinking styles having the generality ascribed by Baron (1985b). Under a contextualist conceptualization, cognitive decontextualization might be expected to display extreme domain specificity. Dispositions for avoiding belief bias such as those discussed in the critical-thinking literature are thus treated with extreme skepticism within the contextualist framework.

In addition to the domain specificity/generality issue, the second contentious theoretical issue in the literature on belief bias effects concerns the normative status of unbiased evidence evaluation. The view predominant in the critical-thinking literature—that avoidance of belief bias leads to more accurate information collection and evaluation—is supported by some of the classic literature on belief adjustment, belief kinematics, and Bayesian reasoning (Fischhoff & Beyth-Marom, 1983; Howson & Urbach, 1993; Kaplan, 1996). This can be most easily seen if Bayes' theorem is expressed in the ratio form (see discussion in chap. 2) where the odds favoring the focal hypothesis (H) are derived by multiplying the likelihood ratio of the observed datum (D) by the prior odds favoring the focal hypothesis:

$$\frac{P(H/D)}{P(\sim H/D)} = \frac{P(D/H)}{P(D/\sim H)} \times \frac{P(H)}{P(\sim H)}$$

From left to right, the three ratio terms represent: the posterior odds favoring the focal hypothesis (H) after receipt of the new data (D); the likelihood ratio composed of the probability of the data given the focal hypothesis divided by the probability of the data given its mutually exclusive complement; and the prior odds favoring the focal hypothesis (see Fischhoff & Beyth-Marom, 1983). The key reasoning principle captured by this form of Bayes' theorem is that the evaluation of the diagnosticity of the evidence (the likelihood ratio) should be conducted independently of the assessment of the prior odds favoring the focal hypothesis. The point is not that prior beliefs should not affect the posterior probability of the hypothesis. In fact, a Bayesian analysis is an explicit procedure for factoring in such prior beliefs. The point is that Bayes' theorem reminds us that they should not be factored in twice. Prior beliefs are encompassed in one of two multiplicative terms that define the posterior probability, but the diagnosticity of the new evidence should be assessed separately from the prior belief. Belief bias occurs when prior knowledge or belief influences the estimation of the likelihood ratio.

Thus, the concern in the critical-thinking literature for segregating prior belief from evidence evaluation appears to receive support from normative models of belief revision. But such a conclusion has not gone unchallenged. There are alternative traditions in developmental and cognitive psychology from which maximizing the decontextualization of the evaluation process might not be viewed as optimal. To reiterate, the contextualist tradition within developmental psychology emphasizes that the optimum exercise of cognitive skills often occurs in highly contextualized situations (Bronfenbrenner & Ceci, 1994; J. S. Brown et al., 1989; Ceci, 1993, 1996; Lave & Wenger, 1991; Rogoff & Lave, 1984). This framework might lead us to question whether detaching prior belief from evidence evaluation should really be viewed as the superior strategy.

The emphasis in the critical-thinking literature on segregating prior belief from evidence evaluation is critiqued not only by the contextualists. Challenges have arisen in the philosophical literature and in other quarters of cognitive science. For example, several philosophical analyses have called into question the normative status of the stricture that evidence evaluation not be contaminated by prior belief. Kornblith (1993) argued that in a natural ecology where most of our prior beliefs are true, projecting our beliefs on to new data will lead to faster accumulation of knowledge:

> Mistaken beliefs will, as a result of belief perseverance, taint our perception of new data. By the same token, however, belief perseverance will serve to color our perception of new data when our preexisting beliefs are accurate. ... If, overall, our belief-generating mechanisms give us a fairly accurate picture of the world, then the phenomenon of belief perseverance may do more to inform our understanding than it does to distort it. (p. 105; see chap. 8 for a further discussion of what is there termed the *knowledge projection argument*)

Such an argument calls to mind the warning of Lopes and Oden (1991), quoted in chapter 3, that with regard to many tasks in the heuristics and biases literature, there is "no support for the view that people would choose in accord with normative prescriptions if they were provided with increased capacity" (p. 209). Do we really know that individuals with more cognitive capacity would use it to decontextualize a reasoning situation? There is particular reason to doubt this outcome because—as Kornblith and the contextualist developmental psychologists have argued—contextualizing could well be the habitual response of those with more cognitive capacity.

Lopes and Oden's (1991) doubts about the directionality of the relationship might be particularly apt in this situation. Perhaps—just as it is rational for individuals to project well-adapted cue validities in making single-trial confidence judgments in the knowledge calibration experiment (Gigerenzer et al., 1991)—it will be found that more cognitively competent individuals are *less* likely to decouple prior knowledge and belief when evaluating arguments and evidence. In short, if the standard position in the critical-thinking literature is correct, people with greater algorithmic capacity should show an enhanced ability to reason independently of prior belief. In contrast, if contextualist theories are correct, and tendencies toward decontextualization are actually maladaptive, then people with increased cognitive capacity might be expected to display greater reluctance to detach world knowledge from their information processing.

That there are two influential but competing traditions within which belief bias effects can be conceptualized (the critical-thinking literature and the contextualist tradition) highlights the need for producing empirical data that can at least partially adjudicate the two positions. Sá, West, and Stanovich (in press) reported one of the few such attempts. The benchmark task was the quintessential paradigm for demonstrating the effects of belief bias—the syllogistic reasoning problem that pits the believability of the conclusion against the validity of the argument (e.g., Evans et al., 1983; Markovits & Nantel, 1989). In this paradigm, the belief bias effect occurs when participants are found to judge the validity of the syllogism more accurately when the believability of the conclusion coincides with the validity of the syllogism than when it conflicts. For example, problems that are invalid and have unbelievable conclusions (All guns are dangerous. Rattlesnakes are dangerous. Therefore, rattlesnakes are guns.) are easier than problems that are logically invalid and have believable conclusions (e.g., All living things need water. Roses need water. Roses are living things).

The purpose of the Sá et al. (in press) study was to compare two tasks in which belief bias has been implicated but that had very different cognitive and response requirements. The syllogistic reasoning task covers the verbal reasoning domain of deductive logic. The comparison task was drawn from the perceptual judgment domain in order to contrast with the verbal reasoning domain of the syllogistic reasoning task. This task was adapted from the work of Nelson, Biernat, and Manis (1990) who had participants judge the heights of pictures of seated and standing men and women. They found that the judgments were related to the actual heights, but that the over- and underestimations of the actual heights were related to the gender of the person in the photograph. That is, although gender is a valid cue in that it is related to actual height, participants tended to overproject this cue. It is important to note that this overprojection was maintained in a condition (termed the matched condition) where the male and female pictures were matched in height and the participants were told of this and warned not to use gender as a cue.

The importance of the matched condition of the Nelson et al. (1990) height judgment task derives from the fact that it mirrors the logic of the syllogistic reasoning task. In both cases, the participant is told to ignore a cue that is normally diagnostic but in the particular situation is not predictive (the truth status of the conclusion in the syllogistic reasoning task and the gender of the stimulus in the height judgment task). In both cases, research indicates that in the aggregate, people are unable to ignore the nondiagnostic cue and evaluate only the information of interest (the validity of the syllogism and the valid cues to height in the photograph, respectively). These tasks are particularly interesting ones for investigating issues of domain specificity/generality because—despite the similarity of the belief bias logic across the two—the stimuli used in the tasks are very different and the judgments are quite different (one is a judgment of logical validity and the other a judgment of height).

Thus, in addition to a syllogistic reasoning task, Sá et al. (in press) examined two versions of the Nelson et al. (1990) height judgment paradigm—one where prior knowledge was predictive and one where it was potentially interfering. In the former—termed the ecological condition—the photographs viewed by the participants were a reasonably representative sample of the actual heights of men and women in North America, and participants were informed of this fact. In the latter condition—the matched condition—participants viewed a sample of photographs where the mean heights of the men and women were matched and participants were informed of the matching (i.e., informed that the gender cue was nondiagnostic). This condition is the one that is structurally analogous to the syllogistic reasoning conflict condition.

To further examine the domain specificity/generality issue, et al. (in press) examined two other reasoning tasks that—although not direct measures of belief bias effects—do reflect the ability to evaluate evidence and argument in the face of potentially interfering prior belief. One, the argument evaluation measure (AET) described previously, involved verbal reasoning; the other, a covariation detection task (Levin et al., 1993), involved processing numerical covariation information but with a prior belief component (see chap. 2 and Stanovich & West, 1998c). Both yield a parameter indicating the ability to evaluate evidence in the face of prior belief. If there is some domain generality to the ability to reason in the face of interfering knowledge and belief, then we might expect performance on the syllogistic reasoning and height judgment tasks to be related to the parameters of these two tasks as well.

Our use of parameters from the height judgment task as indices of individual differences in the tendency to project prior belief was innovative and requires further explanation in order to clarify the presentation of the results of this study. Participants were presented with full-length photographs of men and women seated in a variety of natural settings. The participant's task was to judge as accurately as possible the height of the individuals in each of these photographs. The stimuli in the first height judgment task the participants completed—termed the ecological height judgment task—were sampled to reflect the actual male and female heights in the population. These stimuli consisted of 83 pictured models, 40 men and 43 women (75 of these came from the Nelson et al., 1990, study and were generously provided by those investigators). The mean height of the men in the photographs was 5 ft, 10.5 in., and the mean height of the women in the photographs was 5 ft, 5.5 in. These mean heights are roughly equal to those in the general population to which the participants belonged. The photographs were presented in a randomized order—mixing men and women. The instructions in the ecological height judgment task were as follows:

> This task is designed to assess how accurately people can judge the physical characteristics of individuals based on a small amount of information. You will be looking at photographs of individuals and will be asked to judge the height of each person pictured. The task is fairly difficult because the models are all seated. On each page of this booklet you will find a picture of a person. Your task is simply to look at each photograph and estimate the height of the pictured person. Each person's height was measured when they were wearing the shoes that they are wearing in the picture. Therefore, your height estimate should be an estimate of the person's height while wearing the shoes in the picture. As you flip through these pictures, read outloud to the experimenter your height estimate.

The second version of the height judgment task—termed the matched height judgment task—immediately followed the ecological version. In this version, participants were specifically informed that the gender cue had been rendered nondiagnostic and consequently should be ignored in their ensuing height judgments. Participants estimated the heights of 46 pictured models (23 men and 23 women) where the mean male and female heights were equated at 5 ft, 8.8 in. Again, the stimuli were presented in a randomized order—mixing men and women. The instructions in the matched height judgment task were as follows:

> In the following task, you will be doing exactly what you were just doing before. You will again be looking at several pictured people and estimating their height. This time, however, the men and women pictured are, on average, of *equal height*. That is, we have taken care to match the heights of the men and women pictured (as before, footwear is included in the measurement). For every woman of a particular height, somewhere in this section there is also a man of that same height. Therefore, in order to make as accurate a height judgment as possible, try to judge each photograph as an individual case. *Do not rely on the person's sex to aid your judgment.*

One index of the accuracy of participants' estimates of the heights is the correlation between the estimates (E) and the target heights of the actual models (T). This correlation, $r(T,E)$, was calculated for each participant and ranged from .395 to .766 in the ecological set and and from .091 to .645 in the matched set. The mean value of $r(T,E)$ was higher in the ecological set (.610, *SD* = .071) than in the matched set (.358, *SD* = .109).

One index of the potency of the gender cue in the judgments of each participant is the correlation between the gender of the photograph (G) and that participant's estimates, $r(G,E)$. The mean value of this correlation in the ecological set was .693 (*SD* = .129) and the mean value of $r(G,E)$ in the matched set was .281 (*SD* = .196). The *actual* correlation between gender and the target individuals in the photographs in the ecological set, r(G,T), was .628. Thus, the mean r(G,E) value of .693 in the ecological set represents only slightly more projection of the gender cue than is actually warranted. In the matched condition, the r(G,T) correlation was deliberately constrained to zero (actually .018), so the mean r(G,E) value of .281, which is significantly greater than zero, $t(116) = 15.48$, $p < .001$, represents reliably more projection of the gender cue in this condition than is warranted.

Another metric that captures the degree of projection of the gender cue is simply the mean difference between the estimates of male targets and female targets for each each participant. The mean difference in the ecological condition, $(M - F)_{ecological}$, ranged from 1.53 to 9.37 in., and averaged 4.13 ($SD = 1.25$). This mean is almost 1 in. less than the actual mean difference in the ecological set (5 in.). The mean difference in the matched condition, $(M - F)_{matched}$, was substantially lower (1.21, $SD = 0.91$), but still significantly different from zero, $t(116) = 14.35$, $p < .001$. In the matched condition, despite the instructions emphasizing that the men and women were matched in height, 111 of 117 participants gave mean male height estimates that were larger than female estimates.

There are two indices of accuracy in the height judgment task, each reflecting a different property of estimation efficacy (see N. R. Brown & Siegler, 1993). One has already been mentioned—the correlation between the estimates and the target heights of the actual models, r(T,E). It reflects the tendency to order the targets correctly, but it does not reflect the tendency to use the scale correctly—to arrive at estimates that actually match the target heights. The sum of the absolute deviations between estimate and target (SAD) across all stimuli reflects this property. The smaller this index the higher the absolute accuracy of the estimates. In principle, these two indices are independent. For example, it is possible for r(T,E) to be quite high (indicating highly accurate ordering) but for SAD to also be high (indicating poor absolute accuracy of the estimates—poor scale use). This might occur if someone ordered the photographs nearly perfectly but had each of the estimates 3–4 in. too tall (because the individual believed that, overall, the population is taller than it is).

Because there actually is a correlation between gender and target height in the ecological set (r(G,T) = .628) we might expect that, there, projecting one's knowledge of the gender relationship would be efficacious. This was in fact the case. Using r(G,E) as a measure of the projection of this prior belief, we found that this index correlated highly with both r(T,E) [.697, $p < .001$] and SAD [−.525, $p < .001$]. That is, the more the participant projected the gender/height relationship, the more accurate they were. People who more strongly projected the gender/height relationship in their estimates tended to order the stimuli more accurately and they made estimates that tracked the actual heights more closely in an absolute sense.

In fact, in the ecological set, even the tendency to overuse the gender cue (in short, to stereotype) is efficacious. The explanation of the analysis that indicates this begins with a consideration of the path diagram in the top half of Fig. 6.1. This diagram indicates the outcome when the aggregate height estimates (averaged over all 117 respondents) are regressed on gender and the actual height of the targets. The significant standardized beta weight for gender indicates, in the words of Nelson et al. (1990), that "male targets were judged to be taller, on average, than the female targets, even after the actual difference in height between the male and female targets had been statistically controlled" (p. 665). An analysis of individual differences in this tendency to stereotype based on gender indicates that it is actually associated with more accurate estimates. The regression analysis pictured in Fig. 6.1 was run on each individual participant's scores and 117 separate beta weights for gender and actual height were estimated. The former parameter was positively correlated with r(T,E) ($r = .443, p < .001$) and negatively correlated with SAD ($r = -.314, p < .001$). Thus, the more individuals judged male targets to be taller even after actual differences in male and female targets were statistically controlled, the more accurate they were—both in ordering the stimuli correctly and in their absolute deviations from the actual heights.

As would be expected, this tendency for projecting one's knowledge of the gender relationship to be efficacious did not extend to the matched set. There, the projection index, r(G,E), did not correlate with either r(T,E) (−.172) or SAD (.143)—although the signs on the correlations indicated that the more the participant projected the gender/height relationship, the less accurate they were. The bottom half of Fig. 6.1 presents a path diagram indicating the outcome when the aggregate height estimates (averaged over all 117 respondents) are regressed on gender and the actual heights of the targets. The significant standardized beta weight for gender—although reduced in magnitude from that obtained with the ecological set—indicates that despite the instructions emphasizing that these targets were matched for height across gender, participants persisted in estimating greater male heights. Unlike the case in the ecological set, an analysis of individual differences in this tendency to stereotype based on gender indicates that it is not associated with more accurate estimates in the matched set. The regression analysis pictured in Fig. 6.1 was run on each individual participant and 117 separate beta weights for gender and actual height were estimated. The former parameter failed to correlate positively with r(T,E) ($r = -.181, p < .05$) and negatively with SAD ($r = .148$, ns). In fact, the signs of the correlations were in the opposite direction and significantly so in the former case—more stereotyped responses were less accurately ordered.

We now turn to the question of whether there is any domain generality to the projection of prior belief across verbal and nonverbal tasks. Several correlations in the matrix displayed in Table 6.5 are relevant to this ques-

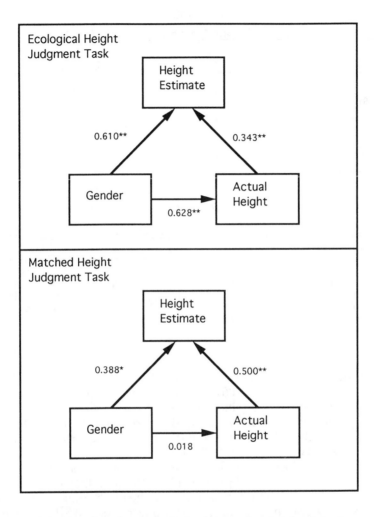

FIG. 6.1. Path diagram predicting the aggregate height judgments in the ecological set displayed on top. Path diagram predicting the aggregate height judgments in the matched set displayed on bottom. Numbers on arrows are standardized beta weights. * = $p < .01$, ** = $p < .001$.

tion. The first two variables listed in the table reflect the degree of projection of the gender relationship on to the estimates, $r(G,E)$, in the matched and ecological sets, respectively. The fourth row of the table indicates that the degree of belief bias on the syllogistic reasoning task (the difference score obtained by subtracting the number correct on the inconsistent items from the number correct on the consistent items) was significantly correlated with the former but not the latter. The correlations were differ-

TABLE 6.5
Intercorrelations Among the Primary Variables

Variable	1.	2.	3.	4.	5.	6.	7.	8.
1. r(G,E), Matched								
2. r(G,E), Ecological	.526							
3. HJ − Adjustment Score	−.396	.342						
4. Syllogisms, Belief Bias	.209	−.095	−.341					
5. AET	−.261	.101	.284	−.236				
6. Covariation Judgment	−.200	.168	.322	−.342	.324			
7. GCA1	−.155	.256	.347	−.445	.449	.493		
8. GCA2	−.215	.263	.461	−.495	.392	.505	.707	
9. AOT	−.130	.057	.119	−.315	.436	.241	.358	.323

Note. Correlations larger than .182 are significant at the .05 level (two-tailed); correlations larger than .237 are significant at the .01 level (two-tailed); and correlations larger than .299 are significant at the .001 level (two-tailed). r(G,E), Matched = correlation between gender and estimates in the matched condition. r(G,E), Ecological = correlation between gender and estimates in the ecological condition. HJ − Adjustment Score = $(M - F)_{ecological}$ minus $(M - F)_{matched}$. AET = argument evaluation test. GCA1 = general cognitive ability composite 1 (WAIS block design and WAIS vocabulary). GCA2 = general cognitive ability composite 2 (Raven matrices and vocabulary). AOT = composite actively open-minded thinking scale.

ent in sign and they were significantly different from each other (.209 vs. −.095, $t(114) = 3.52$, $p < .001$, test for difference in dependent correlations). Thus, it is the condition where the participant is instructed to ignore the relationship between gender and height that correlates with belief bias in the syllogisms task and not the ecological condition where the gender relationship is in fact predictive.

The AET and the covariation task yield parameters reflective of the ability to reason in the face of prior opinion. Although they cannot be interpreted as inverse belief bias indices, these measures of unbiased evaluation of evidence and argument should be related to belief bias if the idea of actively open-minded thinking has the domain generality suggested in the critical-thinking literature. The next two lines of Table 6.5 indicate that they were both significantly correlated with belief projection in the matched set but not with the belief projection in the ecological set. In both cases the signs of the pairs of correlations were different and each pair of correlations is significantly different from each other ($t(114) = 4.30$, $p < .001$ and $t(113) = 4.36$, $p < .001$ for the AET and covariation task, respectively). A greater degree of unbiased processing on the AET and the covariation task was associated with less projection of the gender relationship in the matched set but more projection of the gender relationship in the ecological set. Finally, unbiased processing on the AET and the covariation task were significantly associated with a smaller amount of belief bias on the syllogistic reasoning task (correlations of –.236 and –.342, respectively).

We calculated another index from the height judgment task that reflects the ability to decouple prior knowledge and follow the instructions in the matched set to not use gender as a height judgment cue. The need for this index derives from the fact that the pure projection indices from the matched condition, $r(G,E)_{matched}$ and $(M-F)_{matched}$, should both be zero if the participant fully responds to the instructions and removes all influence of the prior belief—any deviation from the zero value is interpreted as an intrusion of prior knowledge into the height judgments. The problem comes about because reducing these indices to zero may be differentially difficult not because of variation in the belief bias itself but because the strength of the gender stereotype may vary from participant to participant.

To put it simply, it should be easier for a participant who previously thought that there was on average a 2-in. difference between men and women to reduce $(M - F)_{matched}$ to zero than it would be for a participant who thought that there was a 7-in. difference between men and women. The prior belief of the latter participant is much more strongly contradicted by the matched set. Fortunately, in the ecological set we actually have a measure of the participant's prior belief about the strength of the gender/height relationship: $(M - F)_{ecological}$. We used this estimate of the prior belief to construct an index of the degree of adjustment from the ecological set that was achieved in the matched set. This index, HJ Adjustment, was simply $(M - F)_{ecological}$ minus $(M - F)_{matched}$: the mean difference between male and female height estimates in the ecological set minus the mean difference in the matched set. This index captures how much the participant succeeded in reducing their estimates of male–female difference (use of a proportional score rather than a difference score produced very similar results). The mean HJ Adjustment was 2.92 (SD = 1.2)—the average participant decreased the male–female difference in their estimates by almost 3 in. The range in this index was quite large, from .03 in. to 7.41 in.

The third column of Table 6.5 presents the correlations involving the HJ Adjustment index. Its correlation with belief bias on the syllogistic reasoning task was even larger in absolute magnitude than the simpler belief projection index, $r(G,E)_{matched}$ (–.341 vs. .209; the correlation with the former is negative because those showing larger adjustments to the matched set instructions displayed less belief bias in syllogistic reasoning). The HJ Adjustment index was significantly associated ($p < .001$) with performance on both the AET and covariation judgment tasks.

The next two rows of Table 6.5 illustrate the nature of relationships between general cognitive ability and belief bias as well as the ability to reason independently of prior belief. The two composite indices of general cognitive ability, GCA1 (a combination of WAIS [Wechsler Adult Intelligence Scale] block design and WAIS vocabulary) and GCA2 (a combination of Raven matrices and a different vocabulary test), were both negatively correlated with projection in the matched set and positively correlated with projection in the ecological set. In both cases, the correlations with $r(G,E)_{matched}$ and $r(G,E)_{ecological}$ were significantly different $(t(114) = 4.98, p < .001,$ and $t(114) = 6.02, p < .001,$ in the cases of GCA1 and GCA2, respectively). Consistent with these findings are the significant moderate correlations with HJ Adjustment displayed by GCA1 and GCA2 (.347 and .461, respectively). In summary, cognitive ability was positively correlated with belief bias in a perceptual judgment task where prior belief accurately reflected an aspect of the perceptual environment and negatively correlated with belief bias in a perceptual judgment task where prior belief was incongruent with the perceptual environment.

Given the findings on the height judgment task, it then becomes interesting to examine whether cognitive ability is associated with belief bias on a verbal reasoning task as well as the ability to reason independently of prior belief on a verbal task (AET) and on a numerical data inference task (covariation judgment). Both indices of general cognitive ability, GCA1 and GCA2, displayed significant and moderate negative correlations with belief bias on the syllogistic reasoning task (–.445 and –.495). The direction of the correlation was that individuals with more cognitive capacity displayed less belief bias. Similarly, GCA1 and GCA2 displayed moderate correlations (ranging from .392 to .505) with the ability to reason independently of prior belief on the AET and covariation judgment tasks (replicating the results of Stanovich & West, 1997, 1998b).

Finally, the last line of Table 6.5 indicates that a thinking dispositions composite score did not correlate with projecting the gender relationship in the height judgment task, but did display significant correlations with belief bias on the syllogistic reasoning task and performance on the AET and covariation judgment task. This result adds to previous findings indicating that thinking dispositions can predict belief bias in verbal tasks (Kardash & Scholes, 1996; Klaczynski et al., 1997; Schommer, 1990; Stanovich & West, 1997). As is illustrated in Table 6.6, the association remained even after cognitive ability was controlled in the case of two of the four reasoning variables (performance on the AET and the belief bias index of the syllogistic reasoning task). This table presents the results of multiple regression analyses that examined the extent to which performance on each of the reasoning tasks could be predicted by the cognitive ability (the GCA1 composite) and thinking dispositions composite score. The multiple Rs and standardized beta weights for both the cognitive ability composite and the thinking dispositions composite in the final simultaneous equation are presented in the table.

In response to the relatively modest reduction in the gender height stereotype that they achieved with their matched set manipulation, Nelson

TABLE 6.6
**Results of Multiple Regression Analyses Conducted
on the Primary Variables**

	Multiple R	beta, GCA1	beta, TDC
HJ — Adjustment Score	.348***	.341***	.020
Syllogisms, Belief Bias	.476***	−.382***	−.179*
AET	.537***	.336***	.316***
Covariation Judgment	.497***	.467***	.069

Note. GCA1 = general cognitive ability composite 1 (WAIS block design and WAIS vocabulary); TDC = thinking dispositions composite score; beta = standardized beta weight.
* = $p < .05$, ** = $p < .01$, *** = $p < .001$, all two-tailed.

et al. (1990) commented that "people may be largely unable to control the influence of real-life base rates (e.g., the stimulus-response association between sex and height) that have been built up over a lifetime of experience, despite their best attempts to do so" (p. 672). We observed a somewhat more substantial reduction (from a mean height difference of 4.13 in. to one of 1.21 in.), but more important, we have documented very large individual differences in the ability to "control the influence of real-life base rates" and have shown that the ability to control the influence of prior knowledge in this perceptual judgment task is related to the ability to avoid belief bias on a verbal reasoning task and to evaluate evidence in an unbiased manner in two other tasks. Scores on two composite measures of general cognitive ability were also related to the ability to decouple height judgments from the gender stereotype. Thus, people can "control the influence of real-life base rates" but there are large individual differences in the ability to do so—differences that are in part predictable from performance in other reasoning tasks and from their general cognitive ability.

An extreme form of domain specificity—one where the ability to evaluate evidence in an unbiased manner is completely independent from domain to domain—was clearly falsified by the results presented here. A number of analyses indicated that the ability to decouple the influence of prior knowledge from the estimate required in the height judgment task—a perceptual judgment situation—was linked to the ability to decouple prior knowledge from judgments of logical validity in the syllogistic reasoning task—a purely verbal task. Two other tasks yielding parameters reflecting unbiased evidence evaluation ability (the AET and covariation judgment task) also displayed significant correlations with belief bias indices from the height judgment and syllogistic reasoning tasks. As indicated in Table 6.5, all six pairwise correlations involving these four tasks were statistically significant and moderate in size (absolute values = .341, .284, .322, .236,

.342, and .324). These results support the emphasis in the critical-thinking literature on domain-general dispositional traits related to the ability to reason independently of prior belief.

Although an extreme form of the domain specificity view is falsified by these results, it is certainly the case that the magnitude of the correlations leave room for considerable domain specificity in the cognitive mechanisms responsible for biased reasoning. Nevertheless, it should also be emphasized that many of the relationships involving the belief bias index on the syllogistic reasoning task may be underestimated because of the psychometric properties of this index. First, the index is a difference score, which are notoriously unreliable (Cronbach & Furby, 1970; J. R. Edwards, 1995; Thorndike & Hagen, 1977). Second, the components of the difference score are composed of only eight trials each. The task has been developed in the literature as a laboratory measure rather than as a psychometric instrument designed to elucidate individual differences. Schmidt and Hunter (1996) recently cautioned laboratory investigators against expectations of strong relationships when utilizing such measures.

Cognitive ability was associated with skill at decoupling prior knowledge in the syllogistic reasoning task. If contextualist theories were correct, and tendencies toward decontextualization are actually maladaptive, then people with increased cognitive capacity might be expected to display greater reluctance to detach world knowledge from their information processing. Thus, a strong version of the contextualist position—that, because of the primacy of context-based processing (Hilton, 1995; Levinson, 1995), more cognitively able individuals would be more likely to carry over contextual information into an environment where context was inefficacious—was not supported.

Both cognitive ability measures were positively correlated with belief bias in a perceptual judgment task where prior knowledge accurately reflected an aspect of the perceptual environment (the ecological set) and negatively correlated with belief bias in a perceptual judgment task where prior knowledge was incongruent with the perceptual environment (the matched set). Thus, people with more intellectual resources appear to be able to flexibly use prior knowledge depending on its efficacy in a particular environment. They are more likely to project a relationship when it reflects a useful cue, but they are also more likely to decouple prior belief from their judgments when it is *in*efficacious. Our results concerning cognitive ability thus seem to bolster the normative status of the thinking dispositions toward unbiased reasoning that are emphasized in the critical-thinking literature—but with an important caveat emphasized by the contextualist tradition. More intelligent individuals do contextualize the problem more when that context contains cues that can facilitate judgment; but they are less likely to carry over contextual cues into situations where they know the cues are no longer diagnostic.

SUMMARY

The results reported in this chapter indicate that an idealized version of the Apologist's position—every subject performing at the limits of their algorithmic capacity, with no systematic irrationalities at the intentional level—will not be sustained, at least not for most of the tasks considered here. The normative/descriptive gap cannot be entirely explained by computational limitations plus performance errors. Such a view predicts that once capacity limitations have been controlled, the remaining variations from normative responding will be essentially unpredictable (all being due to performance errors). In contrast, it was demonstrated that there was significant covariance among the residualized scores from a variety of tasks in the heuristics and biases literature. Evidence that the residual variance (after partialing cognitive ability) was systematic indicates that at least to some degree the cognitive/behavior model instantiated at the intentional level systematically deviates from the appropriate normative model.

This conclusion was reinforced by findings that the residual variance was also systematically associated with thinking dispositions that were conceptualized as characteristic intentional-level attitudes reflecting epistemic regulation. That cognitive/personality variables can explain normative/descriptive discrepancies that remain after computational limitations have been accounted for again signals a systematically suboptimal intentional-level model of performance. Likewise, domain generality in cognitive decontextualization across two reasoning and judgment tasks of widely varying processing requirements was demonstrated.

In summary, several different multivariate studies discussed here produced evidence indicating that there is systematic variance in performance on heuristics and biases tasks reflective of suboptimal reasoning tendencies. In chapter 7, the processing styles underlying these performance tendencies become the focus.

The Fundamental Computational Bias

What might account for the persistent tendency for performance on reasoning tasks to covary after algorithmic limitations have been accounted for? Some clues as to the cause of these relationships are provided by an examination of the types of thinking dispositions that predicted norma-tive$_s$ responses after computational limitations have been controlled in the Stanovich and West (1997, 1998b; Sá et al., in press) studies. It is argued in this chapter that many of these reflect tendencies toward the types of decontextualizing operations discussed in chapter 6. Consider some examples of the dimensions tapped (and example items from each) in the questionnaires used in those investigations[1]:

- Willingness to postpone closure (Stanovich & West, 1997): example item = "There is nothing wrong with being undecided about many issues."

- Willingness to consider alternative opinions (Stanovich & West, 1997): example item = "A person should always consider new possibilities."

- Willingness to consider contradictory evidence (Stanovich & West, 1997): example item = "People should always take into consideration evidence that goes against their beliefs."

- Openness (NEO scale, Costa & McCrae, 1992): example item = "I believe that laws and social policies should change to reflect the needs of a changing world."

- Disposition toward absolutism (Erwin, 1983): example item = "Right and wrong never change."

---

[1]Recall that when collapsed into a composite measure, all of the subscales are scored in the direction of higher scores indicating stronger tendencies toward actively open-minded thinking.

- Disposition toward dogmatism (Rokeach, 1960): example item = "Of all the different philosophies that exist in the world there is probably only one that is correct."
- Disposition toward categorical thinking (Epstein & Meier, 1989): example item = "I tend to classify people as either for me or against me."
- Disposition toward counterfactual thinking (Stanovich & West, 1997): example item = "My beliefs would not have been very different if I had been raised by a different set of parents" (reverse scored).
- Disposition toward belief identification (Sá et al., in press): example items = "One should disregard evidence that conflicts with your established beliefs," "Someone who attacks my beliefs is not insulting me personally" (reverse scored).
- Need for cognition (Cacioppo et al., 1996): example items = "The notion of thinking abstractly is appealing to me," "It's enough for me that something gets the job done; I don't care how or why it works" (reverse scored).

The items on many of these thinking dispositions subscales are concerned with epistemic regulation—they are probing biases in intentional psychology to recruit prior knowledge to solve problems, to rely on prior belief to aid in judgment, and to bracket existing belief in order to entertain new propositions. They are indirectly tapping the processing style of cognitive decontextualization. Recall the direction of the associations demonstrated in the studies discussed in chapter 6. These thinking dispositions were related to ignoring the content of the belief bias syllogisms. They were related to the tendency to ignore the vivid case evidence in the statistical reasoning problems, and they were related to the ability to reason independently of personal opinions and prior beliefs on a variety of other tasks. Thus, what the tasks had in common among themselves and in common with items on the thinking dispositions questionnaires was that all were directly or indirectly tapping cognitive decontextualization skill.

Another way to conceptualize this commonality is within the context of the dual-process theories discussed in chapter 5 (see Table 5.1). Recalling that discussion, it becomes apparent that many of the decontextualizing cognitive styles mentioned in the previous paragraphs reflect the characteristics of System 2. The degree of overlap might suggest that one function of System 2 that is of preeminent importance is the abstraction of complex situations into a canonical form so that stored syntactic rules can operate efficiently on properly represented information. Additionally, given the complementary set of System 1 properties—and the parallel nature of the two systems (see Evans & Over, 1996)—it is likely that one computational task of System 2 is to decouple (see Navon, 1989a, 1989b) information and context automatically supplied by System 1 that sometimes interferes with the canonical representation needed for the rule system executed by System 2.

Of course, in most cases, the two Systems will interact in concert (Stevenson, 1993) and no decoupling will be necessary. Nevertheless, occasional overrides by System 2 will be necessary because it is the system that responds to the person's intentional-level desires. A potential override situation might occur when System 2 detects that automatic (System 1) processes are thwarting overall goal satisfaction. This will happen occasionally because System 1 processes are adapted to a criterion—genetic fitness (see Dawkins, 1982, chapter 10, for a useful discussion of the complex concept of fitness)—different from utility maximization at the level of the individual (see chap. 5). Thus, the willingness to use the metacognitive control processes of System 2 to override System 1 might well be an intentional-level cognitive style that accounts for the covariance patterns discussed previously. In short, one of the functions of System 2 is to serve as an override system for some of the automatic and obligatory computational results provided by System 1 (Evans & Over, 1996; Fodor, 1983; Pollock, 1991; Stanovich, 1990). This override function might be needed in only a tiny minority of information-processing situations, but they may be unusually important ones (see the discussion that follows and in chap. 8).

It is assumed—along with many other theorists (Brase et al., 1998; Cosmides & Tooby, 1994; Evans & Over, 1996; Gigerenzer, 1996b; Pinker, 1997; Reber, 1993)—that a host of useful information-processing operations and adaptive behaviors are carried out automatically by System 1 (the attribution of intentionality, depth perception, face recognition, frequency estimation, language comprehension, cheater detection, color perception, etc.). Indeed, because this list is so extensive and because System 1 infuses so much of mental life, many theorists (e.g., Cummins, 1996; Evans & Over, 1996; Hilton, 1995; Levinson, 1995; Reber, 1993) have been led to stress the primacy of the implicit, the contextual, and the social—in short, the primacy of the automatic contextualization of System 1 processes. Because this tendency toward the contextualization of information processing by System 1 is so pervasive, it is termed here the *fundamental computational bias* in human cognition.

The fundamental computational bias is meant to be a global term that captures the pervasive bias toward the contextualization of all informational encounters. It conjoins the following processing tendencies: (a) the tendency to adhere to Gricean conversational principles even in situations that lack many conversational features (Adler, 1984; Hilton, 1995), (b) the tendency to contextualize a problem with as much prior knowledge as is easily accessible, even when the problem is formal and the only solution is a content-free rule (Evans, 1982, 1989; Evans et al., 1983), (c) the tendency to see design and pattern in situations that are either undesigned, unpatterned, or random (Levinson, 1995), (d) the tendency to reason enthymematically—to make assumptions not stated in a problem and then reason from those assumptions (Henle, 1962; Rescher, 1988), and (e) the tendency toward a narrative mode of thought (Bruner, 1986, 1990).

All of these properties conjoined together represent a cognitive tendency toward radical contextualization. The bias is termed fundamental because it is thought to stem largely from System 1 and that system is assumed to be primary in that it permeates virtually all of our thinking (e.g., Evans & Over, 1996). If the properties of this system are not to be the dominant factors in our thinking, then they must be overridden by System 2 processes.

The remainder of this chapter deals with several issues surrounding the fundamental computational bias. First, evidence on the pervasiveness of the fundamental computational bias is discussed. I next address the implications of the assumption that the fundamental computational bias is adaptive in an evolutionary sense and the assumption that, as argued in chapter 5, evolutionary rationality in the sense of genetic adaptation to the environment and reproductive success is sometimes not coextensive with normative rationality in the sense of maximizing the organism's utility. The separation of evolutionary rationality from normative rationality in some cases requires that the evolutionarily rational fundamental computational bias be overridden by the personal-utility-maximizing processes of System 2—processes that often operate to strip excess content and context from representations generated by System 1. Briefly mentioned is the fact that a large part of education can be viewed as an attempt to develop controlled processing styles that override the fundamental computational bias and thus enable learned rule systems to operate on decoupled representations. Finally, I argue that the need to override the fundamental computational bias in order to pursue normative rationality increases in a technological, knowledge-based society. Because postindustrial societies increasingly create more and more decontextualized information-processing environments (insurance forms, HMO rules, graduation requirements, taxation statutes), the cognitive environment of present society—and the environment of the future—puts a premium on the ability to selectively override the fundamental computational bias, an ability that studies have shown to be related to both algorithmic-level computational capacity and the thinking dispositions of intentional-level psychology.

THE PERVASIVENESS OF THE FUNDAMENTAL COMPUTATIONAL BIAS

Luria's (1976) work among illiterate Uzbeks in central Asia provides some classic examples of the refusal to adopt a detached, or decontextualizing processing style. The following syllogism was presented to a 37-year-old illiterate man from a remote village: In the Far North, where there is snow, all bears are white. Novaya Zemlya is in the Far North and there is always snow there. What color are the bears there? The exchange between experimenter and participant went as follows:

> P: There are different sorts of bears. [The syllogism is repeated]
>
> P: I don't know; I've seen a black bear, I've never seen any others ... Each locality has its own animals: if it's white, they will be white; if it's yellow, they will be yellow.
>
> E: But what kind of bears are there in Novaya Zemlya?
>
> P: We always speak only of what we see; we don't talk about what we haven't seen.
>
> E: But what do my words imply? [The syllogism is repeated]
>
> P: Well, it's like this: our tsar isn't like yours, and yours isn't like ours. Your words can be answered only by someone who was there, and if a person wasn't there he can't say anything on the basis of your words.
>
> E: But on the basis of my words—in the North, where there is always snow, the bears are white, can you gather what kind of bears there are in Novaya Zemlya?
>
> P: If a man was sixty or eighty and had seen a white bear and had told about it, he could be believed, but I've never seen one and hence I can't say. That's my last word. Those who saw can tell, and those who didn't see can't say anything!
>
> (At this point a young Uzbek volunteered, "From your words it means that bears there are white.")
>
> E: Well, which of you is right?
>
> P: What the cock knows how to do, he does. What I know, I say, and nothing beyond that! (Luria, 1976, pp. 108–109)

Luria (1976) concluded that:

> The most typical responses of the subjects, therefore, were a complete denial of the possibility of drawing conclusions from propositions about things they had no personal experience of, and suspicion about any logical operation of a purely theoretical nature, although there was the recognition of the possibility of drawing conclusions from one's own practical experience. (p. 108)

Of course, such response styles are not restricted to the uneducated or illiterate (Evans & Wason, 1976; Henle, 1962; Wason & Johnson-Laird, 1970). As Schoenfeld (1983) noted, "we need not travel to Liberia; clashes in the 'rules of discourse' between experimenter and subject occur here in our own laboratories" (p. 349).

In both Luria's (1976) examples involving illiterate participants and Henle's (1962) examples involving literate participants, the fundamental computational bias prevented subjects from accepting the framework of a task based on logical validity rather than content. People are also reluctant to accept the consequentialist reasoning of decision theory because of its decontextualizing requirements. For example, Bacharach and

Hurley (1991) pointed out how reasoning consequentially requires a type of decontextualization because outcomes must be considered intrinsically—without reference to external factors that preceded the outcomes and/or provide the context for them: "There is a tendency, and not just among decision-theorists, to assume that there must be some level of description of decision problems at which all acceptable distinctions of context relative to naive characterizations of goods have been captured, and such that no [further] context dependence of evaluation relative to it can be rational" (p. 13). In short, to act in consequentialist fashion, the features of the actual context (intention, etc.) must be abstracted so that only future outcomes are compared.

In a series of studies, Baron (1993a, 1994a, 1998) demonstrated how people routinely fail to do the requisite abstraction and thus reason in a nonconsequentialist fashion. In virtually all of his examples, the violation of consequentialist reasoning occurs because heuristics of System 1 inappropriately contextualize a situation and System 2 processes fail to override by applying rules that subjects actually endorse as superior. For example, the act-omission distinction is hypothesized to arise because harmful acts are usually more intentional than harmful omissions, and this distinction continues to be made even when there is no difference in intention (see Baron, 1993a, 1994a, 1998).

Likewise, in the case of compensation decisions, consequentialist thinking dictates that the amount of compensation should depend only on the nature of the injury when punishment and/or deterrence is not an issue. People give nonconsequentialist responses, Baron (1993a, 1994, 1998) argued, largely because they overgeneralize the desire to punish someone even when that is not part of the decision-making context. The overlearned association between victim compensation and punishment is apparently difficult to override—another case where the inability to decontextualize leads to nonconsequentialist decisions. Similarly, in punishment judgments, deterrence and retribution are so often associated that decisions are determined only by the latter, and the neglect of concerns about deterrence can lead to nonconsequentialist decisions (Baron, 1993a, 1994a). Retribution perhaps dominates because of a vividness effect (see Nisbett & Ross, 1980) that overwhelms considerations of deterrence that might be apparent if one could decouple concerns about retribution that are obligatorily triggered by System 1 heuristics.

Many of the examples discussed by Baron (1993a, 1994, 1998) result from a kind of automatic (see Arkes, 1991) or mindless (see Langer, 1989) appending of contextual features onto a situation—a contextualization that becomes maladaptive when cues that are typically correlated become dissociated. Because System 1 automatically appends contextual features to a task interpretation, situations where these contextual features must be decoupled because they are not applicable require the analytic intelligence of System 2. Thus, failure to override the operation of the fundamental computational bias in these situations becomes the source of nonconsequentialist decision making—situations where people act in contradiction to their own future interests as they themselves see them (Baron, 1993a, 1994a, 1998).

The nonconsequentialist errors discussed by Baron arise because System 1 appends a context to a problem representation when it is inappropriate to do so. But as all of the early heuristics and biases investigators (e.g., Kahneman & Tversky, 1972; Nisbett & Ross, 1980; Tversky & Kahneman, 1974) emphasized, the System 1 processes that contextualize a problem more often than not facilitate reasoning by doing so. The cognitive ecologists—to use Piattelli-Palmarini's (1994) term—have emphasized this point with even more force (e.g., Cosmides & Tooby, 1996; Gigerenzer, 1993, 1996b). Normative and evolutionary rationality most often coincide, and when they do, the automatic contextualization of System 1 will facilitate computation of the normative response. It is only in cases where the contextualization is inappropriate (as in the examples from Baron's work) that people are led astray.

Philosopher Nicholas Rescher (1988) made a similar argument and also emphasized the pervasiveness of the fundamental computational bias in cognitive life. For example, Rescher defended responses that exhibit the gambler's fallacy on the grounds that people assume a model of saturation that is valid in other domains (e.g., food ingestion, sleep) and that:

> The issue may well be one of a mistaken factual supposition rather than one of fallacious reasoning ... one systemic weakness of all such claims of a general penchant to fallacious inference lies in the *enthymematic* character of much human reasoning. We frequently make substantive assumptions about how things stand in the world on the basis of experience or inculcation, and the incorrect conclusions people draw can stem from these *assumptions* rather than from any error of inferential reasoning. (pp. 195–196)

In reviewing the earlier reasoning literature on content effects, Evans (1982) referred to how it is a ubiquitous finding that "in effect, the subject reasons with an augmented problem space, enriched by relevant personal experience" (p. 225). The enthymematic reasoning styles that are a component of the fundamental computational bias are thus natural and nearly universal reasoning styles of human beings; they will facilitate reasoning when context and System 2 processing is compatible and mutually reinforcing (see Stevenson, 1993). But equally obviously they will be maladaptive when the situation demands a non-enthymematic reasoning style.

The enthymematic aspect of the fundamental computational bias thus guarantees that when the environment calls on a person to fix beliefs via a content-free construal, then they will reason poorly. A number of such examples were discussed in chapter 4. Oaksford and Chater's (1994) analysis of the selection task assumes that subjects approach the task as an inductive problem in data selection from the natural environment with assumptions about the relative rarity of the various classes (vowels, odd numbers) of cards (despite the fact the instructions refer to four cards only). Such an approach to the problem is entirely enthymematic. The subject is assumed to be adding details and context to the problem that are not present in the actual instructions. The latter refer to only four cards, but the logic of the inductive approach assumes that the subject is thinking in terms of sampling from classes of cards. Subjects even have implicit hypotheses about the relative rarity of these classes according to the optimal data selection model of Oaksford and Chater. Despite the fact that the instructions speak in terms of determining truth and falsity, most subjects are thought to ignore this and instead to think in terms of inductive probabilities.[2] In short, the deductive requirements of the instructions violate the fundamental computational bias of most subjects who proceed instead to solve a contextualized, inductive version consistent with the bias and for which their System 1 machinery is well adapted (Oaksford and Chater showed that a Bayesian model of optimal data selection fits the choices of most subjects quite well). In contrast, a small minority of subjects—disproportionally those of higher analytic intelligence (see chap. 4)—do construe the task deductively, presumably because, for these individuals, the explicit rule-based processes of System 2 were salient enough to override the more natural inductive construal automatically triggered by System 1.

The analysis of performance on the Linda Problem discussed in chapter 4 implicates a different feature of the fundamental computational bias: its underpinnings in the social and pragmatic contextualization necessary to support a Gricean mechanism of intention attribution (Hilton, 1995; Levinson, 1995). Adler (1991) discussed how an objective perspective confounds all of the biases that interactional intelligence would naturally impose on a problem: "(a) judging probability according to the axioms of probability, (b) representing the alternatives just as they are given, and (c) understanding the problem in terms of no outside, background information. We know that the experimenters want this problem to be viewed as self-contained, as an exam, and not as a particular moment in an on-going inquiry" (p. 276). Instead, the Linda Problem contains a host of features that support pragmatic inferences that justify a reasonably high probability for the conjunction. For example, Macdonald and Gilhooly (1990) argued that it is possible that subjects will "usually assume the questioner is asking the question because there is some reason to suppose that Linda might be a bank teller" (p. 59). Hilton thought the subject assumes that the detailed information given about the target means that the experimenter knows a considerable amount about Linda and conditions lin-

---

[2]Margolis' (1987) conjectures on alternative interpretations of the selection task (see chap. 4) likewise posit highly enthymematic reasoning.

guistic interpretations of the alternatives ("Linda is a bank teller") accordingly. Morier and Borgida (1984) thought that the presence of the conjunction itself prompts an inference that "Linda is a bank teller" really means the complement of the conjunction. With all of these inferences being possible, it is perhaps not surprising that upwards of 80% of subjects display the conjunction fallacy. But all of these inferences are of course as far as one could get from a decontextualized, rule-based (e.g., System 2) representation of the problem. Again, however, a few subjects—disproportionately those of greater cognitive ability—overcome the fundamental computational bias that all of these System 1 inferences reflect and reason according to the conjunction rule of probability theory.

All of these results suggest that a high cognitive ability score (as well as a high score on measures of actively open-minded thinking) is a marker for the tendency of System 2 processes to override the fundamental computational bias. This was certainly true of the study of the belief bias effect in syllogistic reasoning reported by Sá et al. (in press). The task of reasoning about syllogisms with conflicts between factual content and logical form puts a heavy premium on the ability to overcome the fundamental computational bias (responding in terms of the real-world content of the conclusions). In order to concentrate on logical form, the person must decouple (Navon, 1989a, 1989b) the content of the items from the reasoning process and reason as though the terms of the syllogism were neutral symbols rather than words connected to world knowledge in highly overlearned ways. High cognitive ability (as well as high scores on various thinking dispositions) was clearly a marker for the ability to accomplish this decontextualization in the syllogistic reasoning task. Wetherick (1995) implicated the fundamental computational bias in performance on many decontextualized reasoning problems by noting that "subjects do not without specific instruction try to dissect out an abstract model and respond according to that" (p. 429). The results on belief bias in syllogistic reasoning indicate that, even *with* specific instruction, many people have difficulty "dissecting out an abstract model," so strong is the contextualizing bias.

Performance on other tasks displayed an analogous pattern. The causal aggregate statistical reasoning problems examined in several studies were inspired by the work of Nisbett and Ross (1980) on the tendency of human judgment to be overly influenced by vivid but unrepresentative personal and case evidence and to be underinfluenced by more representative and diagnostic, but pallid, statistical evidence. Recognizing the greater diagnosticity of the statistical evidence requires the subject to ignore the salience and seeming personal relevance of the case evidence. This degree of decontextualization again probably requires that an override, or decoupling function be served by System 2, and again Stanovich and West (1998b) observed consistent cognitive ability differences (as well as differences in thinking dispositions) on this task.

All of these results are consistent with the argument of chapter 5 that differences in cognitive ability will be found only on problems that strongly engage both reasoning systems and in which the reasoning systems cue opposite responses. The results from the matched condition of the height judgment task studied by Sá et al. (in press) are consistent with this view. Analytic intelligence is required to decouple the gender cue (which is not diagnostic in this situation) and prevent it from dominating responses. Natural and overlearned environmental cues—perhaps optimized to the natural ecology (Anderson, 1990, 1991; Gigerenzer et al., 1991; Petrinovich, 1989)—must be overridden, and in this case the decoupling is probably of a controlled variety characteristic of System 2.

The results from the ecological condition are perhaps puzzling from this viewpoint, however, because there the overlearned environmental cues should be automatically employed by System 1—yet there was a significant positive correlation between cognitive ability and an index of gender cue projection (the correlation between the gender of the photograph and that participant's estimates, r(G,E)). The mean value of the latter index in the ecological set was .693 and was higher than the actual correlation between gender and the target individuals in the photographs in that set (.628). Thus there was somewhat of an overshoot from proper cue calibration. However, perhaps some of the overshoot represents subjects consciously projecting (from System 2) the gender cue from explicit knowledge of its efficacy. Projection of the gender cue in the ecological condition might occur through both systems, thus creating a relationship with analytic intelligence to the extent that the cue is being projected by System 2 processes. An additional impact from System 2 is consistent with the overprojection of the cue if we assume that System 1 itself is accurately calibrated.

Investigators from a variety of perspectives have emphasized that the fundamental computational bias is a foundational aspect of cognition and that it is sometimes disruptive of normative reasoning. Social psychologists such as Funder (1987) have argued that subjects making errors in social judgment experiments "derive their responses from a wider context than the partial reality the experimenter has in mind. They base their responses on their knowledge of real-world semantics and real-world correlations, on their perceptions of what the experimenter might be 'really' communicating to them or otherwise demanding" (p. 82). Somewhat analogously in the verbal domain, it has long been realized that many departures from the rules of logic reflect adherence to wider pragmatic rules of discourse that are useful in real-world conversation (Braine, 1978; Politzer, 1986; Rumain, Connell, & Braine, 1983). In an article discussing developmental trends in reasoning, Chapman (1993) drew the specific link between the ability to decouple pragmatic knowledge in the interests of reasoning logically: "children who have mastered the pragmatic rules of language may have to unlearn some of these rules when it comes to formal reasoning. More precisely, they may have to learn that particular contexts exist in which those rules do not apply" (p. 104).

Kahneman and Tversky (1982, pp. 132-135) were themselves among the first to discuss an important aspect of the operation of the fundamental computational bias that operates in laboratory experiments: automatic conversational implicatures that subjects draw to contextualize experimental materials. However, Adler's (1984) discussion is perhaps the most complete. In his article titled "Abstraction is Uncooperative," he pointed out that what is called for in many problem-solving and reasoning tasks (and certainly in many tasks in the heuristics and biases literature) is abstraction—extracting from a given problem representation only the features that fit a general pattern. In the process of abstraction "we are rendering information inessential to the formal structure irrelevant" (p. 165). But Adler pointed out that the Gricean cooperative principle is directly in conflict with the demands of abstraction. The cooperativeness principle that everything about the experimenter's contribution is relevant (the instructions, the context, every bit of content that is presented) is diametrically opposed to the requirements of abstraction—that we treat as inessential everything that does not fit a certain formal structure. Hence adherence to Gricean conversational principles—which work directly against the requirements of abstraction—is a critical feature of the fundamental computational bias (see Hilton, 1995; Levinson, 1995; Sperber & Wilson, 1986).

In addition to Gricean relevance principles, the radical contextualization of the fundamental computational bias is often achieved by supplementing formal, often decontextualized, problems with prior knowledge: "Specific features of problem content, and their semantic associations, constitute the dominant influence on thought" (Evans et al., 1983, p. 295). One reflection of this tendency that is often commented on in the heuristics and biases literature is that, even in problems that are viewed purely formally by the experimenter, the slightest bit of real-world information in the problem seems to provoke contextual inferences. For example, even Doherty and Mynatt's (1990; see chap. 2) relatively sparse "Digirosa" selection problem (A patient comes to you with a red rash.... What information would you want.... Below are four pieces of information ...) provokes such a reaction. When Doherty and Mynatt's subjects gave oral explanations for their choices, "many brought real-world knowledge to the task, knowledge about the relations between symptoms and diseases in general and knowledge about rashes in particular" (p. 8). These subject responses exemplify the tendency toward complete contextualization, which Evans, Over, and Manktelow (1993) stressed is often a generally adaptive characteristic of thought: "The purpose of reasoning is best served by drawing inferences from all our beliefs, not just from an artificially restricted set of premises" (p. 175).

Margolis (1987), in describing his notion of scenario ambiguity, described the tendency to fill in with contextual information when a problem is not "narrativized" or provided with personally relevant infor-mation:

> Since our experience in the world is one of dealing with things in context, not as detached set-piece puzzles, a naked puzzle can cause us trouble that goes far beyond what can be accurately accounted for in terms of its intrinsic difficulty.... We will see the problem in terms of some wider context (in terms of some scenario or pattern of experience in the world), even though in this case there is no wider pattern.... In the impoverished environment of the set-piece puzzle, therefore, we may impute a wider context to the problem that is not only not there at all but perhaps is flatly inappropriate. (pp. 143–144)

The tendency to supplement purely formal problems with prior knowledge often takes the form of a constructed narrative that is largely free of the constraints of information actually presented in the problem. Margolis (1987) pointed out that it is not uncommon for a subject to concoct a task construal that is so discrepant from anything in the problem as set (even if narratively coherent in itself) that it represents a serious cognitive error: "an anomalous response will almost always in fact be a reasonably logical response to another question (as Henle has claimed), and in particular to a question that means something in the life experience of the individual giving the response. But the other question will often turn out to be a logically irrelevant or absurd interpretation of the context that actually prompted the response" (p. 6).

The real-life manifestations of this phenomenon are becoming quite problematic in some areas of modern life. For example, many aspects of the legal system put a premium on detaching prior belief and world knowledge from the process of evidence evaluation. There has been understandable vexation at odd jury verdicts rendered because of jury theories and narratives concocted during deliberations that had nothing to do with the evidence but instead that were based on background knowledge and personal experience. For example, a Baltimore jury acquitted a murder defendant who had been identified by four witnesses and had confessed to two people because "they had invented their own highly speculative theory of the crime" (R. A. Gordon, 1997, p. 258). In this particular case, the perpetrator had wanted to plea bargain for a 40-year sentence, but this was turned down at the request of the victim's family. Similarly, in Lefkowitz's (1997) account of the trial of several teenagers in an affluent New Jersey suburb who brutally exploited and raped a young girl who was intellectually disabled, one juror concocted the extenuating circumstance that one defendant thought he was attending an "initiation rite" even though no evidence for such a "rite" had been presented in months of testimony.

The point is that in a particular cultural situation where detachment and decoupling is required, the people who must carry out these demands for decontextualization are often unable to do so even under legal compulsion. Posttrial reports of juries in a "creative," "narrative," or highly enthymematic mode have incited great debate. If the polls are to be believed, a large proportion of Americans were incensed at the jury's acquittal of O. J. Simpson. Similar numbers were appalled at the jury verdict in the first trial of the officers involved in the Rodney King beating. What both juries failed to do was to decontextualize the evidence in their respective cases—and each earned the wrath of their fellow citizens because it is a cultural (and legal) expectation of citizenship that people should be able to carry out this cognitive operation in certain settings. In fact, one of the most important outcomes of schooling is the development of the tendency to override the fundamental computational bias in particular contexts (Luria, 1976; Olson, 1994; Scribner & Cole, 1981; Siddiqui, West, & Stanovich, 1998). A large part of education can in fact be viewed as an attempt to develop controlled processing operations that have the ability to override the fundamental computational bias and thus enable learned rule systems to operate on decoupled representations (Anderson, Reder, & Simon, 1996; Baron, 1993a, 1994b; R. E. Nisbett, 1993; Stanovich, 1996).

However, acknowledging the importance of situations where the fundamental computational bias is at odds with our goals, it should not be forgotten that the bias is helpful in the majority of our interactions with the world. Gigerenzer (1996b) viewed the foundation of thinking as situated in social interaction rather than abstract formalisms and emphasized that contextualization in most cases in the real world is efficacious: "In order to improve reasoning, the mind must take advantage of contextual information and prior knowledge" (Gigerenzer, 1991c, p. 241).

THE FUNDAMENTAL COMPUTATIONAL BIAS AND EVOLUTIONARY ADAPTATION

There is probably a reason that the "specific features of problem content, and their semantic associations, constitute the dominant influence on thought" (Evans et al., 1983, p. 295)—and that reason is that our brains have been shaped by evolution to have this property. The fundamental computational bias is no doubt rational in the evolutionary sense (Anderson, 1990, 1991; Oaksford & Chater, 1994, 1996). Selection pressure was probably in the direction of radical contextualization. An organism that could bring more relevant information to bear (not forgetting the frame problem) on the puzzles of life probably dealt with the world better than competitors and thus reproduced with greater frequency and contributed more of its genes to future generations.

Evans and Over (1996) argued that an overemphasis on normative rationality has led us to overlook the adaptiveness of contextualization and the nonoptimality of always decoupling prior beliefs from problem situations ("beliefs that have served us well are not lightly to be abandoned," p. 114). Their argument here parallels the reasons that philosophy of science has moved beyond naive falsificationism (see Howson & Urbach, 1993). Scientists do not abandon a richly confirmed and well-integrated theory at the first little bit of falsifying evidence, because abandoning the theory might actually decrease explanatory coherence (Thagard, 1992). Similarly, Evans and Over argued that beliefs that have served us well in the past should be hard to dislodge, and projecting them on to new information—because of their past efficacy—might actually help in assimilating the new information (this argument receives further discussion in chap. 8).

Evans and Over (1996) noted the mundane but telling fact that when scanning a room for a particular shape, our visual systems register color as well. They argued that we do not impute irrationality to our visual systems because they fail to screen out the information that is not focal. Our systems of recruiting prior knowledge and contextual information to solve problems with formal solutions are probably likewise adaptive in the evolutionary sense. However, Evans and Over did note that there is an important disanalogy here as well, because studies of belief bias in syllogistic reasoning have shown that "subjects can to some extent ignore belief and reason from a limited number of assumptions when instructed to do so" (p. 117). That is, in the case of reasoning—as opposed to the visual domain—some people do have the cognitive flexibility to decouple unneeded systems of knowledge and some do not.

The studies reviewed in chapter 6 indicate that those that do have the requisite flexibility are somewhat higher in cognitive ability and in actively open-minded thinking. These styles and skills are largely System 2, not System 1, processes. The extra degree of cognitive flexibility displayed by individuals of high cognitive ability and high epistemic openness might translate into higher degrees of normative rationality (the maximization of the individual's utility) for some people. Although the fundamental computational bias appears to operate in the service of evolutionary rationality, it was also emphasized in chapter 5 that normative and evolutionary rationality are not constrained from coming apart (W. S. Cooper, 1989; Skyrms, 1996; Stich, 1990). A conflict between the decontextualizing requirements of normative rationality and the fundamental computational bias may perhaps be one of the main reasons that normative and evolutionary rationality dissociate.

THE REAL-WORLD IMPORTANCE OF COGNITIVE DECONTEXTUALIZATION

Numerous theorists have warned about a possible mismatch between the fundamental computational bias and the processing requirements of many tasks in a technological society containing many abstract and decontextualized symbolic artifacts. Hilton (1995) warned that the default assumption of interactional intelligence may be wrong for many technical settings because:

> Many reasoning heuristics may have evolved because they are adaptive in contexts of social interaction. For example, the expectation that errors of interpretation will be quickly repaired may be correct when we are interacting with a human being but incorrect when managing a complex system such as an aircraft, a nuclear power plant, or an economy. The evolutionary adaptiveness of such an expectation to a conversational setting may explain why people are so bad at dealing with lagged feedback in other settings. (p. 267)

Concerns about the real-world implications of the failure to engage in necessary cognitive abstraction (see Adler, 1984) were what led Luria (1976) to warn against minimizing the importance of decontextualizing thinking styles. In discussing the syllogism, he noted that "a considerable proportion of our intellectual operations involve such verbal and logical systems; they comprise the basic network of codes along which the connections in discursive human thought are channeled" (p. 101). Likewise, regarding the subtle distinctions on many decontextualized language tasks, Olson (1986) argued that:

> The distinctions on which such questions are based are extremely important to many forms of intellectual activity in a literate, society. It is easy to show that sensitivity to the subtleties of language are crucial to some undertakings. A person who does not clearly see the difference between an expression of intention and a promise or between a mistake and an accident, or between a falsehood and a lie, should avoid a legal career or, for that matter, a theological one. (p. 341)

Olson's statement reflects a stark fact about modern technological societies: they are providing lucrative employment only for those who can master complexity, make subtle quantitative and verbal distinctions, and reason in decontextualized ways (Bronfenbrenner, McClelland, Wethington, Moen, & Ceci, 1996; Frank & Cook, 1995; Gottfredson, 1997; Hunt, 1995, in press). Objective measures of the requirements for cognitive abstraction have been increasing across most job categories in technological societies throughout the past several decades (Gottfredson, 1997). This is why measures of the ability to deal with abstraction remain the best employment predictor and the best earnings predictor in postindustrial societies (Brody, 1997; Gottfredson, 1997; Hunt, 1995).

Einhorn and Hogarth (1981) highlighted the importance of decontextualized environments in their discussion of the optimistic (Panglossian/Apologist) and pessimistic (Meliorist) views of the cognitive biases revealed in laboratory experimentation. Einhorn and Hogarth noted that "the most optimistic asserts that biases are limited to laboratory situations which are unrepresentative of the natural ecology" (p. 82), but they went on to caution that "in a rapidly changing world it is unclear what the relevant natural ecology will be. Thus, although the laboratory may be an unfamiliar environment, lack of ability to perform well in unfamiliar situations takes on added importance" (p. 82).

Critics of the abstract content of most laboratory tasks and standardized tests have been misguided on this very point. The issue is that, ironically, the argument that the laboratory tasks and tests are not like "real life" is becoming less and less true. "Life," in fact, is becoming more like the tests! Try using an international ATM machine with which you are unfamiliar; or try arguing with your HMO about a disallowed medical procedure. In such circumstances, we invariably find out that our personal experience, our emotional responses, our stimulus-triggered intuitions about social justice—all are worthless. All are for naught when talking over the phone to the representative looking at a computer screen displaying a spreadsheet with a hierarchy of branching choices and conditions to be fulfilled. Or, consider what a person faces when deciding on whether to apply for a tax deduction for an infirm relative who lived outside Canada for the year 1994. Revenue Canada will advise that person that "Your dependent must be: —your or your spouse's child or grandchild, if that child was born in 1976 or earlier and is physically or mentally infirm; or—a person living in Canada at any time in the year who meets all of the following conditions. The person must have been: —your or your spouse's parent, grandparent, brother, sister, aunt, uncle, niece, or nephew;—born in 1976 or earlier; and—physically or mentally infirm."

Finally, it just seems perverse to argue the "unnaturalness" of decontextualized reasoning skills when tests of such skills are the gatekeepers for an elite educational system that feeds privileged positions in society. If one has the postindustrial goal of, say, "going to Princeton," then the only way to fulfill that goal in our current society *is* to develop such cognitive skills. Tests of abstract thought and of the ability to deal with complexity (often disguised and not labeled as such) will increase in number as more niches in postindustrial societies require these intellectual styles and skills (Gottfredson, 1997; Hunt, 1995). For intellectuals to use their abstract reasoning skills to argue that the "person in the street" is in no need of such skills of abstraction is like a rich person telling someone in poverty that money is not really that important.

To the extent that modern society increasingly requires the fundamental computational bias to be overridden, then dissociations between evolutionary and normative rationality will become more common. For example, once, people grew up eating what was produced in their immediate environments. When they now go to the supermarket, a panoply of foods from all over the world is presented to them, and their choices are conditioned by social custom, active information search, and the influences of an advertising-saturated society that presents messages that they wish to avoid but cannot (Wilson & Brekke, 1994). Thus, in order to achieve one's goals in a technological society where normative rationality and evolutionary rationality have come apart, the evolutionarily adaptive responses of System 1 will increasingly have to be overridden by the strategic, capacity-demanding operations of System 2.

In fact, such dissociations are a major theme in the writings of the cognitive ecologists. Cosmides and Tooby (1996) argued that "in the modern world, we are awash in numerically expressed statistical information. But our hominid ancestors did not have access to the modern accumulation which has produced, for the first time in human history, reliable, numerically expressed statistical information about the world beyond individual experience. Reliable numerical statements about single event probabilities were rare or nonexistent in the Pleistocene" (p. 15). "It is easy to forget that our hominid ancestors did not have access to the modern system of socially organized data collection, error checking, and information accumulation.... In ancestral environments, the only external database available from which to reason inductively was one's own observations" (Brase et al., 1998, p. 5).

Precisely. I am living in a technological society where I must: decide which HMO to join based on just such statistics, figure out whether to invest in a Roth IRA, decide what type of mortgage to purchase, figure out what type of deductible to get on my auto insurance, decide whether to trade in a car or sell it myself, decide whether to lease or to buy, think about how to apportion my TIAA/CREF retirement funds, and decide whether I would save money by joining a book club. And I must make all of these decisions based on information represented in a manner for which my brain is not adapted (in none of these cases have I coded individual frequency information from my own person experience). In order to reason normatively in all of these domains (in order to maximize my own personal utility), I am going to have to deal with probabilistic information represented in nonfrequentistic terms—in representations that the cognitive ecologists have shown are different from my well-adapted algorithms for dealing with frequency information (Cosmides & Tooby, 1996; Gigerenzer & Hoffrage, 1995).

Consider the work of Brase et al. (1998), who improved performance on the notorious three-card problem (Bar-Hillel & Falk, 1982; Falk, 1992; Granberg, 1995) by presenting the information as frequencies and in terms of whole objects—both alterations designed to better fit the frequency computation systems of the brain. In response to a query about why the adequate performance observed was not even higher given that our brains contain such well-designed frequency computation systems, Brase et al. replied that "in our view it is remarkable that they work on paper-and pencil problems at all. A natural sampling system is designed to operate on actual events" (p. 13). The problem is that in a symbol-oriented postindustrial society, we are presented with paper-and pencil problems all the time, and much of what we know about the world comes not from the perception of actual events but from abstract information preprocessed, prepackaged, and condensed into symbolic codes such as probabilities, percentages, tables, and graphs (the voluminous statistical information routinely presented in *USA Today* comes to mind).

Thus, we have here an example of the figure and ground reversals that permeate contemporary rationality studies. It is possible to accept most of the conclusions of the cognitive ecologists but to draw completely different morals from them. The cognitive ecologists want to celebrate the astonishing job that evolution did in adapting to that Pleistocene environment. Certainly they are right to do so. The more we understand about evolutionary mechanisms, the more awed appreciation we have for them. Time and selection are a potent combination as popularizers such as Dawkins (1986, 1996) have so eloquently demonstrated. But at the same time, it is not inconsistent for a thoroughgoing Meliorist to be horrified at the fact that the information Fidelity Investments is sending to millions of Americans is in a form for which they are totally unadapted; or to be likewise horrified that a multi-million-dollar advertising industry is in part predicated on creating stimuli that will trigger System 1 heuristics that many of us will not have the cognitive energy or cognitive disposition to override. For a Meliorist, it is no consolation that the heuristics so triggered were evolutionarily adaptive in their day.

Has Human Irrationality Been Empirically Demonstrated?

The thesis of this book has been that patterns of individual differences, if interpreted in creative ways, can help to shed light on the various reasons why descriptive accounts of human behavior depart from normative models. This thesis has been demonstrated with empirical results that ranged widely over the tasks in the heuristics and biases literature. The data patterns have been varied. In this chapter, I intend to step back from the minutiae of individual tasks and draw more general conclusions. The chapter begins with a brief consideration of performance errors and computational limitations. Considered next are the implications of algorithmic-level limitations for the problem of applying the right normative model to performance. Finally, it is argued that, taken collectively, the results summarized in this volume warrant another broad conclusion. Specifically, after ruling out algorithmic limitations (which makes the normative model not prescriptive for some individuals) there were reliable deviations from normative responding that tended to covary across tasks. This reliable covariation, as well as relationships involving thinking dispositions, suggest that debates about rational thought might benefit from a reversal of figure and ground. Traditionally these debates have foregrounded issues of competence and backgrounded issues of performance. The results discussed in this volume suggest an inversion of these priorities—an inversion that has some unexpected consequences for the debate between the Panglossians, Apologists, and Meliorists. The chapter concludes with some caveats/qualifications and with some speculations about the pretheoretical views that determine study design and data interpretation in these debates.

PERFORMANCE ERRORS

Given the results of the extensive series of studies reported here, it is easy to conclude that performance errors are poor candidates as the sole explanation for the normative/descriptive gap. There is simply too much reliable and predictable variability in the responses across a variety of these tasks. If performance discrepancies from normative responding were mere error variance—reflecting temporary algorithmic-level malfunctions as opposed to stable computational limitations—then we would not expect performance to remain the same on another trial of the same task. It would not be expected that deviations from normative responding on that task would predict deviations from normative responding on another. And, finally, we would not expect deviations from normative responding to be predictable from cognitive/personality variables. But all of these expectations based on the strong performance-error view were repeatedly falsified across a variety of studies that have been discussed. Panglossian theorists will need to invoke other arguments—incorrect norm application, alternative task construals—in order to close the gap completely.

Certainly performance errors occur in these experiments, but performance errors alone are clearly unable to bear the large burden they are assigned in Cohen's (1982) conceptualization, which conceives of only two factors affecting performance on rational thinking tasks: "normatively correct mechanisms on the one side, and adventitious causes of error on the other" (p. 252). In this view, human performance arises from an intrinsic human competence that is impeccably rational, but responses occasionally deviate from normative correctness due to inattention, memory lapses, lack of motivation, and other fluctuating but basically unimportant causes. This is a type of true score plus error model—like that of classical test theory—but one including the strong Panglossian assumption that the true score for every individual is centered on the actual normative response. The problem is that, on a group basis, the reliable variance on each of the tasks indicates that there are systematic departures from normative responding that reflect more than just error variance.

COMPUTATIONAL LIMITATIONS

Throughout this volume, performance errors have been treated separately from stable and predictable computational limitations. In Cohen's (1981) and Stein's (1996) treatment of performance errors, the two are sometimes conflated. It has been argued here that the distinction should be maintained because, from a processing point of view, the two are very different and their implications for individual differences are very distinct. Performance errors represent algorithmic-level problems that are transitory in nature. They might not occur again on a readministration of the same problem. Computational limitations reflect long-term, non-transitory limitations at the algorithmic level that serve to prevent normative models from being computed. Performance errors that cause responses to fall short of the normative ideal are essentially error variance. Computational limitations reflect systematic and replicable processing events. They lead to a distinction between normative and prescriptive ideals, whereas performance errors do not.

Unlike performance errors, which seem unpromising as explanations of the normative/descriptive gap, linkages between measures of cognitive ability (the proxy for computational limitations) and reasoning performance were demonstrated on a variety of tasks drawn from the heuristics and biases literature. Here, though, the situation resembled the proverbial glass half empty and half full. It appears that to a moderate extent, systematic discrepancies between actual performance and normative models can be accounted for by variation in capacity limitations at the algorithmic level. However, the limitations were far from absolute. An extreme Apologist model—every subject performing at the limits of their algorithmic capacity—was not supported by the data. Instead, the vast majority of subjects in a university sample were within a range of cognitive ability where many individuals solved each of the problems (with the possible exception of the abstract selection task, see Fig. 2.2). There appear to be no computational limitations preventing at least half of the college population from producing normative$_s$ performance on most of the tasks investigated.

The magnitude of the associations with cognitive ability left much room for the possibility that the remaining reliable variance might indicate that subjects are systematically computing according to nonnormative rules (and are not necessarily doing so to circumvent limitations in cognitive capacity). The results reported in chapter 6 supported the idea of systematic computation by non-normative models. First, it was not the case that, once capacity limitations had been controlled, the remaining variations from normative responding were unpredictable (which would have indicated that the residual variance largely consisted of performance errors). In contrast, it was shown that there was significant covariance among the residualized scores from a variety of tasks in the heuristics and biases literature. The residual variance (after partialing cognitive ability) was also systematically associated with thinking dispositions that were conceptualized as intentional-level styles relating to epistemic regulation. Both of these indications that the residual variance is systematic support the notion that the normative/descriptive discrepancies that remain after computational limitations have been accounted for reflect a systematically suboptimal intentional-level model of behavior and thought.

In summary, although computational limitations are certainly present, and although performance errors are no doubt implicated in the sizable residual error variance, the remaining systematic variance in the norma-tive/descriptive gap on the tasks discussed in chapters 2 and 6 gives em-pirical support to the Meliorist claim that at least part of the discrepancy is due to non-normative thought patterns.

THINKING DISPOSITIONS AND RATIONAL THOUGHT

As discussed in previous chapters, there are a number of possible impli-cations that could be drawn from the finding that measures of thinking dispositions explain unique variance in reasoning. The types of disposi-tions tapped in the studies reviewed were thinking dispositions in the epistemic domain—the tendency to change beliefs based on evidence and on indication of lack of coherence, resistance to epistemic restruc-turing, etc. Additionally, several of the measures reflected the tendency toward cognitive decontextualization—the tendency to overcome the fundamental computational bias when warranted by the task situation. Some items seemed to be directly tapping the extent to which people are willing to use the metacognitive control processes of System 2 to override System 1 processes.

Whichever aspects of these conjectures are correct, the thinking dis-positions are best viewed as intentional-level psychological attitudes. They do not index the function of algorithmic-level subprocesses but in-stead refer to the individual's goal organization. Knowledge of the latter is what makes behavior predictable without knowledge of algorith-mic-level details. In a discussion of the intentional level of analysis, New-ell (1982) argued that it allows us to "understand behavior without having an operational model of the processing that is actually being done by the agent" (p. 108). Prediction on this basis works "without requiring ... the construction of any computational model" (p. 109). Newell further talked of enduring goal biases and epistemic criteria in a manner that places the thinking dispositions discussed in this volume within the domain of inten-tional-level psychology: "The agent's goals must also be known. ... they are relatively stable characteristics that can be inferred from behavior and (for human adults) can sometimes be conveyed by language" (p. 108).

Within the current conceptualization of thinking dispositions, the exer-cise displayed in Tables 6.4 and 6.6—the prediction of reasoning perfor-mance from a measure of algorithmic-level capacity (cognitive ability) and intentional-level goal structure (thinking dispositions)—should not be thought odd. Newell (1982) explicitly discussed what he called mixed systems of modeling and prediction, and argued that they are quite com-mon in artificial intelligence as well as folk psychology which both tend to mix processing notions from the algorithmic level with goal and belief no-tions from the intentional level. This is why:

> [We] recognize that forgetting is possible, and so we do not assume that knowledge once obtained is forever. We know that inferences are only

available if the person thinks it through, so we don't assume that knowing X means knowing all the remote consequences of X, though we have no good way of determining exactly what inferences will be known.... Having only crude models of processing at the symbol level, these mixed models are neither very tidy nor uniformly effective. (p. 115)

But Newell argued that such mixed models are still often better than models based on only one level of conceptual analysis. Likewise, in artificial intelligence, intentional-level notions are often used to describe components and sequences of operations at the algorithmic level:

Memories are described as having a given body of knowledge and messages are described as transferring knowledge from one memory to another. This carries all the way to design philosophies that work in terms of a "society of minds" and to executive systems that oversee and analyze the operation of other internal processing. The utility of working with such mixed-level systems is evident for both design and analysis. (p. 115)

Dennett (1988) argued that we use the intentional stance for humans and dogs but not for lecterns because for the latter "there is no predictive leverage gained by adopting the intentional stance" (p. 496). In several experiments discussed in this volume, it has been shown that there is additional predictive leverage to be gained by relaxing the idealized rationality assumption of Dennett's (1987, 1988) intentional stance and by positing measurable and systematic variation in intentional-level psychologies. Knowledge about such individual differences in people's intentional-level psychologies can be used to predict variance in the normative/descriptive gap displayed on many reasoning tasks. Consistent with the Meliorist conclusion that there can be individual differences in human rationality, the results show that there is variability in reasoning that cannot be accommodated within a model of perfect rational competence operating in the presence of performance errors and computational limitations.

REVERSING THE FIGURE AND GROUND OF COMPETENCE AND PERFORMANCE

In their discussion of the rationality of emotions, Johnson-Laird and Oatley (1992) conceptualized emotions as interrupt signals supporting goal achievement. They saw such intentional-level constructs as particularly important in the characterization of systems whose behavior is governed by neither fixed action patterns nor impeccable rationality. Johnson-Laird and Oatley's discussion of the rationality of emotions (see also de Sousa, 1987; Oatley, 1992) emphasizes pragmatic rationality—the coordination and achievement of goals (Audi, 1993a, 1993b; Stich, 1990). It is possible that some of the thinking styles discussed previously may be conceived of as signals (e.g., "avoid closure," "keep searching for evidence," etc.) operating in similar ways but serving the ends of *epistemic* rationality—processes of fixing beliefs in proportion to evidence and of maintaining coherent relationships with other beliefs (Harman, 1995; Nozick, 1993; Thagard, 1992).

In short, thinking dispositions of the type that have been have examined here may provide information about epistemic goals at the intentional level of analysis. For example, consider an individual who scores high on measures such as the actively open-minded thinking scales and low on measures such as dogmatism and absolutism that were mentioned in chapter 6—a person who agrees with statements such as "People should always take into consideration evidence that goes against their beliefs" and who disagrees with statements such as "No one can talk me out of something I know is right." Such a response pattern is indicating that belief change in order to get closer to the truth is an important goal for this person. This individual is signaling that they value being an accurate belief-forming system more than they value holding on to the beliefs they currently have (see Cederblom, 1989, for an insightful discussion of this distinction). In contrast, consider a person scoring low on the flexible-thinking scale and high on measures of absolutism and categorical thinking—a person who disagrees with statements such as "A person should always consider new possibilities" and who agrees with statements such as "There are a number of people I have come to hate because of the things they stand for." Such a response pattern is indicating that retaining current beliefs is an important goal for this person. This individual is signaling that they value highly the beliefs they currently have and that they put a very small premium on mechanisms that might improve belief accuracy (but that involve belief change).

The finding that thinking dispositions predicted additional variance in many reasoning tasks after cognitive ability was partialed out indicates that more than just differences at the algorithmic level (computational capacity) is needed to predict performance—something about the epistemic goals of the reasoners must be known. One reason this might be is that the nature of many of the tasks requires that the fundamental computational bias be overridden. For example, some task instructions dictate that prior belief be totally discounted in evaluating evidence, other instructions tell the reasoner to use only the information in the problem, others require implicit calculations to be done and the context of the problem be ignored. Individuals may differ in their willingness/ability to adapt to such instructions. Individuals who put a low epistemic priority on maintaining current beliefs may find the instructions easy to follow. In contrast, those who attach high epistemic value to belief maintenance might find the standard instructions much harder to follow. Thus, epistemic goals might directly affect performance on such tasks independent of the computational capacity that can be brought to bear.

The importance of thinking styles such as these in discussions of human rationality has perhaps not received sufficient attention because of

the heavy reliance on the competence/performance distinction in philosophical treatments of rational thought in which all of the important psychological mechanisms are allocated to the competence side of the
dichotomy. For example, Rescher (1988) argued that:

> To construe the data of these interesting experimental studies [of probabil-
> istic reasoning] to mean that people are systematically programmed to fal-
> lacious processes of reasoning—rather than merely that they are inclined
> to a variety of (occasionally questionable) substantive suppositions—is a
> very questionable step.... While all (normal) people are to be credited with
> the capacity to reason, they frequently do not exercise it well. (p. 196)

There are two parts to Rescher's point here: the "systematically programmed" part and the "inclination toward questionable suppositions"
part. As Rips (1994) noted, such views frame the rationality debate (e.g.,
Cohen, 1981; Stein, 1996) in terms of "whether incorrect reasoning is a 'systematically programmed' part of thinking [or] just a peccadillo" (p. 394).

Rescher's (1988) focus—like that of many who have dealt with the philosophical implications of the idea of human irrationality—is on the issue of
how humans are "systematically programmed." "Inclinations toward
questionable suppositions" are of interest to those in the philosophical debates only as mechanisms that allow one to drive a wedge between competence and performance—thus maintaining a theory of near-optimal
human rational competence in the face of a host of responses that seemingly defy explanation in terms of standard normative models (Baron,
1993a, 1998; Dawes, 1988; Griffiths, 1994; Kahneman & Tversky, 1996;
Shafir, 1994; Shafir & Tversky, 1992; Thaler, 1992; Wagenaar, 1988).

Analogously to Rescher, Cohen (1982) argued that there really are only
two factors affecting performance on rational thinking tasks: "normatively correct mechanisms on the one side, and adventitious causes of error on the other" (p. 252). Not surprisingly given such a conceptualization,
the processes contributing to error ("adventitious causes") are of little interest to Cohen (1981, 1982). Human performance arises from an intrinsic
human competence that is impeccably rational, but responses occasionally deviate from normative correctness due to inattention, memory
lapses, lack of motivation, and other fluctuating but basically unimportant
causes. There is nothing in such a view that would motivate any interest in
patterns of errors or individual differences in such errors.

One of the purposes of the present research program is to reverse the
figure and ground in the rationality debate, which has tended to be dominated by the particular way that philosophers frame the competence/per-
formance distinction. From a psychological standpoint, there may be
important implications in precisely the aspects of performance that have
been backgrounded in this controversy ("adventitious causes," "pecca-
dillos"). That is, whatever the outcome of the disputes about how humans
are "systematically programmed" (Brase et al., 1998; Cosmides & Tooby,

1996; Johnson-Laird & Byrne, 1991, 1993; Johnson-Laird, Byrne, & Schaeken, 1994; Oaksford & Chater, 1994, 1996; O'Brien, Braine, & Yang, 1994; Rips, 1994), variation in the "inclination toward questionable suppositions" is of psychological interest as a topic of study in its own right. The experiments discussed in this volume provide at least tentative indications that the "inclination toward questionable suppositions" has some degree of domain generality and that it is predicted by thinking dispositions that concern the epistemic and pragmatic goals of the individual and that are part of people's intentional-level psychology.

Johnson-Laird and Byrne (1993) articulated a view of rational thought that parses the competence/performance distinction much differently from that of Cohen (1981, 1982, 1986) and that simultaneously leaves room for cognitive styles to play a more important role in theories of individual differences. At the heart of the rational competence that Johnson-Laird and Byrne attributed to humans is not perfect rationality but instead just one meta-principle: People are programmed to accept inferences as valid provided that they have constructed no mental model of the premises that contradict the inference. Inferences are categorized as false when a mental model is discovered that is contradictory. However, the search for contradictory models is "not governed by any systematic or comprehensive principles" (p. 178).

The key point in Johnson-Laird and Byrne's (1993; see Johnson-Laird, in press) account is that once an individual constructs a mental model from the premises, once the individual draws a new conclusion from the model, and once the individual begins the search for an alternative model of the premises that contradicts the conclusion, the individual "lacks any systematic method to make this search for counterexamples" (p. 205). Here is where Johnson-Laird and Byrne's model could be modified to allow for the influence of thinking styles in ways that the impeccable competence view of Cohen (1981, 1982) does not. In this passage, Johnson-Laird and Byrne seem to be arguing that there are no systematic control features of the search process. But epistemically related cognitive dispositions may in fact be reflecting just such control features. Individual differences in the extensiveness of the search for contradictory models could arise from a variety of cognitive factors that, although they may not be completely systematic, may be far from "adventitious" (see Oatley, 1992; Overton, 1985, 1990)—factors such as dispositions toward premature closure, cognitive confidence, reflectivity, dispositions toward confirmation bias, and ideational generativity.

In chapter 6 it was discussed how the panoply of thinking dispositions examined in these studies relate to the cognitive decontextualization that commonly results when System 1 processes are overridden by the analytic intelligence of System 2. The decontextualized nature of many normative$_s$ solutions is a feature that is actually emphasized by many critics of the heuristics and biases literature who, nevertheless, fail to see it as implying a research program for differential psychology. For example, if to contextualize a problem is the natural and nearly universal reasoning style of human beings (the fundamental computational bias), then it is not surprising that many people respond incorrectly when attempting a psychological task that is explicitly designed to require a decontextualized reasoning style (contrary-to-fact syllogisms, argument evaluation, etc.). But the fact that some people *do* give the decontextualized response means that at least some people have available a larger repertoire of reasoning styles (they can flexibly reason so as to override the fundamental computational bias if the situation requires).

For example, Rescher (1988) defended responses that exhibit the gambler's fallacy on the grounds that people assume a model of saturation that is valid in other domains (e.g., food ingestion, sleep) and that "the issue may well be one of a mistaken factual supposition rather than one of fallacious reasoning" (pp. 195–196), and he stressed the enthymematic character of much human reasoning—an issue that was discussed in chapter 7. But, again, the fact remains that many people do not reason enthymematically in this or other reasoning problems and instead give the normative$_s$ response—and this means that at least some people have available a larger repertoire of reasoning styles (they can flexibly reason enthymematically and nonenthymematically as the task requires). Or, at the very least, it means that certain people are more easily shifted out of their natural enthymematic reasoning style.

ALTERNATIVE TASK CONSTRUALS: A PYRRHIC VICTORY FOR THE PANGLOSSIANS

Evans, Newstead, and Byrne (1993) discussed the divide among reasoning researchers between those who see the important task as building idealized competence models and those who feel that it is "the performance factors which prevent subjects exhibiting competence which provide the richest source of psychological data" (p. 268). This volume is obviously dedicated to the second proposition, and there are probably few issues within this second research program more important than accounting for individual differences in how people are prone to contextualize a problem.

There is another reason why those with a pretheoretical bias toward Meliorism find the second research program more congenial. It is the fear that in the domain of reasoning and decision making, any victory for the Panglossian perspective will likely be a pyrrhic one. In the view of investigators working from a Panglossian perspective (e.g., Cohen, 1981; Henle, 1962; Wetherick, 1995), in both linguistics and reasoning, actual performance deviates from the idealized competence model primarily due to performance errors. These errors are most often of trivial consequence in language—slips that make little difference in communication efficiency.

In language, most of the important aspects of the domain are on the competence side of the competence/performance divide. Individual differences are of little practical or theoretical import.

However, in the domain of decision making, and that of fixation of belief, the situation will be exactly reversed. The perfectly normative and uniform competence that is posited by the Panglossians will be useless in explaining precisely what a behavioral scientist is most concerned with understanding in these domains—why some people reason and act differently than others in response to a particular problem. Unlike the case of language, explaining the variability in performance will be extremely important because the errors here are not trivial—they encompass Chernobyl, the savings & loan debacle, overpopulation, neglect of preventive vaccination, depletion of fishing stocks, global warming, animal extinction, medical malpractice, health quackery, and many other real-world problems (Baron, 1998; Dawes, 1988; Gilovich, 1991). In short, all of the interesting practical consequences will be on the performance side of the competence/performance divide. If the Panglossians succeed in preserving perfectly rational competence, it will be a pyrrhic victory because by the time they have abstracted away all of the differing task construals, all algorithmic limitations, all variation in epistemic goals, and a host of other things, we will indeed have identified an abstract reasoning competence with no variability—but the variability in performance factors will in fact be the primary thing that we want to explain.

The situation here is analogous to the alternative construal problem discussed in chapter 4. There, it was shown that one result of a strong tendency to grant subjects their construal of a problem, no matter how bizarre, was that the rational principles that would remain would provide no constraint on behavioral observations at all. The constraints on the rational principles of competence would become so loose that a person could be money pumped but still be transitive in their choices. Recall the example of preference reversal (e.g., Lichtenstein & Slovic, 1971; Slovic, 1995) discussed in chapter 4. In a choice between two gambles, A and B, a person chooses A over B. However, when pricing the gambles, the person puts a higher price on B. Presumably there is an amount of money, M, that would be preferred to A but given a choice of M and B the person would choose B. Thus, we have B > M, M > A, A > B. Transitivity can be preserved by proposing a construal where evaluating the A in the M versus A comparison is not the same as evaluating A in the A versus B comparison. In the latter, choosing A means simultaneously rejecting B and the A alternative here might considered to be a different prospect, and if it is so considered there is no intransitivity.

But how bizarre are we prepared to let the construals become? The Panglossian has no limits on construal implausibility, because perfect competence must be protected at all costs. The Meliorist, in contrast, is not committed to perfect rational competence and thus is not forced to posit bizarre construals in order to protect it. This is an advantage for the Meliorist because any intransitivity can be neutered by the assumption that the subject is reasoning in the following (bizarre) way. Pretend that Bill prefers, successively, object A to object B, B to C, and then C to A—apparent intransitivity. We might posit that, to Bill, the third choice involved not "A" but instead, something that he puts a different value on: "object A offered immediately after a choice involving B." And to him, this bizarre entity—"object A offered after a choice involving B"—is not valued the same as "object A offered after a choice involving C." Thus, an "A offered after a choice involving B" might as well be designated D—and there is no inconsistency at all in preferring A to B, B to C, and then C to D. Bill is now no longer intransitive.

However, despite his perfect transitivity, despite his perfectly rational competence, Bill is still a money pump—and it is very doubtful that his preferences are serving his goals (Baron, 1993a, 1994a). We might still advise Bill that consistent (in his view) or not (in ours) his choices are unwise. I, of course, begin by giving Bill A and C—free of charge. I then offer Bill object B for a little bit of money and for giving me C back. Because Bill prefers B to C, there must some finite, if however small, sum of money that Bill would give me, along with C, to get B. Then, for a little bit of money and object A (which to Bill is "A offered after a choice involving B"), I give Bill object C (which of course Bill prefers to "A offered after a choice involving B"). Now I offer Bill A for a little bit of money and B. And then I can offer Bill B for …

Whether or not Bill's choices are consistent—whether or not they are rational—they have sure led Bill into a lousy deal! And even Bill might agree with that. Nevertheless, the Panglossians still endow Bill with perfect rational competence, with perfect transitivity. But this perfect rational competence that Bill enjoys is utterly uninteresting (and unhelpful to him in the real world in this case). The only interesting thing here is why Bill construes the situation in this bizarre way.

The problem is that the Panglossian has only one degree of freedom—they must posit a construal that makes the choices rational. This of course creates problems when the normative/descriptive gap is quite large. If the competence model is fixed at perfect rationality, the only way to explain an extremely large normative/descriptive gap is by an equally large deviation from the normal construal of the problem. As Bar-Hillel (1991) argued:

> Many writers have attempted to defend seemingly erroneous responses by offering interpretations of subjects' reasoning that rationalizes their responses. Sometimes, however, this charitable approach has been misguided, either because the subjects are quick to acknowledge their error themselves once it is pointed out to them, or because the interpretation required to justify the response is even more embarrassing than the error it seeks to excuse. (p. 413)

The Meliorists are not forced into positing task construals "even more embarrassing than the error they seek to excuse" because they have another mechanism for explaining such gaps—the principles of rational thought can be posited to deviate as well as the subject's task construal. By positing some deviations from rational principles, the Meliorist is not trapped into offering bizarre task construals in order to account for the discrepant behavior.

Margolis (1987) discussed several examples of alternative interpretations of tasks from the heuristics and biases literature that become "even more embarrassing than the errors they seek to excuse." Basically, he agreed with Henle (1962) that the subjects' non-normative responses will almost always be logical responses to some other problem representation. But unlike Henle, Margolis was clear to point out that many of these alternative task construals are so bizarre—so far from what the very words in the instructions said—that they represent serious cognitive errors that deserve attention:

> Like critics such as Henle (1962) and Cohen (1981), I will argue … that what has usually been taken to be incorrect reasoning leading to cognitive illusions in fact is better characterized as normatively plausible responses to a question different from what the experimenters intended. But in contrast to Henle and Cohen, the detailed conclusions I draw strengthen rather than invalidate the basic claim of the experimenters. For although subjects can be—in fact, I try to show, ordinarily are—giving reasonable responses to a different question, the different question can be wildly irrelevant to anything that plausibly could be construed as the meaning of the question asked. The locus of the illusion is shifted, but the force of the illusion is confirmed not invalidated or explained away. (p. 141)

Margolis' (1987) argument is that alternative task construals can be used to insulate reasoning competence from charges of irrationality, but that this ploy simply transfers the irrationality to the stage of problem representation. Irrationality has not been abolished; it simply has been transferred to a different cognitive operation, because for many tasks in the heuristics and biases literature:

> The alternative interpretation necessary to make the usual response logical is either not there at all, or there only under some interpretation so tendentious as to transfer the puzzle about the logic of the response undiminished to an earlier stage. (p. 20)

It simply will not do to argue as Henle (1962) did that "if people were unable to reason logically, so that each arrived at different conclusions from the same premises, it is difficult to see how they could understand each other, follow one another's thinking, reach common decisions, and work together" (p. 374). This is because all of these communicative failures *also* arise if there is variability at the task representation and construal stages of reasoning. Specifically, it is *equally* true that, if people represented different propositions from the same premises, then it would be difficult to see how they could understand each other, follow one another's thinking, reach common decisions, and work together. Communicative success would be just as threatened by unpredictable variability in situation construal as it would be from variations in rational competence. But the Panglossian cannot put limits on the degree of construal implausibility that will be posited, because a boundary on task construal may limit their ability to bring deviant responses into line with perfect reasoning competence.

Shweder (1987) and Churchman (1961, pp. 234–235) discussed how the Meliorist can gradually adjust both the degree of rationality that is posited and the plausibility of the subject's construal to arrive at an interpretation of performance that does not become "even more embarrassing than the error they seek to excuse." Shweder pointed out that "we may end up rejecting the relevance of one or more of the maxims if we are driven to very awkward interpretations of preference or to awkward interpretations of the domain of objects over which choice or preference relations are said to apply" (p. 168). Both of these theorists proposed a process of equilibrium whereby, as suggested in the Bar-Hillel (1991) passage quoted previously, in order to arrive at an interpretation of performance, mutual adjustments are made in the construal that is posited and in the reasoning mechanisms being applied to the task. Shweder clearly indicated that this process of mutual adjustment can stop short of attributing perfect rational competence to all subjects.

Thus, the Meliorist might have begun this inquiry with the question: "Why isn't Bill transitive?" The Panglossian comes along and says, "But you're wrong: He is! Here is a construal that makes his choice rational." We can oblige the Panglossian in this way, but then the interesting question (and it has become no less interesting) is why Bill construes the situation in this weird way. The Panglossian is happy because the question has been transferred from the competence side of ledger (which gets the answer the Panglossian wants—that Bill is rational) to the performance side. But if the Panglossians get their way, *all* of the interesting questions about performance variability will end up on this side.

It is interesting that strong charity advocates (see chap. 1) are drawn to the Panglossian position because of the promise of gaining predictive accuracy from an intentional stance containing such a strong rationality assumption. But the strong charity perspective only garners a gain in prediction in situations where behavior clusters around the modal response. As soon as there is substantial variability—none of which can be explained by the uniform idealized competence—the Panglossian position leads to an unprincipled proliferation of possible construals. The post hoc construal attribution is, of course, predictively worthless because true prediction obviously means that some behavioral pattern is ruled out. But a perfect rational competence view that allows no mechanisms of error in its fundamental operation and that evaluates no construal as irrational can rule out no type of bizarre behavior at all—including someone acting as a money pump.

This is Shweder's (1987) point when he argued that "the problem with the idea of abstract or formal axioms is not that the axioms are false but rather the implication that one can focus on them alone (ignoring content and framing) and still comprehend or predict actual functioning. If you can succeed at predicting functioning, it is because you know more than you realized about the content and the proper way to frame things" (pp. 168–169). Without some constraints on "content and the proper way to frame things" we can predict nothing (see chap. 4), but the Panglossian view refrains from invoking such constraints because all degrees of freedom are needed to preserve the assumption of perfect rational competence. But such a view ends up paying an enormously high price for the assumption of perfect rational competence. When a money pumped person can still be transitive, what good is transitivity as a reasoning principle? Everything that is determining the outcome in the real world that we care about (in this case an awful outcome) is being determined by mechanisms segregated outside of competence on this view.

That is one reason that a victory for the Panglossians would be pyrrhic—individual differences in the domain of reasoning loom much larger in psychological theory. Unlike the case for language, individual differences in reasoning and decision making are of practical importance and they critically determine our view of the human condition. In divesting itself of any implications for individual differences, the Panglossian view undercuts its own importance. Other theorists have argued the point that variation in reasoning errors cannot be dismissed in the same manner as performance errors in the linguistic domain (see Stein, 1996).

Rips and Conrad (1983) argued for a more balanced view when summarizing the results of their study of individual differences in deductive reasoning. They allowed that:

> Although certain logical procedures may be secure and universal parts of our thinking, other rules may be more uncertain, difficult to apply, tied to special circumstances, or overridden by other factors. These latter rules might be likened to technical terms, which increase the expressive power of one's vocabulary but with a possible loss of interpretability. Whereas the rules increase the logical power of the system, they may also give rise to the sort of inter-person differences that we have observed. (pp. 283–284)

Thus beyond a core of deductive rules that are in everyone's competence, there is another subset that create variance in overall deductive competence because they are more salient for some individuals than for others. The "possible loss of interpretability" in this case means that some people will make inferences that are opaque to others.

Adler (1991) emphasized the point that not to make important linguistic, probabilistic, and logical distinctions in a complex social environment has real costs and represents more than just the failure to play an artificial game:

> The conversationally induced problem of a lack of shared understanding is a subtle one, not due to any blatant verbal trick. It is reasonable to conjecture that the subtlety results in part from subjects limited skill with the rule the experimenter wants to study. To be specific: Our greater pragmatic sophistication alone does not explain the differences in the dominant adult responses to the conjunction effect compared to the Piaget class-inclusion studies. The difference between the number of members of a class and the number of a proper sub-class is so obvious to us that we readily permit the conversationally untoward question—"Are there more dimes or coins?"—at face value. Our greater resistance to the violation of the maxims in the conjunction-effect experiment is partly due, I believe, to a certain lack of either accessibility to or confidence in—though not competence with—the conjunction rule for probabilities. If this is so, then the fact that subjects do not understand the experimenter as he intends his words is itself some evidence of a weakness in subjects understanding of the scope of the conjunction rule in everyday reasoning. (p. 265)

Thus, the rule being in human reasoning competence is no consolation if its accessibility in unpropitious circumstances is doubtful due to computational limitations or ineffectual cognitive styles. Simply moving variability in accessibility from the competence side of the ledger to the performance side does not negate the fact that failures of rule accessibility (despite the presence of the rule in reasoning competence) have important social consequences. Lefkowitz (1997) described the trial of some teenagers accused of raping a young girl who was intellectually disabled. A guilty verdict would have been required if either "force or coercion" was used or if the victim was judged not mentally competent to consent. However, several jury members operated under the impression that a guilty verdict necessitated both of these conditions. The jury's "discussion over the course of almost two weeks had been clouded by the misimpression that they had to agree on both the 'mentally competent' and 'force or coercion' charge to find the defendants guilty of first-degree rape. Agreement on only one of the charges would have been sufficient" (p. 410).

In short, the jury confused the connectives *and* and *or* in a real-life situation in which lives were at stake. Presumably there is not a shred of doubt that the ability to use these two connectives was embedded in the reasoning competence of all the jurors. The variability here arises at the stage of problem representation or problem construal. The complexity and stress of a long trial, and the lengthy instructions to the jury, served to obscure for some jurors the proper connective to apply. We can respond to such an example in various ways. One is to frame it in terms of the coexistence thesis articulated by Osherson (1995) whereby normative$_s$ rules exist in the reasoning competence of most people along with heuristics like representativeness that lead to normative$_a$ responses when the conditions are not favorable. The former are manifest in propitious circumstances but are obscured under cognitive load, complexity, and confusing circumstances. The Panglossian alternative is to classify such reasoning errors as due to "adventitious" causes (as a "peccadillo"), consign them to the performance side of ledger, and let out a sigh of relief that perfect rational competence has been salvaged. But given the real-world implications of this particular example, no reasonable person would want to stop there. The ability to represent the right connective in confusing contexts containing many distractions seems clearly to be a most important skill. If some subjects have "a weakness in ... understanding of the scope of the ... rule in everyday reasoning" (Adler, 1991, p. 265), then it seems critically important to embark on a research program to elucidate reasons for variation in "understanding the scope."

ALTERNATIVE TASK CONSTRUALS:
A PYRRHIC VICTORY FOR THE APOLOGISTS

A similar pyrrhic victory also awaits the cognitive ecologists in the Apologist camp, but for different reasons. These theorists emphasize that once many problems in the heuristics and biases literature are properly contextualized and rendered in a form that is compatible with the representations that our evolutionarily adapted inferential systems are designed to deal with (e.g., single-event probability problems turned into frequency estimation problems), then subjects easily solve many problems that had originally yielded non-normative responses (Brase et al., 1998; Cosmides & Tooby, 1996; Gigerenzer & Hoffrage, 1995; Gigerenzer et al., 1991). The cognitive ecologists represent a subtype of the Apologist position. They argue that the brain is well adapted in the evolutionary sense, but not necessarily in the sense of normative rationality. There are computational limitations in this view, but they consist of problem representations being presented to the brain that the brain is unprepared to deal with. A problem can be efficiently solved if represented one way (to coincide with how the modules of the brain are adapted; see Brase et al., 1998) but not if represented in another way (e.g., as single-event probabilities rather than frequencies). The inability to handle a particular type of problem representation could be termed a type of computational limitation, although it is obviously different from processing limitations such as inadequate short-term memory capacity, slow retrieval of memory codes, and inefficient search procedures.

Thus, to the extent that the world (and experimenters) have presented to people problems represented in a form for which their cognitive apparatus was not adapted, then many Meliorist claims to have demonstrated human irrationality will have been proven to have been unfounded. These are situations in which there is a computational limitation due to mismatched representations and thus the normative model is not prescriptive. Furthermore, much ingenious research by the cognitive ecologists has demonstrated that if problem representations are changed in ways more congruent with the appropriate cognitive modules, then performance improves markedly (Brase et al., 1998; Cosmides & Tooby, 1996; Gigerenzer & Hoffrage, 1995).

But this victory for the Apologist camp is also pyrrhic in nature for a variety of reasons. The first problem is that in getting tasks into the appropriate format for evolutionarily adapted modules, it is sometimes the case that the problems become so highly contextualized that the answer is literally handed to the subject on a silver platter. It then becomes difficult to infer whether the subject should really be credited with having an inferential principle in their repertoire. Although many theorists have made this point, Adler (1984) made the argument most eloquently:

> There is a common tradeoff in these studies between the abstractness or unfamiliarity of the material presented and the consensus on the conclusions drawn about subjects' lack of competence ... As we make the material less abstract and more familiar to the subjects, it becomes less clear how much of their successful performance can be attributed to use of that formal rule. First, the background knowledge will have had an influence, so while subjects may be acting in accord with the formal rule, we are less sure how much of that action is due to use of that formal rule. Second, to the extent that such familiarity is requisite for the application of the formal principle, one may doubt if the formal rule is appreciated as a formal rule, i.e., as applicable to any subject matter. (pp. 180–181)

It is just the problem that Adler (1984) outlined that has characterized the literature on the selection task. Early work showing somewhat better performance on concrete versions of the task than on the abstract version was interpreted as showing that the problems containing content facilitated logical reasoning (Dominowski, 1995; Griggs & Cox, 1982; Manktelow & Evans, 1979; Newstead & Evans, 1995). It is now thought that this interpretation is incorrect. Content—especially content such as that involved in the Drinking-Age and Sears Problems discussed in chapter 4—does not appear to facilitate logical thinking at all. Instead the deontic problems trigger System 1 heuristics, Darwinian algorithms, domain-specific modules (depending on one's theory) that all automatically prime the correct choice without implicating analytic System 2 reasoning at all.

Such theories lead inevitably to the question of "whether subjects do much indicative or theoretical reasoning as such in selection tasks" (Manktelow et al., 1995, p. 204). As Dominowski and Ansburg (1996) argued:

> Although the formally-correct cards are selected, there might be no rea-
> soning taking place—i.e., the person might simply have learned what to do
> in the situation presented. At best, success might reflect narrow reasoning
> processes strictly tied to a particular kind of content. No content-free rea-
> soning processes are assumed to play a role. In short, these accounts char-
> acterize successful performance on thematic problems as rather isolated
> behavior. (p. 5)

Margolis (1987) argued similarly that "if it is only under conditions of
strong familiarity that we get fluent performance, then what is happening
looks more like habit than reasoning" (p. 19). In short, the superior performance on the Drinking-Age Problem in no way assuages the concern
about the nature of human reasoning capability that is engendered by the
failure of logical reasoning in the abstract task. Perhaps the logical failure
is less due to irrational thought and more due to computational limitations than had been thought previously (an interpretation reinforced by
data presented in chaps. 2 and 4)—but it is a no less troubling aspect of
human cognition.

In fact, the unavailability of decontextualizing System 2 processes represents a real cognitive limitation. For example, in commenting on Kuhn's
(1991) studies of thinking as argument, Baron (1992) noted that "many
answers that Kuhn counted as inadequate were adequate answers to a
different question.... Perhaps the problem was not in subjects' thinking
but, rather, in their ability to understand interview questions" (p. 64).
Baron went on to argue that:

> If this is true, it would not be entirely uninteresting, and it would not entirely
> undermine Kuhn's account. Kuhn would argue, I think, that subjects cer-
> tainly knew what the words mean (especially given the fact that most ques-
> tions were repeated in different ways), so, if they did not respond
> appropriately, it was most likely because they did not regard the distinctions
> conveyed by the words to be important. Misunderstanding, if it occurred,
> was therefore very likely a result of the very deficits that Kuhn claims to find.
> (p. 64)

In short, the computational limitation revealed by a failure to make critical semantic distinctions is a real and important limitation (if not an irrationality under the view that it does not deviate from a prescriptive
account[1]). Baron's point recalls Olson's (1986) reminder that "a person
who does not clearly see the difference between an expression of intention and a promise or between a mistake and an accident, or between a
falsehood and a lie, should avoid a legal career or, for that matter, a theo-
logical one" (p. 341).

---

[1]However, later in this chapter I address an auxiliary assumption of the Apologist position
that many believe to be false—that computational limits are fixed. Relaxation of this assumption leaves more room for the demonstration of systematic irrationalities.

This quote of Olson's highlights another implication of the Apologist position with which it is possible to take issue: that there is nothing to be gained from being able to understand a formal rule at an abstract level (Bayes' rule, etc.)—and no advantage in System 2 processes that can flexibly override System 1 processes on occasion. But in fact there are real costs involved when logical distinctions are ignored. And there are real costs involved when semantic distinctions go unrecognized. As argued in chapter 7, modern technological society often puts a premium on the use of such abstract tools. And such a society is often deliberately structured so as to extract a price for failure to override System 1 processes. The ubiquitous multi-billion-dollar advertising industry largely creates its added "value" by prompting ill-considered System 1 responses.

Adler (1984) emphasized that the efficiency of the cognitive modules underlying intention attribution and social cooperation just as surely extract certain costs. He argued that such costs occur "in situations where the naturalness of our expectations under the cooperative principle leads us to miss subtle, but significant deviations from those expectations" (p. 174). He cited a now-famous experiment by Langer, Blank, and Chanowitz (1978) where a confederate attempts to cut into a line at a copy machine. In one condition a good reason is given ("May I use the Xerox machine, because I'm in a rush?") and in the other a totally redundant nonexplanation ("May I use the Xerox machine, because I have to make copies?"). Despite the fact that the second explanation is much less informative than the first, the compliance rates in the two conditions did not differ. Langer (1989; Langer et al., 1978) termed the compliance in the second case "mindless" and Adler analyzed it in terms of overly generalizing the Gricean cooperative principle. The default assumption that a contribution will be selectively relevant—in this case, that a real reason will follow the request—is false in this condition, yet it triggers exactly the same compliance behavior because it is not overridden by System 2 processing ("Yes but all of us are in line to make copies. Why should you go first?").

Examples of situations mirroring those studied in the Langer et al. (1978) research are not uncommon. An old aspirin commercial on television claimed "nine out of ten doctors who had a preference" preferred brand X of aspirin. Few viewers probably coded this information correctly as a conditional probability (it is not 90% of all doctors who preferred this brand; it is 90% of those who had a preference). The claim in the ad might well have been true. Of course, because all aspirin is the same, it might well have been the case that 95% of all doctors had no preference. Of the remaining small minority who had a preference for some strange reason (perhaps because they were paid by drug companies), 9 out of 10 preferred brand X—hardly a reason for the consumer to prefer brand X given that it was three times more expensive than generic aspirin (in part to cover the cost of its advertising campaign).

Langer-type examples of mindlessness abound in domains much more important than buying aspirin. *Consumer Reports* ("Buying or Leasing," 1998) chronicles how some dealers put an item costing $500 and labeled ADM on many automobile price stickers. The dealers are hoping that some people will not ask what ADM means. The dealers are also hoping that even after asking and being told that it means "additional dealer markup" that some consumers will not fully process what that means and will not inquire further about what this additional dealer markup feature is that they are paying for. In short, the dealers are hoping that System 2 processes will not methodically plow through this smoke and mirrors to ascertain that ADM is not a feature on the car at all—that it simply represents a request from the dealer to contribute $500 more to the dealership, as if it were a charity. As one dealer put it, "every once in a while somebody pays it, no questions asked" (p. 17). A mindless response here, a failure of System 2 to override, and the consumer could simply throw away a good chunk of hard-earned income. The modern consumer world is simply littered with such traps and, often, the more costly the product, the more such traps there are (e.g., automobiles, mutual funds, mortgage closing costs).

Modern mass communication technicians have become quite skilled at implying certain conclusions without actually stating those conclusions (for fear of lawsuits, bad publicity, etc.). Advertisements rely on the fundamental computational bias (particularly its enthymematic processing feature) to fill in the missing information. The communication logic of relying on System 1 processes to trump System 2 is readily employed by advertisers, in election campaigns, and even by governments—for example, in promoting their lottery systems ("You could be the one!" blares an ad from the Ontario Lottery Commission—thereby increasing the availability of an outcome that, in the game called 6/49, has an objective probability of .0000000000993).

Of course, such techniques are not limited to election and product advertising. The glossy brochures that our universities send out, full of fresh-faced young people in a wholesome learning environment, have the same logic. This logic is now a ubiquitous part of our communication environment. Indeed, "media consumer" courses are currently proliferating—many at the precollege level—in order to teach people to be consciously aware of these influences. The purpose of such courses is to sensitize the reflective processes of System 2 to the media-triggered System 1 responses and to develop habits of overriding such responses. Margolis (1987) warned of the ubiquitousness of this situation in modern society (see Margolis, 1996) in which we are constantly faced with situations in which the fundamental computational bias must be tempered with System 2 reasoning: "We can encounter cases where the issue is both out-of-scale with everyday life experience and contains important novelties, so that habitual responses can be highly inappropriate responses. The opportunity for unrecognized contextual effects akin to the scenario effects of this chapter can be something much more than an odd quirk that shows up in some contrived situation" (p. 168).

QUESTIONABLE TASK INTERPRETATIONS

Analyses of individual differences did not always support the Meliorist task interpretation however. In several instances, the norms applied and/or the task construal championed by the Meliorists seemed questionable and the critiques of the interpretations of these tasks were supported. This was especially true of the noncausal base-rate problems, two of which have been the subject of much controversy in the literature—the Cab Problem and the Disease Problem. Collectively, the normative$_s$ response on these problems received little support from applications of the understanding/acceptance principle. Cognitive ability and normative$_s$ responding on other reasoning tasks were not positively associated with the Bayesian response on the Cab problem. In fact, there were trends in the opposite direction.

A "false positive" version of a noncausal disease problem (the AIDS problem) also displayed the tendency for Bayesian responding to be negatively associated with cognitive ability and normative$_s$ responding on other tasks. A disease problem without the possibly misleading false positive wording did show a mild tendency for Bayesian responding to be positively associated with cognitive ability, but this trend did not hold for need for cognition. Responses to arguments explicating reasons for both normative$_s$ and normative$_a$ responses revealed that the normative$_a$ response appeared more convincing. Greater understanding of these problems seems, if anything, to be more associated with the normative$_a$ (indicant) response. The analyses of individual differences serve to reinforce the critiques of the normative$_s$ interpretations of these tasks and/or the expert consensus on the proper construal of these problems.

With respect to the false consensus effect, the results were ambiguous. Individuals who tended to project their own opinions did not differ from those who projected less in their level of cognitive ability or in their responses on other reasoning tasks. The findings of the Stanovich and West (1998b) experiment were also consistent with the arguments of Dawes (1989, 1990) and others (e.g., Hoch, 1987; Krueger & Zeiger, 1993) that projecting consensus is not necessarily inefficacious. Individuals high in projection tendency were, in fact, somewhat more accurate in their opinion estimates. Although the consensus effect has traditionally been interpreted as an egoistic bias that was unjustified from a normative point of view, there was little evidence for such an interpretation in the data from this experiment.

As with the case of the false consensus effect, an examination of individual differences in the overconfidence bias in the the knowledge calibration experiment indicated that low overconfidence (the absence of calibration bias) failed to correlate with higher scores on any of the cognitive ability measures. Likewise, lack of bias in calibration judgments was not associated with normative$_s$ responding on other reasoning tasks. Thus, from an individual differences point of view, this task did not converge with other reasoning or cognitive ability measures in either direction. Neither the normative$_s$ response (calibration bias of zero) nor the normative$_a$ response (moderate positive calibration bias) displayed consistent correlations with other general ability or reasoning measures.

When an individual differences analysis reveals a lack of association with cognitive ability (as in the case of the false consensus and knowledge calibration situations), the discrepancy between descriptive and normative models of behavior in such a situation cannot be attributed to algorithmic-level limitations. If the gap also cannot be attributed to performance errors, then there are two other important possibilities. One is that some people are systematically computing a non-normative rule and are not constrained by computational limitations from computing the normative one (Baron, 1991b; Kahneman & Tversky, 1996; Shafir, 1993, 1994). The other is that some subjects are adopting an alternative task construal that warrants another normative model, a possibility explored extensively in chapter 4.

These alternatives highlight the need to apportion an equal burden of proof when considering such cases. Recall a previous quote from Cohen (1982), where he called conservatism, compared with a Bayesian model, "not a defect, but a rather deeply rooted virtue of the system" (p. 260). This quote reveals an implication that is carried by many of the critiques of the heuristics and biases literature. Cohen viewed a non-Bayesian response in such a task as not simply an alternative response for which one could muster some degree of support. For Cohen, the non-Bayesian response—a "virtue" of human information processing—is clearly the best response. The modal response in such tasks must be the optimal standard in analyses such as Cohen's (1981, 1982), because he viewed untutored intuition as the sine qua non of normative justification.

It is important to realize that "Cohen is not content merely to defend human rationality in the face of error, but would use these very errors as evidence of the superiority of intuition over supposedly normative prescriptions" (Margalit & Bar-Hillel, 1981, p. 347). Others concur with Cohen (1981) in this view. Levi (1983) argued that "in the examples of alleged base rate fallacy considered by Kahneman and Tversky, they, and not their experimental subjects, commit the fallacies" (p. 502). Similarly, Wetherick (1970) felt that people who fail to give the normative$_s$ response on the selection task "are to be congratulated" (p. 214) because "what Wason and his successors judged to be the wrong response is in fact correct" (Wetherick, 1993, p. 107).

Thus, although some critics of normative$_s$ interpretations are simply arguing for a consideration of different (and equally rational) construals of a problem (see chap. 4), the quotes in the previous paragraph illustrate that not all critics of the standard normative interpretations are arguing that an alternative response pattern is equally rational compared to the normative$_s$ response. These critics are not relativists. They are, in fact, arguing for reflective equilibrium to settle on a different, normative$_a$ response pattern. As in a normative$_s$ analysis, for these critics, some responses are better than others, and according to their critiques, the normative$_s$ response is actually suboptimal. For example, Funder (1987) compared decision-making biases to optical illusions, arguing that we do not characterize an individual experiencing such an illusion as displaying a flaw in judgment or a dysfunctional cognitive mechanism. Indeed, the clear inference to be drawn from this example is that the information-processing system of anyone not subject to the illusion would be suspect. This is how, for example, we interpret the finding that mentally retarded individuals are less susceptible to certain illusions (Spitz, 1979). Those less susceptible to the illusion are expected to be characterized by less efficient information processing because the occurrence of the illusion is seen to result from the operation of adaptive cognitive mechanisms. That is, failing to show the illusion is viewed as maladaptive and indicative of cognitive problems.

The use of the visual illusion analogy invites the same inference with respect to rational thinking tasks where the modal response departs from the normative$_s$ response. The problem here is that the analogy to visual illusions might not be appropriate. Many visual illusions are a product of the operation of modular input systems (Fodor, 1983) with System 1–type properties. Such systems are no doubt evolutionarily adapted. The need to detect edges, depth, and occlusion is as much true now as it was in the Pleistoscene. There is little reason for analytic intelligence to override System 1 processes in these domains. Thus, a cognitive system not showing the illusion would certainly be suboptimal.

But once we leave the domain of vision and move into the domain of reasoning, as was discussed in chapter 5, evolutionary and normative rationality can dissociate—and the possibility arises of the analytic intelligence of System 2 overriding System 1 in order to pursue normative rather than evolutionary rationality. In this domain then, there is the real possibility that individuals less susceptible to the System 1 illusion might be more cognitively competent than those more susceptible. It was argued that this is what is occurring in many of the tasks on which cognitive ability differences were observed—particularly tasks representing strong cognitive illusions such as the Linda Problem and the abstract selection task where only a minority of individuals give the normative$_s$ response.

WHY NORMATIVE RATIONALITY WILL NOT DISAPPEAR

There is one respect, however, in which these conclusions about System 1 versus System 2 processes and normative versus evolutionary rationality might be seen as implying a victory for the Apologists in the debates about human rationality. A small group of subjects (on some tasks) are acknowledged to override System 1 and compute the normative$_s$ response. The majority of individuals with less cognitive capacity compute the System 1 response—an evolutionarily adaptive solution. These individual differences might result because the normative$_s$ response is more computationally complex and is computed only by those individuals with the greatest cognitive capacity. Because for the remaining individuals there are computational limitations and thus because the prescriptive diverges from the normative, even for them the normative/descriptive gap cannot be viewed as an indication of human irrationality.

But this conclusion represents another pyrrhic victory for a number of reasons. First, the ideal of normative rationality is not going to disappear even if we no longer should be imputing irrationality to those who do not achieve it. Such individuals still have a serious cognitive problem that will have negative real-world consequences for them, even if their behaviors are now spared the label *irrational*. If given the choice, most people would prefer that their behaviors be normatively rational (maximizing personal utility) rather than evolutionarily rational (maximizing the reproductive probability of their genes).[2] In situations of system conflict, System 1 responses thus become the equivalent of what Wilson and Brekke (1994) called mental contamination, which they defined as "the process whereby a person has an unwanted judgment, emotion, or behavior because of mental processing that is unconscious or uncontrollable. By unwanted, we mean that the person making the judgment would prefer not to be influenced in the way he or she was" (p. 117).

Thus, Dennett used Dawkins' (1976) argument that "we (and all organisms) are survival machines designed to prolong the futures of our genes. Our interests as we conceive them and the interests of our genes may well diverge, even though were it not for our genes' interests, we would not exist" (Dennett, 1988, p. 503). Anderson (1991) cautioned similarly that there may be arguments for "optimizing money, the happiness of oneself and others, or any other goal. It is just that these goals do not produce optimization of the species" (pp. 510–511). The point is that most people, if given the choice, would take the money!

People want to optimize utility for themselves as people—as opposed to optimizing the fitness function of a collection of subpersonal units called genes. To use Dawkins' (1976) memorable phrase, people don't want to be merely robots for their genes. To say this is not to deny the ex-

---

[2]This is true by the very definition of instrumental rationality—fulfilling one's personal goals (Baron, 1993a, 1994a; Nathanson, 1994; Simon, 1983).

quisite efficiency of our evolutionary mechanisms demonstrated in the excellent empirical work of the cognitive ecologists (Brase et al., 1998; Cosmides & Tooby, 1994, 1996)—for doing what they do. The problem is that sometimes they do not do what we as *people* want them to do. For this reason, normative rationality, which concerns maximizing the goals and desires of individual humans, will remain as a type of standard. Ironically, what from an evolutionary design point of view could be considered design defects, might actually be the reason that normative rationality separates from evolutionary rationality in some cases. That is, inefficient design (from an evolutionary point of view) in effect creates the possibility of a divergence between organism-level goals and gene-level goals—which is an implication of Millikan's (1993) point that "there is no reason to suppose that the design of our desire-making systems is itself optimal. Even under optimal conditions these systems work inefficiently, directly aiming, as it were, at recognizable ends that are merely roughly correlated with the biological end that is reproduction. For example, mammals do not, in general, cease efforts at individual survival after their fertile life is over" (p. 67).

As discussed previously, the cognitive ecologists have shown that some problems can be efficiently solved if represented one way (to coincide with how the brain modules represent information) but not if represented in another way (e.g., as single-event probabilities rather than frequencies). The inability to handle a particular type of problem representation could be termed a type of computational limitation, although it is obviously different from limitations such as inadequate short-term memory capacity, slow retrieval of memory codes, or inefficient search procedures.

Gigerenzer (1991b, 1993; Gigerenzer et al., 1991), for example, demonstrated that many cognitive illusions such as the conjunction fallacy and the overconfidence effect can be attenuated, if not eliminated, if the problems that subjects deal with are couched in terms of frequencies rather than single-event probabilities. However, in the titles and subheadings of several articles, Gigerenzer has used the phrasing "how to make cognitive illusions disappear." This is a strange way to phrase things, because the original illusion has of course not "disappeared." It simply has been shown that the subjects can give the normative$_s$ response to a *different* problem. For instance, Stein (1996) argued that:

> [Gigerenzer's results could be interpreted as underscoring] the irrationality of subjects' responses to the original version of the conjunction experiment. … Gigerenzer's results are consistent with the view that we have the conjunction principle in our reasoning competence, but they are also consistent with the view that we have some context-dependent principle in our reasoning competence that results in our reasoning in accordance with the conjunction principle in contexts involving frequency and violating the conjunction principle in contexts involving probability. For Gigerenzer's results

> to count in favour of the rationality thesis, a specific account of why subjects make performance errors in the standard conjunction task needs to be given. (pp. 100–101)

As Kahneman and Tversky (1996) noted, the Muller–Lyer illusion is removed when the two figures are embedded in a rectangular frame, but this does not mean that the original illusion has "disappeared" in this demonstration. The cognitive illusions in their original form still remain (although their explanation has perhaps been clarified by the different performance obtained in the frequency version), and the situations (real life or otherwise) in which these illusions occur have not been eliminated. Banks, insurance companies, medical personnel, and many other institutions of modern society are still exchanging information using linguistic terms like probability and applying that term to singular events. My physician has on occasion given me a migraine prescription (Imitrex, for instance) with the assurance that he is 90% certain it will work in my case. As many Bayesian investigators in the calibration literature have pointed out, it is likely that I would be quite upset if I found out that for 50% of his patients so advised the medication did not work. In the absence of a training program teaching medical personnel to speak of "in the 100 cases most like yours I have seen, 90 of them were relieved" (which the cognitive ecologists are no doubt correct in recommending), the findings of cognitive illusions involving probability assessment are something to worry about—they are real and they are threats to normative rationality (to people fulfilling their goals) however well people perform on frequentistic versions of the same problems.

The cognitive ecologists have, nevertheless, contributed greatly in the area of remediation methods for our cognitive deficiencies (Brase et al., 1998; Cosmides & Tooby, 1996; Fiedler, 1988; Gigerenzer & Hoffrage, 1995; Sedlmeier, 1997). Their approach is, however, somewhat different from that of the Meliorists. The ecologists concentrate on shaping the environment (changing the stimuli presented to subjects) so that the same evolutionarily adapted mechanisms that fail the standard of normative rationality under one framing of the problem give the normative$_s$ response under an alternative (e.g., frequentistic) version. Their emphasis on environmental alteration provides a much-needed counterpoint to the Meliorist emphasis on cognitive change. The latter, with their emphasis on reforming human thinking, no doubt miss opportunities to shape the environment so that it fits the representations that our brains are best evolved to deal with. Investigators framing cognition within a Meliorist perspective are often blind to the fact that there may be remarkably efficient mechanisms available in the brain—if only it was provided with the right type of representation.

On the other hand, the Apologists and cognitive ecologists have their own blind spots. As exemplified in phrasing such as "make cognitive illusions disappear," they often seem to fail to acknowledge the force of considerations of normative rationality. They also seem to ignore the fact that the world will not always let us deal with representations that are optimally suited to our evolutionarily designed cognitive mechanisms.

For example, in a series of elegant experiments, Gigerenzer et al. (1991) showed how at least part of the overconfidence effect in knowledge calibration studies is due to the unrepresentative stimuli used in such experiments—stimuli that do not match the subjects' stored cue validities that are optimally tuned to the environment. But there are many instances in real life when we are suddenly placed in environments where the cue validities have changed. Metacognitive awareness of such situations (a System 2 activity) and strategies for suppressing incorrect confidence judgments generated by the responses to cues automatically generated by System 1 will be crucial here. Every high school musician who aspires to a career in music has to recalibrate when they arrive at university and see large numbers of talented musicians for the first time. If they persist in their old confidence judgments, they may not change majors when they should. Many real-life situations where accomplishment yields a new environment with even more stringent performance requirements share this logic. Each time we "ratchet up" in the competitive environment of a capitalist economy we are in a situation just like the overconfidence knowledge calibration experiments with their unrepresentative materials (Frank & Cook, 1995). It is important to have learned System 2 strategies that will temper one's overconfidence in such situations (Koriat, Lichtenstein, & Fischhoff, 1980).

THE CULTURAL TRANSMISSION OF NORMS AND THE MALLEABILITY OF COMPUTATIONAL LIMITATIONS

The reference to learning in the previous paragraph highlights a blind spot in the Panglossian position as well as a related blind spot in that of the Apologists. The blind spot of the former is their tendency to downplay the cultural evolution of normative standards. Here again an emphasis on a competence/performance model—with its discrete emphasis on what principles are either in or not in reasoning competence—has impeded the appreciation of the fact that, particularly in the case of reasoning and inductive inference, competence and experience are tightly intertwined (a fact emphasized by the contextualist theorists within developmental psychology; see Ceci, 1996). Instead, Panglossians are prone to extrapolate nativist assumptions from the domain of language into cognitive development more generally. This strong extrapolation of nativist assumptions (see Elman et al., 1996; Quartz & Sejnowski, 1998) ignores the cultural history of norms and thus their potential learnability. Inverting the figure and ground, Jepson et al. (1983) instead stressed the historical contingency of the reasoning tools available to human reasoners: "the correctness of an induction depends not only on the adequacy of one's initial models but also on the conceptual tools one has available for extending or altering them. Changes in concepts and tools can therefore lead to different, and perhaps better, inductions. In other words, induction is a skill in which learning plays an important role" (p. 495).

Because normative models are tools of rationality and because these tools undergo cultural change and revision, there is no idealized human "rational competence" that has remained fixed throughout history. Instead:

> Even if humans lack some principle in our reasoning competence, humans may be able to acquire it and be able to use it on some occasions. For example, it seems possible that, having determined that humans lack the conjunction principle, we might endeavor to teach people to recognize the various situations in which the conjunction principle should be invoked and, then, to apply the conjunction principle in these situations. People trained in this way might still violate the conjunction principle in unfamiliar contexts or when they are rushed, but they might reason in accordance with it more frequently than untrained people would. (Stein, 1996, p. 230)

Braine and O'Brien (1991) made the interesting speculation that:

> Judgments of logical validity may (implicitly) demand a distinction between inferences that depend only on the form of the information given and those that owe something to factual knowledge or pragmatic context (cf. Moshman & Franks, 1986). We speculate that the emergence of logic as a discipline required a level of civilization that included a subclass of intellectuals ready to put energy and persistence into the metacognitive (and metalogical) task. (p. 200)

But through education, everyone now has available for their own thinking the norms of rationality developed by that subclass with the energy and persistence for that metacognitive task. Our task, as learners, is much lightened of metacognitive load because these tools have already been constructed for us. We only have to learn them (or induce them from culture).

The tendency of Panglossians to ignore the cultural history of norms often stems from an adherence to models of idealized competence that are carried over from linguistics into the reasoning domain (see Stein, 1996, for an extensive discussion). But this analogy to the linguistic domain is forced and inappropriate, as argued by Jepson et al. (1983):

> The analogy between language and inductive reasoning fails to recognize that there is far more to language than grammatical competence. Important cultural inventions, such as writing or new vocabulary, increase the effectiveness of language use.... These aspects of language fall outside the usual distinction between competence and performance. Improvements in vocabulary or in other aspects of language effectiveness by a culture or by an individual, do not represent closer approximations to some ideal competence. Instead, there is potentially no limit to the invention of new con-

cepts and new means to communicate them. We contend that effective inductive reasoning is also a skill; that it depends on cultural innovations, such as probability theory; and that it can be improved through education and frequent practice. We also suspect that there are large individual differences. (p. 495)

If Panglossians tend to treat norms that are the product of cultural development as fixed, Apologists make the parallel mistake of downplaying the malleability of human cognitive capabilities. Computational limitations in humans are not fixed in the way they are in a computer (and even there complications arise in the case of neural networks undergoing learning). The computational limits of humans are not as precisely quantifiable as those of nonhuman machines, and the consensus view of developmental psychologists is that they should not be conceived as absolute limitations (Ceci, 1996; Flynn, 1987; Neisser et al., 1996; Perkins & Grotzer, 1997). A host of experiential variables have been shown to effect the cognitive ability of humans, particularly in early developmental periods but not limited to these periods (Brody, 1997; Ceci & Williams, 1997; Cunningham & Stanovich, 1997; Morrison, 1997; Morrison, Smith, & Dow-Ehrensberger, 1995; Myerson, Rank, Raines, & Schnitzler, 1998; Nickerson, 1988; Stanovich, 1993; Stanovich, West, & Harrison, 1995).

Finally, in chapter 6 it was shown that a characterization of aspects of intentional psychology in terms of thinking dispositions related to epistemic regulation can also predict performance on a variety of rational thinking tasks, and to some extent they can predict performance independently of cognitive ability. If, as some theorists (e.g., Baron, 1985a) argue, thinking dispositions are more malleable than cognitive ability, this again provides a lever for attempts to make thinking more normatively rational. Particularly if we accept views in which normative rationality and morality largely coincide (Gauthier, 1986), it is clear that many cultural mechanisms (parents, schools, churches, etc.) have as a practical goal the teaching of rationality. These efforts make sense only if cognitive limitations are not fixed and if we view normative competence in the reasoning domain as in part a cultural product.

EDUCATION AND NORMATIVE RATIONALITY

Thus, the cultural institution of education is in part organized in order to foster those System 2 processes that lead to more rational thought and action (Nickerson, 1988). However, the implicit normative framework of this enterprise is often opaque to teachers. For example, in the current educational literature, teachers are constantly exhorted to "teach children how to think," or to foster "critical thinking" and "creative problem solving." The problem here is that "thinking" is not a domain of knowledge. As Baron (1993b) noted, "We teach Latin or calculus because students do not already know how to speak Latin or find integrals. But, by any reasonable description of thinking, students already know how to think, and the problem is that they do not do it as effectively as they might" (p. 199). Thus, the admonition to educators to "teach thinking skills" and foster "critical thinking" contains implicit evaluative assumptions. The children *already* think. Educators are charged with getting them to think *better* (Adams, 1989, 1993). This of course implies a normative model of what we mean by better thinking (Baron, Badgio, & Gaskins, 1986; Haslam & Baron, 1994).

A somewhat analogous issue arises when thinking dispositions are discussed in the educational literature of critical thinking. Why do we want people to think in an actively open-minded fashion? Why do we want to foster multiplist and evaluative thinking (Kuhn, 1992) rather than absolutist thinking? Why do we want people to be reflective? It can be argued that the superordinate goal we are actually trying to foster is that of rationality (Stanovich, 1994). That is, much of what educators are ultimately concerned about is rational thought in both the epistemic sense and the practical sense. We value certain thinking dispositions because we think that they will at least aid in the former and are essential for the latter. But at least in principle we could imagine a person with excellent epistemic rationality (their degree of confidence in propositions being well calibrated to the available evidence relevant to the proposition) and optimal practical rationality (they optimally satisfy their desires given their beliefs) who was not actively open-minded. We might still want to mold such an individual's dispositions in the direction of open-mindedness for the sake of society as a whole; but from a purely individual perspective, we would now be hard-pressed to find reasons why we would want to change such a person's thinking dispositions if—whatever they were—they had led to rational thought and action in the past.

In short, a large part of the rationale for educational interventions to change thinking dispositions derives from a tacit assumption that actively open-minded thinking dispositions make the individual a more rational person (Baron, 1985a, 1993b, 1994b; Stanovich, 1994). But that puts a burden of proof on the shoulders of advocates of such educational interventions. They must show that thinking dispositions are associated with the responses and thought patterns that are considered normative (and that the association is causal). This is precisely the empirical evidence that was presented in chapter 6 and in the research programs of several other investigators (Kardash & Scholes, 1996; Klaczynski et al., 1997; Kuhn, 1991, 1993, 1996; Schaller, Boyd, Yohannes, & O'Brien, 1995; Schommer, 1990, 1994; S. M. Smith & Levin, 1996). Although the trends are never extremely strong, there has been a consistent tendency for people who are high in actively open-minded thinking to give the normative$_s$ response on hypothesis testing and reasoning tasks, to avoid belief bias in their reasoning, and to properly calibrate their beliefs to the state of the evidence. Thus, the field of education is beginning to develop a normatively justified foundation for its emphasis on critical-thinking dispositions.

CAVEATS AND CLARIFICATIONS

The conclusions drawn in this and other chapters are of course subject to a number of caveats and clarifications. Some of these have been discussed in the relevant chapters. A few that either were not mentioned or deserve a stronger emphasis are discussed in this section.

Assumptions Regarding Evolutionary Rationality and System 1 Processes

Throughout the discussion of evolutionary rationality in chapters 5 and 7, it has been assumed that the computation underlying specifically evolutionarily adapted responses (as opposed to general problem-solving ability) is accomplished entirely by System 1 modules and does not implicate analytic intelligence. This assumption corresponds to one of the alternatives discussed by Oaksford et al. (1997)—that "the cognitive system may implement this analysis [evolutionarily optimized data selection] with a hardwired and cognitively impenetrable (Pylyshyn, 1984) heuristic that has evolved" (p. 443) to deal with the environment (this might be termed the cognitively impenetrable assumption).

An alternative assumption (the cognitively penetrable assumption) is that evolutionarily optimized processes are computed by a mixture of processes—impenetrable (to use Pylyshyn's, 1984, term) System 1 modules and cognitive penetrable central processes of System 2. If this alternative assumption is true, then evolutionary rationality is no longer independent of cognitive ability. To the extent the implementation of evolutionarily optimized data selection implicates System 2, there will be intelligence differences in the ability to execute processes that are evolutionarily adapted. In short, under this assumption, there may well be algorithmic limitations preventing the optimization of evolutionary rationality as well as normative rationality.

The interpretation of the results of the experiments presented in this volume would change in two ways if the alternative assumption (cognitive penetrability) holds. First, situations in which evolutionary and normative rationality dictated different responses would result in the attenuation of cognitive ability differences—rather than the enhancement of such differences as illustrated in Table 4.14. In contrast, large cognitive ability differences would now be consistent with situations where both evolutionary rationality and normative rationality dictated the same response.

The second implication derives from the fact that, under the cognitive penetrability assumption, cognitive ability differences now point in the direction of the evolutionarily optimized response in addition to the normatively rational response. The relations between normative/evolutionary rationality differences and cognitive ability differences thus reverse. Now, large cognitive ability differences mean that normative and evolutionary rationality do not come apart and small differences mean that they do.

However, a consideration of several results discussed previously suggests that this alternative assumption—that evolutionarily adapted responses implicate System 2 processes (and hence general cognitive ability) in their computation—comports poorly with the data. First, on some of the tasks on which it is most likely that evolutionary and normative rationality separate (the abstract selection task and the Linda Problem), the largest cognitive ability differences were displayed. Under the cognitive penetrability assumption, it would follow that both evolutionary and normative rationality are pointing in the direction of the P and not-Q response in the selection task (and against the conjunction fallacy in the Linda Problem). Such an interpretation would, for example, contradict the elegant analysis of optimal data selection in the abstract selection task conducted by Oaksford and Chater (1994, 1996; Oaksford et al., 1997), which is based on an assumption of evolutionary rationality. This is why, in a task such as this, it seems preferable to maintain the earlier assumption that the processes of optimal data selection are carried out by impenetrable System 1 processes, leaving intelligence—an index of System 2 capability and flexibility—to serve as a possible override mechanism in the service of normative rationality.

The cognitive impenetrability assumption—that computation of evolutionarily optimized responses is accomplished entirely by System 1 modules—does have its own interesting implications however. From this assumption, it follows that evolutionary rationality will often become decoupled from normative rationality. To the extent that the mechanisms that compute evolutionary optimized responses are decoupled from processes of analytic intelligence, evolutionary rationality becomes decoupled from normative rationality—because normative rationality is dependent on just such System 2 processes. The connection between normative rationality and the System 2 processes that collectively comprise the construct of cognitive ability is reinforced by much data indicating that job success and the avoidance of harmful behaviors—the very types of outcomes that normative rationality maximizes—are reasonably strongly predicted by the analytic abilities that comprise System 2 (Brody, 1997; Gottfredson, 1997; Lubinski & Humphreys, 1997).

Alternative Interpretations of Relationships With Cognitive Ability

Throughout this volume, cognitive ability measures were interpreted as omnibus indexes of the efficiency of computational components such as working memory, information retrieval speed, and so on—that is, as proxies for overall cognitive power. However, an alternative interpretation might highlight instead the metacognitive functions of intelligence (components having to do with flexible strategy use; see Sternberg, 1985) rather than the elementary information-processing components. This alternative conceptualization views cognitive ability measures not as indicators of basic computational power but as indicators of the tendency to respond to problems with appropriate strategies. These alternative notions of cognitive ability have waxed and waned throughout a century of work on human intelligence (Sternberg, 1990; Sternberg & Detterman, 1986).

Relationships between cognitive ability and normative$_s$ responses can be interpreted with a slightly different emphasis depending on the concept of cognitive ability that is employed. Under the first interpretation, it is assumed that the normative$_s$ response is computationally more complex, and only those with the requisite computational power are able to compute it. Alternatively, under the second interpretation of cognitive ability, the normative$_s$ strategy might not be more computationally complex. It might simply be more efficient and more readily recognized as such by more metacognitively sensitive individuals. This second interpretation was employed only sparingly in this volume because it makes use of metacognitive notions that blur the line between the intentional and algorithmic levels of analysis—a distinction that proved useful in interpreting the results of many of the experiments. Such an interpretation would have had more of a disposition-like implication (Baron, 1985a, 1985b) in cases where we would have attributed a computational limitation under the alternative interpretation: that perhaps better environmental support (e.g., education) might lead the less computationally efficient individuals to the normative solution more quickly.

Finally, as discussed earlier in this chapter, the cognitive ecologists stress a different type of computational limitation that highlights a different way of characterizing overall cognitive ability. From within this framework, computational limitations result from problems being presented to the brain in formats that are incongruent with the representational format used by the relevant cognitive module. Cognitive ability might therefore be characterized as the number of different problem representations with which the individual can cope. The Meliorist—free of the nativist assumptions of many cognitive ecologists and with more emphasis on the cultural malleability of problem representations—would be more likely to see variation in this quantity. Thus, under this representational view, correlations between cognitive ability and the normative$_s$ strategies could be interpreted as indicating that individuals higher in cognitive ability have more alternative problem representations and are thus more likely to have available the representation that is appropriate for the way in which the experimenter has framed the problem.

In short, moving outside of the technical area of computational complexity theory (see Oaksford & Chater, 1992, 1993, 1995) into the looser vocabulary of human abilities research, it might be possible to distinguish three different types of computational limitations: Type A—limitations in the efficiency of basic information-processing components; Type B—limitations in metacognitive control (in the flexible deployment of strategies to solve a problem); Type C—limitations in the types of representations that the cognitive apparatus can deal with and the types of procedures it can implement.

The Plausibility of Computational Limitations in Different Types of Tasks

Simon's (1956, 1957) notion of bounded rationality forms the background for much of the heuristics and biases literature (Kahneman et al., 1982; Nisbett & Ross, 1980). However, Lopes (1992) pointed out that the types of problems in the Newell and Simon (1972) tradition—chess, logic, and cryptarithmetic—are vastly more complex than the one-shot paper-and-pencil-problems in the Tversky and Kahneman (1974, 1983) tradition. Many of the latter—paragraph-length narratives requiring a single numerical response—would seem to be poor candidates for computational limitations ("it could be argued that the laboratory tasks employed by Kahneman and Tversky would have permitted the use of the normative strategy because the amount of information [n] was kept well within manageable bounds," Oaksford & Chater, 1992, p. 227). However, they are only poor candidates for Type A computational limitations. These types of problems still might be characterized by Type B and Type C limitations.

Oaksford and Chater (1992) further pointed out that if a reasoning procedure is not in human competence because it is too costly in terms of Type A limitations, then scaling down the problem will still leave the individual without the necessary procedure. So, for example, if a full Bayesian inference process could not be implemented in the brain, the process simply will not be present. Presenting the individual with a toy problem that could be solved by Bayesian methods cannot make such a process suddenly appear in the brain. Thus, the type of limitation discussed by Oaksford and Chater is very similar to the Type C limitation mentioned previously.

Alternative Construal as a Computational Escape Hatch

Throughout this volume, alternative task understanding was treated separately from computational limitations as an explanation of the normative/descriptive gap. However, the previous discussion of different notions of computational limitations suggests that in some cases these two might be intimately linked. Most briefly stated, sometimes alternative might be computational escape hatches—that is, an alternative construal might be hiding an inability to compute according to the normative model. This could come about in one of two ways—either with or without metacognitive awareness. In the first, the subject is aware of alternative task interpretations and chooses the one with the lowest computational demands. In the second, the computational escape hatch is used automatically and without awareness of the alternative interpretations (in short, in the manner of a System 1 module)—perhaps because there does not exist alternative representations to map the problem (i.e., there is a Type C limitation).

Thus, for example, in the selection task, perhaps some people automatically represent the task as an inductive problem of optimal data sampling in the manner that Oaksford and Chater (1994, 1996) outlined. Alternatively, perhaps some individuals who adopt this construal are aware of the deductive interpretation but avoid it because they intuit—as O'Brien (1995) demonstrated—that the abstract selection task is a very hard problem for a mental logic without direct access to the truth table for the material conditional. If the latter—if subjects are actually choosing different task construals based in part on computational considerations—then such a mechanism may allow for the influence of thinking dispositions. For example, in arguing that it is unlikely that a descriptive model will exactly mirror a normative one, Shafir (1993) argued that "to suppose that a single theory can serve as both a normative guide and a descriptive model of decision making requires that the cognitive processes that guide behaviour conform with our desire to reach rational decisions" (pp. 260–261). "Our desire to reach rational decisions"—clearly captured in the need for cognition, need for closure, and other dispositional constructs mentioned in chapter 6—may vary between individuals and may be what makes one individual choose a normatively rational but computationally costly task construal when an alternative is available.

Finally, in the context of considering differential construal as a computational escape hatch, it is interesting to note that when assessing algorithmic-level computational power there is no allowance made for differential task construal. Unlike the tradition of accepting all task construals when assessing human rationality (e.g., Henle, 1962), the quality of task construals is routinely evaluated when computational power is assessed. For example, Detterman and Thompson (1997) mentioned an instance where a high school student with an IQ of 70 responded to the WAIS–R (Wechsler Adult Intelligence Scale—Revised) vocabulary item of "penny" with the phrase "to buy bubble gum with." This response receives no credit on the WAIS–R even though the individual appears to misinterpret what the examiner is asking for. Nevertheless, it is assumed that this misinterpretation is motivated by the desire to answer an easier question about the meaning of the item and/or by the inability to construe the task as the examiner instructed. Either way, the alternative construal is deemed a computational escape hatch.

Thus, when assessing algorithmic-level capabilities, the tradition is to deem certain task construals as absolutely wrong; whereas when assessing intentional-level rationality, the tradition is just the opposite—to accept whatever task construal the subject arrives at. Or, to put it another way, when a task is misinterpreted it counts against assessments of algorithmic-level capabilities but not against intentional-level rationality. Because alternative task construal is routinely deemed a computational escape hatch in the former, a similar explanation should at least be considered when assessing the latter—particularly in light of the results from certain tasks (nondeontic selection task, Linda Problem) that displayed large cognitive ability differences.

Not All System 1 Overrides Are Efficacious

In this chapter (as well as chaps. 5 and 7), System 2 overrides of System 1 processing have been discussed as if they were always efficacious. But this is not necessarily the case. It certainly is possible for metacognitive judgment to go awry and override System 1 processing when in fact the latter would have served the goals of normative rationality even better than the overriding systems. An example is provided by the work of Wilson and Schooler (1991). They had subjects rate their preferences for different brands of strawberry jam and compared these ratings to those of experts (the ratings in *Consumer Reports*). They found that a group of individuals who were encouraged to be analytic about their ratings made ratings less in accord with the experts than a group who were not given encouragement to be analytic.

Thus, in certain domains and in certain situations, System 1 processes are not only optimally adapted in an evolutionary sense but also best serve the goals of normative rationality as well. This suggests that humans as cognitive systems can make the error of having too low a threshold for System 1 override. Such an overly low threshold for override might be conceived as a Mr. Spock-like hyperrationality that could actually be deleterious to goal achievement.

Normative and Evolutionary Rationality and the Rationality₁ and Rationality₂ of Evans and Over (1996)

It should be noted that the distinction between normative and evolutionary rationality used in this volume is different from the distinction between rationality$_1$ and rationality$_2$ utilized by Evans and Over (1996). They defined rationality$_1$ as reasoning and acting "in a way that is generally reliable and efficient for achieving one's goals" (p. 8). Rationality$_2$ concerns reasoning and acting "when one has a reason for what one does sanctioned by a normative theory" (p. 8). Because normative theories concern goals at the personal (or social) level, not the genetic level, both of the rationalities defined by Evans and Over fall within what has been termed here normative rationality. Both concern goals at the personal level. Evans and Over wished to distinguish the explicit (i.e., conscious) following of a normative rule (rationality$_2$) from the largely unconscious processes "that do much to help them achieve their ordinary goals" (p. 9). Their distinction is between two sets of algorithmic mechanisms (along the lines of Systems 1 and 2 discussed in chap. 5) that can both serve normative rationality.

The distinction in this volume is in terms of the *types* of goals being optimized, whereas theirs is in terms of the *mechanism* used to pursue personal goals (via mechanisms of conscious, reason-based rule following vs. tacit heuristics). In the two-system conception of chapter 5, System 1 was viewed as more directly designed to maximize the evolutionary goals of gene replication. Of course, as discussed there, on most occasions, those goals turn out to be normative goals as well. Thus, we could imagine a partitioning much like Evans and Over's by distinguishing System 1 pursuing the goals of normative rationality from System 2 pursuing the goals of normative rationality. However, the emphasis of this volume was on those situations where evolutionary and normative rationality come apart—where in order for an individual to pursue their personal goals they must use their System 2 processes to override System 1 (which is pursuing not *their* goals but their *genes'* goals). The present emphasis is thus in terms of System 1 pursuing the goals of evolutionary rationality versus System 2 pursuing normative rationality—*when the two sets of goals happen to conflict*.

Normative Rationality in the Belief Bias Situation: The Knowledge Projection Argument

In the discussion of belief bias effects in chapter 6, the decontextualizing response was treated as the normative one and the analysis of individual differences supported this assumption—the analyses of both cognitive ability and thinking dispositions pointed in that direction. In that chapter I also mentioned an alternative normative argument by Kornblith (1993). This argument deserves more attention than it received in chapter 6, because it recurs remarkably often throughout the reasoning literature and it is often hard to recognize because it appears in different guises. The argument as stated by Kornblith was that:

> Mistaken beliefs will, as a result of belief perseverance, taint our perception of new data. By the same token, however, belief perseverance will serve to color our perception of new data when our preexisting beliefs are accurate. … If, overall, our belief-generating mechanisms give us a fairly accurate picture of the world, then the phenomenon of belief perseverance may do more to inform our understanding than it does to distort it. (p. 105)

This argument—that in a natural ecology where most of our prior beliefs are true, projecting our beliefs on to new data will lead to faster accumulation of knowledge—I will term the *knowledge projection argument*, and it reappears in a remarkably diverse set of contexts throughout the reasoning and decision-making literature. For example, Dawes' (1989, 1990) alternative interpretation of the false consensus effect discussed in chapter 3 amounts to essentially the knowledge projection argument. Dawes (1989; see also Hoch, 1987) demonstrated that a Bayesian analysis renders some degree of projection in the opinion prediction experiment normatively appropriate because, for the majority of people, there is actually a positive correlation between own opinion and the consensus opinion. Thus, one's own opinion is, in these social perception paradigms, a diagnostic datum that should condition probability estimates (Krueger & Zeiger, 1993). Or, to put it more colloquially, most people's opinions are in the majority most of the time—this follows from the very definition of majority. Most people's opinions are, more often than not, true of other people—so it makes sense to project them in an opinion prediction paradigm.

Alloy and Tabachnik (1984) echoed the knowledge projection argument in their review of the covariation detection literature on humans and other animals:

> When individuals' expectations accurately reflect the contingencies encountered in their natural environments ... it is not irrational for them to assimilate incoming information about covariation between events to these expectations.... Because covariation information provided in an experiment may represent only one piece of conflicting evidence against the background of the large body of data about event covariations summarized by an expectation, it would be normatively appropriate for organisms to weight their expectations more heavily than situational information in the covariation judgment process. (p. 140)

Of course, Alloy and Tabachnik emphasized that we must project from a largely accurate set of beliefs in order to obtain the benefit of knowledge projection. In a sea of inaccurate beliefs, the situation is quite different (see later discussion).

Koehler (1993) demonstrated that scientists' prior beliefs about the hypothesis in question influenced their judgments of evidence quality. In a Bayesian analysis of whether this evaluation tendency could ever be normatively justified, Koehler found that under certain conditions it could. One of those conditions was that the prior hypotheses influencing evidence evaluation were more likely than not to be true. When evidence is evaluated with reference to a pool of hypotheses that are largely true,[3] that evidence will lead to belief convergence faster if the prior beliefs do influence evidence evaluation—another version of the knowledge projection argument.

Evans, Over, and Manktelow (1993) relied on a variant of the knowledge projection argument when considering the normative status of

---

[3]Of course the counter to this argument is that it is precisely at the frontiers of science where we do not have good reason to believe that our prior hypotheses are true.

belief bias in syllogistic reasoning. They considered the status of selective scrutiny explanations of the belief bias phenomenon. Such theories posit that subjects accept conclusions that are believable without engaging in logical reasoning at all. Only when faced with unbelievable conclusions do subjects engage in logical reasoning about the premises. Evans et al. considered whether such a processing strategy could be rational in the sense of serving to achieve the person's goals, and they concluded that it could. They argued that any adult is likely to hold a large number of true beliefs that are interconnected in complex ways. Because single-belief revision has interactive effects on the rest of the belief network, it may be computationally costly. Evans et al. argued that under such conditions it is quite right that conclusions that contradict one's beliefs "should be subjected to the closest possible scrutiny and refuted if at all possible" (p. 174). Again, the argument works when the selective scrutiny mechanism is applied using a subset of beliefs that are largely true in the domain to which the scrutiny strategy is being applied.

Variants of the knowledge projection argument can show up much further afield however. Mitchell, Robinson, Isaacs, and Nye (1996) found a realist bias in adults in a theory of mind–like task and argued that it represented an instance of mental contamination (Wilson & Brekke, 1994). The forecasts of individuals predicting a protagonist's belief were influenced by facts revealed to them but not the protagonist. Adult subjects thought that a protagonist's behavior would be affected by the facts known to them but unknown to the protagonist. Parallel to children's failures in theory of mind tasks, the adults in the Mitchell et al. experiment had their representation of another's mental state disrupted by (privileged) knowledge they had about the protagonist's world—they inappropriately projected this knowledge. But Mitchell et al. argued that in most cases "since simple factual beliefs would normally be true, a short cut to judging belief is to report reality" (pp. 16–17). In short, the experimental situation is a special one in which what you know is dissociated from what the protagonist knows. In most situations, knowledge will be shared so projecting that knowledge on to a protagonist in order to predict their behavior will work as long as the pool of projected knowledge is shared—another version of the knowledge projection argument.

Finally, K. Edwards and E. E. Smith (1996) found a disconfirmation bias in the evaluation of arguments. Arguments that were incompatible with prior beliefs were subjected to a more intense analysis than those compatible with prior belief. Edwards and Smith developed a selective scrutiny account of this effect similar to that developed for the syllogistic reasoning task by Evans, Over, and Manktelow (1993). Edwards and Smith puzzled over whether such selective scrutiny tendencies could be normative in certain circumstances and, for reasons similar to Evans et al., decided that in appropriate conditions they could be:

> Because the option of searching for a fallacy includes a cost that the option of accepting at face value does not, the former option should be preferred only when a fallacy is likely (i.e., only when the conclusion of the argument is improbable). These ideas map directly onto the disconfirmation model. When an argument is compatible, its conclusion seems probable, and it is unlikely that there will be a fallacy in it; hence, there is little justification for engaging in a mentally costly deliberative search of memory. In contrast, when an argument is incompatible, its conclusion seems improbable, and it is likely that it contains a fallacy; consequently, there is good reason to devote the extra mental work needed to find the fallacy. From this perspective, the bias to disconfirm only incompatible arguments seems rational. (p. 22)

Thus, as in the syllogistic reasoning paradigm, it pays to selectively scrutinize arguments. But K. Edwards and E. E. Smith (1996) also emphasized the caveat mentioned previously—this will be true only when the prior beliefs on which we are conditioning our selectivity are true:

> The preceding considerations indicate that a disconfirmation bias can be normatively justified. Still, we do not want to leave the reader with the impression that all aspects of the behavior of the participants in our experiments were rational. The case for total rationality hinges on the assumption that the prior beliefs involved (which determine whether an argument is compatible or not) were themselves arrived at by a normative process. It seems unlikely that this would always be the case…. Thus, when one looks at the details of the search for disconfirming evidence, irrationalities begin to surface. (p. 22)

Again, the pitfall here is the same as that mentioned previously—when the subset of beliefs that the individual is projecting contains substantial false information, selective scrutiny will delay the assimilation of the correct information.

The latter caveat creates the possibility of observing a so-called "Matthew effect"—a cumulative advantage phenomenon—in the acquisition of knowledge (Stanovich, 1986). Walberg (Walberg, Strykowski, Rovai, & Hung, 1984; Walberg & Tsai, 1983), following Merton (1968), dubbed cumulative advantage effects in education "Matthew effects," after the Gospel according to Matthew: "For unto every one that hath shall be given, and he shall have abundance: but from him that hath not shall be taken away even that which he hath" (XXV:29). In the educational literature, the term springs from findings that individuals who have advantageous early educational experiences are able to utilize new educational experiences more efficiently and thus increase their advantage. How might the knowledge projection process lead to Matthew effects in knowledge acquisition? Imagine two scientists, A and B, working in domain X. The bulk of hypotheses in domain X held by scientist A are true and the bulk of hypotheses in domain X held by scientist B are false. Imagine that they both then begin to project those prior beliefs on the same new evidence in the manner demonstrated experimentally by Koehler (1993)—with stronger tendencies to undermine the evidence when it contradicted prior belief. It is clear that scientist A—who already exceeds B in number of true beliefs—will increase that advantage as new data comes in.

The knowledge projection tendency, efficacious in the aggregate, may have the effect of isolating certain individuals on "islands of false beliefs" from which—because of the knowledge projection tendency—they are unable to escape. In short, there may be a type of knowledge isolation effect when projection is used in particularly ill-suited circumstances. Thus, knowledge projection, which in the aggregate might lead to more rapid induction of new true beliefs, may be a trap in cases where people, in effect, keep reaching into a bag of beliefs that are largely false, using these beliefs to structure their evaluation of evidence, and hence more quickly adding incorrect beliefs to the bag for further projection. Knowledge projection from an island of false beliefs might explain the phenomenon of otherwise intelligent people who get caught in a domain-specific web of falsity and because of projection tendencies cannot escape (e.g., otherwise competent physical scientists who believe in creationism). Indeed, such individuals often use their considerable computational power to rationalize their beliefs and to ward off the arguments of skeptics (Evans, 1996; Evans & Wason, 1976; Margolis, 1987; Nisbett & Wilson, 1977; Wason, 1969).

Further research is needed to examine whether such Matthew effects and knowledge isolation effects can be documented. Nevertheless, a consideration of such effects puts in context the knowledge projection argument as a justification of the normativity of belief bias. It provides a statistical rationale for the presence of such a bias, because across individuals—and across beliefs within an individual—most of what is believed is true. Thus, on an overall statistical basis, knowledge projection may well increase the rate of acquisition of true beliefs. But this does not prevent particular individuals with particularly ill-formed initial beliefs from projecting them and developing beliefs that are even less in correspondence with reality. Neither does it prevent an individual (with an otherwise generally accurate belief network) from getting caught on an island of false beliefs with respect to a particular domain, projecting those beliefs, and with time developing even more bizarre theories about this domain.

Such considerations raise the interesting issue of the metacognitive control of knowledge projection—or what might be termed the calibration of knowledge projection. Specifically, projection tendencies would be much more uniformly efficacious if people had some metacognitive control over them—if they projected more in cases where their confidence is high and less in cases where their confidence was weak. Additionally, on a between-subjects basis, knowledge projection would be more uniformly efficacious if people with more true beliefs were more prone to projection and those with fewer true beliefs less so. The presence of either within-person or across-person knowledge calibration would lower the probability of the formation of truly bizarre beliefs. These different types of metacognitive calibration are currently under investigation.

RATIONALITY AND PRETHEORETICAL BIASES

In a balanced and nuanced essay, Adler (1991) argued that it is best to view an individual facing a reasoning task as balancing different sets of goals and trading one type of real cost for another. He pointed out that many classic problems ask people to trade off predictive accuracy and explanatory coherence. In the Linda Problem, for example, predictive accuracy is lost if the subject displays the conjunction fallacy—it is a bad bet to favor the probability of Linda being a feminist bank teller over the probability of her being a bank teller. To avoid this bad bet, one must ignore Linda's personality description. If, on the other hand, an individual is focused on developing an overall coherent view of Linda—one that might help in developing expectations for her behavior in the future—then paying close attention to the personality description and weighing it heavily would seem to serve this end. Thus, a focus on explanatory coherence will lead one into a bad bet, whereas a focus on predictive accuracy will sacrifice explanatory coherence.

Adler (1991) warned the Meliorists (whom he called the pessimists) that a myopic focus on the static one-shot goals of the problem as set by the experimenter potentially ignores legitimate long-run epistemic goals that individuals may bring to the task. Similarly, he warned Apologists and Panglossians (whom he called optimists) that "the fact that favoring one set of goals over others is reasonable does not eliminate the fact that sacrifice of legitimate objectives has taken place" (p. 274). So, for example, the finding that a frequentist representation of a problem often leads to better performance than the single-event probability version (Cosmides & Tooby, 1996; Gigerenzer & Hoffrage, 1995) does not negate the fact that inaccuracies will result when single-event probabilities must be dealt with. Adler's balanced view contains a warning for both camps:

> Even if subjects' answers are wrong, that does not exclude those answers being appropriate on other relevant evaluative dimensions. Correlatively, if there is a legitimate framework that subjects apply, within which their answers are justified, that doesn't exempt them from criticism. The studies of judgment and reasoning are best understood along a number of evaluative dimensions, and it is the basic weakness of the optimist-pessimist opposition to attempt to reduce these to only one. (p. 274)

Thus, a more nuanced debate would recognize that each of the camps in the rationality debate have their own strengths and their own blind spots. Each has advanced the theoretical and practical debate about human rationality: The Panglossians have demonstrated that the answers to real-world problems are often in human cognition itself (economists have exploited this strategy by assuming that humans are already optimizing in the real-world and that we simply need to properly characterize the optimized processes); the Apologists have demonstrated the power of evolutionary explanations and the necessity of matching stimulus representations to those to which evolution has shaped cognition (e.g., Cosmides & Tooby, 1996); the Meliorists have championed the possibility of cognitive change (e.g., Nisbett, 1993) and warned against the dire consequences of mismatches between human cognitive tendencies and the thinking requirements of a technological society (e.g., Piattelli-Palmarini, 1994).

Correspondingly however: The Meliorists are often too quick to claim flaws in human reasoning and they may miss real strengths in human cognition that could be exploited for behavioral betterment; the Apologists sometimes fail to acknowledge that a real cognitive disability results when a technological society confronts the human cognitive apparatus with a representation for which it is not evolutionarily adapted—and they sometimes fail to stress that representational flexibility is something that can increase with instruction; the Panglossians are often forced into contorted positions in order to excuse human errors and they thus pass up opportunities to remediate correctable cognitive mistakes.

If the trade-offs—and the relevant strengths and weaknesses—are so obvious, why has debate in this area been so contentious? Margolis (1987) humorously noted that "we can see something of the peculiarity of human judgment at work in the tenaciousness with which writers (on the one hand) who view themselves as defenders of human rationality construct reasons why subjects are really being perfectly reasonable in responding in ways that the experimenters (on the other hand) insist can only be reasonably seen as illogical. Both sides agree that someone is being stubborn" (p. 19). As discussed in several previous chapters, some of this stubbornness comes about because although all camps acknowledge the same facts about behavior, they choose to foreground and background different things. Meliorists see a world seemingly full of shockingly awful events—pyramid sales schemes going "bust" and causing financial distress, Holocaust deniers generating media attention, $10 billion spent annually on medical quackery, respected physical scientists announcing that they believe in creationism, savings and loan institutions seemingly self-destructing and costing taxpayers billions—and think that there must be something fundamentally wrong in human cognition to be accounting for all this mayhem. Of course, in the background for the Meliorist are the very things that represent the foreground for the Panglossians and Apologists—all of the cognitive feats that humans perform amazingly well. For these latter two camps, it is a marvel that humans are exquisite frequency detectors (Hasher & Zacks, 1979), that they infer intentionality with almost supernatural ease (Levinson, 1995), that they acquire a complex language code from impoverished input (Pinker, 1994), and perceive three dimensions. These things seem manifestly more important than whether a few people dial up the psychic hotline or not.

The ease with which the figure and ground here can be reversed suggests that we really are dealing with pretheoretical worldviews that are coloring the interpretation of the data. For example, Evans (1982) commented that "many of the 'logical' theorists—including those influenced by Henle—postulate underlying mechanisms in the form of representation and process models. I would argue that the nature of the mechanisms proposed is motivated *not* primarily by a desire to explain the observed behaviour, but by a wish to see the subjects' behaviour as rationally determined" (pp. 212–213). In parallel, Lopes (1991) argued that the interpretation embodied in some Meliorists analyses reflects not the desire to elucidate and reveal underlying psychological processes but the need to label human behavior as irrational.

Obviously, both camps recognize that there are costs and benefits to their positions, but they calculate the probabilities of incurring those costs and reaping the benefits differently. For example, the camps are in strong disagreement about the probability that evolutionarily adapted mechanisms will match the representations called for in many real-world situations that occur in a technological society. The Meliorists (as is evident from the Meliorist bias of this volume) think that there will be many such situations and that it is no consolation to be told that the ill-suited mechanisms that we do possess work marvelously efficiently on some other representation. The Panglossian and Apologists think that the number of such situations is small and that our ability to prepare for them is reduced by Meliorist fixation on attributions of irrationality. In short, the camps make different assumptions about the extent of the ecological match with the cognitive representations that are stored in the brain.

But there may yet be a way out of the impasse caused by the differing worldviews that investigators bring to these studies. Both camps have been guilty of characterizing human cognition too broadly—the Meliorists too broadly attributing irrationalities and the Panglossians employing too encompassing an assumption of rationality. If the variability in human behavior is fully acknowledged by both sides, then it is possible to get all of the camps—and the basic insights that motivate them—into the same focus.

If we relax the Panglossian assumption that everyone, virtually all the time (minus adventitious performance errors) must be rational, we then have room for a minority of individuals to create the egregious incidents—the bizarre beliefs, the disastrous actions—that so worry the Meliorists. For example, the Matthew effects caused by knowledge projection discussed previously are one way that a minority of individuals could have their beliefs detached from reality in ways so extreme that an attribution of irrationality would seem justified. Such a case would be an example of a generally efficacious mechanism resulting in seriously suboptimal belief structures. Knowledge projection is thus a mechanism that could be generally normative in a statistical sense but still be the cause of a minority of actions and beliefs that are seriously irrational.

The operation of such a mechanism would produce data consistent with the overall trend in the analyses of individual differences discussed in this volume—a plurality of individuals giving the normative$_s$ response, a smaller number prevented from doing so by computational limitations, and a residual group who seem to be systematically non-normative. Specifically, virtually all of the tasks showed a continuum of performance. Some responses that deviated from the response considered normative could easily be considered as error variance. Several tasks were characterized by heavy computational loads that made the normative response not prescriptive for some subjects—but these were usually few in number. Finally, a few tasks yielded patterns of covariance that served to raise doubts about the normative models applied to them and/or the task construals assumed by the problem inventors. Although many normative/descriptive gaps could be reduced by these mechanisms, not all of the discrepancies could be explained by factors that do not bring human rationality into question. It does seem that some human behavior is systematically irrational.

References

Ackerman, P. L., & Heggestad, E. D. (1997). Intelligence, personality, and interests: Evidence for overlapping traits. *Psychological Bulletin, 121*, 219–245.

Ackerman, P. L., Kyllonen, P., & Roberts, R. (Eds.). (in press). *The future of learning and individual differences research: Processes, traits, and content.* Washington, DC: American Psychological Association.

Adams, M. J. (1989). Thinking skills curricula: Their promise and progress. *Educational Psychologist, 24*, 25–77.

Adams, M. J. (1993). Towards making it happen. *Applied Psychology: An International Review, 42*, 214–218.

Adler, J. E. (1984). Abstraction is uncooperative. *Journal for the Theory of Social Behaviour, 14*, 165–181.

Adler, J. E. (1991). An optimist's pessimism: Conversation and conjunctions. In E. Eells & T. Maruszewski (Eds.), *Probability and rationality: Studies on L. Jonathan Cohen's philosophy of science* (pp. 251–282). Amsterdam: Editions Rodopi.

Ajzen, I. (1977). Intuitive theories of events and the effects of base-rate information on prediction. *Journal of Personality and Social Psychology, 35*, 303–314.

Akinnaso, F. N. (1981). The consequences of literacy in pragmatic and theoretical perspectives. *Anthropology & Education Quarterly, 12*, 163–200.

Alker, H., & Hermann, M. (1971). Are Bayesian decisions artificially intelligent? The effect of task and personality on conservatism in information processing. *Journal of Personality and Social Psychology, 19*, 31–41.

Allais, M. (1953). Le comportement de l'homme rationnel devant le risque: Critique des postulats et axioms de l'école americaine. *Econometrica, 21*, 503–546.

Allan, L. G. (1980). A note on measurement of contingency between two binary variables in judgment tasks. *Bulletin of the Psychonomic Society, 15*, 147–149.

Alloy, L. B., & Tabachnik, N. (1984). Assessment of covariation by humans and animals: The joint influence of prior expectations and current situational information. *Psychological Review, 91*, 112–149.

Anderson, J. R. (1990). *The adaptive character of thought*. Hillsdale, NJ: Lawrence Erlbaum Associates.

Anderson, J. R. (1991). Is human cognition adaptive? *Behavioral and Brain Sciences, 14*, 471–517.

Anderson, J. R., Reder, L. M., & Simon, H. A. (1996). Situated learning and education. *Educational Researcher, 25*(4), 5–11.

Arkes, H. R. (1991). Costs and benefits of judgment errors: Implications for debiasing. *Psychological Bulletin, 110*, 486–498.

Arkes, H. R. (1996). The psychology of waste. *Journal of Behavioral Decision Making, 9*, 213–224.

Arkes, H. R., & Blumer, C. (1985). The psychology of sunk cost. *Organizational Behavior and Human Decision Processes, 35*, 124–140.

Arkes, H., & Hammond, K. (Eds.). (1986). *Judgment and decision making*. Cambridge, England: Cambridge University Press.

Arkes, H. R., & Harkness, A. R. (1983). Estimates of contingency between two dichotomous variables. *Journal of Experimental Psychology: General, 112*, 117–135.

Audi, R. (1993a). *Action, intention, and reason*. Ithaca, NY: Cornell University Press.

Audi, R. (1993b). *The structure of justification*. Cambridge, England: Cambridge University Press.

Babad, E., & Katz, Y. (1991). Wishful thinking—Against all odds. *Journal of Applied Social Psychology, 21*, 1921–1938.

Bacharach, M., & Hurley, S. L. (1991). Issues and advances in the foundations of decision theory. In M. Bacharach & S. L. Hurley (Eds.), *Foundations of decision theory* (pp. 1–38). Oxford, England: Blackwell.

Baltes, P. B. (1987). Theoretical propositions of life-span developmental psychology: On the dynamics between growth and decline. *Developmental Psychology, 23*, 611–626.

Bara, B. G., Bucciarelli, M., & Johnson-Laird, P. N. (1995). Development of syllogistic reasoning. *American Journal of Psychology, 108*, 157–193.

Bar-Hillel, M. (1980). The base-rate fallacy in probability judgments. *Acta Psychologica, 44*, 211–233.

Bar-Hillel, M. (1984). Representativeness and fallacies of probability judgment. *Acta Psychologica, 55*, 91–107.

Bar-Hillel, M. (1990). Back to base rates. In R. M. Hogarth (Eds.), *Insights into decision making: A tribute to Hillel J. Einhorn* (pp. 200–216). Chicago: University of Chicago Press.

Bar-Hillel, M. (1991). Commentary on Wolford, Taylor, and Beck: The conjunction fallacy? *Memory & Cognition, 19*, 412–414.

Bar-Hillel, M., & Falk, R. (1982). Some teasers concerning conditional probabilities. *Cognition, 11*, 109–122.

Barkow, J. H. (1989). *Darwin, sex, and status: Biological approaches to mind and culture*. Toronto: University of Toronto Press.

Baron, J. (1985a). *Rationality and intelligence*. Cambridge, England: Cambridge University Press.

Baron, J. (1985b). What kinds of intelligence components are fundamental? In S. Chipman & J. Segal (Eds.), *Thinking and learning skills* (Vol. 2, pp. 365–390). Hillsdale, NJ: Lawrence Erlbaum Associates.

Baron, J. (1988). *Thinking and deciding*. Cambridge, England: Cambridge University Press.

Baron, J. (1991a). Beliefs about thinking. In J. Voss, D. Perkins, & J. Segal (Eds.), *Informal reasoning and education* (pp. 169–186). Hillsdale, NJ: Lawrence Erlbaum Associates.

Baron, J. (1991b). Some thinking is irrational. *Behavioral and Brain Sciences, 14*, 486–487.

Baron, J. (1992). Book review of: "The Skills of Argument" by Deanna Kuhn. *Informal Logic, 14*, 59–67.

Baron, J. (1993a). *Morality and rational choice*. Dordrecht, Netherlands: Kluwer.

Baron, J. (1993b). Why teach thinking?—An essay. *Applied Psychology: An International Review, 42*, 191–214.

Baron, J. (1994a). Nonconsequentialist decisions. *Behavioral and Brain Sciences, 17*, 1–42.

Baron, J. (1994b). *Thinking and deciding* (2nd ed.). Cambridge, MA: Cambridge University Press.

Baron, J. (1995). Myside bias in thinking about abortion. *Thinking and Reasoning, 1*, 221–235.

Baron, J. (1998). *Judgment misguided*. New York: Oxford University Press.

Baron, J., Badgio, P. C., & Gaskins, I. W. (1986). Cognitive style and its improvement: A normative approach. In R. J. Sternberg (Ed.), *Advances in the psychology of human intelligence* (Vol. 3, pp. 173–220). Hillsdale, NJ: Lawrence Erlbaum Associates.

Baron, J., & Hershey, J. C. (1988). Outcome bias in decision evaluation. *Journal of Personality and Social Psychology, 54*, 569–579.

Bell, D. E. (1982). Regret in decision making under uncertainty. *Operations Research, 30*, 961–981.

Bell, D., Raiffa, H., & Tversky, A. (Eds.). (1988). *Decision making: Descriptive, normative, and prescriptive interactions*. Cambridge, England: Cambridge University Press.

Berkeley, D., & Humphreys, P. (1982). Structuring decision problems and the "bias heuristic." *Acta Psychologica, 50*, 201–252.

Beyth-Marom, R., & Fischhoff, B. (1983). Diagnosticity and pseudodiagnositicity. *Journal of Personality and Social Psychology, 45*, 1185–1195.

Birnbaum, M. H. (1983). Base rates in Bayesian inference: Signal detection analysis of the cab problem. *American Journal of Psychology, 96*, 85–94.

Block, J., & Funder, D. C. (1986). Social roles and social perception: Individual differences in attribution and "error." *Journal of Personality and Social Psychology, 51*, 1200–1207.

Bornstein, B., & Chapman, G. (1995). Learning lessons from sunk costs. *Journal of Experimental Psychology: Applied, 1*, 251–269.

Braine, M. D. S. (1978). On the relation between the natural logic of reasoning and standard logic. *Psychological Review, 85*, 1–21.

Braine, M. D. S., Connell, J., Freitag, J., & O'Brien, D. P. (1990). Is the base rate fallacy an instance of asserting the consequent? In K. Gilhooly, M. Keane, R. Logie, & G. Erdos (Eds.), *Lines of thinking* (Vol. 1, pp. 165–180). New York: Wiley.

Braine, M. D. S., & O'Brien, D. P. (1991). A theory of "if": A lexical entry, reasoning program and standard logic. *Psychological Review, 98*, 182–203.

Brase, G. L., Cosmides, L., & Tooby, J. (1998). Individuation, counting, and statistical inference: The role of frequency and whole-object representations in judgment under uncertainty. *Journal of Experimental Psychology: General, 127*, 3–21.

Bratman, M. E. (1987). *Intention, plans, and practical reason.* Cambridge, MA: Harvard University Press.

Bratman, M. E., Israel, D. J., & Pollack, M. E. (1991). Plans and resource-bounded practical reasoning. In J. Cummins & J. Pollock (Eds.), *Philosophy and AI: Essays at the interface* (pp. 7–22). Cambridge, MA: MIT Press.

Brenner, L. A., Koehler, D. J., Liberman, V., & Tversky, A. (1996). Overconfidence in probability and frequency judgments: A critical examination. *Organizational Behavior and Human Decision Processes, 65,* 212–219.

Brody, N. (1997). Intelligence, schooling, and society. *American Psychologist, 52,* 1046–1050.

Bronfenbrenner, U., & Ceci, S. J. (1994). Nature-nurture reconceptualized in developmental perspective: A bio-ecological model. *Psychological Review, 101,* 568–586.

Bronfenbrenner, U., McClelland, P., Wethington, E., Moen, P., & Ceci, S. J. (1996). *The state of Americans.* New York: The Free Press.

Brookfield, S. (1987). *Developing critical thinkers.* San Francisco: Jossey-Bass.

Broome, J. (1990). Should a rational agent maximize expected utility? In K. S. Cook & M. Levi (Eds.), *The limits of rationality* (pp. 132–145). Chicago: University of Chicago Press.

Brown, J., & Langer, E. (1990). Mindfulness and intelligence: A comparison. *Educational Psychologist, 25,* 305–335.

Brown, J. S., Collins, A., & Duguid, P. (1989). Situated cognition and the culture of learning. *Educational Researcher, 18*(1), 32–42.

Brown, N. R., & Siegler, R. S. (1993). Metrics and mappings: A framework for understanding real-world quantitative estimation. *Psychological Review, 100,* 511–534.

Bruner, J. (1986). *Actual minds, possible worlds.* Cambridge, MA: Harvard University Press.

Bruner, J. (1990). *Acts of meaning.* Cambridge, MA: Harvard University Press.

Buss, D. M. (1991). Evolutionary personality psychology. *Annual Review of Psychology, 42,* 459–491.

Buying or leasing a car. (1998, April). *Consumer Reports, 63*(4), 16–22.

Byrnes, J. P. (1988). Formal operations: A systematic reformulation. *Developmental Review, 8,* 1–22.

Byrnes, J. P. (1995). Domain-specificity and the logic of using general ability as an independent variable or covariate. *Merrill–Palmer Quarterly, 41,* 1–24.

Byrnes, J. P., & Overton, W. F. (1986). Reasoning about certainty and uncertainty in concrete, causal, and propositional contexts. *Developmental Psychology, 22,* 793–799.

Cacioppo, J. T., Petty, R. E., Feinstein, J., & Jarvis, W. (1996). Dispositional differences in cognitive motivation: The life and times of individuals varying in need for cognition. *Psychological Bulletin, 119,* 197–253.

Campbell, J. D. (1986). Similarity and uniqueness: The effects of attribute type, relevance, and individual differences in self-esteem and depression. *Journal of Personality and Social Psychology, 50,* 281–294.

Campbell, J. D., & Tesser, A. (1983). Motivational interpretation of hindsight bias: An individual difference analysis. *Journal of Personality, 51,* 605–640.

Campbell, R. (1985). Background for the uninitiated. In R. Campbell & L. Sowden (Eds.), *Paradoxes of rationality and cooperation: Prisoner's dilemma and Newcomb's problem* (pp. 3–41). Vancouver: University of British Columbia Press.

Campbell, R., & Sowden, L. (1985). *Paradoxes of rationality and cooperation: Prisoner's dilemma and Newcomb's problem*. Vancouver: University of British Columbia Press.

Carpenter, P. A., Just, M. A., & Shell, P. (1990). What one intelligence test measures: A theoretical account of the processing in the Raven Progressive Matrices Test. *Psychological Review, 97*, 404–431.

Carroll, J. B. (1993). *Human cognitive abilities: A survey of factor-analytic studies*. Cambridge, England: Cambridge University Press.

Carroll, J. B. (1997). Psychometrics, intelligence, and public perception. *Intelligence, 24*, 25–52.

Caryl, P. G. (1994). Early event-related potentials correlate with inspection time and intelligence. *Intelligence, 18*, 15–46.

Casscells, W., Schoenberger, A., & Graboys, T. (1978). Interpretation by physicians of clinical laboratory results. *New England Journal of Medicine, 299*, 999–1001.

Ceci, S. J. (1993). Contextual trends in intellectual development. *Developmental Review, 13*, 403–435.

Ceci, S. J. (1996). *On intelligence: A bioecological treatise on intellectual development* (Expanded ed.). Cambridge, MA: Harvard University Press.

Ceci, S. J., & Williams, S. J. (1997). Schooling, intelligence, and income. *American Psychologist, 52*, 1051–1058.

Cederblom, J. (1989). Willingness to reason and the identification of the self. In E. Maimon, D. Nodine, & O'Conner (Eds.), *Thinking, reasoning, and writing* (pp. 147–159). New York: Longman.

Chapman, M. (1993). Everyday reasoning and the revision of belief. In J. M. Puckett & H. W. Reese (Eds.), *Mechanisms of everyday cognition* (pp. 95–113). Hillsdale, NJ: Lawrence Erlbaum Associates.

Chater, N., & Oaksford, M. (1996). Deontic reasoning, modules and innateness: A second look. *Mind & Language, 11*, 191–202.

Cheng, P. W., & Holyoak, K. J. (1985). Pragmatic reasoning schemas. *Cognitive Psychology, 17*, 391–416.

Cheng, P. W., & Holyoak, K. J. (1989). On the natural selection of reasoning theories. *Cognition, 33*, 285–313.

Cheng, P. W., Holyoak, K. J., Nisbett, R. E., & Oliver, L. M. (1986). Pragmatic versus syntactic approaches to training deductive reasoning. *Cognitive Psychology, 18*, 293–328.

Cherniak, C. (1986). *Minimal rationality*. Cambridge, MA: MIT Press.

Christensen-Szalanski, J., & Beach, I. R. (1984). The citation bias: Fad and fashion in the judgment and decision literature. *American Psychologist, 39*, 75–78.

Churchland, P. M. (1989). *A neurocomputational perspective: The nature of mind and the structure of science*. Cambridge, MA: MIT Press.

Churchland, P. M. (1995). *The engine of reason, the seat of the soul*. Cambridge, MA: MIT Press.

Churchman, C. W. (1961). *Prediction and optimal decision*. Englewood Cliffs, NJ: Prentice-Hall.

Cohen, L. J. (1979). On the psychology of prediction: Whose is the fallacy? *Cognition, 7*, 385–407.

Cohen, L. J. (1981). Can human irrationality be experimentally demonstrated? *Behavioral and Brain Sciences, 4*, 317–370.

Cohen, L. J. (1982). Are people programmed to commit fallacies? Further thoughts about the interpretation of experimental data on probability judgment. *Journal for the Theory of Social Behavior, 12*, 251–274.

Cohen, L. J. (1983). The controversy about irrationality. *Behavioral and Brain Sciences, 6*, 510–517.

Cohen, L. J. (1986). *The dialogue of reason*. Oxford, England: Oxford University Press.

Coleman, J. S., Hoffer, T., & Kilgore, S. (1982). *High school achievement*. New York: Basic Books.

Cooper, L. A., & Regan, D. T. (1982). Attention, perception, and intelligence. In R. J. Sternberg (Ed.), *Handbook of human intelligence* (pp. 123–169). Cambridge, England: Cambridge University Press.

Cooper, W. S. (1989). How evolutionary biology challenges the classical theory of rational choice. *Biology and Philosophy, 4*, 457–481.

Cosmides, L. (1989). The logic of social exchange: Has natural selection shaped how humans reason? Studies with the Wason selection task. *Cognition, 31*, 187–276.

Cosmides, L., & Tooby, J. (1994). Beyond intuition and instinct blindness: Toward an evolutionarily rigorous cognitive science. *Cognition, 50*, 41–77.

Cosmides, L., & Tooby, J. (1996). Are humans good intuitive statisticians after all? Rethinking some conclusions from the literature on judgment under uncertainty. *Cognition, 58*, 1–73.

Costa, P. T., & McCrae, R. R. (1992). *Revised NEO personality inventory*. Odessa, FL: Psychological Assessment Resources.

Cronbach, L. J., & Furby, L. (1970). How we should measure "change"—or should we? *Psychological Bulletin, 74*, 68–80.

Cummins, D. D. (1996). Evidence for the innateness of deontic reasoning. *Mind & Language, 11*, 160–190.

Cunningham, A. E., & Stanovich, K. E. (1997). Early reading acquisition and its relation to reading experience and ability ten years later. *Developmental Psychology, 33*, 934–945.

Daniels, N. (1979). Wide reflective equilibrium and theory acceptance ethics. *The Journal of Philosophy, 76*, 256–282.

Daniels, N. (1996). *Justice and justification: Reflective equilibrium in theory and practice*. Cambridge, England: Cambridge University Press.

Davidson, D. (1984). On the very idea of a conceptual scheme. In D. Davidson (Ed.), *Inquiries into truth and interpretation* (pp. 183–198). Oxford, England: Oxford University Press.

Davis, D., & Holt, C. (1993). *Experimental economics*. Princeton, NJ: Princeton University Press.

Dawes, R. M. (1983). Is irrationality systematic? *Behavioral and Brain Sciences, 6*, 491–492.

Dawes, R. M. (1988). *Rational choice in an uncertain world*. San Diego: Harcourt Brace.

Dawes, R. M. (1989). Statistical criteria for establishing a truly false consensus effect. *Journal of Experimental Social Psychology, 25*, 1–17.

Dawes, R. M. (1990). The potential nonfalsity of the false consensus effect. In R. M. Hogarth (Ed.), *Insights into decision making* (pp. 179–199). Chicago: University of Chicago Press.

Dawes, R. M., Mirels, H., Gold, E., & Donahue, E. (1993). Equating inverse probabilities in implicit personality judgments. *Psychological Science, 4*, 396–400.

Dawes, R. M., & Mulford, M. (1996). The false consensus effect and overconfidence: Flaws in judgment or flaws in how we study judgment? *Organizational Behavior and Human Decision Processes, 65*, 201–211.

Dawid, A. P. (1982). The well-calibrated Bayesian. *Journal of the American Statistical Association, 77*, 605–613.

Dawkins, R. (1976). *The selfish gene.* New York: Oxford University Press.

Dawkins, R. (1982). *The extended phenotype.* New York: Oxford University Press.

Dawkins, R. (1986). *The blind watchmaker.* New York: Norton.

Dawkins, R. (1996). *Climbing mount improbable.* New York: Norton.

Deary, I. J. (1995). Auditory inspection time and intelligence: What is the direction of causation? *Developmental Psychology, 31*, 237–250.

Deary, I. J., & Stough, C. (1996). Intelligence and inspection time. *American Psychologist, 51*, 599–608.

de Finetti, B. (1990). *Theory of probability* (Vol. 1). New York: Wiley. (Original work published 1970)

de Finetti, B. (1989). Probabilism. *Erkenntnis, 31*, 169–223. (Original work published 1931)

Dennett, D. C. (1978). *Brainstorms: Philosophical essays on mind and psychology.* Cambridge, MA: MIT Press.

Dennett, D. C. (1980). The milk of human intentionality. *Behavioral and Brain Sciences, 3*, 428–430.

Dennett, D. C. (1987). *The intentional stance.* Cambridge, MA: MIT Press.

Dennett, D. C. (1988). Precis of "The Intentional Stance." *Behavioral and Brain Sciences, 11*, 493–544.

Denny, J. P. (1991). Rational thought in oral culture and literate decontextualization. In D. R. Olson & N. Torrance (Eds.), *Literacy and orality* (pp. 66–89). Cambridge, England: Cambridge University Press.

de Sousa, R. (1987). *The rationality of emotion.* Cambridge, MA: MIT Press.

Detterman, D. K. (1994). Intelligence and the brain. In P. A. Vernon (Ed.), *The neuropsychology of individual differences* (pp. 35–57). San Diego: Academic Press.

Detterman, D. K., & Thompson, L. E. (1997). What is so special about special education? *American Psychologist, 52*, 1082–1090.

Doherty, M. E., Chadwick, R., Garavan, H., Barr, D., & Mynatt, C. R. (1996). On people's understanding of the diagnostic implications of probabilistic data. *Memory & Cognition, 24*, 644–654.

Doherty, M. E., & Mynatt, C. (1990). Inattention to P(H) and to P(D/~H): A converging operation. *Acta Psychologica, 75*, 1–11.

Doherty, M. E., Mynatt, C., Tweney, R., & Schiavo, M. (1979). Pseudodiagnositicity. *Acta Psychologica, 43*, 111–121.

Doherty, M. E., Schiavo, M. B., Tweney, R. D., & Mynatt, C. R. (1981). The influence of feedback and diagnostic data on pseudodiagnosticity. *Bulletin of the Psychonomic Society, 18*, 191–194.

Dominowski, R. L. (1995). Content effects in Wason's selection task. In S. E. Newstead & J. St. B. T. Evans (Eds.), *Perspectives on thinking and reasoning* (pp. 41–65). Hove, England: Lawrence Erlbaum Associates.

Dominowski, R. L., & Ansburg, P. (1996). *Reasoning abilities, individual differences, and Wason's selection task.* Unpublished manuscript.

Dominowski, R. L., & Dallob, P. (1991, September). *Reasoning abilities, individual differences, and the four card problem.* Paper presented at the Eighth Annual Conference, Cognitive Psychology Section, British Psychological Association, Oxford, England.

Donaldson, M. (1978). *Children's minds.* London: Fontana Paperbacks.

Donaldson, M. (1993). *Human minds: An exploration.* New York: Viking Penguin.

Dougherty, T. M., & Haith, M. M. (1997). Infant expectations and reaction time as predictors of childhood speed of processing and IQ. *Developmental Psychology, 33*, 146–155.

Dulany, D. E., & Hilton, D. J. (1991). Conversational implicature, conscious representation, and the conjunction fallacy. *Social Cognition, 9*, 85–110.

Earman, J. (1992). *Bayes or bust*. Cambridge, MA: MIT Press.

Edwards, J. R. (1995). Alternatives to difference scores as dependent variables in the study of congruence in organizational research. *Organizational Behavior and Human Decision Processes, 64*, 307–324.

Edwards, K., & Smith, E. E. (1996). A disconfirmation bias in the evaluation of arguments. *Journal of Personality and Social Psychology, 71*, 5–24.

Einhorn, H. J., & Hogarth, R. M. (1978). Confidence in judgment: Persistence of the illusion of validity. *Psychological Review, 85*, 395–416.

Einhorn, H. J., & Hogarth, R. M. (1981). Behavioral decision theory: Processes of judgment and choice. *Annual Review of Psychology, 32*, 53–88.

Elgin, C. Z. (1996). *Considered judgment*. Princeton, NJ: Princeton University Press.

Elman, J. L., Bates, E. A., Johnson, M. H., Karmiloff-Smith, A., Parisi, D., & Plunkett, K. (1996). *Rethinking innateness: A connectionist perspective on development*. Cambridge, MA: MIT Press.

Elster, J. (1983). *Sour grapes: Studies in the subversion of rationality*. Cambridge, England: Cambridge University Press.

Ennis, R. H. (1987). A taxonomy of critical thinking dispositions and abilities. In J. Baron & R. Sternberg (Eds.), *Teaching thinking skills: Theory and practice* (pp. 9–26). New York: Freeman.

Ennis, R. H., & Millman, J. (1985). *Cornell Critical Thinking Test*. Pacific Grove, CA: Midwest Publications.

Ennis, R. H., & Weir, E. (1985). *The Ennis–Weir Critical Thinking Essay Test*. Pacific Grove, CA: Midwest Publications.

Epstein, S. (1994). Integration of the cognitive and the psychodynamic unconscious. *American Psychologist, 49*, 709–724.

Epstein, S., Lipson, A., Holstein, C., & Huh, E. (1992). Irrational reactions to negative outcomes: Evidence for two conceptual systems. *Journal of Personality and Social Psychology, 62*, 328–339.

Epstein, S., & Meier, P. (1989). Constructive thinking: A broad coping variable with specific components. *Journal of Personality and Social Psychology, 57*, 332–350.

Erwin, T. D. (1981). *Manual for the Scale of Intellectual Development*. Harrisonburg, VA: Developmental Analytics.

Erwin, T. D. (1983). The Scale of Intellectual Development: Measuring Perry's scheme. *Journal of College Student Personnel, 24*, 6–12.

Estes, W. K. (1982). Learning, memory, and intelligence. In R. J. Sternberg (Ed.), *Handbook of human intelligence* (pp. 170–224). Cambridge, England: Cambridge University Press.

Evans, J. St. B. T. (1982). *The psychology of deductive reasoning*. London: Routledge.

Evans, J. St. B. T. (1984). Heuristic and analytic processes in reasoning. *British Journal of Psychology, 75*, 451–468.

Evans, J. St. B. T. (1989). *Bias in human reasoning: Causes and consequences*. London: Lawrence Erlbaum Associates.

Evans, J. St. B. T. (1995). Relevance and reasoning. In S. E. Newstead & J. St. B. T. Evans (Eds.), *Perspectives on thinking and reasoning* (pp. 147–171). Hove, England: Lawrence Erlbaum Associates.

Evans, J. St. B. T. (1996). Deciding before you think: Relevance and reasoning in the selection task. *British Journal of Psychology, 87,* 223–240.

Evans, J. St. B. T., Barston, J., & Pollard, P. (1983). On the conflict between logic and belief in syllogistic reasoning. *Memory & Cognition, 11,* 295–306.

Evans, J. St. B. T., & Lynch, J. S. (1973). Matching bias in the selection task. *British Journal of Psychology, 64,* 391–397.

Evans, J. St. B. T., Newstead, S. E., & Byrne, R. M. J. (1993). *Human reasoning: The psychology of deduction.* Hove, England: Lawrence Erlbaum Associates.

Evans, J. St. B. T., & Over, D. E. (1996). *Rationality and reasoning.* Hove, England: Psychology Press.

Evans, J. St. B. T., Over, D. E., & Manktelow, K. (1993). Reasoning, decision making and rationality. *Cognition, 49,* 165–187.

Evans, J. St. B. T., & Wason, P. C. (1976). Rationalization in a reasoning task. *British Journal of Psychology, 67,* 479–486.

Falk, R. (1992). A closer look at the probabilities of the notorious three prisoners. *Cognition, 43,* 197–223.

Fetzer, J. (1990). Evolution, rationality, and testability. *Synthese, 82,* 423–439.

Fiedler, K. (1988). The dependence of the conjunction fallacy on subtle linguistic factors. *Psychological Research, 50,* 123–129.

Finocchiaro, M. A. (1980). *Galileo and the art of reasoning.* Dordrecht, Netherlands: Reidel.

Fischhoff, B. (1975). Hindsight ≠ foresight: The effect of outcome knowledge on judgment under uncertainty. *Journal of Experimental Psychology: Human Perception and Performance, 1,* 288–299.

Fischhoff, B. (1977). Perceived informativeness of facts. *Journal of Experimental Psychology: Human Perception and Performance, 3,* 349–358.

Fischhoff, B. (1981). Can any statements about human behavior be empirically validated? *Behavioral and Brain Sciences, 4,* 336–337.

Fischhoff, B. (1982). Debiasing. In D. Kahneman, P. Slovic, & A. Tversky (Eds.), *Judgment under uncertainty: Heuristics and biases* (pp. 422–444). Cambridge, England: Cambridge University Press.

Fischhoff, B. (1988). Judgment and decision making. In R. J. Sternberg & E. E. Smith (Eds.), *The psychology of human thought* (pp. 153–187). Cambridge, England: Cambridge University Press.

Fischhoff, B., & Bar-Hillel, M. (1984). Diagnosticity and the base-rate effect. *Memory & Cognition, 12,* 402–410.

Fischhoff, B., & Beyth-Marom, R. (1983). Hypothesis evaluation from a Bayesian perspective. *Psychological Review, 90,* 239–260.

Flynn, J. R. (1987). Massive IQ gains in 14 nations: What IQ tests really measure. *Psychological Bulletin, 101,* 171–191.

Fodor, J. (1983). *Modularity of mind.* Cambridge, MA: MIT Press.

Foley, R. (1987). *The theory of epistemic rationality.* Cambridge, MA: Harvard University Press.

Foley, R. (1991). Rationality, belief, and commitment. *Synthese, 89,* 365–392.

Fong, G. T., Krantz, D. H., & Nisbett, R. E. (1986). The effects of statistical training on thinking about everyday problems. *Cognitive Psychology, 18,* 253–292.

Frank, R. H., & Cook, P. J. (1995). *The winner-take-all society.* New York: The Free Press.

Friedrich, J. (1993). Primary error detection and minimization (PEDMIN) strategies in social cognition: A reinterpretation of confirmation bias phenomena. *Psychological Review, 100,* 298–319.

Frisch, D. (1993). Reasons for framing effects. *Organizational Behavior and Human Decision Processes, 54,* 399–429.

Frisch, D. (1994). Consequentialism and utility theory. *Behavioral and Brain Sciences, 17,* 16.

Frisch, D., & Jones, J. K. (1993). Assessing the accuracy of decisions. *Theory & Psychology, 3,* 115–135.

Fry, A. F., & Hale, S. (1996). Processing speed, working memory, and fluid intelligence. *Psychological Science, 7,* 237–241.

Funder, D. C. (1987). Errors and mistakes: Evaluating the accuracy of social judgment. *Psychological Bulletin, 101,* 75–90.

Gauthier, D. (1986). *Morals by agreement.* Oxford, England: Oxford University Press.

Gibbard, A., & Harper, W. L. (1978). Counterfactuals and two kinds of expected utility. In C. Hooker, J. Leach, & E. McClennen (Eds.), *Foundations and applications of decision theory* (Vol. 1, pp. 125–162). Dordrecht, Netherlands: Reidel.

Gigerenzer, G. (1991a). From tools to theories: A heuristic of discovery in cognitive psychology. *Psychological Review, 98,* 254–267.

Gigerenzer, G. (1991b). How to make cognitive illusions disappear: Beyond "heuristics and biases." *European Review of Social Psychology, 2,* 83–115.

Gigerenzer, G. (1991c). On cognitive illusions and rationality. In E. Eells & T. Maruszewski (Eds.), *Probability and rationality: Studies on L. Jonathan Cohen's philosophy of science* (pp. 225–249). Amsterdam: Editions Rodopi.

Gigerenzer, G. (1993). The bounded rationality of probabilistic mental models. In K. Manktelow & D. Over (Eds.), *Rationality: Psychological and philosophical perspectives* (pp. 284–313). London: Routledge.

Gigerenzer, G. (1995). The taming of content: Some thoughts about domains and modules. *Thinking and Reasoning, 1,* 324–333.

Gigerenzer, G. (1996a). On narrow norms and vague heuristics: A reply to Kahneman and Tversky (1996). *Psychological Review, 103,* 592–596.

Gigerenzer, G. (1996b). Rationality: Why social context matters. In P. B. Baltes & U. Staudinger (Eds.), *Interactive minds: Life-span perspectives on the social foundation of cognition* (pp. 319–346). Cambridge, England: Cambridge University Press.

Gigerenzer, G., & Goldstein, D. G. (1996). Reasoning the fast and frugal way: Models of bounded rationality. *Psychological Review, 103,* 650–669.

Gigerenzer, G., & Hoffrage, U. (1995). How to improve Bayesian reasoning without instruction: Frequency formats. *Psychological Review, 102,* 684–704.

Gigerenzer, G., Hoffrage, U., & Kleinbolting, H. (1991). Probabilistic mental models: A Brunswikian theory of confidence. *Psychological Review, 98,* 506–528.

Gigerenzer, G., & Hug, K. (1992). Domain-specific reasoning: Social contracts, cheating, and perspective change. *Cognition, 43,* 127–171.

Gigerenzer, G., & Murray, D. J. (1987). *Cognition as intuitive statistics.* Hillsdale, NJ: Lawrence Erlbaum Associates.

Gigerenzer, G., & Regier, T. (1996). How do we tell an association from a rule? Comment on Sloman (1996). *Psychological Bulletin, 119,* 23–26.

Gigerenzer, G., Swijtink, Z., Porter, T., Daston, L., Beatty, J., & Kruger, L. (1989). *The empire of chance.* Cambridge, England: Cambridge University Press.

Gilovich, T. (1991). *How we know what isn't so.* New York: The Free Press.

Goff, M., & Ackerman, P. L. (1992). Personality-intelligence relations: Assessment of typical intellectual engagement. *Journal of Educational Psychology, 84*, 537–552.

Goldman, A. I. (1978). Epistemics: The regulative theory of cognition. *Journal of Philosophy, 55*, 509–523.

Goldman, A. I. (1986). *Epistemology and cognition*. Cambridge, MA: Harvard University Press.

Goldman, A. I. (1993). *Philosophical applications of cognitive science*. Boulder, CO: Westview Press.

Goodman, N. (1965). *Fact, fiction, and forecast*. Cambridge, MA: Harvard University Press.

Goody, J. (1977). *The domestication of the savage mind*. New York: Cambridge University Press.

Goody, J. (1987). *The interface between the written and the oral*. Cambridge, England: Cambridge University Press.

Gordon, R. A. (1997). Everyday life as an intelligence test: Effects of intelligence and intelligence context. *Intelligence, 24*, 203–320.

Gottfredson, L. S. (1997). Why g matters: The complexity of everyday life. *Intelligence, 24*, 79–132.

Gould, S. J. (1991). *Bully for the Brontosaurus*. New York: Norton.

Granberg, D. (1995). The Monte Hall dilemma. *Personality and Social Psychology Bulletin, 31*, 711–723.

Greenwald, A. G. (1980). The totalitarian ego: Fabrication and revision of personal history. *American Psychologist, 35*, 603–618.

Grether, D. M., & Plott, C. R. (1979). Economic theory of choice and the preference reversal phenomenon. *American Economic Review, 69*, 623–638.

Griffin, D., & Tversky, A. (1992). The weighing of evidence and the determinants of confidence. *Cognitive Psychology, 24*, 411–435.

Griffiths, M. D. (1994). The role of cognitive bias and skill in fruit machine gambling. *British Journal of Psychology, 85*, 351–369.

Griggs, R. A. (1983). The role of problem content in the selection task and in the THOG problem. In J. St. B. T. Evans (Eds.), *Thinking and reasoning: Psychological approaches* (pp. 16–43). London: Routledge & Kegan Paul.

Griggs, R. A., & Cox, J. R. (1982). The elusive thematic-materials effect in Wason's selection task. *British Journal of Psychology, 73*, 407–420.

Griggs, R. A., & Cox, J. R. (1983). The effects of problem content and negation on Wason's selection task. *Quarterly Journal of Experimental Psychology, 35*, 519–533.

Griggs, R. A., & Cox, J. R. (1993). Permission schemas and the selection task. *Quarterly Journal of Experimental Psychology, 46A*, 637–651.

Griggs, R. A., & Ransdell, S. E. (1986). Scientists and the selection task. *Social Studies of Science, 16*, 319–330.

Gur, R., & Sackheim, H. (1979). Self-deception: A concept in search of a phenomenon. *Journal of Personality and Social Psychology, 37*, 147–169.

Hacking, I. (1975). *The emergence of probability*. Cambridge, England: Cambridge University Press.

Hacking, I. (1990). *The taming of chance*. Cambridge, England: Cambridge University Press.

Halberstadt, N., & Kareev, Y. (1995). Transitions between modes of inquiry in a rule discovery task. *Quarterly Journal of Experimental Psychology, 48A*(2), 280–295.

Hammond, K. R. (1996). *Human judgment and social policy*. New York: Oxford University Press.

Hardin, G. (1968). The tragedy of the commons. *Science, 162*, 1243–1248.

Hargreaves Heap, S. P., & Varoufakis, Y. (1995). *Game theory: A critical introduction*. London: Routledge.

Harman, G. (1995). Rationality. In E. E. Smith & D. N. Osherson (Eds.), *Thinking* (Vol. 3, pp. 175–211). Cambridge, MA: MIT Press.

Harvey, N. (1992). Wishful thinking impairs belief-desire reasoning: A case of decoupling failure in adults? *Cognition, 45*, 141–162.

Hasher, L., & Zacks, R. T. (1979). Automatic processing of fundamental information: The case of frequency of occurrence. *Journal of Experimental Psychology: General, 39*, 1372–1388.

Haslam, N., & Baron, J. (1994). Intelligence, personality, and prudence. In R. J. Sternberg & P. Ruzgis (Eds.), *Personality and intelligence* (pp. 32–58). Cambridge, England: Cambridge University Press.

Haslam, N., & Jayasinghe, N. (1995). Negative affect and hindsight bias. *Journal of Behavioral Decision Making, 8*, 127–135.

Hastie, R., & Rasinski, K. A. (1988). The concept of accuracy in social judgment. In D. Bar-Tal & A. Kruglanski (Eds.), *The social psychology of knowledge* (pp. 193–208). Cambridge, England: Cambridge University Press.

Havelock, E. A. (1963). *Preface to Plato*. Cambridge, MA: Harvard University Press.

Havelock, E. A. (1980). The coming of literate communication to Western culture. *Journal of Communication, 30*, 90–98.

Hawkins, S. A., & Hastie, R. (1990). Hindsight: Biased judgments of past events after the outcomes are known. *Psychological Bulletin, 107*, 311–327.

Henle, M. (1962). On the relation between logic and thinking. *Psychological Review, 69*, 366–378.

Hilton, D. J. (1995). The social context of reasoning: Conversational inference and rational judgment. *Psychological Bulletin, 118*, 248–271.

Hoch, S. J. (1987). Perceived consensus and predictive accuracy: The pros and cons of projection. *Journal of Personality and Social Psychology, 53*, 221–234.

Holyoak, K. J., & Cheng, P. W. (1995a). Pragmatic reasoning with a point of view. *Thinking and Reasoning, 1*, 289–313.

Holyoak, K. J., & Cheng, P. W. (1995b). Pragmatic reasoning from multiple points of view: A response. *Thinking and Reasoning, 1*, 373–389.

Horgan, T., & Tienson, J. (1993). Levels of description in nonclassical cognitive science. In C. Hookway & D. Peterson (Eds.), *Philosophy and cognitive science* (pp. 159–188). Cambridge, England: Cambridge University Press.

Howson, C., & Urbach, P. (1993). *Scientific reasoning: The Bayesian approach* (2nd ed.). Chicago: Open Court.

Hunt, E. (1978). Mechanics of verbal ability. *Psychological Review, 85*, 109–130.

Hunt, E. (1987). The next word on verbal ability. In P. A. Vernon (Ed.), *Speed of information-processing and intelligence* (pp. 347–392). Norwood, NJ: Ablex.

Hunt, E. (1995). *Will we be smart enough? A cognitive analysis of the coming workforce*. New York: Russell Sage Foundation.

Hunt, E. (in press). Intelligence and human resources: Past, present, and future. In P. Ackerman & P. Kyllonen (Eds.), *The future of learning and individual differences research: Processes, traits, and content*. Washington, DC: American Psychological Association.

Hurley, S. L. (1991). Newcomb's problem, prisoner's dilemma, and collective action. *Synthese, 86*, 173–196.

Jackson, S. I., & Griggs, R. A. (1988). Education and the selection task. *Bulletin of the Psychonomic Society, 26,* 327–330.

Jacobs, J. E., & Potenza, M. (1991). The use of judgment heuristics to make social and object decisions: A developmental perspective. *Child Development, 62,* 166–178.

Jeffrey, R. C. (1983). *The logic of decision* (2nd ed.). Chicago: University of Chicago Press.

Jepson, C., Krantz, D., & Nisbett, R. (1983). Inductive reasoning: Competence or skill? *Behavioral and Brain Sciences, 6,* 494–501.

Johnson-Laird, P. N. (in press). Deductive reasoning. *Annual Review of Psychology.*

Johnson-Laird, P. N., & Byrne, R. M. J. (1991). *Deduction.* Hillsdale, NJ: Lawrence Erlbaum Associates.

Johnson-Laird, P. N., & Byrne, R. M. J. (1993). Models and deductive rationality. In K. Manktelow & D. Over (Eds.), *Rationality: Psychological and philosophical perspectives* (pp. 177–210). London: Routledge.

Johnson-Laird, P. N., Byrne, R. M. J., & Schaeken, W. (1994). Why models rather than rules give a better account of propositional reasoning. *Psychological Review, 101,* 734–739.

Johnson-Laird, P., & Oatley, K. (1992). Basic emotions, rationality, and folk theory. *Cognition and Emotion, 6,* 201–223.

Jones, K., & Day, J. D. (1997). Discrimination of two aspects of cognitive-social intelligence from academic intelligence. *Journal of Educational Psychology, 89,* 486–497.

Jones, W., Russell, D., & Nickel, T. (1977). Belief in the paranormal scale: An objective instrument to measure belief in magical phenomena and causes. *JSAS Catalog of Selected Documents in Psychology, 7*(100), Ms. No. 1577.

Jou, J., Shanteau, J., & Harris, R. J. (1996). An information processing view of framing effects: The role of causal schemas in decision making. *Memory & Cognition, 24,* 1–15.

Jungermann, H. (1986). The two camps on rationality. In H. R. Arkes & K. R. Hammond (Eds.), *Judgment and decision making* (pp. 627–641). Cambridge, England: Cambridge University Press.

Juslin, P. (1994). The overconfidence phenomenon as a consequence of informal experimenter-guided selection of almanac items. *Organizational Behavior and Human Decision Processes, 57,* 226–246.

Juslin, P., Winman, A., & Persson, T. (1994). Can overconfidence be used as an indicator of reconstructive rather than retrieval processes? *Cognition, 54,* 99–130.

Kahneman, D. (1981). Who shall be the arbiter of our intuitions? *Behavioral and Brain Sciences, 4,* 339–340.

Kahneman, D., Knetsch, J. L., & Thaler, R. H. (1990). Experimental tests of the endowment effect and the Coase theorem. *Journal of Political Economy, 98,* 1325–1348.

Kahneman, D., Knetsch, J. L., & Thaler, R. (1991). The endowment effect, loss aversion, and status quo bias. *Journal of Economic Perspectives, 5,* 193–206.

Kahneman, D., Slovic, P., & Tversky, A. (Eds.). (1982). *Judgment under uncertainty: Heuristics and biases.* Cambridge, England: Cambridge University Press.

Kahneman, D., & Snell, J. (1990). Predicting utility. In R. M. Hogarth (Eds.), *Insights into decision making* (pp. 295–310). Chicago: University of Chicago Press.

Kahneman, D., & Tversky, A. (1972). Subjective probability: A judgment of representativeness. *Cognitive Psychology, 3,* 430–454.

Kahneman, D., & Tversky, A. (1982). On the study of statistical intuitions. *Cognition, 11,* 123–141.

Kahneman, D., & Tversky, A. (1983). Can irrationality be intelligently discussed? *Behavioral and Brain Sciences, 6,* 509–510.

Kahneman, D., & Tversky, A. (1984). Choices, values, and frames. *American Psychologist, 39,* 341–350.

Kahneman, D., & Tversky, A. (1996). On the reality of cognitive illusions. *Psychological Review, 103,* 582–591.

Kao, S. F., & Wasserman, E. A. (1993). Assessment of an information integration account of contingency judgment with examination of subjective cell importance and method of information presentation. *Journal of Experimental Psychology: Learning, Memory, and Cognition, 19,* 1363–1386.

Kaplan, M. (1996). *Decision theory as philosophy.* Cambridge, England: Cambridge University Press.

Kardash, C. M., & Scholes, R. J. (1996). Effects of pre-existing beliefs, epistemological beliefs, and need for cognition on interpretation of controversial issues. *Journal of Educational Psychology, 88,* 260–271.

Keating, D. P. (1990). Charting pathways to the development of expertise. *Educational Psychologist, 25,* 243–267.

Kekes, J. (Ed.). (1990). *Facing evil.* Princeton, NJ: Princeton University Press.

Kelley, D. (1990). *The art of reasoning.* New York: Norton.

Kern, L. H., Mirels, H., & Hinshaw, V. (1983). Scientists' understanding of propositional logic: An experimental investigation. *Social Studies of Science, 13,* 131–146.

Kirby, K. N. (1994). Probabilities and utilities of fictional outcomes in Wason's four-card selection task. *Cognition, 51,* 1–28.

Kitcher, P. (1993). *The advancement of science.* New York: Oxford University Press.

Klaczynski, P. A., & Fauth, J. (1997). Developmental differences in memory-based intrusions and self-serving statistical reasoning biases. *Merrill–Palmer Quarterly, 43,* 539–566.

Klaczynski, P. A., & Gordon, D. H. (1996). Self-serving influences on adolescents' evaluations of belief-relevant evidence. *Journal of Experimental Child Psychology, 62,* 317–339.

Klaczynski, P. A., Gordon, D. H., & Fauth, J. (1997). Goal-oriented critical reasoning and individual differences in critical reasoning biases. *Journal of Educational Psychology, 89,* 470–485.

Klaczynski, P., & Laipple, J. (1993). Role of content domain, logic training, and IQ in rule acquisition and transfer. *Journal of Experimental Psychology: Learning, Memory, and Cognition, 19,* 653–672.

Klahr, D., Fay, A. L., & Dunbar, K. (1993). Heuristics for scientific experimentation: A developmental study. *Cognitive Psychology, 25,* 111–146.

Klayman, J., & Ha, Y. (1987). Confirmation, disconfirmation, and information in hypothesis testing. *Psychological Review, 94,* 211–228.

Klayman, J., & Ha, Y. (1989). Hypothesis testing in rule discovery: Strategy, structure, and content. *Journal of Experimental Psychology: Learning, Memory, and Cognition, 15,* 596–604.

Klein, G. (1998). *Sources of power: How people make decisions.* Cambridge, MA: MIT Press.

Koehler, J. J. (1993). The influence of prior beliefs on scientific judgments of evidence quality. *Organizational Behavior and Human Decision Processes, 56,* 28–55.

Koehler, J. J. (1996). The base rate fallacy reconsidered: Descriptive, normative and methodological challenges. *Behavioral and Brain Sciences, 19,* 1–53.

Komorita, S. S., & Parks, C. D. (1994). *Social dilemmas.* Boulder, CO: Westview Press.

Koriat, A., Lichtenstein, S., & Fischhoff, B. (1980). Reasons for confidence. *Journal of Experimental Psychology: Human Learning and Memory, 6,* 107–118.

Kornblith, H. (Ed.). (1985). *Naturalizing epistemology.* Cambridge, MA: MIT Press.

Kornblith, H. (1993). *Inductive inference and its natural ground.* Cambridge, MA: MIT Press.

Krantz, D. H. (1981). Improvements in human reasoning and an error in L. J. Cohen's. *Behavioral and Brain Sciences, 4,* 340–341.

Krueger, J., & Zeiger, J. (1993). Social categorization and the truly false consensus effect. *Journal of Personality and Social Psychology, 65,* 670–680.

Kruglanski, A. W. (1990). Lay epistemics theory in social-cognitive psychology. *Psychological Inquiry, 1,* 181–197.

Kruglanski, A. W., & Ajzen, I. (1983). Bias and error in human judgment. *European Journal of Social Psychology, 13,* 1–44.

Kruglanski, A. W., & Webster, D. M. (1996). Motivated closing of the mind: "Seizing" and "freezing." *Psychological Review, 103,* 263–283.

Kuhberger, A. (1995). The framing of decisions: A new look at old problems. *Organizational Behavior and Human Decision Processes, 62,* 230–240.

Kuhn, D. (1991). *The skills of argument.* Cambridge, England: Cambridge University Press.

Kuhn, D. (1992). Thinking as argument. *Harvard Educational Review, 62,* 155–178.

Kuhn, D. (1993). Connecting scientific and informal reasoning. *Merrill–Palmer Quarterly, 38,* 74–103.

Kuhn, D. (1996). Is good thinking scientific thinking? In D. R. Olson & N. Torrance (Eds.), *Modes of thought: Explorations in culture and cognition* (pp. 261–281). New York: Cambridge University Press.

Kuhn, D., Amsel, E., & O'Loughlin, M. (1988). *The development of scientific thinking skills.* San Diego: Academic Press.

Kunda, Z. (1990). The case for motivated reasoning. *Psychological Bulletin, 108,* 480–498.

Kyburg, H. E. (1983). Rational belief. *Behavioral and Brain Sciences, 6,* 231–273.

Kyburg, H. E. (1991). Normative and descriptive ideals. In J. Cummins & J. Pollock (Eds.), *Philosophy and AI: Essays at the interface* (pp. 129–139). Cambridge, MA: MIT Press.

Kyburg, H. E. (1996). Probabilistic fallacies. *Behavioral and Brain Sciences, 19,* 31.

Kyllonen, P. C. (1996). Is working memory capacity Spearman's g? In I. Dennis & P. Tapsfield (Eds.), *Human abilities: Thier nature and measurement* (pp. 49–76). Mahwah, NJ: Lawrence Erlbaum Associates.

Kyllonen, P. C., & Christal, R. E. (1990). Reasoning ability is (little more than) working memory capacity?! *Intelligence, 14,* 389–433.

Lad, F. (1984). The calibration question. *British Journal for the Philosophy of Science, 35,* 213–221.

Langer, E. J. (1989). *Mindfulness.* Reading, MA: Addison-Wesley.

Langer, E. J., Blank, A., & Chanowitz, B. (1978). The mindlessness of ostensibly thoughtful action: The role of "placebic" information in interpersonal interaction. *Journal of Personality and Social Psychology, 36,* 635–642.

Larrick, R. P., Nisbett, R. E., & Morgan, J. N. (1993). Who uses the cost-benefit rules of choice? Implications for the normative status of microeconomic theory. *Organizational Behavior and Human Decision Processes, 56,* 331–347.

Larrick, R. P., Smith, E. E., & Yates, J. F. (1992, November). *Reflecting on the reflection effect: Disrupting the effects of framing through thought.* Paper presented at the meetings of the Society for Judgment and Decision Making, St. Louis, MO.

Lave, J., & Wenger, E. (1991). *Situated learning: Legitimate peripheral participation.* Cambridge, England: Cambridge University Press.

Leary, D. E. (1987). From act psychology to probabilistic functionalism: The place of Egon Brunswik in the history of psychology. In M. Ash & W. Woodward (Eds.), *Psychology in twentieth-century thought and society* (pp. 115–142). Cambridge, England: Cambridge University Press.

Lefkowitz, B. (1997). *Our guys: The Glen Ridge rape and the secret life of the perfect suburb.* Berkeley: University of California Press.

Legrenzi, P., Girotto, V., & Johnson-Laird, P. N. (1993). Focussing in reasoning and decision making. *Cognition, 49,* 37–66.

Levelt, W. (1995). Chapters of psychology. In R. L. Solso & D. W. Massaro (Eds.), *The science of the mind: 2001 and beyond* (pp. 184–202). New York: Oxford University Press.

Levi, I. (1983). Who commits the base rate fallacy? *Behavioral and Brain Sciences, 6,* 502–506.

Levi, I. (1996). Fallacy and controversy about base rates. *Behavioral and Brain Sciences, 19,* 31–32.

Levin, I. P., Wasserman, E. A., & Kao, S. F. (1993). Multiple methods of examining biased information use in contingency judgments. *Organizational Behavior and Human Decision Processes, 55,* 228–250.

Levinson, S. C. (1995). Interactional biases in human thinking. In E. Goody (Eds.), *Social intelligence and interaction* (pp. 221–260). Cambridge, England: Cambridge University Press.

Lewis, D. (1979). Prisoner's Dilemma is a Newcomb Problem. *Philosophy and Public Affairs, 8,* 235–240.

Liberman, N., & Klar, Y. (1996). Hypothesis testing in Wason's selection task: Social exchange cheating detection or task understanding. *Cognition, 58,* 127–156.

Lichtenstein, S., & Fischhoff, B. (1977). Do those who know more also know more about how much they know? *Organizational Behavior and Human Performance, 20,* 159–183.

Lichtenstein, S., & Fischhoff, B. (1980). Training for calibration. *Organizational Behavior and Human Performance, 26,* 149–171.

Lichtenstein, S., Fischhoff, B., & Phillips, L. (1982). Calibration and probabilities: The state of the art to 1980. In D. Kahneman, P. Slovic, & A. Tversky (Eds.), *Judgment under uncertainty: Heuristics and biases* (pp. 306–334). Cambridge, England: Cambridge University Press.

Lichtenstein, S., & Slovic, P. (1971). Reversal of preferences between bids and choices in gambling decisions. *Journal of Experimental Psychology, 89,* 46–55.

Lipman, M. (1991). *Thinking in education.* Cambridge, England: Cambridge University Press.

Lohman, D. F. (1989). Human intelligence: An introduction to advances in theory and research. *Review of Educational Research, 59,* 333–373.

Loomes, G., & Sugden, R. (1982). Regret theory: An alternative theory of rational choice under uncertainty. *The Economic Journal, 92,* 805–824.

Lopes, L. L. (1981). Performing competently. *Behavioral and Brain Sciences, 4,* 343–344.

Lopes, L. L. (1982). Doing the impossible: A note on induction and the experience of randomness. *Journal of Experimental Psychology: Learning, Memory, and Cognition, 8,* 626–636.

Lopes, L. L. (1991). The rhetoric of irrationality. *Theory & Psychology, 1,* 65–82.

Lopes, L. L. (1992). Three misleading assumptions in the customary rhetoric of the bias literature. *Theory & Psychology, 2,* 231–236.

Lopes, L. L., & Oden, G. C. (1991). The rationality of intelligence. In E. Eells & T. Maruszewski (Eds.), *Probability and rationality: Studies on L. Jonathan Cohen's philosophy of science* (pp. 199–223). Amsterdam: Editions Rodopi.

Lowe, E. J. (1993). Rationality, deduction and mental models. In K. Manktelow & D. Over (Eds.), *Rationality: Psychological and philosophical perspectives* (pp. 211–230). London: Routledge.

Lubinski, D., & Humphreys, L. G. (1997). Incorporating general intelligence into epidemiology and the social sciences. *Intelligence, 24,* 159–201.

Luria, A. R. (1976). *Cognitive development: Its cultural and social foundations.* Cambridge, MA: Harvard University Press.

Lyon, D., & Slovic, P. (1976). Dominance of accuracy information and neglect of base rates in probability estimation. *Acta Psychologica, 40,* 287–298.

Macchi, L. (1995). Pragmatic aspects of the base-rate fallacy. *Quarterly Journal of Experimental Psychology, 48A,* 188–207.

MacCrimmon, K. R. (1968). Descriptive and normative implications of the decision-theory postulates. In K. Borch & J. Mossin (Eds.), *Risk and uncertainty* (pp. 3–32). London: Macmillan.

MacCrimmon, K. R., & Larsson, S. (1979). Utility theory: Axioms versus "paradoxes." In M. Allais & O. Hagen (Eds.), *Expected utility hypotheses and the Allais paradox* (pp. 333–409). Dordrecht, Netherlands: Reidel.

Macdonald, R. (1986). Credible conceptions and implausible probabilities. *British Journal of Mathematical and Statistical Psychology, 39,* 15–27.

Macdonald, R. R., & Gilhooly, K. J. (1990). More about Linda *or* conjunctions in context. *European Journal of Cognitive Psychology, 2,* 57–70.

Maher, P. (1993). *Betting on theories.* Cambridge, England: Cambridge University Press.

Manktelow, K. I., & Evans, J. S. B. T. (1979). Facilitation of reasoning by realism: Effect or non-effect? *British Journal of Psychology, 70,* 477–488.

Manktelow, K. I., & Over, D. E. (1990). *Inference and understanding: A philosophical and psychological perspective.* London: Routledge.

Manktelow, K. I., & Over, D. E. (1991). Social roles and utilities in reasoning with deontic conditionals. *Cognition, 39,* 85–105.

Manktelow, K. I., Sutherland, E., & Over, D. E. (1995). Probabilistic factors in deontic reasoning. *Thinking and Reasoning, 1,* 201–219.

March, J. G. (1988). Bounded rationality, ambiguity, and the engineering of choice. In D. Bell, H. Raiffa, & A. Tversky (Eds.), *Decision making: Descriptive, normative, and prescriptive interactions* (pp. 33–57). Cambridge, England: Cambridge University Press.

Margalit, A., & Bar-Hillel, M. (1981). The irrational, the unreasonable, and the wrong. *Behavioral and Brain Sciences, 4,* 346–349.

Margolis, H. (1987). *Patterns, thinking, and cognition.* Chicago: University of Chicago Press.

Margolis, H. (1996). *Dealing with risk.* Chicago: University of Chicago Press.

Markovits, H., & Nantel, G. (1989). The belief-bias effect in the production and evaluation of logical conclusions. *Memory & Cognition, 17,* 11–17.

Markovits, H., & Vachon, R. (1989). Reasoning with contrary-to-fact propositions. *Journal of Experimental Child Psychology, 47,* 398–412.

Marks, G., & Miller, N. (1987). Ten years of research on the false consensus effect: An empirical and theoretical review. *Psychological Bulletin, 102,* 72–90.

Marr, D. (1982). *Vision.* San Francisco: Freeman.

Matarazzo, J. D. (1972). *Wechsler's measurement and appraisal of adult intelligence* (5th ed.). Baltimore: Williams & Wilkins.

Matthews, D. J., & Keating, D. P. (1995). Domain specificity and habits of mind. *Journal of Early Adolescence, 15,* 319–343.

McCain, R. A. (1991). A linguistic conception of rationality. *Social Science Information, 30*(2), 233–255.

McGeorge, P., Crawford, J., & Kelly, S. (1997). The relationships between psychometric intelligence and learning in an explicit and an implicit task. *Journal of Experimental Psychology: Learning, Memory, and Cognition, 23,* 239–245.

McKenzie, C. R. M. (1994). The accuracy of intuitive judgment strategies: Covariation assessment and Bayesian inference. *Cognitive Psychology, 26,* 209–239.

Mele, A. R. (1987). Recent work on self-deception. *American Philosophical Quarterly, 24,* 1–17.

Mele, A. R. (1997). Real self-deception. *Behavioral and Brain Sciences, 20,* 91–136.

Merton, R. K. (1968). The Matthew effect in science. *Science, 159,* 59–63.

Messer, W. S., & Griggs, R. A. (1993). Another look at Linda. *Bulletin of the Psychonomic Society, 31,* 193–196.

Messick, S. (1984). The nature of cognitive styles: Problems and promise in educational practice. *Educational Psychologist, 19,* 59–74.

Messick, S. (1994). The matter of style: Manifestations of personality in cognition, learning, and teaching. *Educational Psychologist, 29,* 121–136.

Miller, D. T., Turnbull, W., & McFarland, C. (1990). Counterfactual thinking and social perception: Thinking about what might have been. In M. P. Zanna (Eds.), *Advances in experimental social psychology* (pp. 305–331). San Diego: Academic Press.

Miller, P. M., & Fagley, N. S. (1991). The effects of framing, problem variations, and providing rationale on choice. *Personality and Social Psychology Bulletin, 17*(5), 517–522.

Millgram, E. (1997). *Practical induction.* Cambridge, MA: Harvard University Press.

Millikan, R. G. (1993). *White Queen psychology and other essays for Alice.* Cambridge, MA: MIT Press.

Mitchell, P., Robinson, E. J., Isaacs, J. E., & Nye, R., M. (1996). Contamination in reasoning about false belief: An instance of realist bias in adults but not children. *Cognition, 59,* 1–21.

The money in the message. (1998, February 14). *The Economist,* p. 78.

Montgomery, H., & Adelbratt, T. (1982). Gambling decisions and information about expected value. *Organizational Behavior and Human Performance, 29,* 39–57.

Morier, D. M., & Borgida, E. (1984). The conjunction fallacy: A task specific phenomenon? *Personality and Social Psychology Bulletin, 10,* 243–252.

Morrison, F. J. (1997). Nature-nurture in the classroom: Entrance age, school readiness, and learning in children. *Developmental Psychology, 33,* 254–262.

Morrison, F. J., Smith, L., & Dow-Ehrensberger, M. (1995). Education and cognitive development: A natural experiment. *Developmental Psychology, 31,* 789–799.

Morton, O. (1997, Nov. 3). Doing what comes naturally: A new school of psychology finds reasons for your foolish heart. *The New Yorker,* pp. 102–107.

Moshman, D. (1994). Reasoning, metareasoning, and the promotion of rationality. In A. Demetriou & A. Efklides (Eds.), *Intelligence, mind, and reasoning: Structure and development* (pp. 135–150). Amsterdam: Elsevier.

Moshman, D., & Franks, B. (1986). Development of the concept of inferential validity. *Child Development, 57,* 153–165.

Moshman, D., & Geil, M. (1998). Collaborative reasoning: Evidence for collective rationality. *Thinking and Reasoning, 4,* 231–248.

Mullen, B., Atkins, J., Champion, D., Edwards, C., Hardy, D., Story, J., & Vanderklok, M. (1985). The false consensus effect: A meta-analysis of 115 hypothesis tests. *Journal of Experimental Social Psychology, 21,* 262–283.

Myerson, J., Rank, M. R., Raines, F. Q., & Schnitzler, M. A. (1998). Race and general cognitive ability: The myth of diminishing returns to education. *Psychological Science, 9,* 139–142.

Mynatt, C. R., Tweney, R. D., & Doherty, M. E. (1983). Can philosophy resolve empirical issues? *Behavioral and Brain Sciences, 6,* 506–507.

Nathanson, S. (1994). *The ideal of rationality.* Chicago: Open Court.

Navon, D. (1989a). The importance of being visible: On the role of attention in a mind viewed as an anarchic intelligence system: I. Basic tenets. *European Journal of Cognitive Psychology, 1,* 191–213.

Navon, D. (1989b). The importance of being visible: On the role of attention in a mind viewed as an anarchic intelligence system: II. Application to the field of attention. *European Journal of Cognitive Psychology, 1,* 215–238.

Neimark, E. (1987). *Adventures in thinking.* San Diego: Harcourt Brace.

Neisser, U., Boodoo, G., Bouchard, T., Boykin, A. W., Brody, N., Ceci, S. J., Halpern, D., Loehlin, J., Perloff, R., Sternberg, R., & Urbina, S. (1996). Intelligence: Knowns and unknowns. *American Psychologist, 51,* 77–101.

Nelson, T., Biernat, M., & Manis, M. (1990). Everyday base rates (sex stereotypes): Potent and resilient. *Journal of Personality and Social Psychology, 59,* 664–675.

Newell, A. (1982). The knowledge level. *Artificial Intelligence, 18,* 87–127.

Newell, A. (1990). *Unified theories of cognition.* Cambridge, MA: Harvard University Press.

Newell, A., & Simon, H. A. (1972). *Human problem solving.* Englewood Cliffs, NJ: Prentice-Hall.

Newstead, S. E., & Evans, J. St. B. T. (Eds.) (1995). *Perspectives on thinking and reasoning.* Hove, England: Lawrence Erlbaum Associates.

Newstead, S., Pollard, P., Evans, J. S., & Allen, J. (1992). The source of belief bias effects in syllogistic reasoning. *Cognition, 45,* 257–284.

Nickerson, R. (1987). Why teach thinking? In J. Baron, & R. Sternberg (Eds.), *Teaching thinking skills: Theory and practice* (pp. 27–40). New York: Freeman.

Nickerson, R. S. (1988). On improving thinking through instruction. In E. Z. Rothkopf (Ed.), *Review of research in education* (Vol. 15, pp. 3–57). Washington, DC: American Educational Research Association.

Nickerson, R. S. (1996). Hempel's paradox and Wason's selection task: Logical and psychological puzzles of confirmation. *Thinking and Reasoning, 2,* 1–31.

Nisbett, R. E. (1981). Lay arbitration of rules of inference. *Behavioral and Brain Sciences, 4,* 349–350.

Nisbett, R. E. (1993). *Rules for reasoning.* Hillsdale, NJ: Lawrence Erlbaum Associates.

Nisbett, R. E., & Ross, L. (1980). *Human inference: Strategies and shortcomings of social judgment.* Englewood Cliffs, NJ: Prentice-Hall.

Nisbett, R., & Wilson, T. (1977). Telling more than we know: Verbal reports on mental processes. *Psychological Review, 84,* 231–259.

Norman, D. A. (1976). *Memory and attention: An introduction to human information processing* (2nd ed.), New York: Wiley.

Norris, S. P. (1992). Testing for the disposition to think critically. *Informal Logic, 14,* 157–164.

Norris, S. P., & Ennis, R. H. (1989). *Evaluating critical thinking.* Pacific Grove, CA: Midwest Publications.

Nozick, R. (1969). Newcomb's problem and two principles of choice. In N. Rescher (Eds.), *Essays in honor of Carl G. Hempel* (pp. 114–146). Dordrecht, Netherlands: Reidel.

Nozick, R. (1993). *The nature of rationality.* Princeton, NJ: Princeton University Press.

Oakhill, J., Johnson-Laird, P. N., & Garnham, A. (1989). Believability and syllogistic reasoning. *Cognition, 31,* 117–140.

Oaksford, M., & Chater, N. (1992). Bounded rationality in taking risks and drawing inferences. *Theory & Psychology, 2,* 225–230.

Oaksford, M., & Chater, N. (1993). Reasoning theories and bounded rationality. In K. Manktelow & D. Over (Eds.), *Rationality: Psychological and philosophical perspectives* (pp. 31–60). London: Routledge.

Oaksford, M., & Chater, N. (1994). A rational analysis of the selection task as optimal data selection. *Psychological Review, 101,* 608–631.

Oaksford, M., & Chater, N. (1995). Theories of reasoning and the computational explanation of everyday inference. *Thinking and Reasoning, 1,* 121–152.

Oaksford, M., & Chater, N. (1996). Rational explanation of the selection task. *Psychological Review, 103,* 381–391.

Oaksford, M., Chater, N., Grainger, B., & Larkin, J. (1997). Optimal data selection in the reduced array selection task (RAST). *Journal of Experimental Psychology: Learning, Memory, and Cognition, 23,* 441–458.

Oatley, K. (1992). *Best laid schemes: The psychology of emotions.* Cambridge, England: Cambridge University Press.

O'Brien, D. P. (1995). Finding logic in human reasoning requires looking in the right places. In S. E. Newstead & J. St. B. T. Evans (Eds.), *Perspectives on thinking and reasoning* (pp. 189–216). Hove, England: Lawrence Erlbaum Associates.

O'Brien, D. P., Braine, M., & Yang, Y. (1994). Propositional reasoning by mental models? Simple to refute in principle and in practice. *Psychological Review, 101,* 711–724.

Olson, D. R. (1977). From utterance to text: The bias of language in speech and writing. *Harvard Educational Review, 47,* 257–281.

Olson, D. R. (1986). Intelligence and literacy: The relationships between intelligence and the technologies of representation and communication. In R. J. Sternberg & R. K. Wagner (Eds.), *Practical intelligence* (pp. 338–360). Cambridge, England: Cambridge University Press.

Olson, D. R. (1994). *The world on paper.* Cambridge, England: Cambridge University Press.

Ong, W. J. (1967). *The presence of the word.* Minneapolis: University of Minnesota Press.

Ong, W. J. (1982). *Orality and literacy.* London: Methuen.

Osherson, D. N. (1995). Probability judgment. In E. E. Smith & D. N. Osherson (Eds.), *Thinking* (Vol. 3, pp. 35–75). Cambridge, MA: The MIT Press.

Over, D. E., & Manktelow, K. I. (1993). Rationality, utility and deontic reasoning. In K. Manktelow & D. Over (Eds.), *Rationality: Psychological and philosophical perspectives* (pp. 231–259). London: Routledge.

Over, D. E., & Manktelow, K. I. (1995). Perspectives, preferences, and probabilities. *Thinking and Reasoning, 1,* 364–371.

Overton, W. F. (1985). Scientific methodologies and the competence-moderator performance issue. In E. D. Neimark, R. DeLisi, & J. L. Newman (Eds.), *Moderators of competence* (pp. 15–41). Hillsdale, NJ: Lawrence Erlbaum Associates.

Overton, W. F. (1990). Competence and procedures: Constraints on the development of logical reasoning. In W. F. Overton (Eds.), *Reasoning, necessity, and logic* (pp. 1–32). Hillsdale, NJ: Lawrence Erlbaum Associates.

Paul, R. W. (1984). Critical thinking: Fundamental to education for a free society. *Educational Leadership, 42*(1), 4–14.

Paul, R. W. (1987). Critical thinking and the critical person. In D. N. Perkins, J. Lockhead, & J. Bishop (Eds.), *Thinking: The second international conference* (pp. 373–403). Hillsdale, NJ: Lawrence Erlbaum Associates.

Perkins, D. N. (1995). *Outsmarting IQ: The emerging science of learnable intelligence.* New York: The Free Press.

Perkins, D. N., Farady, M., & Bushey, B. (1991). Everyday reasoning and the roots of intelligence. In J. Voss, D. Perkins, & J. Segal (Eds.), *Informal reasoning and education* (pp. 83–105). Hillsdale, NJ: Lawrence Erlbaum Associates.

Perkins, D. N., & Grotzer, T. A. (1997). Teaching intelligence. *American Psychologist, 52,* 1125–1133.

Perkins, D. N., Jay, E., & Tishman, S. (1993). Beyond abilities: A dispositional theory of thinking. *Merrill–Palmer Quarterly, 39,* 1–21.

Perry, W. G. (1970). *Forms of intellectual and ethical development in the college years: A scheme.* New York: Holt, Rinehart & Winston.

Petrinovich, L. (1989). Representative design and the quality of generalization. In L. W. Poon, D. C. Rubin, & B. A. Wilson (Eds.), *Everyday cognition in adulthood and late life* (pp. 11–24). Cambridge, England: Cambridge University Press.

Phillips, L. D., & Edwards, W. (1966). Conservatism in a simple probability inference task. *Journal of Experimental Psychology, 72,* 346–354.

Piaget, J. (1926). *The language and thought of the child.* London: Routledge & Kegan Paul.

Piaget, J. (1972). Intellectual evolution from adolescence to adulthood. *Human Development, 15,* 1–12.

Piattelli-Palmarini, M. (1994). *Inevitable illusions: How mistakes of reason rule our minds.* New York: Wiley.

Pinker, S. (1994). *The language instinct.* New York: William Morrow.

Pinker, S. (1997). *How the mind works.* New York: Norton.

Plous, S. (1993). *The psychology of judgment and decision making.* New York: McGraw-Hill.

Politzer, G. (1986). Laws of language use and formal logic. *Journal of Psycholinguistic Research, 15,* 47–92.

Politzer, G., & Noveck, I. A. (1991). Are conjunction rule violations the result of conversational rule violations? *Journal of Psycholinguistic Research, 20,* 83–103.

Pollard, P. (1982). Human reasoning: Some possible effects of availability. *Cognition, 12,* 65–96.

Pollard, P., & Evans, J. St. B. T. (1987). Content and context effects in reasoning. *American Journal of Psychology, 100,* 41–60.

Pollock, J. L. (1991). OSCAR: A general theory of rationality. In J. Cummins & J. L. Pollock (Eds.), *Philosophy and AI: Essays at the interface* (pp. 189–213). Cambridge, MA: MIT Press.

Pollock, J. L. (1995). *Cognitive carpentry: A blueprint for how to build a person.* Cambridge, MA: MIT Press.

Popper, K. R. (1972). *Objective knowledge.* Oxford, England: Oxford University Press.

Pratt, J. W., Raiffa, H., & Schlaifer, R. (1995). *Introduction to statistical decision theory.* Cambridge, MA: MIT Press.

Putnam, H. (1975). The meaning of "meaning." In H. Putnam (Eds.), *Mind, language, and reality: Philosophical papers* (Vol. 2, pp. 215–271). Cambridge, England: Cambridge University Press.

Pylyshyn, Z. (1984). *Computation and cognition.* Cambridge, MA: MIT Press.

Pyszczynski, T., & Greenberg, J. (1987). Toward an integration of cognitive and motivational perspectives on social inference: A biased hypothesis-testing model. In L. Berkowitz (Eds.), *Advances in experimental social psychology* (pp. 297–340). San Diego: Academic Press.

Quartz, S. R., & Sejnowski, T. J. (1998). The neural basis of cognitive development: A constructivist manifesto. *Behavioral and Brain Sciences, 20,* 537–596.

Quine, W. (1960). *Word and object.* Cambridge, MA: MIT Press.

Rapoport, A., & Chammah, A. (1965). *Prisoner's dilemma.* Ann Arbor: University of Michigan Press.

Rasmusen, E. (1989). *Games and information: An introduction to game theory.* Oxford, England: Blackwell.

Rawls, J. (1971). *A theory of justice.* Oxford, England: Oxford University Press.

Reber, A. S. (1993). *Implicit learning and tacit knowledge.* New York: Oxford University Press.

Reber, A. S., Walkenfeld, F. F., & Hernstadt, R. (1991). Implicit and explicit learning: Individual differences and IQ. *Journal of Experimental Psychology: Learning, Memory, and Cognition, 17,* 888–896.

Reeves, T., & Lockhart, R. S. (1993). Distributional versus singular approaches to probability and errors in probabilistic reasoning. *Journal of Experimental Psychology: General, 122,* 207–226.

Rescher, N. (1988). *Rationality: A philosophical inquiry into the nature and rationale of reason.* Oxford, England: Oxford University Press.

Resnik, M. D. (1987). *Choices: An introduction to decision theory.* Minneapolis: University of Minnesota Press.

Richardson, H. S. (1997). *Practical reasoning about final ends.* Cambridge, England: Cambridge University Press.

Rips, L. J. (1994). *The logic of proof.* Cambridge, MA: MIT Press.

Rips, L. J., & Conrad, F. G. (1983). Individual differences in deduction. *Cognition and Brain Theory, 6,* 259–285.

Robinson, J. P., Shaver, P. R., & Wrightsman, L. S. (1991). *Measures of personality and social psychological attitudes* (Vol. 1). San Diego: Academic Press.

Rogoff, B., & Lave, J. (Eds.). (1984). *Everyday cognition.* Cambridge, MA: Harvard University Press.

Rokeach, M. (1960). *The open and closed mind.* New York: Basic Books.

Ronis, D. L., & Yates, J. F. (1987). Components of probability judgment accuracy: Individual consistency and effects of subject matter and assessment method. *Organizational Behavior and Human Decision Processes, 40,* 193–218.

Rosenthal, R., & Rosnow, R. L. (1991). *Essentials of behavioral research: Methods and data analysis* (2nd ed.). New York: McGraw-Hill.

Ross, J., & Cousins, J. B. (1993). Patterns of growth in reasoning about correlational problems. *Journal of Educational Psychology, 85,* 49–65.

Ross, L., Amabile, T., & Steinnetz, J. (1977). Social roles, social control, and biases in the social perception process. *Journal of Personality and Social Psychology, 35,* 485–494.

Ross, L., Greene, D., & House, P. (1977). The "false consensus effect": An egocentric bias in social perception and attribution processes. *Journal of Experimental Social Psychology, 13,* 279–301.

Rumain, B., Connell, J., & Braine, M. D. S. (1983). Conversational comprehension processes are responsible for reasoning fallacies in children as well as adults: If is not the biconditional. *Developmental Psychology, 19,* 471–481.

Sá, W., West, R. F., & Stanovich, K. E. (in press). The domain specificity and generality of belief bias: Searching for a generalizable critical thinking skill. *Journal of Educationial Psychology.*

Savage, L. J. (1954). *The foundations of statistics.* New York: Wiley.

Schaller, M., Boyd, C., Yohannes, J., & O'Brien, M. (1995). The prejudiced personality revisited: Personal need for structure and formation of erroneous stereotypes. *Journal of Personality and Social Psychology, 68,* 544–555.

Scheffler, I. (1991). *In praise of the cognitive emotions.* New York: Routledge.

Schick, F. (1987). Rationality: A third dimension. *Economics and Philosophy, 3,* 49–66.

Schick, F. (1997). *Making choices: A recasting of decision theory.* Cambridge, England: Cambridge University Press.

Schmidt, F. L., & Hunter, J. E. (1996). Measurement error in psychological research: Lessons from 26 research scenarios. *Psychological Methods, 1,* 199–223.

Schmidtz, D. (1995). *Rational choice and moral agency.* Princeton, NJ: Princeton University Press.

Schneider, S. L. (1992). Framing and conflict: Aspiration level contingency, the status quo, and current theories of risky choice. *Journal of Experimental Psychology: Learning, Memory, and Cognition, 18,* 1040–1057.

Schoenfeld, A. H. (1983). Beyond the purely cognitive: Belief systems, social cognitions, and metacognitions as driving forces in intellectual performance. *Cognitive Science, 7,* 329–363.

Schommer, M. (1990). Effects of beliefs about the nature of knowledge on comprehension. *Journal of Educational Psychology, 82,* 498–504.

Schommer, M. (1993). Epistemological development and academic performance among secondary students. *Journal of Educational Psychology, 85,* 406–411.

Schommer, M. (1994). Synthesizing epistemological belief research: Tentative understandings and provocative confusions. *Educational Psychology Review, 6*, 293–319.

Schommer, M., & Walker, K. (1995). Are epistemological beliefs similar across domains? *Journal of Educational Psychology, 87*, 424–432.

Schrag, F. (1988). *Thinking in school and society.* New York: Routledge.

Schueler, G. F. (1995). *Desire: Its role in practical reason and the explanation of action.* Cambridge, MA: MIT Press.

Schustack, M. W., & Sternberg, R. J. (1981). Evaluation of evidence in causal inference. *Journal of Experimental Psychology: General, 110*, 101–120.

Schwarz, N. (1996). *Cognition and communication: Judgmental biases, research methods, and the logic of conversation.* Mahweh, NJ: Lawrence Erlbaum Associates.

Scribner, S., & Cole, M. (1981). *The psychology of literacy.* Cambridge, MA: Harvard University Press.

Sedlmeier, P. (1997). BasicBayes: A tutor system for simple Bayesian inference. *Behavior Research Methods, Instruments, & Computers, 29*, 328–336.

Sen, A. (1993). Internal consistency of choice. *Econometrica, 61*, 495–521.

Shafer, G. (1988). Savage revisited. In D. Bell, H. Raiffa, & A. Tversky (Eds.), *Decision making: Descriptive, normative, and prescriptive interactions* (pp. 193–234). Cambridge, England: Cambridge University Press.

Shafir, E. (1993). Intuitions about rationality and cognition. In K. Manktelow & D. Over (Eds.), *Rationality: Psychological and philosophical perspectives* (pp. 260–283). London: Routledge.

Shafir, E. (1994). Uncertainty and the difficulty of thinking through disjunctions. *Cognition, 50*, 403–430.

Shafir, E., & Tversky, A. (1992). Thinking through uncertainty: Nonconsequential reasoning and choice. *Cognitive Psychology, 24*, 449–474.

Shafir, E., & Tversky, A. (1995). Decision making. In E. E. Smith & D. N. Osherson (Eds.), *Thinking* (Vol. 3, pp. 77–100). Cambridge, MA: MIT Press.

Shanks, D. R. (1995). Is human learning rational? *Quarterly Journal of Experimental Psychology, 48A*, 257–279.

Shweder, R. A. (1987). Comments on Plott and on Kahneman, Knetsch, and Thaler. In R. M. Hogarth & M. W. Reder (Eds.), *Rational choice: The contrast between economics and psychology* (pp. 161–170). Chicago: Chicago University Press.

Siddiqui, S., West, R. F., & Stanovich, K. E. (1998). The influence of print exposure on syllogistic reasoning and knowledge of mental-state verbs. *Scientific Studies of Reading, 2*, 81–96.

Sieck, W., & Yates, J. F. (1997). Exposition effects on decision making: Choice and confidence in choice. *Organizational Behavior and Human Decision Processes, 70*, 207–219.

Siegel, H. (1988). *Educating reason.* New York: Routledge.

Siegel, H. (1993). Not by skill alone: The centrality of character to critical thinking. *Informal Logic, 15*, 163–177.

Sigel, I. E. (1993). The centrality of a distancing model for the development of representational competence. In R. Cocking & K. Renninger (Eds.), *The development and meaning of psychological distance* (pp. 141–158). Hillsdale, NJ: Lawrence Erlbaum Associates.

Simon, H. A. (1956). Rational choice and the structure of the environment. *Psychological Review, 63*, 129–138.

Simon, H. A. (1957). *Models of man.* New York: Wiley.

Simon, H. A. (1983). *Reason in human affairs.* Stanford, CA: Stanford University Press.

Skyrms, B. (1986). *Choice & chance: An introduction to inductive logic* (3rd ed.). Belmont, CA: Wadsworth.

Skyrms, B. (1996). *The evolution of the social contract.* Cambridge, England: Cambridge University Press.

Sloman, A. (1993). The mind as a control system. In C. Hookway & D. Peterson (Eds.), *Philosophy and cognitive science* (pp. 69–110). Cambridge, England: Cambridge University Press.

Sloman, S. A. (1996). The empirical case for two systems of reasoning. *Psychological Bulletin, 119,* 3–22.

Slovic, P. (1995). The construction of preference. *American Psychologist, 50,* 364–371.

Slovic, P., Fischhoff, B., & Lichtenstein, S. (1977). Behavioral decision theory. *Annual Review of Psychology, 28,* 1–39.

Slovic, P., & Tversky, A. (1974). Who accepts Savage's axiom? *Behavioral Science, 19,* 368–373.

Slugoski, B. R., Shields, H. A., & Dawson, K. A. (1993). Relation of conditional reasoning to heuristic processing. *Personality and Social Psychology Bulletin, 19,* 158–166.

Slugoski, B. R., & Wilson, A. E. (in press). Contribution of conversation skills to the production of judgmental errors. *European Journal of Social Psychology.*

Slusher, M. P., & Anderson, C. A. (1996). Using causal persuasive arguments to change beliefs and teach new information: The mediating role of explanation availability and evaluation bias in the acceptance of knowledge. *Journal of Educational Psychology, 88,* 110–122.

Smith, S. M., & Levin, I. P. (1996). Need for cognition and choice framing effects. *Journal of Behavioral Decision Making, 9,* 283–290.

Spearman, C. (1904). General intelligence, objectively determined and measured. *American Journal of Psychology, 15,* 201–293.

Sperber, D., Cara, F., & Girotto, V. (1995). Relevance theory explains the selection task. *Cognition, 57,* 31–95.

Sperber, D., & Wilson, D. (1986). *Relevance: Communication and cognition.* Cambridge, MA: Harvard University Press.

Spitz, H. H. (1979). Beyond field theory in the study of mental deficiency. In N. Ellis (Ed.), *Handbook of mental deficiency, psychological theory and research* (pp. 121–141). Hillsdale, NJ: Lawrence Erlbaum Associates.

Stankov, L., & Crawford, J. D. (1996). Confidence judgments in studies of individual differences. *Personality and Individual Differences, 21,* 971–986.

Stankov, L., & Dunn, S. (1993). Physical substrata of mental energy: Brain capacity and efficiency of cerebral metabolism. *Learning and Individual Differences, 5,* 241–257.

Stanovich, K. E. (1986). Matthew effects in reading: Some consequences of individual differences in the acquisition of literacy. *Reading Research Quarterly, 21,* 360–407.

Stanovich, K. E. (1989). Implicit philosophies of mind: The dualism scale and its relationships with religiosity and belief in extrasensory perception. *Journal of Psychology, 123,* 5–23.

Stanovich, K. E. (1990). Concepts in developmental theories of reading skill: Cognitive resources, automaticity, and modularity. *Developmental Review, 10,* 72–100.

Stanovich, K. E. (1993). Does reading make you smarter? Literacy and the development of verbal intelligence. In H. Reese (Ed.), *Advances in child development and behavior* (Vol. 24, pp. 133–180). San Diego: Academic Press.

Stanovich, K. E. (1994). Reconceptualizing intelligence: Dysrationalia as an intuition pump. *Educational Researcher, 23*(4), 11–22.

Stanovich, K. E. (1996). Decentered thought and consequentialist decision making. *Behavioral and Brain Sciences, 19,* 323–324.

Stanovich, K. E. (1998). *How to think straight about psychology* (5th ed.). New York: Longman.

Stanovich, K. E., & West, R. F. (1997). Reasoning independently of prior belief and individual differences in actively open-minded thinking. *Journal of Educational Psychology, 89,* 342–357.

Stanovich, K. E., & West, R. F. (1998a). Cognitive ability and variation in selection task performance. *Thinking and Reasoning, 4,* 193–230.

Stanovich, K. E., & West, R. F. (1998b). Individual differences in rational thought. *Journal of Experimental Psychology: General, 127,* 161–188.

Stanovich, K. E., & West, R. F. (1998c). Who uses base rates and P(D/~H)? An analysis of individual differences. *Memory & Cognition, 28,* 161–179.

Stanovich, K. E., & West, R. F. (in press). Individual differences in framing and conjunction effects. *Thinking and Reasoning.*

Stanovich, K. E., West, R. F., & Harrison, M. (1995). Knowledge growth and maintenance across the life span: The role of print exposure. *Developmental Psychology, 31,* 811–826.

Stein, E. (1996). *Without good reason: The rationality debate in philosophy and cognitive science.* Oxford, England: Oxford University Press.

Sterelny, K. (1990). *The representational theory of mind: An introduction.* Oxford, England: Basil Blackwell.

Sternberg, R. (1985). *Beyond IQ: A triarchic theory of human intelligence.* Cambridge, England: Cambridge University Press.

Sternberg, R. J. (1988). Mental self-government: A theory of intellectual styles and their development. *Human Development, 31,* 197–224.

Sternberg, R. J. (1989). Domain-generality versus domain-specificity: The life and impending death of a false dichotomy. *Merrill–Palmer Quarterly, 35,* 115–130.

Sternberg, R. J. (1990). *Metaphors of mind: Conceptions of the nature of intelligence.* Cambridge, England: Cambridge University Press.

Sternberg, R. J. (1997). *Thinking styles.* Cambridge, England: Cambridge University Press.

Sternberg, R. J., & Detterman, D. K. (1986). *What is intelligence?* Norwood, NJ: Ablex.

Sternberg, R. J., & Ruzgis, P. (Eds.). (1994). *Personality and intelligence.* Cambridge, England: Cambridge University Press.

Stevenson, R. J. (1993). Rationality and reality. In K. Manktelow & D. Over (Eds.), *Rationality: Psychological and philosophical perspectives* (pp. 61–82). London: Routledge.

Stich, S. P. (1983). *From folk psychology to cognitive science.* Cambridge, MA: MIT Press.

Stich, S. P. (1985). Could man be an irrational animal? *Synthese, 64,* 115–135.

Stich, S. P. (1990). *The fragmentation of reason.* Cambridge, MA: MIT Press.

Stich, S. P. (1993). Naturalizing epistemology: Quine, Simon, and the prospects for pragmatism. In C. Hookway & D. Peterson (Eds.), *Philosophy and cognitive science* (pp. 1–17). Cambridge, England: Cambridge University Press.

Stich, S. P. (1996). *Deconstruction of the mind.* New York: Oxford University Press.

Stich, S. P., & Nisbett, R. E. (1980). Justification and the psychology of human reasoning. *Philosophy of Science, 47,* 188–202.

Stigler, J. W., & Baranes, R. (1988). Culture and mathematics learning. In E. Z. Rothkopf (Eds.), *Review of research in education* (Vol. 15, pp. 253–306). Washington, DC: American Educational Research Association.

Swartz, R. J., & Perkins, D. N. (1989). *Teaching thinking: Issues & approaches.* Pacific Grove, CA: Midwest Publications.

Takemura, K. (1992). Effect of decision time on framing of decision: A case of risky choice behavior. *Psychologia, 35,* 180–185.

Takemura, K. (1993). The effect of decision frame and decision justification on risky choice. *Japanese Psychological Research, 35,* 36–40.

Takemura, K. (1994). Influence of elaboration on the framing of decision. *Journal of Psychology, 128,* 33–39.

Thagard, P. (1982). From the descriptive to the normative in philosophy and logic. *Philosophy of Science, 49,* 24–42.

Thagard, P. (1988). *Computational philosophy of science.* Cambridge, MA: MIT Press.

Thagard, P. (1992). *Conceptual revolutions.* Princeton, NJ: Princeton University Press.

Thagard, P., & Nisbett, R. E. (1983). Rationality and charity. *Philosophy of Science, 50,* 250–267.

Thaler, R. H. (1980). Toward a positive theory of consumer choice. *Journal of Economic Behavior and Organization, 1,* 39–60.

Thaler, R. H. (1992). *The winner's curse: Paradoxes and anomalies of economic life.* New York: The Free Press.

Thorndike, R. L., & Hagen, E. L. (1977). *Measurement and evaluation in psychology and education* (4th ed.). New York: Wiley.

Tschirgi, J. E. (1980). Sensible reasoning: A hypothesis about hypotheses. *Child Development, 51,* 1–10.

Tversky, A. (1975). A critique of expected utility theory: Descriptive and normative considerations. *Erkenntnis, 9,* 163–173.

Tversky, A., & Kahneman, D. (1974). Judgment under uncertainty: Heuristics and biases. *Science, 185,* 1124–1131.

Tversky, A., & Kahneman, D. (1981). The framing of decisions and the psychology of choice. *Science, 211,* 453–458.

Tversky, A., & Kahneman, D. (1982). Evidential impact of base rates. In D. Kahneman, P. Slovic, & A. Tversky (Eds.), *Judgment under uncertainty: Heuristics and biases* (pp. 153–160). Cambridge, England: Cambridge University Press.

Tversky, A., & Kahneman, D. (1983). Extensional versus intuitive reasoning: The conjunction fallacy in probability judgment. *Psychological Review, 90,* 293–315.

Tversky, A., Sattath, S., & Slovic, P. (1988). Contingent weighting in judgment and choice. *Psychological Review, 95,* 371–384.

Tweney, R. D., & Yachanin, S. (1985). Can scientists rationally assess conditional inferences? *Social Studies of Science, 15,* 155–173.

Vernon, P. A. (1991). The use of biological measures to estimate behavioral intelligence. *Educational Psychologist, 25,* 293–304.

Vernon, P. A. (1993). *Biological approaches to the study of human intelligence.* Norwood, NJ: Ablex.

Verplanken, B. (1993). Need for cognition and external information search: Responses to time pressure during decision-making. *Journal of Research in Personality, 27,* 238–252.

von Mises, R. (1957). *Probability, statistics, and truth.* New York: Dover.

Voss, J., Perkins, D. & Segal J. (Eds.). (1991). *Informal reasoning and education.* Hillsdale, NJ: Lawrence Erlbaum Associates.

Wade, C., & Tavris, C. (1993). *Critical and creative thinking.* New York: HarperCollins.

Wagenaar, W. A. (1972). Generation of random sequences by human subjects: A critical survey of the literature. *Psychological Bulletin, 77,* 65–72.

Wagenaar, W. A. (1988). *Paradoxes of gambling behavior.* Hove, England: Lawrence Erlbaum Associates.

Walberg, H. J., Strykowski, B. F., Rovai, E., & Hung, S. S. (1984). Exceptional performance. *Review of Educational Research, 54,* 87–112.

Walberg, H. J., & Tsai, S. (1983). Matthew effects in education. *American Educational Research Journal, 20,* 359–373.

Wason, P. C. (1966). Reasoning. In B. Foss (Eds.), *New horizons in psychology* (pp. 135–151). Harmonsworth, England: Penguin.

Wason, P. C. (1969). Regression in reasoning? *British Journal of Psychology, 60,* 471–480.

Wason, P. C., & Evans, J. St. B. T. (1975). Dual processes in reasoning? *Cognition, 3,* 141–154.

Wason, P. C., & Johnson-Laird, P. N. (1970). A conflict between selecting and evaluating information in an inferential task. *British Journal of Psychology, 61,* 509–515.

Wason, P. C., & Johnson-Laird, P. N. (1972). *Psychology of reasoning.* Cambridge, MA: Harvard University Press.

Wasserman, E. A., Dorner, W. W., & Kao, S. F. (1990). Contributions of specific cell information to judgments of interevent contingency. *Journal of Experimental Psychology: Learning, Memory, and Cognition, 16,* 509–521.

Watson, G., & Glaser, E. M. (1980). *Watson–Glaser Critical Thinking Appraisal.* New York: Psychological Corporation.

Webster, D. M., & Kruglanski, A. W. (1994). Individual differences in need for cognitive closure. *Journal of Personality and Social Psychology, 67,* 1049–1062.

West, R. F., & Stanovich, K. E. (1997). The domain specificity and generality of overconfidence: Individual differences in performance estimation bias *Psychonomic Bulletin & Review, 4,* 387–392.

Wetherick, N. E. (1970). On the representativeness of some experiments in cognition. *Bulletin of the British Psychological Society, 23,* 213–214.

Wetherick, N. E. (1971). Representativeness in a reasoning problem: A reply to Shapiro. *Bulletin of the British Psychological Society, 24,* 213–214.

Wetherick, N. E. (1993). Human rationality. In K. Manktelow & D. Over (Eds.), *Rationality: Psychological and philosophical perspectives* (pp. 83–109). London: Routledge.

Wetherick, N. E. (1995). Reasoning and rationality: A critique of some experimental paradigms. *Theory & Psychology, 5,* 429–448.

Whynes, D. (1983). *Invitation to economics.* Oxford, England: Basil Blackwell.

Wilson, T. D., & Brekke, N. (1994). Mental contamination and mental correction: Unwanted influences on judgments and evaluations. *Psychological Bulletin, 116,* 117–142.

Wilson, T. D., & Schooler, J. W. (1991). Thinking too much: Introspection can reduce the quality of preferences and decisions. *Journal of Personality and Social Psychology, 60,* 181–192.

Windschitl, P. D., & Wells, G. L. (1997). Behavioral consensus information affects people's inferences about population traits. *Personality and Social Psychology Bulletin, 23,* 148–156.

Wolfe, C. R. (1995). Information seeking on Bayesian conditional probability problems: A fuzzy-trace theory account. *Journal of Behavioral Decision Making, 8,* 85–108.

Yates, J. F., Lee, J., & Shinotsuka, H. (1996). Beliefs about overconfidence, including its cross-national variation. *Organizational Behavior and Human Decision Processes, 65,* 138–147.

Yates, J. F., Zhu, Y., Ronis, D., Wang, D., Shinotsuka, H., & Toda, M. (1989). Probability judgment accuracy: China, Japan, and the United States. *Organizational Behavior and Human Decision Processes, 43,* 145–171.

Zechmeister, E. B., & Johnson, J. (1992). *Critical thinking: A functional approach.* Pacific Grove: CA: Brooks/Cole.

Author Index

A

Ackerman, P. L., 37, 127, 156, 156
Adams, M. J., 237
Adelbratt, T., 64
Adler, J. E., 98, 102, 121, 123, 127, 149,
    192, 197, 200, 204, 222, 224,
    226, 249
Ajzen, I., 2, 68
Akinnaso, F. N., 171
Alker, H., 64
Allais, M., 62, 100
Allan, L. G., 49, 149
Allen, J., 172
Alloy, L. B., 59, 245
Amabile, T., 65
Amsel, E., 164
Anderson, C. A., 164
Anderson, J. R., 9, 10, 11, 58, 135, 148,
    149, 151, 199, 202, 231
Ansburg, P., 133, 140, 224
Arkes, H. R., 2, 46, 109, 109, 115, 171,
    195
Atkins, J., 74
Audi, R., 14, 212

B

Babad, E., 12, 162

Bacharach, M., 102, 194
Badgio, P. C., 237
Baltes, P. B., 157
Bara, B. G., 39, 67
Baranes, R., 175
Bar-Hillel, M., 43, 54, 56, 68, 74, 206,
    218, 220, 229
Barkow, J. H., 150, 151
Baron, J., 2, 3, 4, 23, 26, 27, 36, 37, 40,
    49, 53, 60, 93, 102, 105, 109,
    127, 151, 152, 156, 157, 158,
    159, 162, 166, 171, 175, 176,
    195, 196, 202, 214, 217, 218,
    225, 229, 231, 236, 237, 237,
    240
Barr, D., 44
Barston, J., 35, 172, 178, 192, 200, 202
Bates, E. A., 234
Beach, I. R., 2
Beatty, J., 24
Bell, D. E., 3, 100
Berkeley, D., 2, 102, 103
Beyth-Marom, R., 43, 44, 176
Biernat, M., 178, 182, 186
Birnbaum, M. H., 27, 54, 68
Blank, A., 226
Block, J., 65
Blumer, C., 109
Boodoo, G., 67
Borgida, E., 122, 198

Bornstein, B., 109
Bouchard, T., 67
Boyd, C., 237
Boykin, A. W., 67
Braine, M. D. S., 70, 199, 199, 215, 235
Brase, G. L., 8, 23, 58, 192, 206, 214,
        223, 224, 232, 233
Bratman, M. E., 10, 12, 13
Brekke, N., 171, 206, 231
Brenner, L. A., 117
Brody, N., 67, 67, 143, 150, 204, 236,
        239
Bronfenbrenner, U. 175, 177, 204
Brookfield, S., 162
Broome, J., 15, 98, 100, 101, 102, 105
Brown, J., 171
Brown, J. S., 175, 177
Brown, N. R., 181
Bruner, J., xi, 193
Bucciarelli, M., 39, 67
Bushey, B., 36
Buss, D. M., 157
Byrne, R. M. J., 35, 128, 215, 216
Byrnes, J. P., 67, 137, 172

              C

Cacioppo, J. T., 63, 71, 79, 107, 158,
        160, 191
Campbell, J. D., 55, 87, 118
Campbell, R., 86, 90
Cara, F., 35
Carpenter, P. A., 39, 157
Carroll, J. B., 37, 39, 67, 94, 127, 143,
        157
Caryl, P. G., 39
Casscells, W., 71
Ceci, S. J., 67, 175, 177, 204, 234, 236
Cederblom, J., 213
Chadwick, R., 44
Chammah, A., 88
Champion, D., 74
Chanowitz, B., 226
Chapman, G., 109
Chapman, M., 199
Chater, N., 3, 4, 9, 12, 35, 36, 37, 58, 66,
        129, 132, 134, 135, 137, 139,
        149, 151, 196, 202, 215, 238,
        239, 240, 241, 242
Cheng, P. W., 42, 137, 128, 129

Cherniak, C., 3, 37
Christal, R. E., 39
Christensen-Szalanski, J., 2
Churchland, P. M., 18
Churchman, C. W., 220
Cohen, L. J., 1, 2, 5, 6, 8, 24, 25, 27, 29,
        30, 32, 33, 57, 58, 61, 64, 65,
        67, 68, 95, 96, 102, 106, 209,
        214, 215, 216, 229
Cole, M., 202
Collins, A., 175, 177
Connell, J., 70, 199
Conrad, F. G, 34, 221
Cook, P. J., 204, 234
Cooper, L. A., 157
Cooper, W. S., 22, 23, 148, 149, 150, 203
Cosmides, L. 8, 23, 58, 67, 68, 72, 74,
        83, 84, 128, 137, 192, 196, 206,
        214, 223, 224, 232, 233, 249,
        250
Costa, P. T., 167, 190
Cousins, J. B., 67
Cox, J. R., 128, 129, 131, 224
Crawford, J., 137, 147
Crawford, J. D., 121
Cronbach, L. J., 188
Cummins, D. D., 129, 137, 143, 147,
        151, 192
Cunningham, A. E., 236

              D

Dallob, P., 140
Daniels, N., 25
Daston, L., 24
Davidson, D., 20
Davis, D., 6, 116
Dawes, R. M., 2, 8, 25, 53, 54, 71, 75,
        93, 214, 217, 228, 245
Dawid, A. P., 56
Dawkins, R., 148, 149, 150, 152, 192,
        207, 231
Dawson, K. A., 2
Day, J. D., 147
Deary, I. J., 39, 157
de Finetti, B., 27, 56
Dennett, D. C., 5, 9, 10, 11, 12, 16, 18,
        21, 22, 27, 65, 148, 212, 231
Denny, J. P., 171
de Sousa, R., 212

Detterman, D. K., 39, 151, 240, 242
Doherty, M. E. , 25, 44, 63, 79, 80, 96, 200,
Dominowski, R. L., 128, 131, 133, 140, 224
Donahue, E., 71
Donaldson, M., 170
Dorner, W. W., 39, 44, 46, 47, 149
Dougherty, T. M., 39
Dow-Ehrensberger, M., 236
Duguid, P., 175, 177
Dulany, D. E., 54, 122, 123, 149
Dunbar, K., 67
Dunn, S., 39

E

Earman, J., 16
Edwards, C., 74
Edwards, J. R., 188
Edwards, K., 246, 247
Edwards, W., 64
Einhorn, H. J., 2, 44, 67, 102, 105, 204
Elgin, C. Z., 25
Elman, J. L., 234
Elster, J., 13, 15, 21, 98
Ennis, R. H., 156, 157, 162, 175
Epstein, S., 40, 142, 145, 168, 169, 191
Erwin, T. D., 168, 190
Estes, W. K., 157
Evans, J. St. B. T., x, 2, 3, 33, 35, 36, 66, 115, 128, 129,131, 135, 136, 137, 138, 139, 142, 143, 144, 145, 146, 147, 171, 172, 173, 178, 191, 192, 193, 194, 196, 200, 202, 203, 216, 224, 245, 246, 248, 251

F

Fagley, N. S., 63, 106
Falk, R., 206
Farady, M., 36
Fauth, J., 36, 45, 63, 158, 162, 164, 169, 186, 237
Fay, A. L., 67
Feinstein, J., 63, 71, 79, 107, 158, 160, 191
Fetzer, J., 35, 66

Fiedler, K., 125, 233
Finocchiaro, M. A., 35
Fischhoff, B., 25, 43, 44, 56, 64, 116, 117, 118, 176, 234
Flynn, J. R., 236
Fodor, J., 192, 230
Foley, R., 7, 14, 15, 16, 101
Fong, G. T., 35, 68, 74, 173
Frank, R. H., 204, 234
Franks, B., 67
Freitag, J., 70
Friedrich, J., 44
Frisch, D., 16, 102, 107, 108, 109, 110, 111
Fry, A. F., 39, 157
Funder, D. C., 65, 67, 199, 230
Furby, L., 188

G

Garavan, H., 44
Garnham, A., 172
Gaskins, I. W., 237
Gauthier, D., 8, 25, 236
Geil, M., 63
Gibbard, A., 86, 87
Gigerenzer, G., 1, 2, 3, 8, 24, 28, 36, 55, 56, 57, 58, 63, 66, 67, 68, 72, 74, 95, 102, 104, 116, 117, 125, 128, 137, 143, 144, 149, 151, 177, 192, 196, 199, 202, 206, 223, 224, 232, 233, 234, 249
Gilhooly, K. J., 121, 122, 123, 127, 197
Gilovich, T., 43, 55, 74, 217
Girotto, V., 35, 173
Glaser, E. M., 163
Goff, M., 156
Gold, E., 71
Goldman, A. I., 3, 16, 20, 37, 38
Goldstein, D. G., 3, 8, 63, 116
Goodman, N., 25
Goody, J., 171
Gordon, D. H., 36, 45, 63, 158, 162, 164, 169, 186, 237
Gordon, R. A., 201
Gottfredson, L. S., 150, 204, 205, 239
Gould, S. J., 142
Graboys, T., 71
Grainger, B., & 238, 239
Granberg, D., 206

Greenberg, J., 164
Greene, D., 55, 74
Greenwald, A. G., 55, 118
Grether, D. M., 100
Griffin, D., 35, 56, 117
Griffiths, M. D., 214
Griggs, R. A., 54, 127
Griggs, R. A., 42, 128, 129, 131, 134, 224
Grotzer, T. A., 236
Gur, R., 13

H

Ha, Y., 44
Hacking, I., 24
Hagen, E. L., 188
Haith, M. M., 39
Halberstadt, N., 44
Hale, S., 39, 157
Halpern, D., 67
Hammond, K. R., 2, 145
Hardin, G., 9
Hardy, D., 74
Hargreaves Heap, S. P., 88
Harkness, A. R., 46
Harman, G., 3, 14, 16, 159, 213
Harper, W. L., 86, 87
Harris, R. J., 103
Harrison, M., 236
Harvey, N., 12
Hasher, L., 250
Haslam, N., 118, 237
Hastie, R., 2, 117, 118
Havelock, E. A., 171
Hawkins, S. A., 117, 118
Heggestad, E. D., 127, 156
Henle, M., 98, 193, 194, 216, 219, 242
Hermann, M., 64
Hernstadt, R., 137, 147
Hershey, J. C., 40
Hilton, D. J., 1, 54, 98, 100, 121, 122,
        123, 127, 144, 149, 151, 188,
        192, 197, 200, 204
Hinshaw, V., 42
Hoch, S. J., 55, 75, 78, 94, 228, 228, 245
Hoffrage, U., 8, 56, 68, 72, 74, 116, 117,
        177, 199, 206, 223, 224, 232,
        233, 234, 249
Hogarth, R. M., 2, 44, 67, 102, 105, 204
Holstein, C., 40

Holt, C., 6, 116
Holyoak, K. J., 42, 128, 129, 137
Horgan, T., 9
House, P., 55, 74
Howson, C., 56, 176, 203
Hug, K., 128, 137
Huh, E., 40
Humphreys, L. G., 39, 67, 143, 150, 239
Humphreys, P., 2, 102, 103
Hung, S. S., 247
Hunt, E., 39, 157, 204, 205
Hunter, J. E., 40, 153, 156, 188
Hurley, S. L., 86, 87, 90, 91, 102, 194

I

Isaacs, J. E., 246
Israel, D. J., 10, 12, 13

J

Jackson, S. I., 42
Jacobs, J. E., 67
Jarvis, W., 63, 71, 79, 107, 158, 160, 191
Jay, E., 156, 157, 162
Jayasinghe, N., 118
Jeffrey, R. C., 15
Jepson, C., 8, 23, 25, 27, 35, 173, 234,
        235
Johnson, J., 162, 175
Johnson, M. H., 234
Johnson-Laird, P. N., 35, 39, 67, 133,
        172, 173, 194, 212, 215
Jones, J. K., 16
Jones, K., 147
Jones, W., 168
Jou, J., 103
Jungermann, H., 8, 105
Juslin, P., 116
Just, M. A., 39, 157

K

Kahneman, D., 1, 2, 3, 4, 6, 8, 16, 27,
        31, 43, 54, 56, 63, 67, 68, 93,
        102, 103, 104, 107, 108, 109,
        116, 121, 122, 123, 124, 125,
        127, 142, 143, 147, 148, 196,
        200, 214, 229, 233, 241

Kao, S. F., 39, 44, 45, 46, 47, 149, 179
Kaplan, M., 176
Kardash, C. M., 63, 158, 169, 186, 237
Kareev, Y., 44
Karmiloff-Smith, A., 234
Katz, Y., 12, 162
Keating, D. P., 147, 156
Kekes, J., 9
Kelley, D., 171
Kelly, S., 137, 147
Kern, L. H., 42
Kirby, K. N., 137, 173
Kitcher, P., 23, 157
Klaczynski, P. A., 36, 45, 63, 134, 158,
    162, 164, 169, 186, 237
Klahr, D., 67
Klar, Y., 129, 137
Klayman, J., 44
Klein, G., 145
Kleinbolting, H., 8, 56, 116, 117, 177,
    199, 223, 232, 234
Knetsch, J. L., 109, 116
Koehler, D. J., 117
Koehler, J. J., 27, 36, 43, 66, 67, 68, 71,
    245, 247
Komorita, S. S., 9
Koriat, A., 234
Kornblith, H., 36, 59, 66, 177, 244
Krantz, D., 8, 23, 25, 27, 35, 68, 74, 102,
    173, 177, 234, 235, 244
Krueger, J., 55, 75, 76, 228, 245
Kruger, L., 24
Kruglanski, A. W., 2, 157, 158, 160
Kuhn, D., 162, 164, 225, 237
Kunda, Z., 13, 162, 164
Kyburg, H. E., 54, 59, 66, 68, 96
Kyllonen, P. C., 37, 39

L

Lad, F., 56
Laipple, J., 134
Langer, E. J., 171, 195, 226
Larkin, J., 238, 239
Larrick, R. P., 61, 63, 97, 106, 151
Larsson, S., 62
Lave, J., 175
Leary, D. E., 117
Lee, J., 2

Lefkowitz, B., 201, 222
Legrenzi, P., 35, 173
Levelt, W., 9
Levi, I., 54, 66, 68, 96, 229
Levin, I. P., 45, 46, 63, 106, 127, 144,
    179, 237
Levinson, S. C., 98, 121, 127, 143, 145,
    147, 149, 151, 188, 192, 197,
    200, 250
Lewis, D., 90
Liberman, V., 117
Liberman, N., 129, 137
Lichtenstein, S., 56, 64, 101, 116, 118,
    217, 234
Lipman, M., 162, 175
Lipson, A., 40
Lockhart, R. S., 124
Loehlin, J., 67
Lohman, D. F., 157
Loomes, G., 100
Lopes, L. L., 2, 8, 9, 54, 59, 64, 65, 67,
    94, 102, 177, 241, 251
Lowe, E. J., 35, 66
Lubinski, D., 39, 67, 143, 150, 239
Luria, A. R., 171, 193, 194, 202, 204
Lynch, J. S., 129
Lyon, D., 43, 54, 68

M

Macchi, L., 71
MacCrimmon, K. R., 62
Macdonald, R. R., 1, 95, 103, 121, 122,
    123, 127, 197
Maher, P., 27
Manis, M., 178, 182, 186
Manktelow, K. I., 21, 35, 36, 66, 104,
    128, 129, 134, 137, 200, 224,
    245, 246
March, J. G., 59, 60, 97
Margalit, A., 229
Margolis, H., 35, 53, 98, 127, 130, 146,
    197, 201, 219, 225, 227, 248,
    250
Markovits, H., 67, 172, 178
Marks, G., 55, 74
Marr, D., 9, 11
Matarazzo, J. D., 39
Matthews, D. J., 147

McCain, R. A., 24
McClelland, P., 204
McCrae, R. R., 167, 190
McFarland, C., 40
McGeorge, P., 137, 147
McKenzie, C. R. M., 44
Meier, P., 168, 169, 191
Mele, A. R., 13
Merton, R. K., 247
Messer, W. S., 54, 127
Messick, S., 157
Miller, N., 55, 74
Miller, D. T., 40
Miller, P. M., 63, 106
Millgram, E., 16
Millikan, R. G., 232
Millman, J., 162
Mirels, H., 42, 71
Mitchell, P., 246
Moen, P., 204
Montgomery, H., 64
Morgan, J. N., 63, 97, 151
Morier, D. M., 122, 198
Morrison, F. J., 236
Morton, O., 151
Moshman, D., 63, 67, 156, 157
Mulford, M., 75
Mullen, B., 74
Murray, D. J., 8
Myerson, J., 236
Mynatt, C. R., 25, 44, 63, 79, 80, 96, 200

N

Nantel, G., 172, 178
Nathanson, S., 9, 14, 15, 16, 98, 231
Navon, D., 172, 173, 174, 191, 198
Neimark, E., 171
Neisser, U., 67
Nelson, T., 178, 182, 186
Newell, A., 9, 10, 11, 12, 211, 241
Newstead, S. E., 35, 35, 128, 131, 172,
    216, 224
Nickel, T., 168
Nickerson, R. S., 35, 36, 66, 129, 132,
    139, 156, 162, 175, 236
Nisbett, R. E., 4, 6, 8, 18, 21, 23, 25, 26,
    27, 35, 59, 61, 63, 68, 74, 97,
    102, 106, 128, 151, 172, 173,

    195, 196, 198, 202, 234, 235,
    241, 248, 250
Norman, D. A., 164
Norris, S. P., 157, 162
Noveck, I. A., 123
Nozick, R., 14, 16, 23, 86, 87, 88, 90,
    159, 213
Nye, R., M., 246

O

Oakhill, J., 172
Oaksford, M., 3, 4, 9, 12, 35, 36, 37, 58,
    66, 129, 132, 134, 135, 137,
    139, 149, 151, 196, 202, 215,
    238, 239, 240, 241, 242
Oatley, K., 212, 215
O'Brien, D. P., 49, 70, 138, 215, 235, 242
O'Brien, M., 237
Oden, G. C., 2, 64, 65, 67, 94, 177
Oliver, L. M., 128
O'Loughlin, M., 164
Olson, D. R., 171, 202, 204, 225
Ong, W. J., 171
Osherson, D. N., 2, 3, 27, 105, 222
Over, D. E., x, 2, 21, 35, 36, 66, 104, 115,
    129, 129, 134, 135, 136, 137,
    139, 142, 143, 144, 145, 146,
    191, 192, 193, 200, 202, 203,
    245, 246
Overton, W. F., 58, 67, 215

P

Parisi, D., 234
Parks, C. D., 9
Paul, R. W., 171
Perkins, D. N., 36, 156, 157, 162, 236,
Perloff, R., 67
Perry, W. G., 168
Persson, T., 116
Petrinovich, L., 116, 199
Petty, R. E., 63, 71, 79, 107, 158, 160,
    191
Phillips, L. D., 56, 64, 116, 118
Piaget, J., 170, 171
Piattelli-Palmarini, M., 2, 53, 58, 196,
    250
Pinker, S., 23, 58, 192, 250
Plott, C. R., 100

Plous, S., 2, 3
Plunkett, K., 234
Politzer, G., 123, 199
Pollack, M. E., 10, 12, 13
Pollard, P., 35, 128, 172, 173, 178, 192, 200, 202
Pollock, J. L., 10, 12, 13, 14, 16, 144, 145, 146, 192
Popper, K. R., 24
Porter, T., 24
Potenza, M., 67
Pratt, J. W., 15
Putnam, H., 26
Pylyshyn, Z., 9, 238
Pyszczynski, T., 164

Q

Quartz, S. R., 234
Quine, W., 16

R

Raiffa, H., 3, 15
Raines, F. Q., 236
Rank, M. R., 236
Ransdell, S. E., 42
Rapoport, A., 88
Rasinski, K. A., 2
Rasmusen, E., 88
Rawls, J., 25
Reber, A. S., 137, 139, 145, 146, 147, 192
Reder, L. M., 202
Reeves, T., 124
Regan, D. T., 157
Regier, T., 144
Rescher, N., 193, 196, 214, 216
Resnik, M. D., 27, 60, 87, 105
Richardson, H. S., 16
Rips, L. J., 31, 34, 214, 215, 221
Roberts, R., 37
Robinson, E. J., 246
Robinson, J. P., 168
Rogoff, B., 175, 175
Rokeach, M., 159, 168, 191
Ronis, D. L., 118
Rosenthal, R., 124, 134

Rosnow, R. L., 124, 134
Ross, J., 67
Ross, L., 4, 6, 26, 35, 55, 65, 74, 172, 195, 196, 198, 241
Rovai, E., 247
Rumain, B., 199
Russell, D., 168
Ruzgis, P., 156

S

Sá, W., 178, 190, 191, 198
Sackheim, H., 13
Sattath, S., 103
Savage, L. J., 15, 62, 100
Schaeken, W., 215
Schaller, M., 237
Scheffler, I., 156
Schiavo, M., 44, 63
Schick, F., 15, 98, 100, 105
Schlaifer, R., 15
Schmidt, F. L., 40, 153, 156, 188
Schmidtz, D., 8
Schneider, S. L., 107, 108
Schnitzler, M. A., 236
Schoenberger, A., 71
Schoenfeld, A. H., 194
Scholes, R. J., 63, 158, 169, 186, 237
Schommer, M., 158, 160, 169, 186, 237
Schooler, J. W., 243
Schrag, F., 157
Schueler, G. F., 16
Schustack, M. W., 46
Schwarz, N., 98
Scribner, S., 202
Sedlmeier, P., 233
Segal J., 162
Sejnowski, T. J., 234
Sen, A., 15, 102, 104
Shafer, G., 59, 103
Shafir, E., 2, 49, 86, 87, 88, 90, 93, 151, 173, 214, 229, 242
Shanks, D. R., 149
Shanteau, J., 103
Shaver, P. R., 168
Shell, P., 39, 157
Shields, H. A., 2
Shinotsuka, H., 2, 118
Shweder, R. A., 15, 102, 105, 220, 221

Siddiqui, S., 202
Sieck, W., 63, 106, 108
Siegel, H., 8, 156, 171
Siegler, R. S., 181
Sigel, I. E., 170
Simon, H. A., 3, 15, 37, 63, 202, 231, 241
Skyrms, B., 22, 23, 27, 88, 105, 148, 149, 150, 151, 203
Sloman, A., 158
Sloman, S. A., x, 115, 142, 144, 145, 147
Slovic, P., 2, 43, 54, 59, 62, 63, 64, 68, 78, 92, 97, 101, 103, 106, 128, 217, 241
Slugoski, B. R., 2, 123
Slusher, M. P., 164
Smith, E. E., 61, 63, 106, 246, 247
Smith, L., 236
Smith, S. M., 63, 106, 127, 144, 237
Snell, J., 16
Sowden, L., 86, 90
Spearman, C., 67, 94
Sperber, D., 35, 200
Spitz, H. H., 230
Stankov, L., 39, 121
Stanovich, K. E., 34, 35, 36, 37, 38, 39, 41, 44, 47, 49, 53, 68, 69, 72, 75, 79, 107, 109, 118, 121, 124, 129, 137, 139, 149, 154, 157, 159, 163, 168, 172, 178, 186, 190, 191, 198, 202, 228, 236, 237, 247
Stein, E., xi, 2, 6, 16, 18, 21, 22, 24, 25, 26, 27, 29, 32, 33, 34, 44, 56, 58, 60, 67, 151, 209, 214, 221, 232, 235
Steinnetz, J., 65
Sterelny, K., 9, 10, 11, 38
Sternberg, R. J., 46, 67, 137, 151, 156, 239, 240
Stevenson, R. J., 156, 192, 196
Stich, S. P., xiii, 3, 12, 16, 18, 21, 22, 27, 38, 44, 50, 52, 148, 151, 203, 212
Stich, S. P., 25, 26, 61, 106
Stigler, J. W., 175
Story, J., 74
Stough, C., 39, 157
Strykowski, B. F., 247
Sugden, R., 100

Sutherland, E., 129, 134
Swartz, R. J., 156
Swijtink, Z., 24

T

Tabachnik, N., 59, 245
Takemura, K., 63, 106, 144
Tavris, C., 175
Tesser, A., 118
Thagard, P., 18, 21, 23, 27, 59, 61, 105, 159, 203, 213
Thaler, R. H., 6, 34, 36, 109, 109, 110, 116, 214
Thompson, L. E., 242
Thorndike, R. L., 188
Tienson, J., 9
Tishman, S., 156, 157, 162
Toda, M., 118
Tooby, J., 8, 23, 58, 68, 72, 74, 83, 84, 192, 196, 206, 214, 223, 224, 232, 233, 249, 250
Tsai, S., 247
Tschirgi, J. E., 40, 66, 67
Turnbull, W., 40
Tversky, A., 1, 2, 3, 4, 6, 8, 15, 27, 35, 43, 54, 56, 62, 63, 64, 67, 68, 78, 86, 87, 88, 90, 92, 93, 99, 102, 103, 104, 105, 106, 107, 108, 117, 121, 122, 123, 124, 125, 127, 128, 142, 143, 147, 148, 196, 200, 214, 229, 233, 241
Tweney, R. D., 25, 44, 63, 134

U

Urbach, P., 56, 176, 203
Urbina, S., 67

V

Vachon, R., 67, 172
Vanderklok, M., 74
Varoufakis, Y., 88
Vernon, P. A., 39, 157
Verplanken, B., 63

von Mises, R., 56
Voss, J., 162

W

Wade, C., 175
Wagenaar, W. A., 54, 214
Walberg, H. J., 247
Walkenfeld, F. F., 137, 147
Walker, K., 160
Wang, D., 118
Wason, P. C., 35, 65, 66, 128, 130, 133,
        148, 171, 173, 194, 248
Wasserman, E. A., 39, 44, 45, 46, 47,
        149, 179
Watson, G., 163
Webster, D. M., 158, 160
Weir, E., 162
Wells, G. L., 27
Wenger, E., 175
West, R. F., 34, 35, 36, 37, 38, 39, 41, 44,
        47, 49, 68, 69, 72, 75, 79, 107,
        109, 118, 121, 124, 129, 137,
        139, 149, 154, 159, 163, 168,
        172, 178, 186, 190, 191, 198,
        202, 228, 236

Wetherick, N. E., 1, 5, 35, 54, 65, 66, 67,
        95, 133, 140, 141, 198, 216,
        229
Wethington, E., 204
Whynes, D., 6
Williams, S. J., 236
Wilson, A. E., 123
Wilson, D., 200
Wilson, T. D., 171, 206, 231, 243, 248
Windschitl, P. D., 27
Winman, A., 116
Wolfe, C. R., 44
Wrightsman, L. S., 168

Y

Yachanin, S., 134
Yang, Y., 215
Yates, J. F., 2, 61, 63, 106, 108, 118
Yohannes, J., 237

Z

Zacks, R. T., 250
Zechmeister, E. B., 162, 175
Zeiger, J., 55, 75, 76, 228, 245
Zhu, Y., 118

Subject Index

A

Actively open-minded thinking, 159–160, 190–191
AIDS problem, 71–74, 83–85, 228
Algorithmic level of analysis, 10–12, 37–38
Algorithmic limitation, *see* Computational limitations
Allais paradox, 100
Alternative hypothesis, 43–48, 79
Alternative task construal, *see* Construal of tasks
Analytic intelligence, *see* Intelligence
Analytic processing, 135, 144
Apologist position, 7, 28, 37, 52, 153, 159,189, 210, 223–228, 233–236
Argument evaluation task, 36, 154, 162–169, 179
Associative system, 142, 191–192

B

Baserates, 43, 56, 68–74, 81–83, 228
Bayes' rule, 43, 176
Bayesian reasoning, 43, 54, 64, 69
Belief bias, 34–35, 162–163, 176–180, 198–199, 244–249

Belief formation, 12–13
Beliefs, 12–14

C

Cab problem, 54, 68–71, 228
Charity, principle of, 17–21
Cognitive ability, 38–39, 49–52, 239–240, *see also* Intelligence, *see also* g
malleability of, 234–236
Cognitive capacity, 156–159, 171–172
Cognitive decontextualization, *see* Decontextualized reasoning
Cognitive ecologists 58, 206–207, 223–228, 232–235
Cognitive resource limitation, *see* Computational limitations
Cognitive science, 9–12
Cognitive styles, 156–159, 166–169, 171–172, 175, 190–191
Conjunction fallacy, 56, 121–128
Competence/performance distinction, 24, 95–96, 212–216
Computational limitations, 3, 7, 28, 33, 37–39, 49–52, 61, 153–154, 189, 209–211, 223, 234–236, 240–243
Consequentialist reasoning, 194–196

Construal of tasks, 6, 15, 28–29,
    98–102, 216–223, 241–243
    rational construal, 99–103, 148–152
    System 1 and System 2 and,
    146–147
Contextualist tradition, 175–176
Contextualization, 192
Cornell Critical Thinking Test, 162
Covariation detection, 39–40, 45–47,
    179, 245
Critical thinking, 162–163, 170–171,
    174–176
Cultural transmission of norms,
    234–236

D

Decontextualized reasoning, 169–174,
    191, 193–196, 203–207, 216,
    see also Cognitive
    decontextualization, 169–174
    empirical tests, 174–188
Decoupling, 174, 191
Desires, 12–14
Descriptive model, 3–7, 59–60
Domain generality, 174–176, 180–188
Dual-process models, *see*
    Two-process theories

E

Economics, 6
Education and rationality, 202, 236–237
Emotions, 212
Ennis-Weir Critical Thinking Essay
    Test, 162
Enthymematic thinking, 192–193, 196
Epistemic regulation, 159–160,
    190–191, 211–213
Evolution and rationality, 22–24,
    148–152, 192, 202–203,
    230–234, 238–239
Evolutionary optimization, 192–193
Expert reflective equilibrium, 26–27,
    105–107
Explicating normative rules, 78–86,
    95–96

F

False consensus effect, 55, 74–78, 228,
    245
Falsification research strategy, 44
Framing effects, 103–104, 106–107
Fundamental computational bias, 146,
    192–202, 216
    evolutionary adaptation and, 192,
    202–203

G

g, 39

H

Height judgment task, 179–184, 199
Heuristic processing, 135, 144–146
Heuristics and biases approach, 2, 6
Hindsight bias, 117–121
Hypothesis testing, 40

I

Inappropriate norm argument, 6, 28,
    53–56, 228–229
Independence axiom, 62, 100
Intelligence, 39, 61, 143, *see also* Cog-
    nitive ability
Intention-attribution, 143
Interactional intelligence, 143–144
If/only bias, 40
Illusions, visual vs. cognitive, 230, 233
Inconsistency detection, 12–13
Individual differences, 2, 153–156,
    212–216
Individuating outcomes, 100–101
Intentional stance, 11, 17–22, 212
Intentional level of analysis, 11–17,
    154, 159, 192, 211–213
Intuitions, 27

K

Knowledge calibration, 116–121
Knowledge projection argument,
    244–249

L

Laboratory task vs. real world, 204–207
Levels of analysis, 9–12, 158–159
Likelihood ratio, 43–46, 79, 176, *see also* P(D/~H)
Linda problem, 121–124, 197–198, 249
Linguistics, 24–26, 235–236
Literacy and cognitive decontextualization, 171–172, 193–194

M

Matthew effects in knowledge projection, 247–249
Meliorist position, 7, 28, 52, 53, 212, 216–220, 249–252
Mensa protocol, 130–131
Mental contamination, 246
Mental models, 215
Modularity, 145–146, 192, 224, 230, 238–239

N

Narrative mode of thought, 193
Naturalistic fallacy, 58–60
Need for cognition, 71, 79, 107, 159, 191
Newcomb's problem, 86–88
Norm abstraction method, 29
Normative/descriptive gap, 2, 5–6, 9, 28–30, 153–154, 189, 208, 231
Normative model, 3–7, 23–24, 53, 59–60
Normative rationality, 31, 148–152, 193, 202–203, 230–234, 238–239, 243–244

O

Optimal data selection, models of, 129, 134–135, 139–140, 238–239
Outcome bias, 40
Overconfidence effect, 56, 116–121, 228–229

P

Panglossian position, 5–7, 17, 28–30, 52, 53, 57–58, 209, 216–223, 234–236, 249–252
P(D/~H), 43–48, 79
Performance errors, 6, 28, 32–37, 48–49, 154, 189, 209
Personality traits, 158–159
Positive manifold, 67–68, 94
Preconceived norm method, 30
Prescriptive model, 3–7, 38, 50–52, 153, 159, 210
Prisoner's dilemma, 88–92
Probabilistic reasoning, 56
Probability theory, 55–56

R

Rational level of analysis, 10–12
Rationality₁ and rationality₂, 243–244
Rationality, 1–2, 4–9, 12–17, 23–24, 153–154, 159, 208, 231, 249–252
  as cultural product, 23–24, 27
  broad theory of, 16–17
  construal of tasks, rationality of, 99–103
  epistemic, 14–16, 213
  instrumental, 14, 101–102, 231
  practical, 14–16
  pretheoretical commitments, 4–9, 249–252, *see also* Apologist position, *see also* Meliorist position, *see also* Panglossian position
  theoretical, 14
  thin theory of, 15, 101
Reflective equilibrium, 24–27, 95–96, 105–107
Reject-the-norm strategy, 57–58
Remediation of cognition, 7–9
Resource limitations, *see* Computational limitations
Rule-based system, 142, 191–192

S

Scholastic Aptitude Test, 39
Selection task, 35, 51, 65, 128–133, 196–197, 224–225

deontic selection task, 128–129,
     134–135
models of performance on,
     133–141
Statistical reasoning, 35, 154, 198
Sunk cost problems, 109–115
Syllogistic reasoning, 34–35, 50, 154,
     178–179, 198, 245–246
individual differences and, 63–67,
     95–96
task construal and, 105–107
System 1/System 2, 144–147, 150–152,
     191–192, 195–198, 226–227,
     230, 234, 238–239, 243

T

Theory of mind, 246

Thinking dispositions, 156–159,
     166–169, 171–172, 175,
     190–191, 211–213, 215
Two-process theories, 135–140, 142,
     144–147, 191–192

U

Understanding/acceptance principle,
     61–63, 78, 92–94
Utility maximization, 192–193

W

Watson-Glaser Critical Thinking Ap-
     praisal, 163
Wishful thinking, 12

BLOOD GAME

AN EVANS NOVEL OF THE WEST

BLOOD GAME

EDWARD GORMAN

M. EVANS & COMPANY, INC.   NEW YORK

Library of Congress Cataloging-in-Publication Data

Gorman, Edward.

  Blood game / Edward Gorman.
    p. cm. — (An Evans novel of the West)
    ISBN 0-87131-596-3
    I. Title. II. Series.
  PS3557.0759B57 1989   89-23267
  813'.54—dc20

M. Evans and Company, Inc.
216 East 49 Street
New York, New York 10017

Manufactured in the United States of America

9 8 7 6 5 4 3 2 1

For Barb and Al Collins—the Beauty and the Best—
this homage to our friends Nolan and Quarry.

Chapter One

The boys were Mexican. They were about eighteen. Inside a rope ring each was stripped to the waist. Each wore snug brown leather gloves. They had ribs like hungry dogs'. The one boy had a decent left jab. The other boy had nothing at all. They had been sparring for half an hour in the sun. A dozen people stood in the small boxing camp in the alley of this midwestern town, and not one of them paid any attention to the two boys.

Guild sat on the edge of a rain barrel drinking lemonade and smoking a cigarette. A dog kept coming over with his wet black nose, and Guild kept petting him. In the sun Guild's hair was pure white, his eyes pure blue. The scar on his cleft chin had faded under his sunburn. He had spent the past three and a half weeks riding shotgun for one of the last stage lines in the Midwest. This was the summer of 1892, and as all the newspapers made note, the sun was merciless.

When one of the Mexican boys grunted and fell to the ground, Guild looked up and shook his head. He disliked boxing. He had once seen a redheaded kid go into convulsions, and ever since he'd had no stomach for the whole thing.

He would not have been here today if he wasn't, as usual, in need of money. The bounty-hunting business was going through one of its occasional lulls when the only criminals within five hundred miles seemed to be pimple-faced young clerks who had embezzled a few hundred dollars from mean employers. Having worked for his share of mean employers, Guild wished the pimple-faced young clerks well.

"You Guild?"

"Right."

"You come with me?"

"Sure."

The man wore a three-piece worsted suit far too heavy for the ninety-degree temperature. He carried a white surrender hand-kerchief in his hand and kept dabbing at his angular, pale face with it. He had nervous brown eyes. He wore a big navy Colt strapped in a creaking holster around his middle. The gun looked all wrong on him, like a pink garter on a nun.

They went in the rear entrance of the Northern Hotel and up a narrow flight of stairs, their boots making sharp rapping sounds on the wood.

They came out on the second-floor landing. The sunlight through the hall window was blinding white. In the center of it a hefty gray cat who looked capable of both stealth and wisdom rolled on his back in the light. Guild watched the cat as they continued their way down the hall. He reminded Guild of a cat he'd had during his married days.

When they came to room 246, the young man knocked three times with one knuckle. It almost appeared to be a code.

"Who is it?"

"Stephen."

"You're five goddamn minutes late."

"I'm sorry."

"When I say two o'clock, I mean two o'clock."

"Yes, sir."

2

"I don't mean two-oh-five."

"Yes, sir."

On the other side of the door, footsteps started coming toward them.

In a whisper, Stephen said, "That's my father. I'm sorry if that embarrassed you. He's just got one of those tempers is all."

Guild watched how the young man's right hand had begun to twitch. Stephen's face looked as if somebody had hit him very hard. He dabbed at his face again with the white handkerchief.

The door opened. A tall, stout man in a white shirt and tailored gray trousers and shiny black riding boots stood there. He held a drink of copper-colored bourbon in one hand and a dollar cigar in the other. His face looked fleshy but handsome. The expression he wore suggested he found the world had never quite lived up to his standards. Guild saw why a son of this man would be given to twitching.

"You're Guild?"

"Yes."

"Come in."

"Thank you."

"Oh. I'm Stoddard. John T. Stoddard."

He didn't offer to shake hands.

"You've heard of me?"

Guild nodded. "You're a boxing promoter."

"That's right, and a goddamned good one."

He said this with no irony. He said it, indeed, as a challenge.

"That's what I've heard," Guild said, as John T. Stoddard obviously expected him to say. When he was between good jobs like this, he did not mind on occasion eating a one-pound bag of shit. It was the two-pound bags that gave him problems.

Guild sat in a chair the color of dirty greenbacks. The room was heavily trimmed in mahogany. Deep maroon carpeting and white flocked drapes gave the place the feel of an expensive lawyer's office. John T. Stoddard sat in the center of a vast leather couch. He spread his arms out wide on either side of him. He gave the air of a potentate granting an interview with peasants.

3

"Did Stephen tell you about the job?"

"No."

"Good. He usually gets things wrong."

The cruelty of the remark caused Guild to look up at Stephen Stoddard. He stood to the right of the couch like a servant awaiting his next command. He refused to meet Guild's eyes, but Guild could see the faint pulsing twitch of his right arm.

"He does all right," Guild said to John T. Stoddard.

"I didn't bring you up here to talk about my son."

"All right."

"Do you know who Victor Sovich is?"

"Maybe."

"Are you being smart?"

"No."

"I don't like people being smart."

"I said 'maybe' because the name is familiar but I'm not sure who he is exactly." Now Guild felt like the young man. He wondered if his right arm, too, would begin to twitch.

"He's a boxer."

"Oh."

"Just about the best boxer in the United States."

"I see."

"You could show a little more goddamn enthusiasm."

"I guess I should tell you."

"Tell me what?"

"I don't much care for boxing."

"And just why not?"

"I don't like to see people do that to each other. You should only do it when you have to."

"I asked the sheriff here who would be good for this job, and he said there was a bounty hunter in town. I didn't expect a bounty hunter to be a nelly."

Guild flushed. A two-pound bag of fecal matter had just been pushed his way. He pushed it right back.

Guild stood up and said, "I want you to know something, Mr. Stoddard. In your small circle of friends and admirers, you're probably a very big deal. But you're nothing to me or most of the world. Do you understand that?"

Guild wanted to smash the man's face.

"It's just the way he is, Mr. Guild," Stephen Stoddard said. "He almost can't help it."

"Well, somebody better teach him to help it."

"I'm sorry I made that remark, Guild," John T. Stoddard said. "A lot of decent people are opposed to boxing. I probably would be myself if I didn't make so goddamn much money from it."

Stephen Stoddard gestured to his father. "You see, Mr. Guild. He isn't so bad."

"Right," Guild said. "He's a sugar baby."

"Please sit down, Mr. Guild. Please. My father really needs your help."

Guild looked at the young man and wondered why he acted so nice to a man who took every opportunity to berate and humiliate him.

Probably because he was curious, Leo Guild sat down.

John T. Stoddard gave Guild a cigar, and then Stephen Stoddard got them lemonade, and then John T. Stoddard started talking.

Chapter Two

The thing was, John T. Stoddard said, white people liked to see colored people get the hell kicked out of them. This was in general. While John T. Stoddard personally had nothing against colored people and had in fact supported the Union in the war, as a boxing promoter he would be foolish not to give the boxing public what it was looking for.

He used three examples. A year ago in San Francisco a kid named John L. Sullivan had fought a black man named Peter Jackson. The fight had gone sixty-one rounds. The crowd loved it. A month earlier a black man who was considered "the colored champion" had packed an arena when he'd fought Jake Kilrain. He'd lost to Kilrain. Then there was the business in Texas when a white man named O'Toole fought a mulatto named Waylou. The fight, according to one newspaper account John T. Stoddard read, had gone seventy-two rounds and ended only when Waylou's right eye popped out of its socket. Waylou stuffed it back in, but the referee, bowing to the outspoken demands of some Lutheran ladies who'd come to monitor the fight, called the fight over.

7

"My problem has been," John T. Stoddard said, "finding the right colored man to fight Victor."

"Victor Sovich?"

"Victor Sovich."

"And you've come up with a colored man?"

"Indeed I have, Mr. Guild. Or better yet, you call me John and I'll call you Leo."

John T. Stoddard smiled as if he'd just ceded the Louisiana Territory to Guild.

"If you've got the colored man, and the public wants to see a black man and a white man fight, I guess I don't understand what you need me for." Guild tried to call him "John," but it didn't work. He couldn't get the word to leave his mouth.

"The problem," John T. Stoddard said, "is Victor."

"Victor?"

"He's mad at me."

The way he said it, as if they were playmates in a spat, almost made Guild smile.

"Why is he mad at you?"

"That part doesn't matter, Leo. What matters is that we convince him to get back here in time for the fight Saturday afternoon."

"Where is he?"

"Across town."

"Doing what?"

"If I know Victor, he's soaking up the suds and spending all the time he can with Mexican women. He loves Mexican women, just before they go to fat. You understand?"

Guild nodded. "So what am I supposed to do?"

"Get him for me."

"How am I supposed to do that?"

"Take him this envelope. When he sees it, he'll come along."

"If it's so easy, why don't you do it?"

"Because he wouldn't even give me the chance to hand him the envelope. He'd just start swinging."

Stephen Stoddard said, "He's a genuine madman, Mr. Guild,

8

Victor is. A genuine madman. I once saw him knock a Brahma bull out with one punch."

"Great," Guild said, "and I'm supposed to go get him."

"The sheriff said that's the sort of thing you do," John T. Stoddard said.

"If you mean Sheriff Cardinelli," Guild said, "he only says things like that after about three or four schooners. He always gets sentimental and likes to talk about how tough all his former deputies are. I suppose it reflects on how well he trained us thirty years ago."

"You worked for him here?"

"No. Up in the territory. Near the border."

"Oh."

Guild sighed. "I'm not your man."

"What?" John T. Stoddard looked shocked.

"I'm fifty-five years old. I've got a crimped right knee from a riding accident, and I'm used to dealing with criminals, who most of the time are willing to have you bring them in because they're tired of running and hiding. Victor doesn't sound as if he'll be happy to see me at all."

"You're afraid of him, then?" John T. Stoddard said.

"Of course."

"I can't believe you're admitting this."

"Why wouldn't I admit it?"

"Well, because."

"Because as a bounty hunter I'm supposed to be big and strong and brave?"

"I guess something like that."

Guild stood up, fanned at his sweaty face with his Stetson. He was playing something of a game and he was about to see if all his theatrics were about to pay off. He had immediately sized up John T. Stoddard as a cheapskate, a man who would expect a man to accept whatever pittance he felt like paying. Obviously, there weren't many men in this town willing to deliver the envelope to Victor, whatever the fee. Guild figured he should get a good dollar.

"You're leaving?" John T. Stoddard said.

"I'm leaving."

"I'd think pride alone would make you take this job."

"Well, you'd be wrong."

Now John T. Stoddard stood. "How much do you think I was going to offer you?"

Guild considered a moment. He wanted to name a price that would establish a high ceiling. "Fifty dollars."

"Fifty dollars!" John T. Stoddard moved with the large, melodramatic motions of an opera star in his dying moments on stage. "Who would pay you fifty dollars just to deliver an envelope?"

"I wouldn't take fifty dollars, anyway. I'd want seventy-five."

"Seventy-five!"

Guild fanned himself some more with his hat and waited for what he sensed was the right moment and then turned to go.

"Do you realize how many young boys you're letting down?"

This one was so good Guild had to stop halfway to the door and turn around. "Beg pardon?"

"Young boys. In this town. Do you know how many of them have their hopes up to see Victor Sovich?" He paused and threw a wild hand toward the heavens. "Do you read magazines, Leo?"

"Sometimes."

"Have you ever read articles on how disappointment can stunt a young boy's mental development?"

"I see," Guild said. "If they don't see Victor on Saturday, they might be mentally stunted."

"You can scoff if you like, Leo. But that's exactly what we're dealing with here."

"Sixty-five dollars," Leo Guild said.

John T. Stoddard glared at Guild as if he were one of those socialists now stirring up labor trouble around the country. "You would put your own pocketbook above the well-being of eight-year-old boys?"

Guild shook his head. "Yeah, I guess that's the kind of low-down son of a bitch I really am."

Stephen Stoddard, whom Guild already liked anyway, had the good grace to laugh. At least until his father glared at him.

Chapter Three

He had sixty-five dollars' worth of John T. Stoddard's green-backs in his wallet, he was smoking one of John T. Stoddard's stogies, and he was sitting across the aisle in the streetcar from a very nice looking fortyish woman in a big picture hat. Her occasional glances at the six-foot Guild in his white boiled shirt, black suitcoat, black serge trousers, and black Texas boots said that he was probably a rapscallion, but an interesting one. Only when her soft brown gaze fell to the .44 strapped around his waist did her lips purse in that social disapproval city folks display for people not their kind.

In addition to watching the woman, Guild just enjoyed the ride. He liked the way the streetcar ran down the center of the sprawling town with its three- and four-story buildings and all its buggies and rigs and wagons. He enjoyed watching all the men in straw boaters and high-buttoned suits and the women in flowered hats and twirling red and blue and yellow parasols, and he liked seeing all the big shiny store windows filled variously with high-button shoes and fresh bakery goods and pharmaceuticals and barbers in dark suit coats and handlebar mustaches stropping their razors and patting shaving cream on sagging faces. There was a music to the city that he sometimes longed for, the announcing clang of streetcars, the hoarse whistle of the factory changing shifts, the traffic policeman's street corner instructions to keep moving, keep moving, the sweet passing laughter of women he could at least dream about.

The woman he'd been playing eye games with got off about three blocks before he did, and as usual he felt a vast and personal disappointment, as if she'd been the woman he'd been meant to marry only she hadn't understood this and had gone shopping for rutabagas instead, and with not so much as a glance back at him. Not a glance.

The city changed abruptly. Where the stone and brick and wooden business buildings had given way to wide streets lined with forbidding iron gates and what passed for mansions in a midwestern town this size, so then did the mansions give way. Now the streets narrowed and the houses grew smaller and uglier in appearance, immigrant houses already sixty years old, older than the town's incorporation itself. Wild, filthy children ran the streets, and a cornucopia of garbage—the red of tomato rinds, the yellow of gutted squash, the tainted brown of sun-rotting fly-infested beef—filled curbstones and gutters alike.

Mothers bellowed harshly for their children, threatening enormous violence if the kids did not show their faces soon. Drunks wound and wove amid it all, one poor bastard puking into a garbage can, puking blood. There were cats and dogs and a few horses, all rib-gaunt and glassy-eyed from malnutrition, and here and there you saw a man smack a woman hard in the face or belly, and you saw a woman bash a man with a broom. White faces, black faces, brown faces, red faces, all showed the toil taken by living here. The sadness so easily became rage, and the rage so easily became despair. This was the part of city life Guild hated, the eternal poor and their eternal doom.

When he stepped off the platform of the streetcar, he took from the pocket of his coat the piece of paper John T. Stoddard had given him containing Victor Sovich's address.

The house stood two stories tall. It looked as though it had once been green. Now there was so much grime it was hard to tell what color it was. Not a single window remained intact. Cans, newspapers, pages of magazines, and plump brown dog turds covered the thin grass of the front yard. A small mulatto child, perhaps a year and a half, lay naked on the front step, fondling himself and crying.

A woman with a leaf-shaped paper fan bearing the name of a funeral home on its front side leaned in the doorway, watching Guild approach. Next to her squatted a dog with dirty white fur. From what he could see of the woman, she looked Mexican.

"Hello."

"What do you want?"

"I'm looking for a man named Victor Sovich."

"I don't know a man named like that."

Beneath the thin white cotton of her dusty dress, a beautiful, breathtaking set of breasts rose and fell with her breathing.

Guild sensed eyes watching him from all the windows of this tightly packed neighborhood. A word from her and two or three young men would no doubt appear, and Guild, if he wasn't quick and ruthless enough with his .44, would most likely be sorry.

"I have some money for him. Five hundred dollars."

He felt sorry for the quick, cheap light in her brown eyes. She had so little money, the child at her feet obviously malnourished, that mention of it made her almost ugly with desire. "Money you say?"

"Money. Five hundred dollars."

"For this Victor?"

"For Victor. Yes."

Guild would never be sure what happened next. No matter how many times he tried to reconstruct it, he just couldn't get the sequence straight.

Apparently Victor Sovich had been hiding in the vestibule right behind the woman. No other position would have allowed him to catapult out of the house. Or maybe he didn't catapult out of the house. Maybe Sovich came from behind him. Or from the side. Not that it mattered.

The man with the fancy tattoos and the gray chest hair and the slick-shaven head and the biceps like coconuts started his attack by hitting Guild in the ribs.

Not that Sovich gave him a chance to do anything about it.

Before Guild's fists came up reflexively, Sovich hit him twice in the face and once more in the stomach.

Guild knew that he was bleeding, knew that he had peed his pants, and knew that he was making some kind of vague mewling sound.

Then Sovich slammed a right cross straight into Guild's crotch.

If Guild was not precisely unconscious at that point, he certainly was when his head slammed against the ground.

Chapter Four

"You keep this one there," the Mexican woman said twenty minutes later, bending into Guild's face with her soft breasts and her breath smelling of spicy Mexican food.

Guild lay on a red daybed in a white room. The hot sunlight shone directly on him through the room's single window. The room stank of food and tobacco smoke and heat. His head hurt and his jaw hurt, but neither hurt half so much as his groin. In the hallway outside, he could hear kids running up and down the wooden steps, screaming and laughing. One of them kept saying the dirtiest word Guild ever heard anybody say. The kid couldn't have been more than five.

"He lost his temper, Victor."

Guild tapped his sports coat. "He also took his money."

"You know what he did with the money?"

"What?"

"He burned it."

"What?"

He saw tears in her eyes. She shook her head in anger and a curious kind of fascination. "Look."

She showed him the white envelope John T. Stoddard had given him. She opened it up like an oyster. He peeked inside. Black curled ashes filled the white envelope.

"He is crazy sometimes."

"I'm sorry."

"He was cheated."

"Victor?"

She nodded. "I do not blame him for being mad."

"Who cheated him?"

"Stoddard."

"How much did he cheat him out of?"

"Many, many thousands. They have a—what is the word? Paper you sign?"

"Contract?"

"Yes. Contract. They have contract giving Victor half of everything. He gets nothing except five hundred dollars every three or four months. It is not fair."

"Where is Victor now?"

"He's in the kitchen."

Guild raised his head. He could never recall being hit so hard or so often without being able to swing back.

"What's he doing in the kitchen?"

"He's waiting for you."

"He wants to hit me again?"

"No. He only wants to talk."

"To me?"

"Yes."

Guild patted his right hip. His .44 was there. He drew it out and looked it over. "I'm taking this into the kitchen with me."

"He will understand. He knows how he can get."

"You tell him if he tries to hit me again, I'll kill him right on the spot."

She surprised him by smiling. "He scares you?" There was a certain pride in her voice.

"Absolutely. Now you go tell him."

She went away with her sweet, swaying breasts and long, good legs and bare, slapping feet. Guild sat up. He moaned several times and cursed. He checked his Ingram. He had been out for over half an hour. He focused his eyes. There was no evidence of concussion that he could tell. His groin was so painful, he was afraid to move.

The Mexican woman came back. "He asked if you would like a glass of beer."

"That would be nice, yes."

"He asked if you would like a cigarette."

"That would be nice, too." He paused. "Did you tell him what I said about killing him if he tries to hit me?"

"He is calm now. The only time you have to worry about Victor is when he is not calm."

Guild tried to stand up.

The undignified mewling sound came from his chest again.

The Mexican woman reached down and helped him stand. She put her arm around his shoulder and walked him across the sun-hot floor and down a small hallway past walls the kids had drawn circles and lines and sort of Aztec faces on with pencils.

The kitchen was a tiny room with a wobbly wooden table and four chairs and a stove and an icebox. It smelled of sour milk and beer and beans. Fat black flies squatted everywhere, the webs of their wings iridescent blue and green in the sunlight.

Victor sat naked to the waist behind the table. His shaven head was sleek and sweaty in the yellow daylight. From a bucket of beer he poured two glasses. He set one on the table for himself. The other one he shoved toward Guild.

"You'll be all right," Victor Sovich said.

"Thanks for the diagnosis, doctor."

"I've hit men a lot harder than I hit you, and they've been fine." He nodded to an empty chair. "You going to sit down?"

"The woman told you what I said?"

"About killing me?" He grinned.

"I'm glad you find it funny."

17

"Look, friend, your pride's been hurt. You'll get over it."

Guild knew there wasn't anything else to do. He sat down. He drank the beer. It was warm and cheap, with too much grain.

"How'd you get hooked up with John T.?" Victor Sovich said.

"The sheriff told him about me."

"The sheriff?"

"I'm a bounty hunter."

"Nice job."

"So is bashing people's heads in."

He laughed. "I guess you got me there, friend."

"You burned the money."

"Yeah, I burned the money, and I want you to tell John T. I burned the money. He won't believe it. He'll throw one of his goddamn fits. You wait and see."

"So you're not going to fight Saturday?"

"Sure I am."

"What?"

"Sure. We go through this in half the towns we're in. I walk off and he sends somebody after me and I beat that somebody up and then he agrees to pay me a certain amount up front before the fight. It's just a game."

Guild's groin sent pain all the way down into his ankles. "Some game."

"He's cheated hell out of me over the years. 'Expenses,' he'd always say. That's why there was always so little to split up at the end. Expenses, my ass. So last year I got smart. I started making him pay me my share up front." He had some beer. When he took the glass away he had a white foam mustache. It should have been comic. It just made him look meaner. "Tell him I want two thousand or nothing."

"That seems like a lot."

"It is a lot, but he's going to make a lot. I saw this colored kid. He's going to be good."

"You mean he's tough?"

"No, I mean he'll help me put on a good show. Didn't John T. tell you how it works?"

"Apparently not."

"The colored kids, they don't try to win. They can't win. They get paid by the round. They get paid for every round they stay on their legs. And they get paid more as the fight goes on." He smiled. "Of course John T. cheats them, too."

"How long do they usually last?"

"Five, six rounds. If they're lucky. Boy in Ohio went twenty rounds. He was a good one."

"He must have been a mess."

"Didn't John T. tell you that, either?"

"Tell me what?"

"About the boys I killed."

"Killed?"

"Yeah. He uses that in the advertising. How I've killed six boys in the last four years. It really gets the yokels worked up. You know how boxing fans are. A part of them wants to see a good clean fight, but another part of them wants to see somebody die." He shrugged meaty shoulders. "Anyway, this boy in Ohio, he went twenty rounds all right, but he was dead before they could get him out of the ring." He had some more beer. "The goddamn church groups went nuts, let me tell you. We had to leave town within two hours."

"You think you'll kill this new colored boy?"

He smiled again. "I take it you don't care for boxing."

"Not much."

"I won't kill him unless it just happens that way. I don't have much time for niggers, but I don't kill them on purpose, if that's what you mean." He stared at Guild. "You expected me to be dumb, didn't you?"

"I suppose."

"You're looking at the only boxer in the United States with a high school diploma."

"I'm impressed."

"You should be. Do you have a high school diploma?"

"No."

"I didn't think so."

"You want to know why I went into boxing instead of banking or something?"

"Why?"

"I enjoy killing people. Now, that may sound like a contradiction. Just a minute ago I said I don't kill people on purpose, and I don't. But when I *do* kill people, well, I can get away with it legally as long as it's in a ring. It gives me a certain kind of satisfaction. It really does."

A lot of tough guys like to tell you how tough they are. They like to sit over schooners for hours on end and tell you how tough they've been and how tough they are and how tough they're going to be in the future. With most of them it's bragging, because finally they're not tough at all. They just like to bully people with their words. But sometimes you meet a man who is truly tough, and he likes to tell you about it, too. Those are the ones you can't figure. They don't have to brag because you already believe them, but they brag anyway. Maybe they're just bored.

Victor Sovich was that way. After what he'd done to Guild, Guild had no doubt that the man was a genuine killer, nor any doubt even that he took pleasure in the killing. But this little speech was all sideshow barker horseshit, and Guild was sick of it and sick of Sovich.

Guild stood up. "I'll go tell Stoddard you burned the money."

"He'll throw a fit. You wait and see. A regular fit."

Guild snugged down his Stetson and started for the door.

Victor Sovich said, "You know something, Guild?"

"What's that?"

"I really think you would shoot me if I gave you half a chance."

Then he started laughing. The sound was loud and harsh in the small, sunny kitchen.

On his way out Guild passed the Mexican woman, who had been eavesdropping in the hallway.

Guild took her by the elbow and walked her to the door with him. "You owe it to your kids not to get mixed up with somebody like that. You understand me?"

She nodded. She had tears in her eyes. "I can't help it. I love him."

Guild shook his head and went on down the stairs.

Chapter Five

Stephen Stoddard stood in the open doorway. Guild pushed him out of the way and went straight across the room to the couch where John T. Stoddard sat so baronially.

Stoddard saw what was about to happen. He tried to climb backward up the couch, but it didn't work.

Guild shoved the barrel of the .44 directly into his face. From his shirt pocket he took a receipt and shoved this in Stoddard's face, too.

"What's this?" Stoddard said.

"What the doctor charged to look me over, you son of a bitch."

"You've got a temper, cowboy."

It was the wrong thing to say. Guild hit Stoddard hard enough in the mouth to cut his lip pretty badly. Thick red blood flowed from a pink wound on Stoddard's lower lip. He made the sort of mewling sound Guild had made earlier.

Peripherally Guild saw Stephen Stoddard move toward him. He had made a fist of his hand. It wasn't much of a hand to begin with and it sure as hell wasn't much of a fist.

"Please, kid," Guild said. "You're a nice boy. Let this be between your old man and me."

John T. Stoddard said, "He's right, Stephen. You go on down to the restaurant and have some dinner."

"But—"

"You go on now."

Guild had never heard Stoddard speak so softly or courteously to the young man.

Stephen Stoddard sighed and nodded. "You aren't going to hurt him anymore, are you, Mr. Guild?"

"Not unless he forces me to."

"He isn't so bad. He really isn't."

Guild's jaw set. "Kid, don't try and sell him to me, all right? You've got your opinions and I've got mine."

"You go on now, Stephen," John T. Stoddard said.

Stephen sighed again and left the room.

"You want a drink, Leo?"

"Don't call me Leo."

"It's all right if you call me John."

"I don't want to call you John, and I don't want you to call me Leo."

"You're one pissed-off man."

"He told me it was a game."

"Who told you what was a game?"

"Sovich told me that you and he do this sort of thing all the time. You hire somebody to get him back here, and sometimes he beats them up."

"Let me reassure you, this is no game. There's twenty thousand dollars at stake here on Saturday."

"Twenty thousand dollars?"

"You figure up all the wagers and that's just what you get."

"And how much do you make?"

"Are you going to put that goddamn gun away or what?"

Guild sighed. "You two deserve each other. You and Sovich. He tells me he killed some colored boys in the ring."

"Those things happen."

Guild wanted to hit him again, but he knew how Stoddard's son would get. The kid had plenty of grief already.

Guild waved the receipt at him again. "I want you to reimburse me for this right now, and then I never want you to bother me again. For anything. You understand that?"

"You're a strange man, Guild. No offense." Stoddard reached in his pocket. He paid in greenbacks.

A minute later Guild walked out. He slammed the door as hard as he could.

Chapter Six

Eating wasn't so easy. He ate a piece of steak that he had to cut up into tiny pieces, he ate American fries which he had to mash down, and he ate peas which were just fine. It was his jaw; it was sorer now than it had been six hours ago when he'd been hit.

He sat at a front window table of the Family Steak Restaurant, watching dusk bleed from the sky and the stars come out.

Nearer by, streetlights came on, lending the buildings wan light and deep shadows. People, mostly couples, strolled the business district, pointing out things in windows or simply standing on corners and taking in the air. You could smell rain coming, clear and clean and fine. The temperature had dropped fifteen degrees. After the heat today, the chill was a pure blessing.

Guild ate his custard and sipped his coffee. Because of cuts inside his mouth, he had to let the coffee cool, so he read the local paper, most especially "The City in Brief," which included such items as:

Ten businessmen were caught in a crap-shooting game last night.

Two young people eloped on bicycles from Oquawka, Illinois, and were married at Ottumwa.

Our compositors made Reverend Dr. Tilden's subject for yesterday morning read "Infidelity and Her Crown," when it should have read "Fidelity and Her Crown." (This struck Guild as very funny.)

Mr. Frank Redmond, a new baritone in our city, will sing at the Elks Minstrels tomorrow night.

Geo. Williams carries a full line of Blatz and Schlitz bottled beer for family use. Telephone No. 133.

Try a Turkish Bath at Ford's. You will like it.

Guild smoked a cigar with his second cup of coffee. Then he noticed the woman. She was one of those women it would be difficult not to notice.

She sat alone four tables away, gazing out the window. The first thing he noticed about her was how prim and pretty she was in her frilly, high-necked dress and sweet, angled little hat. He supposed she was forty or so. The second thing he noticed was the high, beautiful color of her skin. She was most likely a mulatto. In midwestern cities women who could "pass" were allowed to eat in white restaurants.

If she was aware of Guild's presence, she kept it a secret to herself.

Given the lingering pain in his jaw, he needed a distraction. She provided it. Like most lonely people, he speculated on the lives of strangers. What they did. What they wanted. Where they'd come from and where they were going. The trouble was, this woman being a mulatto, his usual line of speculation didn't work. Mulattos were especially despised. The only thing he could think she would want was to be left alone by men who wanted her carnally and by good citizens who wanted to express their contempt.

The hell of it was, that this woman with her dark eyes and full, exotic mouth did not look at all as if she needed Guild's understanding or pity. Indeed, there was even a certain haughtiness in the way she sat there, dismissing everyone who passed by with a disinterested glance, returning her gaze inevitably to the street

28

and the clip-clop of fancy buggies and the first silver drops of rain sliding down the window.

Several times he started to go to her table and introduce himself, but he always stopped. He wasn't good at this sort of thing. His heart would get to hammering and his throat would twist into a snake of silence and his palms would get sweaty. He would stand there and everyone would stare at him and he would stand there some more and they would stare at him some more and finally he'd just sort of nod and leave, his face burning with embarrassment and his mind already flaying himself for his terrible performance.

When it came time for sex, he stuck to brothels. He didn't get crushes on whores; whores never broke his heart.

By this time, still sitting at his window table in the Family Steak Restaurant, Guild was reduced to little eye games. He'd pretend to be vastly interested in whatever was going on in the street. Then he'd kind of ease his gaze back to her, convinced that this time she'd be noticing him.

Only she never did notice him, of course.

And at 9:03, when he very slyly brought his gaze back around again to see if she was watching him, she was gone. He glimpsed her long, graceful back at the cash register, her sweet little hat floating just above the heads of the crowd at the front door, and then—

Gone.

He supposed he was being asinine, but loneliness was a burden sometimes and seemed especially a burden tonight.

He paid his bill and splurged on a fifty-cent cigar and went out to walk the streets. He could hear the vaudeville show over at the opera house, the harmonies of the popular ballads melancholy and irresistible.

Chapter Seven

He tried a whorehouse, but just standing downstairs in the vestibule convinced him. Whores couldn't help him tonight.

He did the second-best thing. He started at one end of a long city block and drank his way, beer-and-shot, beer-and-shot, to the other end of the block. There were nine saloons on that block. Nine of them.

In the morning when he awakened in the hotel, he found a plain white envelope on the stand next to the bed. The envelope depressed him. Not knowing where it had come from or what it contained reminded him that he'd been pretty bad last night. He did not drink liquor that often or that much, but when he did, and did so indulgently, the hangover always brought on memories of the little girl he'd shot and killed. Now he saw her six-year-old face and her patched gingham dress as she moved from the shadows of her cabin. By then it had been too late. He had already fired.

He looked at the way the dust motes glinted gold in the sunlight. He stared out the window at the hard blue sky until the little girl's face vanished. His bladder was full and his mouth was dry. His head pounded. Jesus, was he stupid.

He had just returned from the bathroom down the hall ten minutes later when the knock came.

He was dressed and already packing. He wanted to get out of this town. He had come here to try to earn some money, but instead he'd only met Stoddard and been beaten for his troubles. His bones still ached from the beating, but the hangover ached more.

He opened the door on the fifth knock. He jerked it open with some aggravation. He was not good at hangovers and tended to take them out on other people.

"You found the envelope, Mr. Guild?" Stephen Stoddard asked.

"How the hell did it get here?"

"I had the clerk bring it up last night."

"What is it?"

"You mean you haven't looked inside?"

"I'm too goddamned hung over for games, kid. What's in the envelope?"

"A hundred and fifty dollars."

"For what?"

"My father's money needs protection."

"You want to know what I think of your father, kid?"

"I'm willing to make it two hundred, Mr. Guild. For two days' work."

Even dehydrated and somewhat shaky, Guild thought the idea of two hundred dollars for two days' work sounded good.

"I need some breakfast," Guild said.

"They serve a very fine one here. I ate here yesterday. Toast and scrambled eggs and ham."

Guild smiled. "You sound like an ad in the newspaper." His stomach made noises. He'd done a lot of drinking last night but not enough eating. He went back, leaving Stephen Stoddard in the doorway, picked up the envelope, and said, "Let's go get some breakfast."

* * *

"I finally had to grab the shotgun and put it right to his face. I've seen Victor pretty mad before, but nothing like last night. Not even close, Mr. Guild."

"Will you do me a favor?"

"What?"

"Stop calling me Mr. Guild."

"Oh. Sure."

"Leo will do fine."

For the next few minutes Guild went back to his eggs over easy and his American fries and his two thick slices of ham.

Stephen Stoddard knew enough to just let him eat.

As he sipped his coffee, Guild said, "You really think Victor wanted to kill him?"

"Yes, he did."

"He just barged into your hotel room?"

"Just barged in."

"And ran over to your father and started hitting him?"

"Yes. And that's when I grabbed the rifle." He shook his head. "I put it right up against his cheek. I would have killed him, too, the way he was beating Dad."

Guild frowned and looked around the restaurant. It was beautifully decorated with flocked red wallpaper and gathered white drapes and mahogany appointments. Sunlight came in golden and warm through the front windows. Fancy men in three-piece suits sat talking to each other with great amounts of self-confidence. Women in big picture hats spoke more quietly.

"I believe Victor," Guild said, looking back at Stephen Stoddard.

"About what?"

"About your father cheating him."

Stephen Stoddard dropped his eyes. "My father doesn't cheat people."

"Sure he does, kid, and you know it." Guild realized how harsh he sounded. "I'm sorry I had to say that, but in case I decide to take your two hundred dollars I want you to know where I stand."

"I don't suppose it's important that you respect Dad, as long as you protect him."

Guild grinned. "I couldn't protect myself from Victor yesterday. What makes you think I can protect your father?"

"You'd kill Victor if he tried anything. I know you would. The sheriff told my dad all about you."

Whenever people said that to Guild, he wondered if they knew about the little girl. There were a lot of lies told about Guild in and out of the territory. Most of them had started over the death of the little girl.

Guild said, in a softer tone, "Why do you stay with him, kid? The way he treats you and all."

"You don't know anything about him." For the first time Stephen Stoddard sounded angry. For the first time Guild felt a little respect for the kid.

"Such as what?"

"Such as how he had to raise me after my mother ran off with a drummer ten years ago. Or how he was raised in the worst white slum in New York. Or how he was taken prisoner in the war and tortured by three Confederates."

Guild sighed. You could make a case for anybody. You could even make a case for Guild, a man who'd killed a six-year-old girl.

"I guess I was getting a little pompous there," Guild said.

Stephen Stoddard calmed down. "He really is a decent man. After all is said and done, I mean."

"He shouldn't have sent me over to Victor's."

"He really thought Victor would take the money and come back."

Guild asked him a question he'd been curious about since yesterday. "If Victor's so hot on the idea your father is cheating him, why doesn't he go to some other boxing promoter?"

In the strong sunlight, Stephen Stoddard blushed. "I'm not sure."

"You're lying, kid. Your father's got something on him, doesn't he?"

"Please don't ask me any more about that, Mr. Guild."

Guild stared down at the envelope between them. He could live four or five months on the money in there.

He told himself he had no right to judge John T. Stoddard. He couldn't figure out if he was just saying that to allow himself to take the money. As for Victor—Victor didn't scare him anymore. The kid was right. If Guild signed on, he'd be prepared to shoot the boxer. That was the only way he could be sure he'd survive the two days.

"So you're not going to tell me what your father's got on him?"

"No," Stephen Stoddard said softly. "No, I'm not."

Chapter Eight

At sight of Victor Sovich, Guild drew his .44 and aimed it directly at the boxer's middle. This was an hour after finishing breakfast with Stephen Stoddard.

Sovich, dressed in the type of black suit and white shirt and red-lined cape you would expect to see on an opera baritone, walked into the boxing camp smiling.

Guild, John T. Stoddard, and Stephen Stoddard all stood staring at him.

"You'd better tell Guild here that guns don't always frighten me," Sovich said, strolling up.

It was hot in the alley, just as it had been yesterday afternoon, though thunderheads had begun massing in the flat blue midwestern sky and there was a promise of a brief respite from the heat.

The two Mexican boys were in the rope ring again. They would precede Sovich and the black man. Guild just hoped the skinnier of the boys somehow learned to box between now and tomorrow afternoon.

A small group of reporters stood in the wide mouth of the alley, to the left of the livery stable, where you could smell heat and iron and smoke, talking to a small, prim group of churchwomen who were here to protest fisticuffs in general and any fight with Victor Sovich in particular.

"I wish I could turn you loose on them," John T. Stoddard said, nodding to the women.

"I wouldn't do it," Guild said. "I agree with them, remember?"

By now Sovich was directly in front of them.

Guild glanced up, sensing Stephen Stoddard's eyes on him. The kid could obviously sense what Guild was thinking.

Here was Sovich coming back to a partnership in which he was constantly cheated. Yesterday he had burned Stoddard's money. He had been through with the relationship. His presence here today could only mean that Stoddard had telephoned or sent a note—reminding Sovich that if money hadn't wooed him back, then maybe a certain memory would.

Guild wondered what Sovich had done.

John T. Stoddard said, "Victor, I don't expect any trouble between us. I've agreed to give you half the purse tomorrow. But I want Guild here to make sure that everything runs smoothly. I want tomorrow to be a good day for us."

"You just keep Guild out of my way," Sovich said, glaring at Guild.

"He'll be with me, Victor. That's the whole point of having him. But he won't bother you unless he needs to. Right, Guild?"

Guild felt as if he were stepping into the middle of an argument between two ten-year-olds.

"He'd better be damn good with that gun," Sovich said, "for his own sake."

"We'll have those boys take a rest," John T. Stoddard said, "and you can get in there and work out with Barney. I hope you didn't hit the bottle too hard last night."

"It wasn't the bottle," Sovich grinned. "It was the woman. Those goddamn hips of hers never stop."

Unlikely as it seemed, John T. Stoddard slid his arm around

Sovich's bear shoulders, and together they walked back to the two rooms in the livery stable used for dressing.

Halfway there, however, John T. turned around and nodded his head at Guild.

He wanted him to come along.

Given Sovich's power and temperament, that was probably a good idea.

John T. Stoddard hadn't been exaggerating. There was every possibility that Victor Sovich was the best fighter in the country.

His sparring partner, Barney, was a rangy man with red hair and small but astonishingly quick fists. Even Sovich had occasional trouble with the other man's speed.

But for the most part Sovich, dressed in black pants and black boots, had no trouble at all pounding Barney, dressed in black pants and red boots; no trouble at all.

The body blows were almost as impressive as the head shots, something you rarely saw. Twice Sovich hit Barney so hard in the ribs that he lifted the man off the canvas. He hit him so hard in the kidneys that he drove him to his knees.

After twenty minutes, both men were sleek and rancid with sweat.

The reporters had deserted the churchwomen and come over for a look at Sovich.

"Listen to how those goddamn punches sound when they land," said one reporter in a derby and checkered suit. "They sound like he's throwing bricks."

They fought for another twenty minutes until Barney's bleeding got bad, especially from the nose. He started choking on his own blood, and John T. Stoddard stepped in and said, "Why don't you quit now, Barney? We're going to need you again tomorrow."

For all his sweat, for all the redness in his face, Victor Sovich did not seem tired at all. Indeed, he seemed refreshed in some unimaginable way, as if punishing the other man so severely had made him younger, stronger, sharper.

When he stepped between the ropes, he looked up at Guild and said, "Remember yesterday afternoon, Guild? Remember how it felt?" He smiled. "Next time, you're going to look like Barney when I get through with you."

Guild hadn't realized until just now, looking at the boxer, what was really wrong with him.

Victor Sovich was insane.

Driving cattle, riding shotgun, serving as lawman, tracking bounty, Guild came across them occasionally, insane men. They weren't the laughing, sneering people he saw in melodramas. Usually it was just something in their eyes, some rage or grief that was frightening when he finally recognized it.

There was no grief in Sovich's dark eyes. Just rage.

He walked past Guild, back to the dressing room.

John T. Stoddard came up and stood next to Guild. "You stick right by me, you understand, Guild?"

"I understand."

"I hope you realize that the son of a bitch wants to kill us both."

Guild nodded. "Yeah, that's sort of what I was thinking."

John T. Stoddard shook his head. "I was going to take him along to see the colored man, but the hell with him. You and I will go."

From inside the livery you could hear Sovich yelling at one of the trainers. He really was crazy.

Chapter Nine

The town had a colored section adjacent to the mixed-race section. The buildings all seemed to lean at impossible angles, as if ready to collapse. You could smell cooking and heat and filth. A white policeman in a fancy blue uniform and a kepi-style hat walked up and down the street with a murderous-looking nightstick in his hand. Ragged children ran after him, trying to be nice. He wasn't nice back. He was just fat and Irish-looking and mean. The people here stared at Guild and John T. Stoddard with white, forlorn eyes out of black, forlorn faces.

Rooney was the name of the colored fighter. Unlike Sovich he did not have a training camp. He worked outside against another Negro in tufty grass behind a bar where an ancient Jamaican man played a squeeze box. There were maybe thirty black men in a circle around the two fighters. Some of them wore the bright clothes of the bayou they originally came from. Most wore the drab rags of stoop laborers. Most of them were drunk. The sparring served to take their minds off their problems. They sounded as if they had only one real concern in this world, and that was how good Rooney looked.

"Come on, Rooney, you take him out, hear?"

"Come on, Rooney, quit playin' and do the job."

"Come on, Rooney, show him your real punch."

Rooney was as squat and massive as Victor Sovich. He appeared to be a talented fighter capable of a good right hook and an even better left uppercut, but he did not have Sovich's skill at moving left and right as he threw his combinations. The other fighter pegged him several times with punches Rooney should have been able to avoid. Guild could imagine what Sovich would do to this man.

"He looks good, doesn't he?" Stoddard said.

"You know what Sovich will do to him."

"Sure. But Rooney here will put on a good show. You'd be surprised at how many people will bet on him. A lot of white people secretly believe that colored boxers are stronger. And that's what you have to play on—that belief."

It was then that Guild saw the woman start to draw something from her purse, something that glinted suspiciously in the sunlight.

"Shit," Guild said, and took off running to the other side of the crowd, where the woman stood.

John T. Stoddard shouted at Guild to stop, but Guild didn't slow down.

The men around here were too drunk and too involved in the fight to see what she was about to do.

Guild got her just as she was leveling the small revolver at Rooney's back.

He grabbed her wrist and tugged her free of the crowd. He must have grabbed her wrist very hard because she started crying almost immediately.

He pulled her inside the tavern. The place was shadowy and stank of the outhouse just outside the door.

"What the hell are you trying to do?" Guild said.

She just kept crying.

The bartender eased over for a better look at the two of them. Obviously he thought Guild had smacked her around some.

"I wanted to kill him," she said.

This was the beautiful mulatto woman he had seen last night in the restaurant. She wore the same sort of frilly white lace at her neck, but today her dress was of blue silk and her small angled hat of a darker blue silk. She was still beautiful, but Guild's impression of her fragile nature had been altered somewhat by the fact that she had just tried to kill a man.

"I know you wanted to kill him," Guild said. "What I want to know is why."

She glanced up at the bartender, who was still eavesdropping. "I don't want to talk with him listening."

"Let's go for a walk, then."

"Why are you so interested?"

"You wouldn't be interested in a woman who pulls out a gun and almost shoots a man?"

She sighed. "I suppose I would be."

They left a few minutes later. The bartender looked disappointed he hadn't gotten to hear what happened.

Guild knew he should be back with Stoddard, but instead he walked with the mulatto woman. Several times she tried to walk away from him. Each time, he grabbed her elbow and jerked her back. "What's going on here?" Guild would ask. "What's shooting Rooney all about?" But she'd say nothing.

They walked out of the colored section to a park where children splashed chill silver water in a marble pool and where nurses pushed strollers. Dogs yipped and jumped at balloons and a three-year-old got chocolate all over her face.

When they reached the river, he pulled her into a tavern where the bar was nothing more than rough planks. The place smelled of heat and hops and wine and vomit. He could see she hated it in here. The men filled their ignorant eyes with her.

After two beers—his, not hers; she wouldn't drink—he took her out behind the place and threw her up hard against a shed.

"I'm going to slap you," he said, "if you don't talk."

She didn't talk, and he slapped her very hard.

She immediately started sobbing.

"My name is Clarise Watson. I'm from Chicago. Rooney killed my brother a year ago."

"In the ring?"

"Supposedly."

"What's that mean?"

"It means that he put poison in my brother's drinking water right before the fight. It made my brother very groggy. He couldn't defend himself. He died right in the ring."

He could see she was fighting tears again.

They had been walking once more, back to the colored section.

The block they were on was filled with children and teenagers. The latter stared long and hard at the beautiful mulatto woman. Guild could not quite tell if they liked her or despised her. Their stares seemed to convey both feelings.

The sunlight showed her skin to be a beautiful coffee color. In the daylight her features were even more beautiful. Only the lines in her neck betrayed her age. She had to be nearly forty.

"I'm sorry I keep crying."

"Nothing to be sorry for."

"I loved him."

"I'm sure you did. You sure about the poison?"

"One of Rooney's trainers admitted it to me."

He looked at her closely. "He admitted it?"

She smiled without pleasure. "I had to help him. I gave him some bourbon and then I gave him myself."

"I see."

"You don't sound as if you approve."

"I don't."

"I wanted to know the truth."

"You probably could have figured out another way."

"Could I?"

They walked another quarter block in silence. Guild felt jealous. It was ridiculous, feeling jealous. Then he felt ashamed. He realized then that he was still hung over.

He stopped and turned her toward him. "You going to try it again?"

"I don't know. I've waited so long for today—built up to it so much. And then right at the last second you stopped me and—"

"I'm going to turn you over to the law. You tried to kill a man."

"What?"

"You're not giving me any choice."

"You've got my gun."

"You can always buy another one."

"Maybe I won't try. Maybe coming this close was good enough."

"'Maybe' isn't something I can count on."

"Do you have a brother, Mr. Guild?"

"I had two of them. They both died in the war."

"I'm sorry."

He took a cigarette from his shirt pocket and lighted it up. The smoke tasted nutty in his throat and felt soft and blue in his lungs.

"I'm going to ask you again. You going to try to shoot him?"

She made a face. "I suppose not."

"You're a hell of a lot of help."

She laughed. She had a wonderful laugh. "I don't suppose I am, am I?"

"You staying anyplace special?"

"The Carleton Arms. The manager is out of town. The desk clerk said I could stay till the manager gets back. He hates Negroes."

"Why don't you meet me tonight in the Carleton dining room?"

She looked at him carefully. "What are you after, Mr. Guild?"

"I'm not sure yet."

"I guess that's fair enough."

He paused. "Rooney wouldn't be worth hanging for."

"Did you ever get over the death of your brothers?"

"Not really."

"Then you know what I'm going through, Mr. Guild."

With that, she walked off, making it clear that she didn't want him to accompany her.

He watched her go down the block. The children came up to her and felt her beautiful blue dress and looked more closely at her beautiful face.

She looked back at him only once. She looked happy that the children were so accepting of her and seemed to like her so much.

She walked around the corner with them. Even from here he could hear their laughter. It was silver on the sudden cool breeze. His hangover did not bother him so much now. He thought of the man she'd had to sleep with. He felt angry, and stupid that he felt angry.

He went back to find John T. Stoddard.

Chapter Ten

Sometimes he forgot the name of the town he was in. With the coming of streetcars and tall buildings, with the coming of large glass display windows and crowded sidewalks, towns all began to look alike.

He could not, standing at the hotel window and looking down at the street, recall the name of this town, for instance.

He puffed on his cigar and continued to watch late afternoon passengers board the streetcar.

He looked at his pocket watch.

He was supposed to meet Reynolds downstairs in five minutes.

He turned around and said, "I'm going to go downstairs to get some cigars. I'll come right back up."

"Do you want me to go with you?"

"No. I don't think Victor will bother me anymore today. We got through our meeting. He'll be with his Mexican woman and his booze. It's tomorrow I'm really going to need you."

Guild smiled at him. "You're not going to need me tonight?"

"Not after dinner. I'd appreciate it if you'd sit downstairs with me and help keep some of the reporters at bay."

"Sure."

"Then you can take off if you'd like."

"Fine."

He stared at Guild a moment. He was not the sort of man he could understand quickly. Stoddard never knew when he was going to irritate Guild; he never knew when Guild was going to take offense. He would be glad when it was all over, when Reynolds had done his job, and when he no longer needed men such as Guild for protection.

The streetcar rattled away now. He had been paying particular attention to a woman in a white picture hat. He still loved to look at women, even though the last three years he had suffered the embarrassing loss of his manliness when he'd actually been with them. He wondered what it was, disgust over his wife leaving him or just age, that slow creaking crawl to the grave he saw in so many men around him, closed off to all experience but making money. He felt tears in his throat as he looked out once again at the town. He wondered if this would be the sort of place he would die in—big and anonymous—and without even knowing its name.

He put the flocked curtain back in place and went over to where Guild played solitaire.

"I'll be going downstairs now."

"You all right?"

"Why wouldn't I be all right?"

"You look sort of strange."

"I didn't hire you to be my goddamn priest."

Guild sighed and turned over a red eight of hearts. "You can leave anytime, as far as I'm concerned."

He had succeeded in pissing off Guild again. He almost felt good about it. He liked to see Guild upset and squirming.

It was always pleasant to walk into a taproom. He liked the smell of smoke and the hubbub of laughter and conversation. He liked the boozy heat of arguments about politics and sports. He liked the barmaids he tried to pick up for later and the bartenders he tried to intimidate with his self-confidence and his tips. It was fun to see them jump.

This taproom was fashioned after those in Chicago, everything done in stained oak, with brass fixtures along the bar and a huge mural of a naughty vaudeville lady named Ruby Lee stretching across the back wall. He had actually spent a night with Ruby Lee once. She'd had enormous breasts and equally enormous feet. He'd never seen feet that size on a woman.

Reynolds was at a rear table. He sat alone, a shot glass and a schooner sitting untouched in front of him. He was in his early thirties but older looking because he was balding. He was thin and wore a drab three-piece brown suit. He had small hands and nervous fingers. There was a certain air of sadness about him. He was one of the best thieves in the Midwest.

Stoddard sat down. When the waitress came over, he ordered a bourbon. When the waiter left, he said, "Are you all set for tomorrow?"

There was so much noise in the taproom that Stoddard did not have to worry about being overheard.

"There's only one thing."

"What's that?"

"You sure Victor isn't going to figure it out and come for me?"

"How's he going to figure it out?"

"You think he's going to believe it?"

Stoddard shrugged. "Robberies happen all the time. I'll leave Guild in the back room guarding the cash. If Victor blames anybody, it will be Guild. He hates him."

"He could still figure it out."

"Not if we're careful."

David Reynolds looked around. "This Guild, is he tough?"

"Not as tough as he thinks."

"He going to give me any problems?"

"Not if you do what I tell you."

"Which is?"

"Shoot him."

"What?"

"You want to make this look convincing, don't you?"

"Jesus, Stoddard, I'm a thief, not a killer."

"I didn't say kill him."

"Jesus."

"In the arm, maybe. Or the shoulder."

"I don't know. I've never shot a man before."

Stoddard smiled. "Then it's probably the only thing you haven't done before." Stoddard tried to know things about everybody he worked with. "You've developed yourself quite a reputation. Even for a man in your line of work. You get in and out, and there's supposed to be no trouble."

"After this is all over, I have to live in this town."

"Meaning?"

"Meaning if there's violence, the police are going to be looking for the thief double hard."

Stoddard took out a cigar and lit it. The afternoon light was dying in the window. A pretty barmaid passed by just now. He did not want to be talking to this frightened little man.

"You might even enjoy it, Reynolds."

"I doubt it."

"Some men get accustomed to it."

"I'm a thief," he said again with a certain obstinate pride.

"I don't want to have to worry about you. You're getting a nice little nut for half an hour of work."

"I don't have any objections to the nut, Mr. Stoddard."

"Good. Then you'll do it?"

Reynolds smiled. "You're a cold son of a bitch."

"I just want to relax and have a quick drink here before I have to go back upstairs. And I can't relax if I think you're not going to do it right tomorrow."

"Oh, I'm going to do it right."

"You're going to shoot him?"

Reynolds hesitated only a moment. "I'm going to shoot him."

"Good, then. It's settled."

"You really are a cold son of a bitch, you know that?" Reynolds said. But his words were not without a certain harsh admiration.

Chapter Eleven

Victor Sovich said, "You want to come with me?"

The woman looked at him. "Where you have in mind?"

"The next town, wherever that is."

"My children?"

"Your mother's across town."

"I leave my children?"

"It's no life for them, believe me."

"But my children. I love them."

"We'd come back through here every three or four months. The Midwest is good for me. I'd have to come back through here anyway."

They were in bed. The sheets smelled of their sweat and their lovemaking and the wine they'd had just before. He sat propped up against the wall and took in the smells. He enjoyed them. In the window the light was dying. It had turned yellow and pink. Now it was purple dusk. Through the smashed window he could see the quarter-moon. He smiled to himself. She was going to go with him. Oh, she would protest and tell him what a good mother she was. They always did. They needed that dignity. There was no other way they could face what they were about to do. He knew they wouldn't last long. These women never did. There would come a night or afternoon, some idle moment when he was shaving or bathing or reading a magazine, when he would suddenly have had enough of her, and then he would want to see her no longer. Then he would not be able to endure her touch or look at her body, clothed or unclothed, ever again.

"You like Maria."

"She's cute."

"Couldn't we at least take Maria?"

"I'd like to. It just wouldn't be good for her."

"Bobby, then. Perhaps it would be more appropriate for a boy to travel."

"It wouldn't be good for him, either."

Now was her time to sulk. She rolled over in the bed, away from him. He put his hand on her warm back, feeling the graceful curve of it, how it so fetchingly gave way to her plump, tender buttocks and the magnificent sweep of her long legs.

"Don't," she said.

Now it was his turn to roll away.

He lay on his side, staring at the wall. He could see the dirty handprints the kids had left on it. He could smell where the cat shit in the corner. Maybe he didn't want to take her with him tomorrow after all.

He kept staring at the quarter-moon and wondering about tomorrow. The nigger. He hated niggers and he wasn't even sure why. Something happened to him when he fought colored men. Something even he was slightly afraid of. He never liked to feel out of control, but with niggers in the ring that was usually the way he felt, out of control.

He remembered the first time he'd killed one. How the crowd had become silent so abruptly, how the referee kept saying, "Goddammit, boy. Goddammit, you wake now, you hear?" But the nigger had been dead already. The way all niggers should be.

After the fight a reporter came back to his dressing room. The reporter kept asking him how he felt. He knew Stoddard would get angry if he said the wrong thing. There had been more than one hundred ring deaths in the past two years, and church groups were really protesting prizefights. He did not say anything stupid. His livelihood depended on his not saying anything stupid. He said instead the expected things. That he was sorry. That he hoped the boy's family would understand. That he would say a prayer for the boy, in fact.

By the second time he had killed a colored boy, it was something most desirable for him to do. And not only for Stoddard's sake, but for his own. He enjoyed killing.

She was crying now.

He said, "You're a good mother. It's not like you're deserting them."

"They're my children."

"We'll see them often. I promise."

"What would the priest think?"

He scowled. "The hell with the priest." He remembered watching his sister die from smallpox. How the priest hovered. How the priest swooned. How the priest talked about an afterlife as if he really believed in it. As if we weren't like cats and dogs and rats, animals that died and rotted. He had had no time for priests ever since.

She only cried all the more. "I suppose you would like me to give up my faith, too?"

He stayed on his side, looking at the quarter-moon.

It was always like this with them. They cried and then they got indignant and then they got angry. But they always came along.

Always.

Stephen Stoddard liked to walk the streets at dusk, just as the first fireflies appeared in parks and the electric lights appeared on the streets.

He passed from the downtown, with its barbershops and millinery stores and banks and jewelers and ice parlors, to an address he'd found in the newspaper.

Most cities these days had Evening Home Clubs, where young men could gather to discuss the issues of the day without consorting with the type of people you met in pumprooms and taverns.

He was most interested in discussing the gold standard, finding it the one topic that always provoked immediate and prolonged conversation.

Given the letter he carried in his suit coat, however, he wondered how able he would be to focus on a debate.

Now, as he walked, Stephen Stoddard shook his head. Incredibly the ex-Pinkerton he'd secretly hired a year ago had finally found Stephen's mother. She lived in Portland, Oregon, half a continent away, and in the ten years since he'd last seen her, she'd gone on to start a whole new family. According to the photograph the ex-Pinkerton had enclosed with the letter, his mother was now plump, gray-haired, and surrounded by children bobbing around her like apples in a barrel.

His mother. He remembered soft, slender fingers and sweet songs hummed in the darkness. He remembered bread baking in the oven and the wet, clean scent of her long auburn hair just after she'd washed it. He remembered the sunlight on the new bicycle she'd bought him and moonlight on the silver ice of the skating rink.

He remembered her tears, too, how he'd been unable to stop them and felt the lesser for being so unable. The harshness of those tears. The increasing frequency of those tears.

Then she'd been gone, and gone forever.

Why, he'd never been able to understand exactly, nor had his father been able or willing to explain.

Now he held in his possession a letter that promised to tell him. The letter had come the day before yesterday. He had still not opened it. He did not know if he was frightened or simply savoring this first word from his mother in all these years.

Whatever, each time his soft, slender fingers touched the envelope, they jumped away, as if stung or shocked.

There would be an appropriate time, an appropriate place, to open the letter.

Soon now, he told himself as he moved along the sidewalk in and out of the shadows cast by the streetlight.

Soon now.

Guild had to be careful with the stuff. Put too much on and he smelled too sweet. A little was all he needed.

As he stood fresh from his bath in new black trousers, Leo Guild looked at the way the flesh of his chest had started to sag some beneath the wiry salt-and-pepper hair.

As if the stuff would magically make him younger, he splashed on a generous amount of the bay rum he'd bought at the barbershop a few days earlier. He next combed his hair and then pulled on a newly laundered white boiled shirt.

Putting on a false grin so he could get a look at his teeth, Guild at the same time began patting his stomach. Even if his chest was starting to go, his stomach was pretty damn flat for a man his age. Pretty damn flat.

He went over and sat on the bed and pulled on clean white socks and then his black Texas boots.

He wanted a steak and some bourbon. Most especially he wanted the company of Clarise Watson.

He started thinking of the little girl. It was usually like this. Anytime he was about to have himself some fun, the little girl came to mind. A priest had explained to him that this was one way of continuing to punish himself. The little girl was always there to remind him of that day. Of his mistake. Of his guilt.

He went over and sat on the edge of the bed. He looked around the hotel room. He thought of all the men who had stayed in this room before him. Of their pleasures and of their shame, of their loneliness for families far away. It was as if this room was haunted by all of them, a jumble of ghostly voices and griefs, but no voice, no grief was any clearer than that of the little girl's. He had never given a name to her, even though during the course of the trial—Guild ultimately acquitted—he heard it daily. But a name made her real in a way he could not deal with. She would always be just "the little girl." It was easier that way, somehow.

He opened the door on the third knock. He carried his .44 along with him. When he saw who it was, he leveled the gun to point directly at the man's stomach.

Victor Sovich was once again dressed like an opera star, complete with cape. This time he'd even added a top hat and cane. He said, "What's that smell?"

Guild flushed. He felt like an eight-year-old discovered doing something terrible. Sovich was referring to the bay rum. Guild said, "Some goddamn man before me must have spilled a bottle of bay rum."

Sovich sniffed. Then he smirked. "That must be it, Guild. Some man before you must have spilled a bottle of bay rum." He seemed to take as much pleasure from mocking Guild as he had yesterday from beating him.

"What do you want, anyway?" Guild said.

"I wonder if you'd like to talk some business."

"What kind of business?"

Sovich said, "Why don't we go downstairs and have a drink?"

"You can tell me right here."

"Is it all right if I come in?"

"No."

"You're still mad about yesterday?"

Guild didn't say anything.

"It wasn't anything personal, Guild. It's just that you're working for Stoddard. You know how it is."

"Why are you working for Stoddard?"

"What?"

"You heard me. You keep saying he cheats you yet you keep right on coming back. There's only one way to explain that."

"And what would that be?" The smirk was back.

"He's got something on you. Something he could use against you with the law."

Now the smirk grew icy. "I'm going to assume Stoddard didn't tell you anything, that you had this notion yourself."

Guild just wanted Sovich out of his sight. "What kind of business do you want to talk about?"

"He's going to short-count me again. He'll take eighty percent and give me twenty percent. If I'm lucky."

"That's between you and Stoddard."

"He'll probably have you guard the gate money and the betting money."

"So?"

"So you could take it all and give it to me."

Guild hefted the .44 again. "Now why the hell would I do that?"

Just then an old man in a flannel robe came down from the bathroom. He smelled of hot water and sweat. It was much too hot for a flannel robe. He kept walking, but he gave them both a big blue-eyed stare.

After the old man passed down the hall, Sovich said, "You'd do it because I'd pay you to do it. Fifteen percent of what you take from Stoddard you keep."

"Maybe the fight won't be as successful as you two think. Some of these fights people just don't show up for."

"Oh, they'll show up for this one." He smirked again. This expression was slightly different from the others. It was colder. "White folks always show up when a nigger's going to get killed."

"You ever think it could go the other way?"

"I never think that at all. Because it's not going to."

"I won't do it."

"You could make yourself a lot of money."

"I could make you a lot of money, you mean. And that I'm against on principle."

"You're going to be old pretty soon, Guild. Principle won't get you jack shit then. You'll need money."

Guild waved the .44 at Sovich. "Go on. Get out of here."

"Fifteen percent, Guild. You could make yourself a lot of money."

Guild slammed the door, but not before Sovich had a chance to smile again.

Guild went and sat on the edge of the bed until it was time to leave. He thought of the little girl. He wondered what she'd be doing now if she'd lived. Getting ready for the fall and high school, he thought. That was how he measured her years. Where she'd be in school.

Ninth grade now.

But of course that wasn't going to happen.

He had seen to that.

Chapter Twelve

"Well," said Clarise Watson, "I was born in Illinois and I moved to Connecticut when I was twelve, where a white man was very much taken with me. He saw to it that I was educated and that I learned how to dress properly and that I had proper dental work. He was grooming me to work in his house, which meant, among other things, being his mistress. His wife was this very cold white-haired woman who was difficult for everybody to get along with, including her husband. I'm told that he'd had other mistresses before. She knew about them and would tease him with them. She would get one of the mistresses' undergarments and leave it under his pillow. Or a gift he had given his mistress would be on his desk in the morning. She was the one with all the money, and all the power, and she never wanted to let him forget it. Finally she would make him so nervous and anxious that he couldn't have sex with his mistress. He'd keep trying, but his wife leaving all these little hints would undo him. She took more pleasure in handling it this way than in just throwing the girls out. She liked humiliating him.

"As I said, I was told all this. When it was my turn—he liked his mistresses to have just turned sixteen—he took me by the hand and led me out to this guest house they kept down by a stream. He took me inside and took my clothes off one layer at a time. I've never seen a man more appreciative of a woman's body. He was crying, and it was with pleasure.

"He carried me over to the bed and set me down on it and started to kiss me, and then it happened. I had no idea what was going on. He just started making these funny noises in his chest and throat, and then his eyes sort of started bugging out. I tried to help him, but I didn't know what to do. I ran up to the mansion to get somebody to help, and I was so terrified that I didn't even care that I was naked. Then she saw me, his wife. She came running out of the house with a riding crop, and I kept screaming that her husband was dying. But instead of running down to the cabin to see if she could help him, she started beating me. She must have beaten me for fifteen minutes. Finally I just passed out. She had them put me in the barn, in the haymow. They were under strict orders not to help me in any way. I stayed there for four days. I had to drink from the same trough the horses did. I got the chills so badly one night that I had to steal a blanket from a horse who was cold, too. I never forgot the look in his eyes. He seemed to know what I was doing and forgave me for doing it.

"The husband didn't live. The wife went to my family and told them that if they wanted to continue to work for her they'd have to send me to the city to live. She wanted to force me into prostitution.

"My father and mother had fourteen children. They had to look at the greater good—the well-being of thirteen children versus one child. I'm sure my mother never got over it, but they sent me anyway. I never did go into prostitution. I became a decorator for rich people. I even married a white man, but he could never forgive me for being a 'high yellow' as he always called me. Whenever he got drunk he beat me. He couldn't forgive me for being part colored, and he couldn't forgive himself for loving me.

"By then my brother had started boxing. I left my husband and traveled around with my brother until Rooney gave him that drink and killed him. And all this led me here, to try to kill Rooney.

"I'm sort of a disreputable woman, wouldn't you say?"

She said she didn't mind if he had an after-dinner cigar, so as they strolled along the river, he smoked.

On the dark water, the reflections of yellow and white city lights shimmered. Ducks floated and quacked. Rowboaters angled downstream toward the rush and roar and silver splash of the dam.

A soft breeze flowed over the grassy banks. Fireflies flickered and died. Lost in bushes, and happy to be lost, lovers giggled. An earnest young man in a straw boater sat on a park bench with a bored young woman and tried to impress her with his ukulele playing. An old immigrant sat in rags, despondent, staring at the shimmering water.

They walked upstream past the boat dock and the icehouses and pavilion where church ladies were carting off the last of the picnic baskets from a social.

"Have you even wanted a life like theirs?" Clarise asked Guild.

"I'm not sure."

"You ever tried it?"

"Sort of, I suppose."

"Sort of?"

"It's not worth talking about."

"Were you married?"

"For a time."

"Were you happy?"

"That's the part that's not worth talking about."

"I see."

They walked some more. He finished his cigar, tossing the red eye of it into the black water.

Electric poles hummed and thrummed in the dark night along the graveled river road.

A white-nosed fawn stumbled out of undergrowth like a lost

child, standing dazed in a circle of moonlight. Clarise went over to it and fell to her knees and hugged it as if she had borne it, and Guild was moved enough that he, too, went over and knelt and began petting the frightened animal.

At last came the fawn's mother, a loose-fleshed animal that seemed, seeing them, both scared and angry. You could smell the night's heat on the mother, and fecal matter.

The fawn disappeared back into the undergrowth with its mother.

Clarise and Guild went on their way.

They walked another mile. The river angled gently east. At its widest point the moon made the surface pure silver. Laughter came sharply from upriver, like gunshots, as two rowboats oared away from them.

They walked over and sat in the long grass on a ragged clay cliff above a backwash.

Clarise picked sunflowers, tucking one behind her ear. The other sunflowers she twirled, tossing them finally into the water below.

He was afraid to kiss her, but he kissed her anyway and she seemed quite pleased about it.

As they lay in the long grass, they could hear night birds and roaming dogs and distant cows. Nearer by, they could hear the soft lap of water on the shore and the wooden creak of rowboat oars and a young man singing a soft song, presumably to his girl.

He was scarcely aware of where his moments with Clarise were leading so suddenly.

"I can't help the way I am," Clarise said. "I don't like most men, and it's been a long time for me."

"Will you roll me one of those?"
"Sure."
"A lady oughtn't smoke."
"I suppose not."
"But then a lady, a real lady, oughtn't do what I just did."
"Aren't we a little old for oughtn'ts?"

She laughed. "Speak for yourself."

He rolled the cigarettes and got them going red in the dark night. He gave her a cigarette and then lay down again with her. They'd put their clothes back on in case somebody came along.

"You seem like a troubled man, Guild."

He did not want to talk about the little girl and spoil everything for them. He said, "And you seem like a troubled woman."

They said nothing for a long time. They just listened to the soft lapping of water on the shore and the reedy sound of breeze through the long grasses.

"I enjoyed myself, Guild."

"So did I."

"I guess I don't care if you think I'm a whore or not."

"I don't."

"That's what most white people think of us."

"You want me to tell you what most white people think of me?"

She laughed again. "Look at that moon. You ever wonder what's going on up there, in the parts that look like continents?"

"Sure. I wonder about that a lot."

"Wouldn't it be funny if there were people up there and they were just like us?"

"No," Guild said. "I hope they're not. I hope they're very, very different."

"In what way?"

He sighed. "I hope they don't have politicians the way we do, and I hope they don't let people go hungry, and I hope they don't kill children."

He felt her shudder. "Kill children? That's a terrible thing to think of."

"Yes," Guild said. "It's the worst thing you can think of."

"Then stop thinking about it."

She drew him back to her then, and the wonderful softness and heat and moisture of her mouth pressed to his again.

Chapter Thirteen

"Another one?"

"Please."

"You're all alone tonight, Mr. Reynolds." The bar was small, a narrow walk-in just off Church Street. The smell of whiskey and sawdust and stale ham from the free lunch filtered through the air.

"Yes." He left it at that. He did not want to talk about Helen anymore, or her marriage two months ago to a bank clerk. Everything had been fine with Helen until she learned by accident that he was a thief. She still loved him enough that she had not turned him over to the law, but nothing since then had gone right for Reynolds. Nothing. There had been, for instance, an easy breaking-and-entry job in Milan, Illinois, two weeks ago. He'd been going in through the back window when the entire casement fell down on his head, knocking him out. The incident had very nearly been comic. He'd come to with time enough to get out of the empty house with its walls filled with expensive paintings, its drawers filled with money and silver. Then he had tried breaking into the liquor store over on Harcourt Street. Two steps in he'd noticed a copper walking past the back door, a looming shadow. A copper. He'd cased the job for a week. Coppers were not supposed to come by for twenty minutes. But for some reason one did this night. He'd been forced to flee with nothing. And it all started when Helen told him she was going to marry the boy she'd graduated eighth grade with.

"You going to see the fight tomorrow, Mr. Reynolds?" the bartender asked.

"Isn't everybody?" Reynolds tried to make a joke of it.

"Darn near, from what I hear. You have tickets?"

"I bought one today, matter of fact."

"You're lucky. I have to work."

"It'll be some fight."

"The colored guy's going to get killed. You've heard about Sovich, haven't you?"

"He's killed several colored boys, from what I gather."

"You gather right."

Reynolds eyed him. "You like prizefighting?"

"Sure. Don't you, Mr. Reynolds?" The bartender had sort of a high voice for somebody who was so chunky and had such massive hands.

"I don't know. I always think I'm going to like it, and then the blood starts flowing—" He shook his head. "I just don't know if I do or not."

"Well, tomorrow's going to be special."

It sure is, Reynolds thought. *I'm going to have to shoot somebody. And with the way things have been going, I'm going to kill him by accident.*

"Special? You mean Sovich?"

The bartender nodded, wiped out the inside of a schooner with his white towel. "Sure, Mr. Reynolds. It isn't likely a town this size is going to see him again."

Six customers came in through the front door. They were laughing and slapping each other on the back. One, very drunk, was singing. He sounded Swedish. He was off-key.

The bartender moved down the bar to serve them.

This was what Reynolds had wanted, anyway. Solitude. He liked to stand at a bar and think through his problems and plan his robberies.

Tonight he'd gone to an alley with the Navy Colt his old man had owned. He needed to practice firing. His ineptitude with firearms was obvious. People assumed because you were a good thief you were also good with a gun. In fact, most of the robbers Reynolds knew were peaceful men. They would rather give themselves up than be shot or shoot at somebody.

He agreed with Stoddard that the robbery would look more believable if somebody was shot. Victor Sovich was less likely to be suspicious.

But he wondered how it would feel, shooting a man like that. Just shooting him.

He had a few more drinks—thankfully, the bartender got to talking with the group that had just come in and left Reynolds alone—and then of course he started thinking about Helen again.

Things had been very, very good with Helen. They'd made a lot of plans, including a family and a cabin by a lake they could share with her cousin in Wisconsin. They were even talking about what parish they were going to belong to (Helen was partial to St. Michael's; he to All Saints), and then it just had all gone to hell. He wished he were better at crying. Being a small man, though, he'd carefully taught himself not to cry. He needed every vestige of manliness he could summon. But sometimes crying would feel good, and he knew it. To just goddamn sit down and bawl like a baby. He'd seen his old man do it in the last failing months of the old man's life, when the black lung had gotten especially bad and when he coughed up blood more and more. He could never have imagined the old man crying. But there he was in bed, with his wife holding him as if he were her child and not her husband, and he was bawling away without shame. The old man didn't have her faith in the afterlife. He thought we were just like road dogs, nothing but ribs and a skull left of you, and then not even that after a time.

"Why don't you have a drink on me, Mr. Reynolds?"

"Sure. What's the occasion?"

"The fight tomorrow. Those men down there rode all the way over from Chicago to see it. They say it's going to be one hell of a fight, and the colored guy's going to be lucky he doesn't get killed."

The bartender poured him a drink.

"You be sure and go now, Mr. Reynolds."

"Oh, I'll be sure. Don't worry about that."

He wished there was some way he could explain to this Guild that he was really sorry he had to shoot him.

"Well, you not only be there but you enjoy yourself, you hear now, Mr. Reynolds?"

Sometimes Reynolds suspected that the bartender fixed himself good, hard drinks when nobody was watching. You could see this in the way he walked after a certain hour.

"I'll try to enjoy myself," Reynolds said. "I'll do my damnedest."

"That's the spirit, Mr. Reynolds. That's the spirit."

Reynolds had two more drinks and then walked back to his sleeping room. He propped the window up with a book and stripped down to his shorts and lay on the bed and smoked a cigarette. The smoke was gray in the leaf-shadowed light from the street. He thought of Helen and going with her dressed up to mass every Sunday. Jesus, but how sweet that would have been. Then he thought of this Guild he had to shoot tomorrow. He was going to get him in the calf and make it fast. In the calf there wouldn't be any way he could go wrong. If he tried to shoot him in the arm, maybe he'd hit the chest. Then things could go very wrong.

He lay there finishing his cigarette and then they started, the tears. He had to keep them down because the man on the other side of the wall would hear them and tell everybody in the boardinghouse.

He lay on the bed in the leaf-shadowed light all curled up like a little kid. His thin body jerked and started with his silent tears. He tasted them in his throat and his mouth and his nose.

He kept thinking of Helen and how he still loved her and how he would always love her. All she'd asked was that he'd give up being a thief, and at first it had seemed easy, but after a few weeks he'd realized that that was all he knew and that working a time clock job was just never going to work.

He wondered now who he was crying for, himself or Helen. Probably both of them.

He had another cigarette. Gradually his tears stopped. He reached over to the nightstand and picked up the Navy Colt.

He pointed it at the wall and made a small popping sound with his mouth, imitating the sound a gun makes.

He wished it were tomorrow afternoon. He wished it were over with.

Chapter Fourteen

They started arriving early on Saturday morning. They came by train, stagecoach, buckboard, horse. They came in ones and twos and threes and whole families. They came from farms and factories and neighboring towns. The local newspaper would make note that one man had been four days traveling and had come better than two hundred miles. Many of them hit restaurants and hotels and the local YMCA, but the majority of them sought out taverns and pumprooms. This was the sort of occasion you started getting drunk for early in the day.

Out on the edge of town, where the bleachers had been set up and a large canvas ring was in the process of being erected, there were already more than three hundred fans who had come early for the best possible seats. It was not yet eight A.M., and two men had already been arrested for drunk and disorderly and another for indecent exposure, the result of taking a pee behind a tree without noticing the fact that a family was having a picnic nearby. The temperature was nearing ninety, the humidity oppressive. Many of the police wore the tan khaki of the auxiliary policeman.

These cops looked especially young, trying to swagger around with their hands on their nightsticks but not quite knowing how to do it without looking somewhat ridiculous. The pickets had arrived, too, ten ladies in crisp summer pastels bearing signs that read BOXING IS IMMORAL and WE ARE NOT ANIMALS. A reporter from Quincy spent an hour with them, making note of their various complaints and trying to hide his own delight over the fact that today he was finally going to see Victor Sovich fight.

Downtown at the train depot, all the taxis were taken up as well as the ten buggies the city had provided for the occasion. The latter were reserved for the gentry, the men who wore three-piece suits and derbies despite the heat, the ladies in lace and contempt. These people were dispatched to the small city's two best hotels, where they immediately proceeded to ruin the days of bellhops, desk clerks, serving maids, and other guests.

Even most of the people who claimed disinterest in the fight had to admit that the town had never seen anything like this. It was as if the place had been set upon by vandals. Every square inch of ground, it seemed, was being stood upon, sat upon, or claimed for later by somebody who'd come here to watch Victor Sovich. In three taverns downtown there were large photographs of Sovich behind the bar. As a joke, one man from Chicago got behind the bar and lighted a candle to Sovich, the way Catholics light candles to honor statues of saints. The prank got five solid minutes of applause from the crowd and free drinks from the bartender, who considered the man a real crowd pleaser and therefore good for business.

In the city park an additional contingent of churchwomen had gathered to decry fisticuffs in any form, but especially the form in which it was done for money.

Two more people got arrested, one for being with another man's wife, and the second for drunkenly believing he was Victor Sovich. For no reason anybody could understand, the man simply began punching his friend until said friend was unconscious and perhaps dead. He'd taken a bad, twisting fall, striking his head on the curbing on his way down.

It was not yet nine A.M.

Guild said, "I'm not sure yet."

He was having breakfast in the hotel restaurant with Clarise. She had just asked him where he would go when the fight was over. "How about you? Where are you going?"

She smiled. "I'm not sure yet, either."

"We're quite a pair."

The waiter came. He was sweaty and angry, his hair plastered in wet ringlets to his skull. It was hot in here. Management didn't want to open the windows because the black flies would get in.

"You're having a bad time of it, I take it," Guild said.

The waiter, who was probably close to Guild's age, said, "They kept warning us about the fight and how the crowd would be and all. I thought they were exaggerating."

"They weren't, huh?"

"Most of these people are drunk already."

Clarise looked around. "You know, Leo, I think he's right."

The waiter poured them more coffee. Its stream looked red in the morning sunlight.

"Well, by the end of the day, it'll be all over with."

"Yes," the waiter said with a certain theatrical flourish, "or I will be."

"Stoddard's going to make a lot of money," Clarise said.

"Stoddard and Sovich. I don't think Stoddard will be dumb enough to cheat him this time. I think Sovich would kill him if he tried."

Her small, beautiful mouth wrinkled into a frown. "As long as Rooney doesn't make anything."

"He gets so much per round. That's how these things work. If he can stay on his feet ten rounds he can make himself some nice money."

"Maybe he'll get killed."

Guild sighed and looked out at the room filled with stout men in suits and thick mustaches, at women in chenille dresses, at curtains that looked like golden waterfalls with sunlight blasting through them.

Guild said, "You've got to forget about Rooney."

"That isn't very easy."

"I'm not sure you'd want to see him get killed, anyway."

"Why not?"

"Because there's a difference between wanting somebody dead and actually seeing them dead. No matter how much you hate them, you always start to feel a little sorry for them."

"I take it you're talking about your bounty hunting now."

Guild shrugged. "I suppose. You track them a few months and take them in, and by then you start to wonder if they are really guilty and what's going to happen to them in prison and what's going to happen to their families while they're gone."

"I haven't met many people like you, Guild."

"I haven't met many people like you, either, Clarise."

"Is that a compliment?"

"Of course."

"I just wanted to make sure."

Guild reached over and put his hand on hers. "You know what you should do?"

"What?"

"Get on a train this morning and leave this town."

"Why?"

"So you can break your tie to Rooney."

"What tie?"

"Following him around, always waiting for something bad to happen to him. He's got you."

"Got me? What're you talking about?"

"You hate him so much you can't let go of him. It's like being in love with somebody. You can't let go of him then, either."

"I hope Sovich kills him."

"Given Sovich's record, I'd say that that's at least a possibility."

"I know how I sound, Guild. So hateful. It's not very Christian. But I can't help myself. My brother was a decent man."

"I'm sure he was."

She paused, stared out at the blue sky and the golden sunshine. "You really think I should get on a train?"

"Right now."

"And go where?"

"Anywhere you can start a life for yourself."

"But I'd always think about him. About Rooney, I mean."

"But maybe after a while you won't think about him so much." He looked down at the remnants of his over-easy eggs, sausage, and toast. With the last remaining slice of toast, he wiped up a long, juicy streak of egg yolk and jelly. It tasted wonderful. He finished this off with coffee. He picked up a toothpick and got to work.

Clarise stared down at her long, delicate hands. They looked dark against the white tablecloth. In the hard light you could see all the crumbs from breakfast on the cloth. They seemed the size of pennies.

"I'm scared," she said.

"Of what?"

"Of not knowing where to go or what to do. At least trailing Rooney around gives my life a shape."

"I still think you should take a train out right now."

"You wouldn't be trying to get rid of me, would you?"

The waiter interrupted, saying, "We are supposed to ask all customers if they would mind giving up their seats when they're done with breakfast. The crowd in the lobby is out on the sidewalk and around the block."

Guild shook his head. "No, I've got to be getting up to Stoddard's room, anyway."

Clarise nodded, dabbed daintily at her mouth with a blood-red cloth napkin, and then stood up. She looked wonderful again this morning in a blue silk dress with a brocaded top. "I'll see you out at the fight this afternoon."

"I still wish you were taking that train."

"Don't worry, Guild. I can't shoot Rooney or anyone. You've got my gun." She smiled at him with very white teeth.

He walked her out to the lobby. The place was worse than the waiter had said. Everybody was shoving. It was like being on board a sinking ship. He managed to kiss Clarise on the cheek. She vanished into the mob.

Chapter Fifteen

He had worked as a field hand until he was fifteen. Perhaps because of his ugliness, which was considerable, and perhaps because of his surliness, which was also considerable, the white people who ran the plantation had never considered using him in the house. His father and mother were in the house. His sisters and brothers were in the house. But not him. No, he went out into the sweltering fields, where they put the worst of them—as they defined the worst of them, anyway—those fit not for social skills or the subtle machinations of being a servant. He was fit only for stoop labor where his hands got bloody from pulling everything from turnips to cotton from the ground and where on a lucky day in the corn he might have sex with a young girl.

He broke his first jaw when he was fifteen. A white man had watched as Franklin Rooney had at first resisted and then given in to the taunts of another black boy. Rooney went up to him and broke the boy's jaw with a single punch. How the boy had wailed. How the boy had backed away, terrified.

By age seventeen Rooney was a fixture on an eastern "colored" circuit of boxers. While the whites scorned him, as whites always did, the advantage to being a fighter was that it earned respect from certain types of black people, especially those who inhabited the taverns and brothels of Rooney's choice. Men feared him and women adored him. Sometimes even white women came to watch him fight, and there was no mistaking what he saw in their soft blue eyes.

But early on Rooney knew that despite his cunning, stolid body, his deft right hand, and a certain amount of ring skill, he would never be major. He watched other fighters, black and white, work their way up, but somehow it never happened for him. He stayed on the "circuit," as folks called it, and watched as other men, lesser men, succeeded. He was told it was because he "just wasn't ready for it." He knew it because he was so ugly, the nose too splayed, the lips comically thick, the eyes seeming to pop from his head. People who followed the fights wanted their man to look, if not heroic, at least decent. No matter what he did, Rooney couldn't look good. He fussed with his hair, he grew a beard, he had his teeth worked on, he took to wearing a gray cutaway and matching top hat. It didn't matter. No matter what you did to Rooney's face, you couldn't alter it. It was the sort of face that, no matter how long you stared at it, you never quite got used to.

He beat Jackson in '88 and Salivar in '89. He even beat a Chilean named Estafen. He awakened one day and noticed how gray his hair was getting. A few weeks later, fighting a plump kid he should have had no problem with, he nearly got knocked out. It wasn't that the kid was so good. It was that Rooney was getting so bad. Strength, endurance, quickness—by the time he was age thirty they had all left him. And they would never come back.

Wifeless, even finding few prostitutes who were willing to welcome him into their beds, he spent his life trying to make some sense of forces he sensed but could not understand. Why had he been born not only colored but so ugly? Why were less gifted men promoted when he was not? Would he ever know anything remotely like a normal life? The other day, walking up the street, he'd noticed a small cottage surrounded by a picket fence. A man and woman had stood in the yard, hand in hand, watching a dazzling little blonde girl play with a calico dog. Rooney had almost been overcome by a feeling that started out envy but ended up sadness. Would he ever have a life like that? Ever?

"You know what we're looking for, Rooney."

"I know."

"We want a show."

Rooney nodded.

"A good show, Rooney."

Rooney nodded again.

"He hits you, you get up. Meanwhile, you hit him every chance you get."

"You ever see Carter anymore?"

"Not anymore." John T. Stoddard's eyes dropped, and Rooney wondered what was wrong.

"He head east?"

"I'm not sure where he headed. He—died," Stoddard replied.

"Died?"

"In the ring."

"Carter?"

"Had you seen him in a while?"

"Not for a while, no."

"He'd started to get old suddenly." Stoddard shook his head. "You know how it gets with fighters."

"Yeah. I know."

"He found this kid from Pennsylvania. This really strapping bastard."

"A kid killed him?"

"Nineteen. But a punch you just can't believe."

Rooney got up from the chair. The three of them were in a small room on the east edge of the raw board building adjacent to the ring. The room smelled of heat and tobacco. The building was a warehouse for a tobacco wholesaler. Rooney was already stripped to the waist because of the heat.

"Carter. Dead." Rooney shook his head. "He was a decent man for a—"

Stoddard grinned and turned to the man he called Guild. "He was going to say 'a decent man for a white man.' You see, Guild, they think of us what we think of them." He laughed in a booming way that revealed anxiety beneath.

Rooney kept pacing. "Victor still hates colored folks?"

"I'm afraid he does."

"What we ever do to him?"

"You know how Victor is." Stoddard tapped his skull to indicate he was crazy. "You go fifteen rounds with him, you could be sitting pretty, Rooney. Sitting very pretty."

"I go fifteen rounds with him, I could be dead is what I could be."

"Victor's not so young anymore."

"That why he killed a fighter just last spring?"

"To be honest, that guy wasn't much of a fighter. He really wasn't."

Stoddard looked over at Guild. There was some doubt in his expression. "Now you're not going to go out there and just lay down, are you, Rooney?"

"We have an agreement. I'm going to stick to that agreement. I'm going to do everything I can."

"I need at least twelve rounds."

"I need my head on my shoulders, too." Rooney allowed a certain belligerence to come into his voice.

Stoddard glanced over at Guild again, then back at Rooney. "Why don't you show me a little something?"

"I ain't in the mood."

"Just a little something, Rooney. So I know you're fit and all ready to go." He patted his stomach. "You've been putting on weight, boy."

"I'm gettin' old."

Stoddard smiled. "Old is going around. Like the flu. Everybody seems to be catching it."

Rooney finally relented and showed him a few things. He

showed him a few right hooks and a few right crosses and a few uppercuts. He stood in the sunny corner and fought his quick moving shadow. The shadow was not quite as black as Rooney.

When he finished, there was a sheen of sweat on his back and arms. He went over and sat on the edge of a chair. He was panting. As he had told Stoddard, he was getting old. He'd fought many one-hundred-round matches in his youth. Today he was up against two things—the loss of that youth and the unforgiving hands of Victor Sovich.

"You know something, Rooney?"

"What?"

"You look scared."

"I got a right to look scared."

"You're going to be fine."

"He hates us folks."

"Victor isn't exactly a spring chicken himself anymore."

"That's what you said. That don't necessarily convince me."

"I need a good show, Rooney. A damn good show. There's going to be a lot of people out there."

"Sure. A man who kills other men always gets a crowd."

Stoddard paused. "You're forgetting something, Rooney."

"What?"

"You killed a man, too."

"Not on purpose."

Stoddard smiled. "That story kind of hangs on."

"What story?"

"That you poisoned his drinking water before the fight."

"That's bull."

"It's what I hear."

"It's not the truth."

"You just put on a show today, Rooney. That's all I care about. The past is the past."

Rooney noticed how interested Guild seemed since the conversation had come round to the fighter Rooney was accused of poisoning.

"I won't look good if you don't look good," Stoddard said. "You just try and remember that, all right?"

"All right."

Stoddard came up. He looked as if he were going to pat Rooney on the back. But you could see in his eyes the distaste he felt for the boxer's sweating body. He brought his hand back to his suit coat and put it in a pocket.

Rooney said, "You tell Sovich not to kill me."

"I'll tell him, Rooney."

"You promise?"

"I promise."

"I ain't got nothing against him. He shouldn't have nothin' against me."

"I'll talk to him, Rooney. You can bet I will."

Rooney sighed. "Maybe I'll retire after this one."

Stoddard said, "That's something to think about, Rooney. That sure is something to think about."

He and Guild left soon after.

Rooney sat in the chair. There was a fly in the room. Every few minutes Rooney tried to slap it down. He had no luck.

He thought about the fighter he'd poisoned that time. The kid wasn't supposed to die. All Rooney had wanted was to slow him down enough to beat him good. Then the kid up and died.

Rooney got up and paced. The sweat was now chill on his back, even with the heat. He was thinking of picket fences and small thatched cottages. He was thinking of a good woman with wide hips and a real way with children.

But he knew better, Rooney did. He knew it wasn't going to happen for him. Ever.

He stared out the window at the first hundred or so fans who surrounded the large ring.

There was only one thing they'd come here to see today, and Rooney knew only too well what that was.

Chapter Sixteen

Twenty minutes later, inside the office where the gate receipts would be kept, John T. Stoddard handed Guild a Sharps and said, "I want you to shoot anybody who comes through that door during the fight."

"Somehow I don't think your permission is enough. To kill somebody, I mean."

"Anybody who tries to get through there is doing so for only one reason. To take the gate money."

The office was snug, with two oak rolltop desks on the east and west walls, a bookcase filled with leather-bound legal volumes, a map of Dakota Territory, and one wall lined with advertisements for various brands of pipes and smoking tobacco. Sunlight fell hot on the floor. In the corner Stephen Stoddard sat at a noisy typewriter filling up a white sheet of paper with black-lettered information. He wore a white straw boater. Inside his coat was a lump that had to be a gun.

"I'll keep the Sharps, but I'll be using it only as a last resort."

"I wouldn't put anything past Victor."

"He probably wouldn't put anything past you."

Stoddard surprised Guild by taking his gibe seriously. "That supposed to mean something?"

Stephen Stoddard turned away from the typewriter. He was curious about his father's reaction to Guild's harmless remark.

"I said, is that supposed to mean something?"

"No, it isn't."

"Then why'd you say it?"

"I was making a joke."

"I don't find it one damn bit funny."

"You could always get somebody else for this job."

"A little late, isn't it, Mr. Guild? Two goddamn hours before the first preliminary fight starts?"

"Dad, I really don't think he meant anything by that," Stephen Stoddard said. He wore a white shirt with a high, starched collar, red arm garters, and a white straw boater. His trousers were dark blue and his shoes white.

"Did I ask you, Stephen?"

"No, I suppose not but—"

"Then you keep your goddamn nose out of my business, you hear me?"

"But Dad, all I said was—"

Stoddard moved across the room with easy grace. He poked a plump pink finger in Stephen's face. "Out of my goddamn business, you understand me?"

Stephen managed to look more miserable than usual. He could not meet his father's gaze.

"You understand me?"

Stephen scarcely whispered, "Yes, sir."

"Now you come on with me and walk the grounds."

For the first time, a look of anger showed clearly on Stephen's face. "I'm going to stay here, Dad, with Guild."

"The hell you are."

"The hell I'm not."

"Don't you dare talk to me that way."

"That's just the way I'm talking, Dad. Just the way."

Stoddard glared at his son and began to sputter something but stopped himself.

His glare turned to Guild. "You'd better watch yourself, Guild. You'd better watch yourself pretty damn close."

Stoddard turned and was gone.

Stephen Stoddard could not meet Guild's eyes. He went back to the typewriter and began pounding away again.

Guild watched him. He knew it wasn't his place to say anything, but he didn't have any choice. "You don't owe him, son."

Stephen continued to type, his back to Guild. "It's none of your affair, Mr. Guild."

"I don't like to see people suffering."

"I'm not suffering."

"Sure you are, son. Sure you are."

Stephen turned around and faced Guild. "He's my father."

"I know he's your father. He's also a bastard, and he's particularly a bastard to you, his own son."

"He means well."

"The hell he does. Your father has never meant well in his life."

"You're suggesting what?"

"That you leave. Get a job of your own. Show him you won't take his abuse anymore."

"It would kill him."

"Because you left?"

"Yes."

Guild rubbed at his face and sighed. "Son, he doesn't care about you."

"I'm the only family he's got."

Guild sat down in the office chair. He angled it away from Stephen. He put his Texas boots up on the rolltop desk and took out a cigarette and lighted it.

"You're some kid."

Stephen was already back to his typing. "I don't want to talk about it anymore. If you don't mind, I mean."

Guild inhaled deeply. He watched the blue smoke emerge from

his mouth. He tried a couple of smoke rings. They almost worked, but not quite. "You want to stay here with me?"

"Why? You don't want me to stay?"

"Fine with me. As long as you know what you're getting into."

"What am I getting into?" Stephen asked this with just a hint of mockery in his voice.

"There's always some risk when you have this much money."

"I've been around this much money before."

"But we're isolated here. Thieves could get in and out—"

Stephen shook his head. The white straw boater jiggled some. "I'm ready for any eventuality, Mr. Guild." From inside his blue coat he took out a Colt .45. "After all, it's the family money at stake."

"I'm not sure it's 'family' money, son. A big part of it is supposed to belong to Victor."

"Oh, yes," Stephen said, almost as an afterthought. "Victor." It was going to be a very long afternoon, Guild thought.

"God did not mean for us to mingle the races, even in fisticuffs!" the man shouted to passersby. "The Bible expressly forbids mingling in any way!"

He stood at the bottom of the bleachers, an open Bible in one hand and the skull of an ape in the other. "It is from the ape that the colored man is descended. But it is from God that we white men spring. Please, stop this travesty!"

His pockmarked face, his sunken, exhausted gaze, his thin red lips that seemed always to be trembling, lent him the visage of a man not only mad but perhaps dangerous, too. Even the most swaggering of fans walked wide of him, unsettled by his presence in some way they could not define.

And so he stood in his ministerial frock coat, crying out as he had cried out on street corners and on trains and stagecoaches and in mainstream churches; cried out to be heard; cried out so that he could share at least some of the burden of his hatred.

"Help me end this travesty!" he called. "Help me end this tragedy!"

They kept on walking wide of him.

Chapter Seventeen

The streetcar was so crowded the conductor had to keep asking people to move back, otherwise he wouldn't be able to steer.

Reynolds stood near the rear, somebody's elbow pressed against his rib, somebody's shoulder against his shoulder blades. A stout woman's huge picture hat covered half of his face.

When the streetcar finally stopped, he was glad for the two-block walk to the arena. His legs needed stretching and he needed fresh air. He also needed to calm himself. The closer the time came to the shooting, the more anxious he became. He wished he had not agreed to this job, but backing out was the sort of thing he just couldn't do. Word would get around, and then people would begin to wonder if he would back out on *them*.

He bought a ticket and entered the carnival-like arena. A furious rumbling shook the wooden bleachers, the effect of so many people talking, shouting, screaming, laughing, cursing. He sat down and bought peanuts from a vendor. He dropped the shells on the bleacher and crunched them with his shoe. He stared down into the empty ring.

He still wished he had not agreed to this.

"You think he's going to kill him?"

Reynolds was distracted from his thoughts. A petite woman in a pink summer dress and a white straw hat held down by a gauzy piece of pink chiffon stared at him.

"You think he's going to kill him?"

"Oh. The fight."

"Yes. The fight."

"Well, I don't know. I don't actually follow boxing all that carefully."

"Well, I do and I think he's going to kill him. Victor's going to kill the colored man, I mean."

"It'll probably be exciting."

He knew immediately that his style of response did not please the woman. She glared at him as if he were some kind of circus freak and then turned back to her female companion.

He wished he had not agreed to do this.

The woman was now whispering something about him to her companion. Her companion smiled.

Blushing, Reynolds stood up. Now was a good time to check out the office, figure a way in and a way out.

When he turned back to the woman to see if he might not have been imagining her whispered insults, he saw that they were now both smirking.

Suddenly he became self-conscious about the way he moved. He tried to be more purposeful in his motions.

God, he wished there were not so many people out here.

God, he wished it were not so hot out here.

God, he wished he had not agreed to do this.

She took a carriage from the hotel. She liked the smart way the sleek black horse in traces picked up and put down its shoed feet. She liked the smart way the driver cracked his whip just over the horse's back so that the animal wasn't hurt in any way.

She sat back on the tufted blue silk seat and watched the buildings of the business district give way to small frame houses and then to real mansions, with wide stone gates and windbreaks of firs offering privacy.

She was aware that the driver turned back every minute or so for a glance at her. He was smitten, obviously. But he was also leery. He was white and he obviously suspected that she was not. Still, he could not quit staring.

It was hot in the carriage. She fanned herself with a black, Spanish-style hand fan.

Images of her brother filled her mind.

When he was seven.

When he was nine.

When he was dead there in the ring.

The driver was staring at her again. "You all right, ma'am?"

"Yes, thank you."

"You look troubled."

She smiled. "I am troubled. I'm impressed that you were sensitive enough to notice."

The man flushed. "It's just your face—well, it's easy to see what's in your soul, is what I'm trying to say."

"So you believe in the soul?"

"Yes, ma'am."

"A lot of men don't."

"I was raised Methodist."

"That's odd."

"What is, ma'am?"

"So was I."

"Methodist?"

"Yes. And most people think we're all Baptists."

"'Us,' ma'am?"

"Yes. Us." She paused, giving her word all the dramatic power she could summon. "Coloreds."

She watched his eyes. She was not disappointed. He looked as if he'd just suffered a sharp kick to the stomach. "You're colored?"

"You mean you didn't guess?"

"No, ma'am." He sounded miserable.

"You wanted me, didn't you?"

"Ma'am?"

"You desired me, didn't you, until you found out I was colored?"

He turned his head back to the street.

She wasn't sure why she'd wanted to hurt him. It was just this need that came on her from time to time. She needed to feel someone else's hatred sometimes. It revived her, brought her in touch with herself again. The hatred of others was a definition of all the things she could never be, no matter how badly she might want to be. The hatred of others told her very definitely who and what she was.

She said, "I'm sorry I embarrassed you."

But he wouldn't turn around now. He would take her out to the boxing arena and deposit her and leave as soon as possible.

"I really am sorry," she said. "You seem like a decent man, and I shouldn't have hurt your feelings."

The horses stepped smartly forward.

The day was very hot.

She wondered if, in the end, she would have enough courage for what she had ahead of her.

"Do you plan on killing him, Mr. Sovich?"

The kid had red hair and freckles and wore a cheap, loud suit and spoke an octave higher whenever he got nervous, as now. The older reporters gathered in Victor Sovich's dressing room let the kid talk because he was kind of funny to watch.

"Son, that's not a decent thing to ask me." Victor Sovich winked at the older reporters. "I just go out there and do my job, and if the boy happens to fall and not get back up, there isn't much I can do about that, is there?"

"Do you regret killing those other colored people?"

"Now you're getting serious, aren't you?"

"Yes, sir."

Victor Sovich, bare chested and fitted out with fine leather gloves, smiled toward John T. Stoddard, who stood in the corner.

"There's only one type of question Mr. Stoddard has asked me not to answer."

"What kind is that, sir?"

"The serious kind."

Several of the older reporters laughed.

But the redheaded kid persisted. "Do you ever get scared?"

"Me?"

"Do you ever think maybe you could be the one who gets killed?"

Sovich offered the onlookers another wink. "Maybe you know something I don't, kid. You think I *should* be scared?"

"No, sir," the kid said, writing something on the tablet he held out before him. "I just wonder if it ever crossed your mind."

"Do you have any idea how many fights I've had?"

"No, sir."

"Do you have any idea how many of those fights I've won?"

"No, sir."

"Well, I've had one hundred two fights and I've won one hundred two fights. Now, does that sound like a reason for me to get scared?"

The kid gulped. He had a huge Adam's apple. "No, sir. I guess not."

John T. Stoddard nodded to Victor and left the dressing room. He hated Victor's swaggering before the press. Victor swaggered enough as it was.

He felt grateful for the heat and the crowd. The crowd was invigorating.

He walked the aisles between the bleachers, noting how everything was going smoothly, from the vendors to the ice tents. After the "robbery," he was going to have a great deal of money.

One thing remained. He needed to get his son out of the office. He did not want Stephen there when the shooting started.

He headed back for the office, and it was then he saw Reynolds.

John T. Stoddard knew immediately that he had made a terrible mistake counting on Reynolds. Severe dark rings encircled the lower part of the man's eyes. His entire body seemed to twitch.

John T. Stoddard watched as Reynolds went inside the office building, obviously preparing for the "robbery" later this afternoon.

The door opened and a tall, gray-haired man stood there. "Help you?"

Reynolds couldn't find his voice. "Uh, I was just wondering if there was a toilet in here."

"There are latrines outside."

"I just wondered if there was a toilet in here."

"Afraid we can't help you."

"All right. Thank you."

When the door closed, Reynolds fell back against the wall. His chest heaved. His head pounded.

Could he go through with it?

He heard footsteps coming up the stairs. He should run, hide. He should not be seen anywhere near this office.

But somehow he couldn't move. He tried, but he couldn't.

"Jesus Christ," a harsh voice said, and when he opened his eyes there was John T. Stoddard. "You're supposed to be a professional."

He swallowed, wanting to defend his honor. "I am a professional, Mr. Stoddard. A professional thief."

"It's too late for me to get somebody else. I've got to depend on you."

"Couldn't I just knock him out?"

"You knock Guild out? Don't be absurd. You'd never get that close." He shook his head. "Listen, you miserable little bastard. We had an agreement, and I expect you to stick to it. Do you understand?"

"I'm going to be all right."

"You should see yourself—"

"I'm going to show you that I've got a lot more grit than you think."

"—pasty white and dark little eyes, and your left hand keeps shaking and—"

Reynolds moved away from the wall. "I said I'm going to show you, Mr. Stoddard. I'm going to show you."

He wasn't sure what he was talking about and felt he was just babbling, but he was tired of Stoddard's scorn. That was for sure. So now he tried to make himself appear as strong as possible.

"You've got a gun?" Stoddard asked.

"Yes."

"It's loaded?"

"I'm not a child, Mr. Stoddard."

"It's loaded?"

"Yes, it's loaded."

"And you're ready?"

"I'm ready, Mr. Stoddard. Yes, I'm ready."

"Then don't let me down, Reynolds. Don't let me down."

"I won't."

"You promise?"

"I promise."

After leaving the building, Reynolds walked over to a latrine and started vomiting. The stuff was orange. He closed his eyes so he wouldn't have to see.

Behind him a hick voice said, "Whooee! Whatever that little guy is drinkin', I don't want no part of!"

Rough male laughter filled Reynolds's ears.

He lurched from the latrine and walked with as much dignity as he could muster back toward the bleachers.

Chapter Eighteen

The first money came in a steel box latched with a lock. A hefty man in a three-piece suit and a walrus mustache delivered it. Guild opened the door for him. The man stared down at Guild's .44. "That Stoddard, he don't trust nobody, does he?" the man said. He was laughing.

He brought the box into the office, walked over, and set it on the desk.

"This is Stoddard's son, Stephen," Guild said, hoping the man would take a hint and not insult the father in front of the son anymore. Guild couldn't help it; he felt sorry for the boy.

"Yeah, I met him," the man said.

Stephen Stoddard pulled a piece of paper from inside his coat. He dropped to his haunches and held the paper up to the steel box. The paper held the combination to the lock. Stephen worked quickly, deftly. In seconds the lock was open and he was throwing back the lid.

The man whistled. "Your old man is having a good day, kid."

The box was packed tight with greenbacks.

"This is the biggest haul I've ever seen around these parts," the man said.

Stephen slammed the lid and latched the box again. He carried it over to the corner and set it on a small desk.

"I'll be back in another hour or so with the next box. It's already half full." He snorted. "The way them yokels is streamin' in, it may not take another full hour."

He went to the door. "Your old man said we wasn't to be drinkin' no beer today. That still hold?"

"Yes, it does," Stephen said.

The man offered them a sour expression and left.

Guild went over to the rolltop desk where he'd been sitting. He put his feet up and laid the .44 in his lap. He took a five-cent cigar from his pocket and lighted it. He watched the way the blue smoke turned the golden dust motes silver.

Stephen went over and stood by the money box. He touched it as if it were the most precious thing he had ever seen.

"Both Dad and Victor are going to make out all right on this one," Stephen said. "This is the one they've both been waiting for."

Guild took a drag on his cigar. "I don't think you should be here."

"What?"

"You're not hired to be a guard. I am."

"You think I'm afraid?"

"No."

"You think I couldn't cut it if I had to?"

"No."

"Then why would you want to get rid of me?"

"Because I've got a funny feeling is all."

"What kind of funny feeling?"

"The kind of funny feeling this kind of money always gives me."

"I'm his son."

"I'm surprised he would want you here."

"Meaning exactly what, Leo?"

"Meaning if you were my boy, I'd want you out walking around the stands. Putting a good face on things for the public. I wouldn't want you anywhere near the money."

"Dad trusts me."

Guild didn't want to say what he thought: *Your dad doesn't care enough about you to move you out of the way.* Instead he said, "Anyplace in particular you'd want to settle?"

"Beg pardon?"

"Anyplace you been thinking of settling when the time comes?"

"I couldn't leave Dad."

"I mean if something happened and you had to leave your dad. Where would you settle?"

He seemed afraid to even speculate. "I've just never thought about it." But his quickly averted eyes said that he was lying.

"You ever seen the ocean at Atlantic City?"

"Yes."

"Beautiful, isn't it? And all those girls on the beach."

Softly Stephen said, "It's very nice."

"You ever seen Vermont in autumn? I've never seen anything like the leaves in the hills. Like they're on fire."

"No, I've never seen them."

"Or a dairy farm in New Hampshire? The grass gets so green that the black and white cows really stand out against it on a sunny day. And it's so peaceful in the shade—"

"What the hell are you trying to do?"

"Just passing the time."

"No, you're not."

Guild sighed. "If you were my boy, you wouldn't be guarding the money, and that's for goddamn sure." He was angry at the three of them—at Stoddard for using his son this way, at his son for being used, and at himself because he could not seem to let things lie where they were.

"I'm not your son and I'm tired of your running down my dad. I should tell him some of the things you've said."

He had pushed too far. He had lost the boy. He could not help the kid now because the kid wouldn't let him.

He said, "You should ask for a cut."

"What?"

"You should ask your old man for a percentage of the take."

"I know you're trying to help, Leo, and I appreciate it, but you're really talking crazy."

"You work hard, kid. You deserve a percentage. That way when you're finally ready to leave—"

"You're getting kind of one note."

Guild stared at him. "You deserve a life of your own, Stephen. You really do."

Stephen walked to the door. "I'm going to go get some lemonade. You want a glass?"

"That would be fine."

"Big glass or small glass?"

"Big glass."

"I know you're just trying to help."

"I don't seem to be doing a very good job."

"He isn't as bad as you claim."

"Maybe not."

"He's my father. He raised me."

"I know."

Stephen said, "I'm going to stay with him till he dies, Leo, and that's the way things are." He spoke with a quiet determination that was all the more convincing for its lack of bluster.

He nodded and left.

Chapter Nineteen

Her four-year-old son said, "You will go far away?"

"Not far away."

"You will go with Victor?"

"Yes."

"I don't like Victor."

"I know."

"Maria, she is scared."

"I know she is scared."

"And I'm scared, too."

"I will not go far away, and I will return often."

"You promise?"

"I promise."

They stood in the center of the living room. The place looked better than it had in months. Victor had given her money to fix the place up. There was a new yellow spread for the couch, and two of the windows were fixed with new panes of glass. Where there had been a picture of the Virgin there was now a photograph of Victor. He had asked for it to be this way. Teresa had brooded about this for several days. Something about the Virgin made Victor uncomfortable. When she'd asked him what, he'd said, "It makes you look like a cheap Mexican. All these religious things on the walls." But of course Victor made her uncomfortable about many things. He had struck her several times with exceeding force, and sometimes when his teeth nibbled on her during lovemaking he seemed to take undue pleasure from the pain he inflicted.

Now her mother appeared in the doorway.

Her son ran to the older woman and hugged his grandma's thigh. He began sobbing immediately. "She is going to go, Grandma. She is going to go."

"You be a good boy and go play outside," the grandmother said softly. She knelt down to wipe away the boy's tears. She kissed him tenderly on the cheek and then patted him on the bottom and sent him on his way outside.

In the doorway the boy looked back at his mother.

Teresa raised her hand and waved good-bye.

The boy stood staring at her as if it would be the last time he ever saw her.

"Go play," his grandmother said.

The boy vanished.

The grandmother was scarcely five feet tall. She had skin the color of coffee and eyes the color of a midnight sky. She wore a loose-fitting white dress and sandals. She came over and sat on the couch, careful not to wrinkle the new yellow spread when she sat down.

"I do not want you to go," she said.

"I have already told him I will."

"It does not matter, Teresa, what you told him."

"He is expecting me."

"Your children are expecting you."

"They love you. They will be happy you are around them."

"Can you imagine what the priest will say?"

"He will say nothing to me."

"Oh?"

"Victor does not believe in priests. He does not want me to see the priest."

"It's terrible what you do."

"It's not. I will lose my looks in a few years. Then I will have only regrets."

"I have had three daughters."

"Yes."

"And I should be thankful."

"Thankful, yes. For our good health."

"And for one other thing, too."

"What?"

There was craft and malice in the old woman's gaze. "Only one of them turned out to be a whore."

Teresa flushed. "You do not understand."

"You think I was not young once, Teresa, as you are young—and beautiful, as you are beautiful?"

"It is different in the modern world, Mama."

"He made you take down the picture of the Virgin?"

"Yes."

"And he does not want you to see a priest?"

"No, he does not want me to see a priest."

"And he wants you to leave your children?"

Teresa said nothing. She did not want to be called a whore again.

"Does this not tell you about the man, Teresa? About what is in this man's heart?"

"He's a good man."

"In bed he may be good. No other place."

"We will be back often."

"You don't really believe that. I can see the lie in your face, Teresa." She wrung her brown hands. "You are so stupid."

"He loves me."

The old woman scoffed. "He puts gaudy dresses on your back. He makes you promises. He puts his seed in you. These things are not love."

"He said we will live in a fine house in St. Louis."

"You are forgetting your cousin Donna."

At mention of the name, Teresa lowered her head. "He is not like the man Donna was with."

"Oh, no? And what makes him different, Teresa? What makes him different?"

"Victor is a man of honor."

"So was her man until he got tired of her. And do you remember what he did then?"

"Please. You know how I hate to talk about it."

"He threw fire in her face so that she would be in agony and no other man would ever want her. He could not even give her the rest of her life, a chance to live well without him. He would not even do this much for her. So he burned her."

"Please."

"Do you know how she lives today?"

"I know."

"She lives in the cellar of her parents' basement because she looks so horrible that no one can stand to set eyes on her."

"He is not like this."

"Oh, no. He is a most honorable man. He makes you take down the picture of the Virgin, and he persuades you to leave your children."

She got up and walked across the room to where Teresa sat in a chair. She slapped her very hard across the side of the face.

Teresa began sobbing.

"Because he puts his seed in you does not mean he loves you, Teresa."

The old woman shook her head sadly, then went out the door and down the steps to play with her grandchildren in the sunlight.

Chapter Twenty

The referee was a man named Macatee. Stoddard had requested a man named Simek but Simek was sick with gout.

Stoddard knew nothing about Macatee, whose first name was George, and this made him nervous. He stood inside Macatee's dressing room, watching a bluebottle fly perch at an angle on the windowsill.

Outside the open window four women in crisp summer dresses carried placards back and forth. Obviously they knew this was where Macatee was getting ready. They wanted him to understand their seriousness.

Stoddard tried a nervous smile. "You can't escape them these days. They're in every town with more than one hundred people."

"Oh, they're all right."

"They are?"

"Sure. They just don't like to see people get hurt. Nothing wrong with that, is there?"

Stoddard continued to smile. "I like to see men get hurt. When men get hurt, I have a good payday. So do you."

Macatee had been shining his black boots with a coarse-bristled brush. The room they were in was smaller than many closets. There was a chair, a bureau with a mirror, and a spittoon.

As they passed by the window this time, the ladies leaned in toward Macatee. One of them, a redhead in an emerald-green picture hat, waved.

Macatee waved back.

"You know her?" Stoddard said.

Macatee, a tense little man with freckles on a white bald head, nodded and said, "I should. She's my wife."

"You have a wife who protests boxing?"

"It's her right. Just as it's my right to referee."

"Oh, I'm glad I came over here, Mr. Macatee. To see you, I mean."

"You are?"

"I certainly am. Do you know how many people are going to be here today?"

"How many?"

"The estimate is four thousand now."

Macatee whistled. He took a cigar from his shirt pocket, ran a lucifer along the front of the bureau. "Four thousand. That's the biggest sporting event this town has ever seen."

"That's one of my concerns."

"What is?"

"That the event lives up to the billing."

Macatee looked at him with eyes as green as his wife's hat. "What are you trying to say, Mr. Stoddard?"

"They tell me you're a good referee."

"I try to be."

"But I wouldn't want you to be too good."

Macatee blew heavy cigar smoke in Stoddard's direction. The blue-tailed fly was noisy in the corner. "Wish I had a swatter," Macatee said. "That goddamn thing's driving me crazy."

"You ever hear of the Sorgenson fight?"

"Sorgenson?"

"Over in Omaha about four years ago. Hmmm. Four years ago exactly this summer."

"I think I've heard of it. But what about it?" Macatee went back to shining his boots with the brush. He wore a short-sleeve shirt. He might be a small man, but he had outsize biceps for his size.

"Sorgenson was supposed to knock out his opponent pretty early in the fight. Everybody expected it. But Sorgenson was so good that he put the other fellow to the canvas in the first round."

Macatee whistled again. He didn't look up from his brushing. "Guess I should pay more attention to this Sorgenson."

"That isn't the point of the story."

"Then what is?" He still didn't look up. He seemed fascinated with getting the oxfords to shine perfectly.

"It's what happened after the first round. Sorgenson ran back in the ring at the top of the second and really started hitting the other man. Knocked him down again. Knocked him down so hard that the referee got scared."

"It can get scary in there."

"The referee stopped the fight."

"Oh. I see."

"Maybe you don't. He stopped the fight and a riot started."

"A riot?"

"It was a hot day, just like today. There was a huge crowd, just like this one. One man was predicted to win, just as Victor is supposed to win today. But the crowd still wanted a match. They didn't want to see it end too soon. They rioted. They took over the town and made it impossible for decent people to be anywhere near them for the night."

For the first time Macatee stopped his brushing. He raised his very green eyes to Stoddard. "You don't want to see this stopped today?"

"Not too soon."

"What if the colored boy gets hurt real bad?"

"He knows what he's getting into."

Macatee studied Stoddard's face for a long minute. "That story wasn't true, was it, Mr. Stoddard? About Sorgenson?"

"It was meant to illustrate a point."

"But it's not true."

"Not strictly speaking."

"Meaning there was no Sorgenson?"

"No."

"And no Omaha fight?"

"Not exactly."

"And no riot?"

"No, no riot."

Macatee had inhaled on his cigar. He was still studying Stoddard. "You're worried I'm going to lose you money, aren't you?"

"Yes, Mr. Macatee, I am. Especially now that I know your wife is carrying a placard."

Macatee picked up the shoe brush once again. He returned to his polishing. "I'm not going to let him get killed."

"Meaning what exactly, Mr. Macatee?"

"Meaning I'll stop the fight before it goes too far."

"Afraid of your wife?"

Macatee tapped his bald head. "Afraid of my conscience. I don't want to be responsible for a man's death. Even if he's colored."

"Just because a man gets hurt real bad, that doesn't mean he's going to die or anything like it."

"I know you want a show, Mr. Stoddard, and I intend to help give you a show. Just not at the expense of a man's life."

"You'll stop the fight, then?"

"When it's appropriate. I'm going to keep watching the colored boy's face close. When he looks like he's had enough, I stop the fight."

"The colored fellow wants to make some money. Remember, he's getting paid for every round he can get through. He'd sure appreciate all the money he could earn."

"It's nice you're so concerned for him," Macatee said. "The colored fellow, I mean."

"There's no call to get sarcastic."

"The mayor's office hired me because they don't want the responsibility of a death on their hands. If they hadn't hired me, or someone else with my attitude, Mr. Stoddard, you wouldn't have gotten your permit. A boxer dying may be all in a day's work to you, but not to the mayor's office. You have a fellow die in a ring like that and the state newspaper starts to paint you as an uncivilized place, and once that starts then businesses get real nervous about settling in your town, and pretty soon, before you know it, you've become a little fork in the road again and nothing more."

"That crowd's going to get awful mad if they don't see a fight."

"In Houston, I hear a crowd took its money back."

Stoddard said, "I'm just asking you to be fair, Mr. Macatee."

"How about if his eyes roll back in his head? Is that a fair time to stop the fight, Mr. Stoddard?"

"Eyes rolling back don't always mean anything."

"How about if he starts strangling on his own blood from his mouth being cut up so bad inside? Is that a fair time to stop the fight, Mr. Stoddard?"

"He takes a little salt water, he'll be fine."

"Or how about if his arms start twitching because his nervous system has been damaged? Is that a fair time to stop the fight, Mr. Stoddard?"

"He could be just arm-tired."

Macatee put the shoe brush down and dropped his leg from the chair. He stood up straight, touching a hand to a crick in his back. "I'm sure glad you're not going to be referee, Mr. Stoddard. You know that?"

Stoddard slid the white envelope from his pocket. He dropped it on the chair. "I like to give referees a little bonus. Before the fight."

Macatee stared down at the envelope. He leaned over and

picked it up. He hefted it, estimating the number of bills inside. He handed it back unopened to Stoddard. "I don't believe in bonuses, Mr. Stoddard. Especially before a fight."

A minute later, after stuffing the envelope back inside his pocket, Stoddard was gone.

Chapter Twenty-One

He went over to one of the thirty different beer tents. He knew it was the last place he should go.

He had a sausage sandwich and two mugs of beer. He figured that the food would help offset any damage the beer would do.

He hated it out here. It was too hot, the sunlight almost a bleached white, and too dusty. The dust smudged his clothes and got in his eyes and even down his throat.

He was eager now to get it over with.

He would go in and not even hesitate. He would shoot Guild right in the leg. When Guild was trying to recover, he would grab the money and flee. He would vanish into the crowd. That was the reason Stoddard had hired him. He was no good as a gunnie, but he was very good at vanishing.

So that not even Victor Sovich could find him.

He stood in the beer tent, hearing the first of the preliminary bouts announced.

A few more hours, he figured. A few more goddamned hours.

* * *

"I'm sorry I got so pissy."

"It's fine, son. We all get pissy."

"I know you're only trying to help."

"It isn't my business, and I shouldn't put my nose in it."

"It's just I wish you knew him better before you passed judgment on him."

"Maybe you're right. Maybe he's a wonderful man."

"You're being sarcastic, aren't you, Leo?"

"No, son, I'm not. Maybe he's a wonderful man and it's just my blind spot."

"He took right over as soon as my mother left."

Guild smiled at him. "He couldn't ask for a better son. You know that?"

Just then the crowd shouted and whistled and began stomping their feet.

"The prelim must have started," Stephen Stoddard said.

Guild picked up the rifle from where it stood next to the chair he was sitting in. He laid it across his lap. "Should be some more money coming our way pretty soon."

"I really am sorry I got so pissy, Leo. I hope you understand."

"Oh, I understand, son. I understand fine."

Stephen Stoddard grinned. "Maybe when this is all over, the three of us will go out and have some drinks. Would you go along if we asked you?"

"Sure."

Stephen Stoddard sat back and shook his head. "I've got a feeling you're good for him, Leo. He seems to act a little better when you're around."

"That's me," Leo Guild laughed. "A good influence on everybody I meet."

He rolled himself a smoke and checked out the rifle again.

Chapter Twenty-Two

They started rubbing Rooney with liniment half an hour before schedule. He was tightening up, and the bald, lanky man John T. Stoddard had appointed as Rooney's trainer could see why.

Rooney was obviously afraid he was going to die, and probably with good reason. Rooney, from everything Simpson, the trainer, could see, was no longer much of a fighter.

Oh, there had undoubtedly been a time when Rooney had been respected enough giving and taking in the ring, but he had probably always been one of those men who look more ferocious than they really are. Harold Simpson had been watching Rooney work out the past three days. If he were Rooney, he'd be afraid, too.

The liniment smelled of alcohol and another sharp odor. In the tiny dressing room the odor was overpowering.

"You probably should talk."

"Huh?" Rooney said, glancing up from his reverie.

"Talk. It would probably be good for you. You're real tight."

"I was remembering this fishing hole in Arkansas."

"Nice, huh?"

"Biggest snappers a man ever saw. And the water so blue and cold in the morning with steam coming up off the lake."

"Sounds pretty."

"Real pretty. Real pretty."

"You remember what I told you about his right hand. The son of a bitch comes up from nowhere."

But Rooney wasn't listening. "Then when it got hot you could lay back on the shore and look at the clouds. I never had it so peaceful before or since." Rooney was still back there fishing in Arkansas.

"You got to keep moving, first to your left, then to your right. It's your best chance, Rooney." He wanted to say your *only* chance, but he knew how that would sound.

"Sometimes I'd stay there right through the night," Rooney went on. "I'd get me a fire going by the shore, and I'd clean the snapper and put it in a pan and cook it right there. It was beautiful, the way the fire glowed in the darkness. Downright beautiful."

"You keep moving and his punches won't land clean. And if his punches don't land clean, he's going to get frustrated. And if he gets frustrated, you got a chance of hitting him back, Rooney."

Rooney turned his ebony torso toward Simpson. "You ain't been listening to me, have you?"

"You ain't been listening to me, either, Rooney."

"I was telling you about this fishing spot in Arkansas."

"And I was telling you about how to get out of that ring alive." Simpson said this with such vehemence that Rooney had no choice but to forget about Arkansas and face the situation at hand.

"I need to go fifteen rounds anyways," Rooney said. "I need the money bad, Simpson."

"He could hurt you a lot in fifteen rounds."

"Not if I keep moving like you said."

Simpson thought of the thick, ponderous body he'd seen working out yesterday. At some point in the past five years or so, Rooney had been hurt. The arms didn't come up quite right, the legs were always wobbly, and sometimes, for no reason, he'd start to shake.

Fifteen rounds could kill him for sure.

"You ever want to go with me?"

"Where, Rooney?"

"Back to Arkansas. That's where I'm going when this is all over."

"You are, huh?"

"Yes, I am. I'm getting me a pole and some elderberry wine and some good cigars, and I'm going to do nothing but fish for a month and watch the steam come up off the lake every morning."

"It sounds like it's going to be swell."

"It is. You wait and see."

Simpson had the impression that Rooney was gone again, was refusing to face the battle at hand by slipping into dreamy dialogue about fishing holes in Arkansas.

But suddenly Simpson knew better.

When he looked down at Rooney, he saw him starting to cry. "I'm scared, Harold. I'm scared."

Simpson put a white hand on the black shoulder. "It'll be all right, Rooney. You wait and see."

But Simpson knew better. Simpson was scared, too.

"This'll probably be the last big box," the guard said as he put the strongbox on the desk next to the other two strongboxes.

John T. Stoddard took the cigar from his mouth and nodded. Guild watched Stoddard as he obviously resisted the impulse to start running his hands through all the greenbacks.

Stephen Stoddard, standing next to his father, said, "Dad and Victor are certainly going to be on easy street after this one."

Guild said, "If this is the last big strongbox, why don't I take it all to the bank right now instead of letting it sit here the rest of the afternoon?"

John T. Stoddard turned and looked at him. "The agreement was that you'd guard the money, Mr. Guild."

"The agreement was," Guild said, "that I'd make sure your money was safe. It'd be a lot safer in a bank vault than here."

"You've got a rifle, don't you?"

"You know I do. You're looking at it."

"Then my money should be safe."

"The banker said we could bring it in anytime up till three o'clock. That gives us forty-five minutes. If we put the strong-boxes on a buckboard, we could make it."

John T. Stoddard put the cigar back in his mouth and shook his head. "You ever do a job without offering your own opinion?"

"I'm not arguing with you. I'm just making a point."

"Well, you've made your point. Now I'm making my point. I want you to stay here with the money the rest of the afternoon while Stephen and I make sure everything's going all right in the grandstand."

"But Dad, I told Leo I'd stay with him."

"I want you to help me out, Stephen." John T. Stoddard seemed to make a point of being casual. But, watching him carefully, Guild saw that his eyes had begun to flicker anxiously. "Unless you've got a contrary opinion like our friend Guild here."

"I just thought I'd kind of help him out."

"I want you to help me out, Stephen. Do you understand that? I want you to help me out, and I don't want any more goddamn back talk about it."

Stoddard's attempt at casualness was now gone.

The office crackled with his anger.

Stephen went over and sat on the edge of the desk. He put his head down and said, "Yes, sir."

But his father wasn't done yet. "I'm getting good and sick of having to tell you everything. You know that?"

Stephen was shrinking into himself. "Yes, sir."

John T. Stoddard obviously needed to unload his formidable temper. He went over by the strongbox and slammed his fist on the desk. He whirled suddenly and jabbed his finger in Stephen's face. "The next time I tell you to do something, I want you to do it, and no back talk."

"Yes, sir."

"Now you stand up and precede me out of this office"

"Yes, sir."

Guild couldn't watch any longer.

Stephen would never be free of his father. Never.

Stephen glanced over at Guild. He looked ashamed of himself and ashamed of his father. He put his head down and walked out the door.

When the kid was gone, Guild said, "I think you finally got to him, Stoddard."

"Meaning what?"

"Meaning that I think you finally broke him."

"Did I ask your opinion?"

Guild stood up. He wanted to smash in Stoddard's face. "You want to keep him a little boy, don't you?"

Stoddard thumped the pocket watch in his vest. "In a few more hours, Mr. Guild, it is going to be my pleasure to pay you off and get you out of my life forever."

"I wish you'd do the same favor for your son."

"You just take good care of my money."

Guild said, "Something's going on, isn't it?"

"What the hell are you talking about?"

"There's a reason you're not letting me take this money to the bank, isn't there?"

"Are you calling me a liar?"

"No, Stoddard, I'm calling you a lot worse than that."

But Stoddard was already on his way out the door. "You'll be all finished in a couple hours, Mr. Guild. In the meantime, you just take care of the money."

After Stoddard slammed the door, Guild went over and locked it. Next he propped a chair under the doorknob so nobody could force his way in.

Finally he went over and sat directly in front of the door, his .44 in his lap.

He wasn't sure what John T. Stoddard was up to yet, but he now knew for sure that he hadn't hired Guild simply as a guard. He had hired Guild as some sort of patsy.

Chapter Twenty-Three

"I told her how you are about seeing women right before a fight."

"It's all right," Victor Sovich said to Kane, his pudgy trainer.

She stood in the doorway after Kane left. She looked crisp in her white dress, and beautiful. In her right hand was a suitcase.

Sovich smiled as she walked into the dressing room. "You did it, huh?"

"My mother is not happy."

"She'll survive."

"She says you'll get tired of me and throw me away. Or do something worse."

"You know how mothers are."

She came over and stood by the table he sat on. He had been rubbed down. He smelled harsh. The gloves had been put on his hands. "You seem so calm."

"I am calm."

"You don't ever get afraid?"

"What's to be afraid of?"

"Do you suppose you'll ever marry me?"

"I thought we were talking about boxing?"

"Is my mother right, Victor? Are you that kind of man?"

He brought her to him and put his face into her soft breasts. "I'm not exactly forcing you to go with me at gunpoint."

"Do you want me to go with you?"

"What did I tell you about the next time you asked me that? I said I wouldn't tell you anymore."

"Are you ashamed to tell me your feelings?"

He laughed. "No. But I am tired of repeating myself."

If he wouldn't repeat himself, she would repeat himself for him. "You told me you wanted me to go with you."

"If I said it, I must have meant it."

"You told me that I was beautiful and that you have never felt this way about any woman."

"I'm pretty good with the words, aren't I?"

"You said that if everything went all right that perhaps some-day we would be married."

"Oh, I did, did I?"

"Yes."

"And how much did I have to drink?" He smiled and brought her tender body to his again.

"It was very hard saying good-bye to my children."

"I'll bet."

"They cried so hard I could hear them three blocks away."

"They'll get over it. You know how kids are."

"You don't care about them, do you?"

Just then his trainer knocked again. He held up a bottle. "This'll be your last drink before the fight."

He was happy for the chance not to get into the mess about her children. He held out his thick arm. "I could use some water."

He took the bottle and drank. The water tasted odd. He assumed it was from the well out here.

Finished, he handed the trainer back the bottle.

The trainer left.

Victor said, "Let's not talk anymore. Let me just hold you."

"You don't care about my children, do you?" she said. There were tears in her voice.

Victor sighed. "This isn't what I need right now. You understand?" He paused, then spread his arms for her. At first she would not come into the circle he made for her. She stood and stared like a frightened animal. Her tears made her seem much younger and quite vulnerable. Victor found this very erotic.

More softly he said, "Come here. Please."

"Will you say you love me?"

"Yes. If that's what you want me to say."

"I want you to say it because you want to say it."

Women were so simple, he told himself. All you had to do was shave and wear clean clothes and know when to tell them the right lies and they were yours.

So of course he told her that he loved her, and he told her that it was something that he wanted to say.

Her tears then were not of remorse but of gratitude. She thanked him in the same little-girl way she thanked him after they had made love.

But even as he held her, he was tiring of her. This would not be a long one. He liked them with some fight in them, and there was almost no fight left in her at all anymore.

Chapter Twenty-Four

The fight started at 3:43 that afternoon.

In all, 4,341 paying customers watched it. An additional one hundred policemen, army personnel from a nearby fort, and Mesquakie Indians from a reservation witnessed the bout.

In faces were pipes, cigarettes, cigars, and turdy lumps of chewing tobacco; in hands were soda pop, spafizzes, lemonade, and beer; on tongues were cheers for Sovich, curses for the colored man, and boos whenever the referee had the audacity to remind Sovich that there were, after all, rules to this contest.

It was ninety-four degrees when the fight started, and there was no wind. The latrines, filled with piss and feces, were rancid enough to spoil some people's enjoyment of the boxing match. The people in the confection tents worried that they would not have enough soda pop and beer to last the fight, particularly if the colored man surprised everybody and managed to stay upright for any length of time.

Occasional female faces dotted the crowd. These women generally fit into two classes—the girlfriends (as opposed to brides) of men who wanted to feel their girls were good sports, and the odd woman who had developed a genuine taste for the blood game. The former tended to squeal and bury their faces in a manly shoulder when things got nasty in the ring. The latter showed a silence and fascination stonier even than the men's.

The first round surprised everybody. Rooney did not do so badly. He did not do all that well, true, but he managed to avoid several uppercuts and to dance away from two hard right crosses Sovich tried to inflict on him. Once Rooney even managed to duck a bolo punch he saw only peripherally. Even the meanest of white men had to pay him begrudging respect for that one. If nothing else, Rooney's first-round performance implied that this might be, for a time anyway, something resembling a real boxing match rather than a carnival sideshow.

The second round immediately put the fight back in the sideshow category. Sovich threw three left hooks, each one of which caught Rooney square on the jaw. The second time he dipped to one knee and shook his wide, ugly head to clear it of cobwebs. With this, he brought the white crowd alive. They started yelling "Nigger," and when whites yelled "Nigger," the fight was only starting.

The third round was more even. Rooney landed two fair punches on Sovich's shoulders and one on Sovich's head. These blows did not seem to hurt Sovich especially, but they did infuriate him. Sovich had been hoping that the colored boy would have been set down for good by now. He rallied, of course, pasting Rooney with several powerful body shots, one of which lifted Rooney half an inch off the canvas.

By this time the temperature had risen to ninety-seven degrees.

In the fourth round, Sovich took complete command again. Two ringing shots to the head and three quick kidney punches once more brought Rooney to one knee. For the first time the referee began seriously evaluating Rooney's demeanor and behavior. He paid special attention to Rooney's eyes.

In the fifth round, Rooney shocked everyone, most especially himself, by slamming a roundhouse right to Sovich's forehead and pushing him back into the ropes, where he followed up with some solid but not spectacular body blows.

Sovich got out of the round, but barely.

"What the hell's going on in there, Victor?" John T. Stoddard asked in the corner while they waited for the next round to begin.

Sovich's entire torso was heaving. "Must be the heat."

"Do I need to remind you how much we've got riding on this?"

"You think he's going to beat me?" Sovich managed a smile that did not quite convince either himself or Stoddard of his skills at the moment.

"Forget about giving them a show. Just put him to the canvas. You understand?"

The bell rang.

"You understand?" Stoddard shouted into Sovich's ear.

"Yes," Victor Sovich said, spitting a mouthful of saliva and blood next to Stoddard's shoe. "Yes, you son of a bitch. I understand."

He rushed back to the center of the ring, determined to get the fight over with and soon.

Sovich felt angry. He liked it when he felt angry. Such a feeling always proved good for him and most unfortunate for his opponent. Especially if the opponent was colored.

At the top of the sixth, Sovich landed two smashing rights to Rooney's stomach. Rooney dropped backward to the canvas, landing on his bottom.

The white crowd shouted, screamed, cheered, and stamped its feet. They wanted to see one hell of a lot more of this kind of action.

The temperature was now ninety-eight degrees.

The fight continued.

Chapter Twenty-Five

Reynolds watched the first five rounds and then began working his way toward the office, making stops at a beer tent, a beef tent, and a foul-smelling latrine. Sweating had kept him sober, kept him intent on the plan that now seemed not only ingenious but inevitable. Just outside the office door where Guild sat, Reynolds would collect papers and rags and set a fire. There being only one way out, Guild would have to come to the door to find out what was going on. Reynolds would then shoot him in the arm, sneak in during all the confusion, grab as much money as possible, and escape. He had spent most of the past half hour looking at a route for himself that ran adjacent to a railroad bed running east. A fast creek ran below a small forest of poplar and pines, and he could easily wade into the water and move unseen downstream.

Now he was getting almost excited about using a gun.

He found the rags and paper he needed in a storeroom in the back of the office building. He soaked these in kerosene that was also conveniently stored in the same room and then proceeded up to the front of the building.

"Your father's going to have a nice payday, son."

"It sure looks that way."

"Though the fight isn't going exactly as he planned, I bet."

"No. I'd have thought Victor would have put Rooney away by now."

"You can't always tell with colored people." The gate man, one of the first people John T. Stoddard had hired in this town, touched his hand to the brim of his Stetson in a sort of half salute and then moved down the fencing to help out a man who looked both confused and irritated, standing half drunk in the heat and the hard white sunlight.

Stephen Stoddard turned back to the fight. At this point, midway in the ninth round, Rooney seemed as startled as any of the spectators. Not only was Victor Sovich not putting the black man to the canvas, he was beginning to lose the fight. Rooney had just delivered some slashing blows to the head and was now moving in with some heavy body punches.

The crowd did not know how to respond. It was as if a bishop had climbed into the ring and had begun singing dirty ditties.

It was very confusing. Rooney was supposed to be flat on his back at this point.

Stephen Stoddard wondered what Guild would make of all this. Guild usually had something interesting to say about nearly everything. Stephen decided to go tell him.

He wadded newspaper and rags into a single mass of flammable material and set it in front of the door.

He knelt next to it, taking a lucifer from his pocket as he did so. Calculating the direction the smoke would take, he pushed the material a little east of the door itself.

He struck the lucifer.

He sat back to wait for the smoke to start oozing beneath the door and for Guild to come out and see what was going on.

He had his gun drawn.

He was trembling so badly he had to hold his weapon steady with his other hand.

"What the hell you doing in there?" Victor's trainer shouted following the end of the ninth round.

"Heat," Sovich managed to say.

"Heat my ass. Your arms are dragging. You got to keep them up. You got to keep him from hitting you. That's the problem, Victor. He keeps hitting you, and you're not doing a goddamn thing about it."

The bell rang for the next round.

His trainer watched Sovich rise ponderously to his feet. He wavered, then wobbled as he put one glove on the ropes and started to walk to the center of the ring.

What the hell was going on here?

Guild, still seated at the rolltop desk with his feet up, thought he smelled something peculiar. Then he decided it was nothing more than all the combined odors, good and bad, of this afternoon.

The rags did not burn properly. Reynolds watched in frustration and anger as the flame reached the kerosene only to have it sputter out before any useful amount of smoke could be generated.

He snatched up the rags and ran back down the stairs to the storeroom for more kerosene.

The knock startled Guild, who had just been on the verge of falling asleep. He had started dreaming about the little girl he'd killed and was grateful to be awakened.

With his .44 in hand, he moved to the door and said, "Yes. Who is it?"

"Me. Stephen."

"I thought your old man didn't want you in here."

"You hear about the fight?"

Now that Guild listened, the crowd sounded almost surly. He wondered what was going on.

"Victor's losing."

"What?"

"Rooney seems to be getting stronger and Victor seems to be getting weaker."

"I'll be damned."

"Let me in, Leo. I brought some lemonade for both of us."

Guild shook his head and opened the door. He kept his .44 ready.

Stephen Stoddard stood in the open doorway with a pitcher of lemonade and two glasses.

"Figured you could use a break," Stephen said. "Probably gets pretty boring in here."

"I'm earning some decent money, kid. I don't mind it."

Stephen set down the pitcher and the glasses. He said ironically, "You changing your mind about my father?"

"Long as he pays me, I don't have any complaint."

Stephen sat down, poured them lemonade, and sat back in a squeaking office chair. "If Victor loses, my dad may be ruined."

"I'm sure he's been ruined before. He'll come back somehow."

"Not at his age." Stephen made a sour face. "There's just no way Victor should be losing."

"Maybe Rooney's a better boxer than we gave him credit for."

Stephen shook his head. "We watched him in three different towns, just to make sure he was the man we wanted. We figured he could give Victor a decent fight but he'd never win." He shook his head again. "Now look."

Guild sipped his lemonade and lighted a cigarette. He felt, as usual, pity for the kid and an inability to do anything about his pity. Maybe it would be for the best if the old man lost all his money. Maybe in doing so he'd have to cut the kid free.

Stephen said, "I told you about my mother."

Guild nodded.

"What I didn't tell you is that I hired this ex-Pinkerton to find her for me."

"Why now? After all these years?"

Stephen shrugged. "I suppose it's like a bad tooth, Leo. You never quit worrying about it."

"So did this ex-Pinkerton find her?"

"Yes."

"What's she doing?"

"Living her new life. Pretty happily, from what the detective said." He paused. Sorrow filled his eyes. "She's got a lot of new kids."

Guild sighed. "Makes you feel kind of bad, doesn't it? Knowing she started a new family and forgot about you?"

"Yes. Makes me wonder if she ever thinks about me or Dad at all."

"Maybe you should try to look her up sometime."

"She wrote me a letter."

"She did?"

"Yes."

"What'd it say?"

"I haven't read it yet."

"Why not?"

"Scared to, I guess."

"Probably be better if you'd read it, don't you think?"

"Maybe that's why I came back here."

"Why?"

"So I could read it in front of you. Maybe you could help me with it. Afterward, I mean. If I get real bad or something."

"Sure, kid."

"I don't want to hate her anymore, Leo. I'm tired of hating her. It takes too much out of me after all these years." He stared out the window. "Maybe she had a reason."

"Maybe she did." Gently, he said, "Why don't you open up the envelope?"

Stephen looked down at his hands and then brought his right hand to the inside of his coat. He took a plain white envelope from the pocket and set it on his knee.

"I'm kind of scared, Leo. I really am."

"You want me to read it to you?"

"Would you, Leo? Would you?"

Stephen sounded no more than eight.

"Sure." Guild reached out to take the envelope, and it was then he smelled the smoke.

This time Reynolds had gotten it going nicely. The smoke was an oily black snake slithering beneath the door.

On one knee now, his weapon aimed directly at the door, he waited for Guild to appear.

Leo Guild said, "Sit right there, Stephen, and don't move."

Guild handed him back the envelope unopened. "Afraid that's going to have to wait."

Guild took out his .44 and eased up to the door.

"What's the smell, Leo?"

"Kerosene smoke. Somebody wants to play a little trick on us."

"What kind of trick?"

All this time Guild was easing up to the door, flattening himself on one side of it so he could get a clean shot off when he opened it up.

"They want us to think there's a fire in the hallway. This gets me to open up the door, and then they come running in and take the money."

"Don't give them the money, Leo. Please."

"Just sit there, and let me handle it."

Guild was now up to the door. He dropped to his haunches and put a hand on the knob.

He flung the door open in a single motion, and that's when the firing started, as he had assumed it would. The bullets came at chest height, where he would normally have been if he hadn't ducked down.

The smoke was so thick Reynolds couldn't see anything. When the door opened, he fired by impulse.

Moments later he heard a harsh cry and then listened as a body slumped to the floor somewhere on the other side of the smoke.

Leo Guild turned just in time to see Stephen Stoddard fall from his chair to the floor. The bullets had gone so wild they'd taken the kid by accident.

Expecting more gunfire but hearing none, Guild crawled back along the floor to Stephen.

Even from here he could see there wasn't anything he could do for the kid. One of the bullets had entered through the forehead. The back of Stephen's head would look like a terrible purple flower suddenly in bloom.

Behind him he heard footsteps.

From the smoke emerged a short, slight man with a gun in his hand. He was coughing from the greasy smoke, and Guild saw no reason not to shoot him just because he was indisposed at the moment.

He shot him in the chest and the groin, and then he moved back up to the man's face. Just as the man began to crumple, he shot him in the forehead, right where the man had shot Stephen.

Standing, he walked to the front of the office and down into the smoke. Coughing himself now, he went down to the basement, where he found two water buckets. He filled them and carried them back upstairs. Putting out the fire was no problem. He put the smoldering rags and newspapers in one of the empty buckets and took everything back downstairs.

Back in the office, he got the kid propped up against a desk. He was still dead, but somehow he didn't look quite so vulnerable in this position.

He went back to the robber. He kicked the man twice hard in the ribs. He could hear bone cracking. The sound did not displease him.

Just then the crowd roared, and he realized that nobody had come running after the gunshots because most likely nobody had heard the shots. Not above the noise of the crowd.

He saw the white envelope on the floor near where Stephen had fallen from the chair.

He went over and picked it up. Red spatters of blood covered the front of it.

He wondered why she had left them. It seemed a terrible and incomprehensible thing to do. Maybe not to leave some son of a bitch as mean as John T. Stoddard but to leave the boy they'd raised together.

He folded the envelope twice and slid it down the back pocket of his black trousers.

He went back to the dead robber. He went through his coat and then his pants. For a time he was afraid he was not going to find what he was looking for.

But it was there, all right.

Oh, it was there.

He hunched there looking at the man's bad complexion. He stared at where the bullet had gone in the man's forehead.

He tried to tell himself the kid hadn't been happy alive, that maybe he would be happy dead.

He stood up and went over to the door and locked it securely behind him. Then he went looking for John T. Stoddard.

Chapter Twenty-Six

Victor Sovich went down for the first time midway through the eleventh round. What was so surprising for the crowd was that he was scarcely hit. Rooney had thrown a right hand, but it had glanced off Sovich's shoulder. It was not the sort of punch that could put a man down, but Sovich went to one knee, where he remained for a time while the referee counted off the seconds. Sovich, obviously dizzy, looked with dismay at his corner. What was going on here?

When he regained his feet and the fight went on, Sovich obviously made a decision—to throw his strongest punches against Rooney. The roundhouse, for example, was exactly the kind of punch that had killed people in the past, and probably would have this time—if it had landed. Still suffering from dizziness, Sovich threw three roundhouses during the remaining minutes of the round—but none connected, each missing Rooney's jaw by an inch or so.

The round concluded with Sovich wobbling his way back to his corner.

His trainer, trying to make some sense of what he was seeing, said, "You're letting him beat you, Victor."

"I don't feel well."

The trainer got angry. "Too much partying. Too many Mex women."

Sovich shook his head belligerently. "That water you gave me." He looked around for the water bottle. "It tasted funny."

"It isn't the water you should be worrying about. It's the partying you did last night."

Sovich scowled. "We'll settle this after the fight, you son of a bitch."

The bell rang.

"You'd better finish him this round, Victor. He's getting stronger and you're getting weaker."

Victor Sovich stood up on trembling legs and moved ponderously back into the ring.

The doc checked for vitals. He glanced up at Guild. Nothing.

The doc was a hefty man in a white boater and a yellow shirt and white trousers. He had come out here for a good time, and now he was spending his afternoon with a corpse. The doc, whose name was Fitzgerald, shook his head and got to his feet, his knees cracking as he did so.

He was about to say something to Guild, but just then the door crashed open and there stood John T. Stoddard. Guild had asked one of the boxing people to find him.

Stoddard's first reaction to being called back here was anger, then terror as he saw his son's pale hand on the floor from behind the table.

"My God," Stoddard said.

Guild looked away. He did not like Stoddard, but he did not want to take any pleasure in seeing the arrogant man's face begin to reflect the waiting sorrow.

Dr. Fitzgerald started to say something to Stoddard. "Be quiet," Stoddard said.

Stoddard's footsteps were heavy on the wooden floor. One,

two, three, four. He walked over and stood above his son.

"Who did this?"

"You know who did it."

Stoddard seemed shocked by Guild's harsh response.

"Reynolds did it," Guild said. "The man you hired to rob you. He wasn't much of a shot, Stoddard. Maybe you should have thought of that beforehand." He thought of what he'd found in Reynolds's pocket, the office key and a layout of the building. Only Stoddard could have given it to him. He smacked the key on the table.

Stoddard broke then.

He stood swaying miserably above his son, crystal tears on his jowly face. The sounds he made were intolerable for Guild to hear. Guild had sounded not unlike this one night shortly after the little girl's death.

Guild took Dr. Fitzgerald's arm and led him out to the hallway, where Reynolds was being wrapped in a blanket.

"What the hell's going on in there?" Dr. Fitzgerald demanded.

Guild shook his head. "He played it a little too cute, and it didn't work." He thought of Stephen. He slammed a fist into the wall.

"That's a good way to break some knuckles," Dr. Fitzgerald said.

But right now Guild didn't give a damn. He didn't give a damn at all.

Chapter Twenty-Seven

Sportswriters would later say that it was round twelve that proved decisive.

Rooney could scarcely believe what was happening. He started landing vicious body blows at will and then spent the second half of the round concentrating on Victor Sovich's face, opening up a wide cut above the right eye and even cutting him on the chin.

Sovich, so long accustomed to winning, began using almost pathetic defenses, limply putting his hands up in front of his face, only to have them smashed away by Rooney's blows.

For the second time in the fight, Sovich fell down. This time it was on both knees, not just one, and this time it was Sovich who had some difficulty getting back up. He knelt there, his wide white body sleek with sweat, one glove placed on the lowest rope as he struggled to regain his footing.

Fortunately for Sovich, the bell rang. His corner people rushed in and dragged him back to the corner.

* * *

"I didn't mean for it to happen this way," Stoddard said as they walked back into the office.

"Why the hell'd you have me come in here, anyway?"

"Because I want you to believe me."

"You want me to forgive you, Stoddard, and I can't do it. You set up the robbery so you could pretend to Victor that somebody else took his money. Only it didn't turn out so good."

Stoddard took some whiskey, stared down at the dead face of his son. "I treated him like hell, didn't I?"

"You know the answer to that."

Stoddard started sobbing. He put his face in his hands and wept.

Guild stood up and walked around. His boots were heavy on the floor. He went over, exasperated, and sat on the edge of the desk, where all the money was, and had a cigarette. He looked at the money and hated it as if it were a living thing. Then Guild remembered the letter.

He said, "He found your wife."

"What?"

"Awhile back he hired an ex-Pinkerton to look up your wife."

"What the hell are you talking about?"

"Here." Guild tossed him the envelope. "Stephen never opened it."

"Why not?"

"He said he was afraid to."

"He went to all that trouble, and he was afraid?" Stoddard's voice had started to rise in anger, the way it always did when Stephen had displeased his father. "I'm sorry. I shouldn't have taken that tone."

"It's the tone you always took with him."

"You want to hit me, don't you, Guild?"

"No."

"No?"

"Hitting you would be easy. You're going to have to live the rest of your life with how you treated him. That's going to be the hard part."

Something resembling a sob came from Stoddard. He lifted the flask and had another drink. "I wasn't always terrible to him."

"I know."

"I loved him."

"That's the hell of it."

"What is?"

"I really think you did. And you still treated him the way you did."

"It wasn't easy for me."

"I don't suppose it was."

"He never got over his mother leaving us, and I had to be both parents to him. Or try to be."

"Don't start feeling sorry for yourself, Stoddard. He's the one who died, not you."

Stoddard glanced up. "You going to tell Victor?"

"Right now I don't give a damn about Victor. I want you to give me my money, and I want to get out of here."

Stoddard brought his fist down on the desk. "I'm giving the orders around here."

"I want my money or I'll go and tell Victor myself what happened here."

Guild walked over and snapped his fingers and put his hand out. "I want my money right now."

But for the first time Stoddard was looking at the envelope on his lap.

Even before he opened the envelope, Stoddard was crying. Guild wasn't sure why, exactly. He just supposed Stoddard was a little bit insane now. Guild would have been.

Guild walked over to the desk with the money and started counting greenbacks. When he'd counted out his fee, he rolled the bills up and put them in his pocket.

Stoddard paid no attention.

He just kept reading the letter. He rocked back and forth and sobbed. Guild had seen Indian women mourn this way. It was not becoming to see it in a man.

Finished with the letter, Stoddard dropped it to the floor. He put his face in his hands and began his slow rocking again. He cried so violently Guild expected him to vomit.

Guild went over and picked up the letter from the floor and started reading it.

Chapter Twenty-Eight

Clarise sat in her hotel room, watching the street below for sight of the wagon that would take her to the train depot. She kept looking at the clock on the mahogany bureau. It was nearly five-thirty. The train left at six-thirty. She wanted to be certain not to miss it.

The heat, waning now, had left her feeling unclean. She hated that feeling. She rose and went over to the porcelain pitcher and basin on the bureau. Even warm, the water felt good on her face and hands. She opened her lacy blouse and massaged clean water onto the tops of her breasts. She thought of last night with Leo Guild. She had not liked a man, least of all a white man, in some time. But there was a humility about Guild she liked. That was the only word for it. Humility.

Going to the bed, she sat on the edge of the mattress, the box springs squeaking slightly beneath her weight. She looked at the yellow bowl of red apples against the light blue wall. In the sunlight the bowl and the apples and the wall looked like a painting. She stared at it until the tears came.

There should not be tears now, of course. She had waited so long for this day that she should feel nothing but joy.

The poison she had put in Victor Sovich's water bottle would be taking effect by now. His punches would be ineffectual. He would die in the ring, just as her brother had died in the ring.

At first Rooney would see this as a day for celebration. A mediocre boxing career would have been turned around. Rooney would have big plans.

The light in the room was the purple of dusk. In the street below was the clatter of buggies and wagons and the faint sound of laughter from the porch where oldsters passed the time by whittling on white wood and lying to each other about the past.

She wished her brother were here with her now. He would be pleased with what she had done.

A knock. "Taxi's here, miss."

"Thank you."

"He says shake a leg."

"I'll be right down."

"They like to have you there early for the train."

"Right down," she said again.

The room had enveloped her in melancholy, and she found herself reluctant to leave. The soft song of birds, the gray light in the window, the scent of perfume spilled in her carpetbag. She did not want to leave. If she closed her eyes she could be a little girl again. Her brother would not be dead and Guild—

She knew what Guild would think of what she had done. The words he would use.

She stood up, sighing.

She gathered her two carpetbags quickly and left the room, turning back only once to look for the last time on the peculiar half-light trapped in the corners of the place.

She wondered if death would be this soft and eerily beautiful. She hoped so, she hoped so.

"Hurry now, miss. Hurry now," the desk clerk said, looking her over again, still undecided if she was black or white.

Chapter Twenty-Nine

Portland

June 7, 1892

Dear Stephen,

When the detective came to my door, I was very frightened. I knew that at last my past had found me, the past I wonder about when I can't sleep at night.

If you have children of your own someday, you will know the particular hell I am describing, the hell of deserting your own flesh and blood. How many times over these past years have I wondered what you would look like as a young man. How many times have I heard the tears you surely cried when I left.

I know that no apology can undo what I did. I must accept my blame without any attempt at justifying myself. The worst thing I ever did was to desert my own son.

There is no point in castigating your father. I'm sure you

know by now how difficult he can be, and how he delights in belittling and bullying people. I can only say that I stood it as long as I could and then left. I should have taken you. I was afraid, however, that he would never rest if I took you, and he would someday find me, too.

The detective tells me that you work for your father and that you've grown into a healthy and handsome young man. When he saw me, he said that you still favor me. I suppose it sounds vain, but I'm glad you do. It's as if we still have a special bond between us, and the looks we share prove that bond.

Reading this over again, I see that your father was probably right—I was, and remain, a silly woman, spoiled by my own father and sheltered from the world in convent school. Even today I feel more like a girl than a woman, and when I look at the children I've had with my husband, Ralph, I feel a peculiar alienation—the same alienation I felt from your father and now my husband, Ralph. I know you won't believe this, but the only person I've ever felt close to—except to my father, who never had any time for me—was you. I think about you constantly. I hear a sentimental song and I think of the songs I used to hum to you when I rocked you in your cradle. I see a painting or a book—remembering how taken you were with paintings and books—and I want to buy it for you and send it to you.

I think it would spoil things if we met, Stephen. Tempting as it is, I think you would hate me the more for inflicting myself on you at this late date. And Ralph, to be truthful, would not understand. Long ago he tired of my tears and moods where you are concerned. He warned me that he would ask me to leave if I "moped" about you any longer.

At my age, darling, I can't afford to be on the street, and Ralph, handsome and rich as he is, would not think twice about putting me there. He is known to keep company with other women, and I assume at least a few of them would be more than happy to become his next wife.

But there I go, doing what I said I didn't want to—inflict my troubles on you.

I pray to sweet Jesus that you can someday find it in your heart to forgive me. I pray to sweet Jesus that someday I can forgive myself.

Love,

Your mother

Guild was outside the business office, smoking a cigarette, when the boy he'd sent as a runner came back with the fat, beer-smelling sheriff's deputies. Guild explained to them what had happened, carefully leaving out that John T. Stoddard himself had set up the robbery.

"His son got it, huh?"

"Yes."

"This doesn't look like Stoddard's day."

"Oh," Guild said, "what else?"

"The nigger."

"The fighter?"

"Yeah." The deputy wore a khaki uniform. Great dark circles of sweat ringed the areas beneath his arms. "He's winning."

"What?"

"He's knocked Sovich down four times now."

Something was wrong in the ring. Guild didn't know what, but Rooney had no chance against Sovich. None. "We'd better go tell Stoddard."

"Wasn't like Reynolds to carry a gun," the deputy said. "We all knew him. He was a robber, and a good one. But never carried any gun."

"He did this time."

"You have to kill him?"

Guild stared at the man. "Yes, I did, Deputy. I had to kill him."

The deputy shrugged. "Just asking." He nodded over to a

wagon. Two sleek black horses stood in traces. "We can use that to take the bodies back to town."

"Fine."

"I'll go make arrangements. Why don't you go tell Stoddard."

Guild nodded and went back inside the building. Dusk shadows filled the hallway now. Reynolds lay sprawled beneath a blood-soaked blanket. Guild stepped over him and went inside the office where Stoddard sat in a chair next to his son's body. Stoddard dumbly held a letter in his hand. Guild knew the letter was the one Stephen had been carrying but had been afraid to open. Stoddard stared down at Stephen.

"I don't know what to do, Guild."

"There's nothing to do," Guild said harshly. "You live with it, that's all."

"I didn't know he was going to die. I didn't want him to be here when Reynolds came in."

"Well, he was."

John T. Stoddard looked up. All the arrogance was gone from his face. He appeared to be a large, ponderous animal that had been wounded very badly. His eyes were red from crying. "You still don't like me, do you?"

"No."

"Can't you believe I'm sorry about this?"

"You're sorry for yourself, not for Stephen."

"I loved him."

"No, you didn't." He nodded to the letter. "Any more than she did."

"She didn't want to see him." He stared down at Stephen again and began sobbing. His great shoulders moved to the rhythms of his grief. He let the white letter fall to Stephen's chest. Red blood soaked it immediately. "He couldn't have asked for two worse parents."

Guild didn't say anything. He was tired of it all. He wanted to see that the kid was loaded on the wagon along with Reynolds, and then he wanted out of here.

The deputy appeared in the doorway. He glanced down at Stoddard and shook his head. He seemed disgusted with a man who would cry for any reason. He said, "You tell him about the nigger?"

"No, I didn't. Not yet."

"You better. Things are getting worse in there. Things are getting a lot worse."

Chapter Thirty

She watched him die. At first Teresa thought he was just having a bad time of it. She attributed this to the heat and all the food and liquor he'd had last night. The colored man was hurting Victor because of Victor's own excesses. For a few rounds she thought this might even be a good thing for Victor. Perhaps it would teach him some humility. Perhaps he would begin taking better care of himself and better care of her. Perhaps, though she knew this was very unlikely, perhaps he would even agree to take the children with them now.

Sitting in the front row, her head pained by all the hoarse shouting going on around her, she thought again of her mother's contempt and disgust. She had never seen such an expression on her mother's face nor heard such ugliness in her mother's voice.

The shouting got worse.

Teresa looked up just in time to see Victor get knocked down for the first time. It was then she knew he was going to die and that she could do nothing about it. It was more than just fear. It was some sense she had. As he was falling to the canvas, he turned his face so that he seemed to look right at her. She saw how vague his eyes had become, the way pain had wrinkled his mouth. Nothing broke his fall. Canvas and his head smashed together.

He got up. The crowd around her took this as a sign that the fight would turn back Victor's way. They shouted and clapped and stamped their feet. But she knew better, knew exactly what was going to happen to him.

You get used to being bad. You get used to seeing your once stone-fisted punches become as nothing against the face of your opponent. You get used to the feeling of strangling on your own blood from cuts inside your mouth, and you get used to the blindness that sets in after you've been hit so many times. When you get paid by the round, all you can hope is that you somehow manage to stay upright long enough to make good money for your day's work.

Today was different.

Today was the sort of day Rooney dreamed about when he'd had several schooners of beer and was sitting at a fishing hole. His punches were crisp and deadly once more. His opponent was driven to the canvas several times. Rooney, loose now with self-confidence and a real sense of how to take his man out, was once again a man others needed to fear.

He had lost count of how many times Sovich had pitched to the canvas by now. And it didn't matter. All that did matter was that Rooney was moving in slowly, cutting off the ring and making escape for Victor Sovich impossible.

He kept punching, punching.

She did not want to watch him die.

She sensed that even the crowd, that great roaring white beast that seemed to have its masculinity at stake here, knew he was going to die.

Its chanting fell to ragged silence.

Its boastfulness became soft curses.

Its anger became fear.

She took it as a sign from God. He did not want her to desert her children, and this was His way of letting her know.

She stood up just as Victor was knocked down for the fourth time. She was crying, quiet silver tears, as much for herself as for Victor, and she slipped from the arena without a single look back at the ring.

No, she did not want to see because seeing was a curse. If she saw him in his last moments, she would never be able to forget. In the night when it was hot and she could not sleep, she would see his dying face. Or in the winter when the hard winds came and woke her, then too she would see his dying face and her heart would turn bitter over things that might have been but, alas, were not.

She did not look back once. She went home to her children and her mother.

When he put his head down, the nigger hit him on top of the head. When he moved his body away, the nigger hit him in the kidney. When he fell to the canvas, the nigger hit him in the face on the way down. There was no escaping the nigger now.

Victor knew it was the water that had done this to him. But as the rounds pressed on, as the pain carried him into a kind of purgatory where all normal human reactions were suspended, he thought less about the water. Now there was just the blindness setting in, the sensation of pissing his pants, the right hand from nowhere inflicting more pain.

For a time he'd hoped that he could still turn the fight around. By now he knew better. As he bobbed and ducked and tried to retaliate, odd images began forming. He saw his father, Slavic-rough and Slavic-mean, tossing a baseball to a six-year-old Victor. He saw his sister Peg singing "Ave Maria" at Victor's first communion. He saw the first girl he'd ever slept with smiling at him knowingly in the shadows afterward.

More blows, abruptly. The referee, clamping his hands on Victor's face and forcing his eyes open, shouted right into Victor's face, "How are you feeling? Can you go on?"

Could he go on?

A nigger beating Victor Sovich?

Instinctively, Victor pushed the man aside and staggered in the direction of Rooney, swinging wildly as he did so.

The crowd roared for the first time in long minutes.

Rooney hit him very hard on the forehead again. Victor felt himself start to sink to his knees. A coldness came, then a darkness. He had experienced neither before.

His sister again, and the "Ave Maria."

His father slapped him for spilling too much beer in the bucket Victor always ran down and got him. (He'd never been able to please the old man. Never.)

The chewy breasts of Teresa. What an odd thing to want now with the coldness and the darkness setting in—sex.

The referee's hands on his shoulders, pushing him to the corner. "You're bleeding from your penis," the referee shouted into his face. "There's blood all over your legs."

He wanted, despite all the pain and confusion, to get Rooney.

And wanted Teresa, the musk of her sex, the soft brown sadness of her eyes.

Blindness was total now, and the coldness.

God, the coldness.

Chapter Thirty-One

The crowd was without voice. Where only minutes before it had urged its raging best on Victor Sovich, now it was nothing more than a whimpering beast, softly cursing its disbelief.

Dr. Fitzgerald was in the ring, bending over the unmoving form of Victor Sovich.

Rooney crouched on his haunches in the corner, keeping his massive, ugly head down, obviously trying not to pay any attention to the taunts and jeers directed at him by various white fans nearby. "He better not die, nigger. You hear that?" said one man as Guild pushed past to the ring.

The first drops of rain began to fall now, too, the sun disappearing altogether, the plump black rain clouds bringing not only darkness but chill, too. Rooney started rubbing himself. Seeing this, his trainer brought him a robe and threw it over his shoulders.

John T. Stoddard climbed up through the ropes. He was dazed

in such a way that his face looked dead, his mouth open, spittle a silver cord down the side of his jaw, his eyes shocked into a flat, unseeing blue.

"What happened here?" the trainer said to the referee as Stoddard wandered around looking lost.

"Rooney just came on strong."

"Bullshit."

"You asked me a question. I'm just telling you what happened."

"And I say bullshit. There's no way Rooney could have done this to Sovich."

"It's what happened. I'm telling you—it's what happened. The only thing I can think of is that Victor complained about the water."

"What water?"

"You gave him a bottle to drink from right before the fight. Maybe you still have the bottle."

"Back in the dressing room."

"Maybe we better have a look at it."

Stoddard came over now. The dazed look was still in his eyes. He stared dumbly down at Victor.

"He's dead," the referee said.

Stoddard said nothing.

"Dead, Mr. Stoddard. Dead."

The rain came harder now, cold and almost painful to the skin. The fans in the bleachers began to scatter. Where before there had been thousands, now there were only scores. Those who remained seemed not to notice the rain. They stood in their places, watching the ring.

Guild stared down at Sovich. He had not liked the man, did not like him still, yet there was an angry dignity to the man's Slavic face in the repose of death. His eyelids were cut badly and his nose had been broken and two of his front teeth were nothing more than stumps. His legs were covered with blood.

"Let's get his body back to the dressing room," Guild said to the trainer.

Guild got Sovich by the feet, the trainer by the shoulders. They eased him over onto a stretcher.

The referee said, "I've never had a man die on me before."

The sky opened up fully. The silver rain came in waves, in walls, in chill, shifting patterns that quickly drenched the parched ground beneath the bleachers and obscured everything in steam.

Somewhere in the middle of the downpour, they could hear an isolated fan shout toward the ring, "Is he dead?"

And the referee shouting back, "Yes, he's dead."

There was no sense in hurrying. Guild was already soaked. They carried Victor Sovich back on a stretcher covered by a sheet. The sheet got soaked immediately and clung tightly to Sovich, lending him the aspect of sculpture.

Guild tried not to think about the water bottle Victor had drunk from, but of course he had already begun to suspect what had happened. He thought of a woman whose brother had been given poison. Her brother had been a boxer, as had his killer.

They moved slowly back through the bleachers and along the rope fence and to the business office.

Guild said nothing. There was nothing to say.

Stoddard trailed along. He seemed barely able to pick up his feet. He said nothing.

They put Sovich on the rubdown couch. Dr. Fitzgerald checked him again. He shook his head.

The room smelled of liniment and trapped heat.

Guild got a cigarette going. He was watching John T. Stoddard sink into memories of his son when Sovich's trainer appeared holding a glass bottle half filled with water. "Here's what we're looking for."

Guild took the bottle and sniffed it. "Can't smell anything." He held it up to the light. "Looks clear."

"There are a number of poisons we can't detect right away," Dr. Fitzgerald said. "Not being able to see them or smell them doesn't mean anything." He looked at Stoddard heaped in the corner and said, "Mr. Stoddard, I'm going to pour you a glass of whiskey. I want you to drink it. Then I want you to get out of your wet clothes and lie down on that cot in the other room. Whether you know it or not, you're in a state of shock." He nodded for the trainer to help Mr. Stoddard into the other room.

Stoddard came suddenly and violently back to life. He jerked his arm away from the trainer's hand. "Mr. Guild here doesn't approve of me," he announced in a formal, almost theatrical way. He sounded as if he were right on the edge of tumbling into insanity. "He didn't think I was good enough for him, and he didn't think I was good enough for my son. He has a pretty goddamn high opinion of himself."

"Why don't you go in and lie down, Stoddard?" Guild said.

"Are you happy I'm ruined, Leo? Are you going to get drunk and tell all the men in the bar that John T. Stoddard is ruined?"

"Come on now," Dr. Fitzgerald said. "You go with the trainer and lie down and get a nap for yourself."

"He thinks it's funny," Stoddard said. "He thinks it's funny that I'm wiped out."

The tears were coming again. They were hard, bitter tears, and he might never recover from them. But they were better than his silence.

The trainer eased him out of the room and into the next. He got the door closed, but Guild could hear Stoddard's sobs.

Dr. Fitzgerald handed Guild a folded piece of paper. The faded bloodstains told Guild what it was. "Have you read this, Mr. Guild?"

"Yes."

"The poor kid."

"Yes."

Dr. Fitzgerald nodded to the door. "Is he really ruined?"

"I suppose."

"You don't like him, huh?"

"No."

"He's in a bad way."

"He deserves to be in a bad way."

"You're kind of a hard son of a bitch."

"You wouldn't say that if you knew how he'd treated the kid."

"Sometimes we treat people we love pretty badly."

"I guess so."

Dr. Fitzgerald looked at the door again. "No matter how much you hate him, Mr. Guild, right now he hates himself a whole lot worse."

The doctor's remarks cooled Guild's anger. Stoddard was probably not the villain Guild had turned him into. He was probably just as helpless and pathetic as Guild himself, living with his remorse over his son just as Guild lived with his remorse over the little girl.

The door from the hallway slammed open. A young man with freckles and a soaked gray suit stood there. "Didn't you hear it?" he said to Guild.

"Hear what?"

"The gunshot."

"Not above the rain."

"Somebody shot the nigger."

"Rooney?"

"Yeah. Rooney."

"Jesus," Guild said. "Jesus."

Chapter Thirty-Two

Guild recognized the man right away, the tall, frenzied man in the ministerial frock coat and the insane dark eyes. He sat in a corner. Reverend Feely. The fat deputy stood next to him. The deputy said, "In this town you're in trouble even if you shoot a colored."

"He killed a white man. Coloreds have gone far enough. Don't you agree?"

"Whether I agree or not don't matter none. They still put you behind bars in this town when you shoot somebody."

"Even a colored?"

"Even a colored."

"I tell you they've gone far enough, and we've got to put a stop to it."

"This is the gun you shot him with?"

"You think I'm ashamed of shooting him?"

"No. I s'pose not."

"And I ain't going to be ashamed when I go before a judge, neither."

Guild knocked on the door that led to the interior room being used for dressing. When the door opened, he stepped back so Dr. Fitzgerald could step inside first.

Rooney lay on the training cot. In his black face his white eyes bulged. Silver sweat stood in cold beads on his face. His big hands favored the massive hole in his chest.

His trainer said, "We got the guy, Rooney. Deputy's got him outside."

Rooney seemed not to hear. He just stared up at the ceiling with those bulging eyes. Guild wondered what he was thinking about.

Dr. Fitzgerald went over and started examining him. Once Rooney moaned, as if enduring intolerable pain. He started crying soon after. "I'm gonna die, ain't I, Doctor?"

"You're going to be fine."

"You're lying and you know it. I'm gonna die. I beat Sovich and a white man shoots me. It ain't fair."

"You lie there now and let me have a closer look at that wound."

"It ain't fair."

Guild watched Rooney's eyes. They were quick now with panic and fear.

As Dr. Fitzgerald bent over him, Rooney said, "They got a priest around here?"

"Lie still now. I don't think they have a priest."

"I got to tell somebody what I did." He writhed then with his pain. He was delivering death just as a birthing woman delivered life. Rooney looked over at Guild. "I poisoned this man, this nigger. He was a boxer. I shouldn't ought to done that. I just wanted to get ahead, was all. That was all."

His entire body jerked. His bulging eyes bulged even more. His body jerked again. His eyes closed, white eyes replaced by dark lids.

"He was lucky to make it this long," Dr. Fitzgerald said.

Chapter Thirty-Three

An hour and twenty-two minutes later, Guild stepped off the streetcar. His clothes were dry. He needed a shave. He was shaking and he wasn't sure why.

He stood on the street corner, letting well-dressed pedestrians swirl by him on their way to the opera house and the vaudeville parlor. He stared for a long time at the hotel. He wondered which floor she was on. He wondered if she'd left.

Dropping his hand instinctively to his .44, he crossed the street, waiting for a hansom cab to pass by, sleek and black in the streetlight. He liked the fresh smell of the city following the rain. It felt as though it had been purged of something foul.

In the lobby he went up to the desk. He asked the clerk if Clarise had checked out.

"No, she hasn't, sir."

"You're sure?"

"She was going to. Said she changed her mind."

"Thank you." He started away from the desk. "Oh. I need her room number."

"Four-oh-six," the clerk said without looking it up. His blue eyes said that he'd been smitten, and smitten most seriously by Clarise.

On the carpeted stairs Guild passed more people in evening dress going out. In his rumpled clothes, he seemed to elicit both amusement and disgust.

On the fourth floor he went down a long hall. At 406 he leaned forward to see if he could hear anything. Nothing.

He knocked.

Still he heard nothing. He glanced around the hallway and at the same time took his .44 from its holster. He tried the door-knob. Open.

He peered into the darkness of the room. Through a gauzy white curtain, plumped out from the window on a breeze, he saw a ghostly streetlight. The furnishings, bed, bureau, reading chair, and lamp were silhouetted against the glowing curtain.

He went inside.

The place smelled of Clarise's perfume. Despite himself, he allowed himself a moment's pleasure by closing his eyes and recalling last night by the river, the wonderful floating death of his orgasm and the fast roar of the water and the sweet, soft scent of her perfume.

She took one step from the shadows behind the door and quite skillfully got him square across the back of the head.

He was unconscious before he hit the floor.

"You figured it out, didn't you?"

"Yes."

"I don't want you to hate me, Leo."

"You killed two men tonight."

"Sovich has killed enough colored people. I don't worry about him. And you know what Rooney did. I wanted him to be blamed. I figured white folks would make his last minutes a lot more miserable than I could."

"A minister killed him. A crazy white man. But you knew a white man would kill him, didn't you?"

"That's what I was hoping. White folks don't like black folks who kill whites."

"You should have seen him, Clarise. There at the last."

"Did he suffer?"

"He suffered a lot. He was really scared, Clarise. The way you're going to be. The way I'm going to be."

"He killed my brother."

"I know."

"I tried to forgive him, Leo. I couldn't." She sighed and walked over to the window. In the street below, the clatter of hooves was sharp. "Back at the arena, I didn't think I could go through with it. I looked at him for the first time. Really looked at him. I saw that he was just human like the rest of us. You ever convince yourself somebody's not human and then all of a sudden you see they're a scared animal just like you?"

"All the time."

She turned back to Guild. She came over and sat on the edge of the bed. Her brown, gentle hands were folded in her lap. "I prayed God to forgive me, Leo, but somehow I couldn't warn Rooney. I wanted to. I wanted to get up and shout out that—"

She started crying.

Guild rolled himself a cigarette and watched her. He took two long drags, and then he got up and went over and sat next to her, taking her gently into the crook of his arm, putting her warm, wet cheek on his shoulder. Her whole body trembled.

"I wish I could feel good, Leo," she said. "I wish I could feel some satisfaction." She cried harder again. "I deserve what happens to me, Leo. I shouldn't have done it. I surely shouldn't have."

Guild walked over to the dresser. He took her bag and started throwing her things into it. He was neither gentle nor orderly.

"What are you doing?" she asked.

"You've got to go," he said. "Fast."

"But Leo, I killed a man this afternoon."

"He killed your brother."

"But I still didn't have any right to—"

"I said hurry."

Looking at him in a kind of shocked disbelief, she rose from the bed and moved like an uncertain child to the closet.

"Hurry," Guild said again.

She began taking dresses down from the closet and folding them in half. When she was finished, Guild took the dresses and put them inside the bag.

"Come on," he said.

"Where?"

"Depot."

"Depot?"

"There's a train pulling out of here in fifteen minutes."

"To where?"

"Does it matter? Now, come on."

Downstairs she paid the room clerk. He gave Guild, who was obviously nervous, a queer look.

In the street Guild kept her arm, steering her through the foot traffic and across the wide wagon-packed streets.

A block away they could hear the train getting ready to pull out. People's loud good-byes floated on the air like colorful balloons.

He made her sit as he bought her a one-way ticket at the counter.

On the way to the train, their footsteps loud on the wooden platform, she said, "You sure you should be doing this, Leo?"

"You let me worry about this."

At the car she boarded, she turned and said, "I wish we were going to be together again, Leo."

"It wouldn't work."

"Why?" she said.

Without humor, he replied, "We're too much alike. Now get on up there."

She started crying. "Leo, please, won't you reconsider? We could—"

"Board!" shouted the strolling conductor, checking his Ingram pocket watch. "Board!"

"You get up there," Guild said. "You get up there right now."

She leaned forward and kissed him quickly on the mouth.

He felt the kiss inside and out. He looked at her and felt alone. He wished there were some way she could stay.

"Board!" shouted the conductor.

The crowd pressed in, and she was lost in the midst of it, buoyed up the steps of the car as she moved inside with the others.

Guild knew better than to wait and wave.

He needed no more pain today.

Chapter Thirty-Four

In the morning Guild came down from his hotel room carrying his carpetbags. He had slept ten hours without any alcohol. Alcohol would just have made things worse.

He stood on the steps in the shade of the overhang. The bright day was already so hot the livery man down the street was sloshing water on horses.

From behind him a voice said, "I'd like to talk to you a minute."

Guild turned to find John T. Stoddard standing there, carrying carpetbags of his own. Guild said nothing to him, just turned away and started down the steps, heading for the railroad station where he'd taken Clarise yesterday.

As he walked, he heard Stoddard coming up behind him, panting, change jingling in his pockets.

"I'm sorry about the way I treated Stephen," Stoddard said. "If I could do it all over again—"

Guild set his bags down in the middle of the street and turned around and faced Stoddard. "I don't have any right to judge you,

Stoddard. I've done some pretty terrible things in my own life."
He frowned. "But don't ask me to forgive you, all right? That's
something I can't do."

"He liked you, Guild. Did he—" He paused, looking
aggrieved. "Did he ever say anything about me?"

"He said he loved you. He said that I didn't know anything
about your suffering and that I shouldn't judge you. That's
exactly what he said."

Guild picked up his bags and turned back in the direction of the
depot. He walked as fast as he could. He didn't want to see Stoddard ever again.

"Guild! Guild!" Stoddard shouted after him. "Please! Talk to
me, Guild! Talk to me!"

But then a streetcar came, and John T. Stoddard vanished
behind it. Not even his voice could be heard now, not even his
voice.